Orthodoxy
Its Truths And Errors

by

James Freeman Clarke

Orthodoxy
Its Truths And Errors
by James Freeman Clarke

Copyright © 2024

All Rights reserved.

ISBN: 978-93-65788-10-5

Published by

DOUBLE 9 BOOKS

2/13-B, Ansari Road
Daryaganj, New Delhi – 110002
info@double9books.com
www.double9books.com
Tel. 011-40042856

This book is under public domain

ABOUT THE AUTHOR

James Freeman Clarke (1810–1888) was an influential American theologian, minister, and writer known for his contributions to religious thought and reform. Born in Boston, Clarke was educated at Harvard University, where he developed a deep interest in theology and religious studies. His career as a Unitarian minister saw him serving several prominent congregations, including those in Boston and Brooklyn. Clarke is best remembered for his critical examination of Christian doctrine, particularly through his work Orthodoxy: Its Truths and Errors. This book reflects his commitment to scrutinizing traditional religious beliefs and advocating for reform. Clarke's writings often challenge established orthodoxy, aiming to reconcile faith with modern understanding and spiritual insights. A proponent of liberal Christianity, Clarke sought to address doctrinal discrepancies and promote a more inclusive and progressive approach to religion. His works also include discussions on comparative religion and the evolution of belief systems. Clarke's impact extends beyond his theological critiques, influencing the broader discourse on religious reform and the development of modern Unitarian thought.

CONTENTS

Preface

The Protestant Reformation has its Principle and its Method. Its Principle is Salvation by Faith, not by Sacraments. Its Method is Private Judgment, not Church Authority. But private judgment generates authority; authority, first legitimate, that of knowledge, grows into the illegitimate authority of prescription, calling itself Orthodoxy. Then Private Judgment comes forth again to criticise and reform. It thus becomes the duty of each individual to judge the Church; and out of innumerable individual judgments the insight of the Church is kept living and progressive. We contribute one such private judgment; not, we trust, in conceit, but in the hope of provoking other minds to further examinations.

Chapter I
Introduction

§ 1. Object and Character of this Book

The peculiarity of the book now offered to the religious public by the government of the American Unitarian Association, is this—that it is an honest attempt to find and state the truth contained in the doctrines of their opponents. It is, perhaps, something new for an association established to defend certain theological opinions, and baptized with a special theological name, to publish a work intended to do justice to hostile theories. The too usual course of each sect has been, through all its organs, to attack, denounce, undervalue, and vilify the positions taken by its antagonists. This has been considered as only an honest zeal for truth. The consequence has been, that no department of literature has been so unchristian in its tone and temper as that of sectarian controversy. Political journals heap abuse on their opponents, in the interest of their party. But though more noisy than the theological partisans, they are by no means so cold, hard, or unrelenting. Party spirit, compared with sectarian spirit, seems rather mild.1

It is true that theologians do not now use in controversy the epithets which were formerly universal. We have grown more civil in our language than were our fathers. It is also true that we often meet with theological discussions conducted in a spirit of justice towards one's opponents.2 But to say, "Fas est ab hoste *doceri*," is a step as yet beyond the ability of most controversialists. To admit that your antagonist may have seen some truth not visible to yourself, and to read his work in this sense,—in order to learn, and not merely to confute,—is not yet common.

This we are about to undertake in the present treatise. We stand in the Unitarian position, but shall endeavor to see if there be not some truths in Orthodoxy which Unitarians have not yet adequately recognized. To use the language of our motto—we come "not as deserters, but as explorers" into the camp of Orthodoxy. We are satisfied with our Unitarian position, as a stand-point from which to survey that of others. And especially are we grateful to it, since it encourages us by all its traditions, by all its ideas and principles, to look *after* as well as before—to see if there be no truth behind us which we have dropped in our hasty advance, as well as truth beyond us to which we have not yet attained.

§ 2. Progress requires that we should look back as well as forward

Such a study as this may be undertaken in the interest of true progress, as well as that of honest inquiry. For what so frequently checks progress, causes its advocates to falter, and produces what we call a reaction towards the old doctrines, as something shallow in the reform itself? Christians have relapsed into Judaism, Protestants into Romanism, Unitarians into Orthodoxy—because something true and good in the old system had dropped out of the new, and attracted the converts back to their old home. All true progress is expressed in the saying of Jesus, "I have not come to destroy, but to fulfil." The old system cannot pass away until all its truths are *fulfilled*, by being taken up into the new system in a higher form. Judaism will not pass away till it is fulfilled in Christianity—the Roman Catholic Church will not pass away till it is fulfilled in Protestantism—Orthodoxy will not pass away till it is fulfilled by Rational Christianity. Judaism continues as a standing protest, on behalf of the unity of God, against Trinitarianism.

And yet we believe that, in the religious progress of the race, Christianity is an advance on Judaism, Protestant Christianity an advance on Roman Catholic Christianity, and Liberal and Rational Christianity an advance on Church Orthodoxy. But all such advances are subject to reaction and relapse. Reaction differs from relapse in this, that it is an oscillation, not a fall. Reaction is the backward swing of the wave, which will presently return, going farther forward than before. Relapse is the fall of the tide, which leaves the ships aground, and the beach uncovered. Reaction is going back to recover some substantial truth, left behind in a too hasty advance. Relapse is falling back into the old forms, an entire apostasy from the higher stand-point to the lower, from want of strength to maintain one's self in the advance.

The Epistle to the Hebrews deserves especial study by those who desire to understand the philosophy of intellectual and spiritual progress. It was written to counteract a tendency among the Jewish Christians to relapse into Judaism. These Christians missed the antiquity, the ceremony, the authority of the old ritual. Their state of mind resembled that of the extreme High Church party in the Church of England, who are usually called Puseyites. They were not apostates or renegades, but backsliders. They were always lamenting the inferiority of Christianity to Judaism, in the absence of a priesthood, festival, sacrifices. It hardly seemed to them a church at all. The Galatians, to whom Paul wrote, had actually gone over and accepted

Jewish Christianity in the place of Christianity in its simplicity and purity. The Hebrews had not gone over, but were looking that way. Therefore the writer of the Epistle to the Hebrews endeavors to show them that all which was really good in the Jewish priesthood, temple, ritual, was represented in Christianity in a higher form. It had been fulfilled in the New Covenant. Nothing real and good can pass away till it is fulfilled in something better. Thus the Roman Catholic Church stands, as a constant proof that Protestant Christianity yet lacks some important Christian element which Romanism possesses. Orthodoxy, confuted, as we suppose, over and over again, by the most logical arguments, stands firm, and goes forward.

Let us, then, reëxamine the positions of our antagonists—not now merely in order to find the weak places in their line of battle, but to discover the strong ones. Let us see if there be any essential, substantial truth in this venerable system, to which we have as yet not done justice. If there be, justice and progress will both be served by finding and declaring it.

We ask, What are the substantial truths, and what the formal errors, of Orthodoxy? But what do we mean by these terms?

§ 3. Orthodoxy as Right Belief

By Orthodoxy in general is meant the right system of belief. This is the dictionary definition. But as the world and the Church differ as to *which* is the right system of belief—as there are a vast multitude of systems—and as all sects and parties, and all men, believe the system they themselves hold to be the right belief—Orthodoxy, in this sense of right belief, means nothing. In this sense there are as many orthodoxies as there are believers, for no two men, even in the same Church, think exactly alike. Unless, therefore, we have some *further* test, by which to find out *which* orthodoxy, among all these orthodoxies, is the true orthodoxy—we accomplish little by giving to any one system that name.

Here, for instance, in New England, we have a system of belief which goes by the name of Orthodoxy; which, however, is considered very heterodox *out* of New England. The man who is thought sound by Andover is considered very unsound by Princeton. The General Assembly of the Presbyterian Church, in 1837, cut off four synods, containing some forty thousand members, because they were supposed not to be sound in doctrinal belief. But these excommunicated synods formed a New School Presbyterian Church, having its own orthodoxy. Andover considers itself more orthodox than Cambridge; but the New School Presbyterians think themselves more orthodox than Andover—the Old School Presbyterians think themselves more orthodox than the New School. But the most orthodox Protestant is called a heretic by the Roman Catholics. The Roman Catholics, again, are called heretics by the Greek Church. So that orthodoxy, in this sense, seems an impossible thing—something which, if it exists, can never be certainly ascertained.

Whenever a body of believers assumes the name of Orthodox, intending thereby that they are right, and their opponents wrong, they evidently assume the very point in dispute. They commit the fallacy called in logic a *petitio principii*. They beg the question, instead of discussing it. They put will in the place of reason. They say, in the very title page of their book, in the first step of their argument, that their book is satisfactory and their argument conclusive. It would be more modest to wait till the discussion is concluded before they proceed thus to state what the conclusion is. This is an arrogance like that which the Church of Rome commits, in calling itself Catholic or Universal, while excluding more than half of Christendom from its communion.3

A political party does not offer such an affront to its opponents. It may name itself Democratic, Republican, Federal; it may call itself the Conservative party, or that of Reform. By these titles it indicates its leading idea—it signifies that it bears the standard of reform, or that it stands by the old institutions of the country. But no political party ever takes a name signifying that it is all right and its opponents all wrong. This assumption was left to religious sects, and to those who consider humility the foundation of all the virtues.

The term "Evangelical" is, perhaps, not as objectionable as Orthodox, though it carries with it a similar slur on those of other beliefs. It says, "We are they who believe the gospel of Christ; those who differ from us do not believe it." It is like the assumption by some of the Corinthians of the exclusive name of Christians. "We are of Christ," said they—meaning that the followers of Paul and Apollos were not so.

Probably the better part of those who take the name of Orthodox, or Evangelical, intend no such arrogance. All they want is some word by which to distinguish themselves from Unitarians, Universalists, &c. They might say, "We have as good a right to complain of your calling yourselves 'Rational Christians' or 'Liberal Christians'—assuming thereby that others are not rational or liberal. You mean no such assumption, perhaps; neither do we when we call ourselves 'Orthodox' or 'Evangelical.' When we can find another term, better than these, by which to express the difference between us, we will use it. We do not intend by using these words to foreclose argument or to beg the question. We do not mean by Orthodoxy, right belief; but only a certain well-known form of doctrine."

This is all well. Yet not quite well—since we have had occasion to notice the surprise and disgust felt by those who had called themselves "The Orthodox," in finding themselves in a community where others had assumed that title, and refused to them any share in it. Therefore it is well to emphasize the declaration that Orthodoxy in the sense of "right belief" is an unmeaning expression, signifying nothing.

§ 4. Orthodoxy as the Doctrine of the Majority. Objections

The majority, in any particular place, is apt to call itself orthodox, and to call its opponents heretics. But the majority in one place may be the minority in another. The majority in Massachusetts is the minority in Virginia. The majority in England is the minority in Rome or Constantinople. The Archbishop of Canterbury, the Primate of all England, gave Mr. Carzon a letter of introduction to the Patriarch of Constantinople, the head of the Greek Church. But the Patriarch had never heard of the Archbishop of Canterbury, and inquired, "Who is he?"

Nevertheless, it is a very common argument that such and such a doctrine, being held by the great majority of Christians, must necessarily be true. Thus it is said that since the great majority of Christians believe the doctrine of the Trinity, that doctrine must be true. "Is it possible," it is said, "that the great majority of Christian believers should be now, and have been so long, left in error on such a fundamental doctrine as this?" Even so intelligent a man as Dr. Huntington seems to have been greatly influenced by this argument in becoming a Trinitarian. The same argument has carried many Protestants into the Roman Catholic Church. And, no doubt, there is a truth in the argument—a truth, indeed, which is implied all through the present work—that doctrines thus held by great multitudes during long periods cannot be wholly false. But it by no means proves them to be wholly true. Otherwise, truth would change as the majorities change. In one century the Arians had the majority; and Arianism, therefore, in that century would have been true. Moreover, most of those who adhere to a doctrine have not examined it, and do not have any defined opinion concerning it. They accept it, as it is taught them, without reflection. And again, most truths are, at first, in a minority of one. Christianity, in the first century, was in a very small minority. Protestantism, in the time of Luther, was all in the brain and heart of one man. To assume, therefore, that Orthodoxy, or the true belief, is that of the majority, is to forbid all progress, to denounce all new truth, and to resist the revelation and inspiration of God, until it has conquered for itself the support of the majority of mankind. According to this principle, as Christianity is still in a minority as compared with paganism, we ought all to become followers of Boodh. Such a view cannot bear a moment's serious examination. Every prophet, sage, martyr, and heroic champion of truth has spent his life and won the admiration and grateful love of the world by opposing the majority in behalf of some neglected or unpopular truth.

§ 5. Orthodoxy as the Oldest Doctrine. Objections

Some people think that Orthodoxy means the *oldest* doctrine, and that if they can only find out what doctrine was believed by the Church in the first century, they shall have the true orthodox doctrine. But the early Church held some opinions which all now believe to be false. They believed, for instance, that Jesus was to return visibly, in that age, and set up his church in person, and reign in the world in outward form—a thing which did not take place. They therefore believed in the early church something which was not true—consequently what *they* believed cannot be a certain test of Orthodoxy.

The High Church party in the Church of England, in defending themselves against the Roman Catholic argument from antiquity, have appealed to a higher antiquity, and established themselves on the supposed faith of the first three centuries. But Isaac Taylor, in his "Ancient Christianity," has sufficiently shown that during no period in those early centuries was anything like modern orthodoxy satisfactorily established.4 The Church doctrine was developed gradually during a long period of debate and controversy. The Christology of the Church was elaborated amid the fierce conflicts of Arians and Athanasians, Monothelites and Monophysites, Nestorians and Eutychians. The anthropology of the Church was hammered and beaten into shape by the powerful arm of Augustine and his successors, on the anvils of the fifth century, amid the fiery disputes of Pelagians, Semi-Pelagians, and their opponents.

Many doctrines generally believed in the early church are universally rejected now. The doctrine of chiliasm, or the millennial reign of Christ on earth; the doctrine of the under world, or Hades, where all souls went after death; the doctrine of the atonement made by Christ to the devil,—such were some of the prevailing views held in the early ages of the Church. The oldest doctrine is not certainly the truest; or, as Theodore Parker once said to a priest in Rome, who told him that the primacy of Peter was asserted in the second century, "A lie is no better because it is an old one."

§ 6. Orthodoxy as the Doctrine held by all

But, it may be said, if Orthodoxy does not mean the absolutely right system of belief, nor the system held by the majority, nor the oldest doctrine of the Church, it may, nevertheless, mean the *essential* truths held in all Christian Churches, in all ages and times; in short, according to the ancient formula—that which has been believed always, by all persons, and everywhere—"*quod semper, quod ab omnibus, quod ubique.*"

In this sense no one would object to Orthodoxy. Only make your Catholicity large enough to include every one, and who would not be a Catholic? But this famous definition, if it be strictly taken, seems as much too large as the others are too narrow. If you only admit to be orthodox what all Christian persons have believed, then the Trinity ceases to be orthodox; for many, in all ages, have disbelieved it. Eternal punishment is not orthodox, for that, too, has often been denied in the Church. Sacraments are not orthodox, for the Quakers have rejected them. The resurrection is not orthodox, for there were some Christians in the Church at Corinth who said there was no resurrection of the dead.

§ 7. Orthodoxy, as a Formula, not to be found

Any attempt, therefore, rigidly to define Orthodoxy, destroys it. Regarded as a precise statement, in a fixed or definite form, it is an impossibility. There is no such thing, and never has been. No creed ever made satisfied even the majority. How, indeed, can any statement proceeding from the human brain be an adequate and permanent expression of eternal truth? Even the apostle says, "I know in part, and I prophesy in part, but when that which is perfect is come, then that which is in part shall be done away." The apostle declares that his sight of truth is only partial, and that everything partial is imperfect, and that everything imperfect must pass away; so that our present knowledge of truth is transient. "Whether there be knowledge, it shall pass away." If the apostle Paul declared that he had not the power of making a perfect and permanent statement of truth, how can we believe that any one else can ever do it?

§ 8. Orthodoxy as Convictions underlying Opinions

If, therefore, every doctrinal statement is changeable and changing; if the history of opinions shows the rise and fall of creeds,—one after the other becoming dominant, and then passing away; if no formula has ever gained the universal assent of Christendom; if the oldest creeds contained errors now universally rejected,—what then remains as Orthodoxy? We answer, no one statement, but something underlying all statements—no one system of theology, but certain convictions, perhaps, pervading all the ruling systems. Man's mind, capable of insight, sees with the inward eye the same great spiritual realities, just as with his outward eye he sees the same landscape, sky, ocean. According to the purity and force of his insight, and the depth of his experience, he sees the same truth. There is one truth, but many ways of stating it—one spirit, but many forms.

"The one remains, the many change and pass;

Heaven's light forever shines, earth's shadows fly."

Are there any such great convictions underlying and informing all the creeds? I think there are. I think, for example, it has always been believed in the Church that in some sense man is a sinner, and in some sense Christ is a Saviour from sin; that Christianity is in some way a supernatural revelation of the divine will and love; that Scripture is somehow an inspired book, and has authority over our belief and life; that there is a Church, composed of disciples of Jesus, whose work in the world is to aid him in saving the lost and helping the fallen and wretched; that somehow man needs to be changed from his natural state into a higher state, and to begin a new life, in order to see God; that there is such a thing as heaven, and such a thing as hell; that those who love God and man belong to heaven, and that the selfish and sensual belong to hell. These ideas have been the essential ideas of the Church, and constitute the essence of its Orthodoxy.

Orthodoxy, then, is not any definite creed, or statement of truth. It is not of the letter, but of the spirit. The letter kills. Consequently those who cling to the letter of Orthodoxy kill its spirit. The greatest enemy of Orthodoxy is dead Orthodoxy. The old statements retained after their life is gone, — the old phrases made Shibboleths by which truth is to be forever tested, — these gradually make the whole system seem false to the advancing intellect of the human race. Then heresies come up, just as providential, and just as necessary, as Orthodoxy, to compel the Church to make restatements of the eternal truth. Heresies, in this sense, are as true as Orthodoxy, and make part, indeed, of a higher Orthodoxy.

By Orthodoxy, therefore, we do not mean the opinions held by any particular denomination in New England or elsewhere. We do not mean the opinions of New England Calvinists or of Southern Presbyterians; not the creed of Andover, of New Haven, or of Princeton: but we mean that great system of belief which gradually took form in the Christian Church, in the course of centuries, as its standard theology. The pivotal points of this system are sin and salvation. In it man appears as a sinner, and Christ as a Saviour. Man is saved by an inward change of heart, resulting in an outward change of life, and produced by the sight of the two facts of sin and salvation. The sight of his sin and its consequences leads him to repentance; the sight of salvation leads him to faith, hope, and love; and the sight of both results in regeneration, or a new life. This system also asserts the divinity of Christ, the triune nature of God, the divine decrees, the plenary inspiration of Scripture, eternal punishment, and eternal life.

§ 9. Substantial Truth and Formal Error in all great Doctrinal Systems

Within the last twenty-five years, a new department of theological literature has arisen in Germany, which treats of the history of doctrines. The object of this is to trace the doctrinal opinions held in the Church in all ages. By this course of study, two facts are apparent—first, that the same great views have been substantially held by the majority of Christians in all ages; and, secondly, that the forms of doctrine have been very different. The truths themselves have been received by Christians, as their strength, their hope, and their joy, in all time; but the formal statement of these truths has been wrought out differently by individual intellects. The universal body of Christians has taken care of Christian truth; while the Church Fathers, or doctors, have held in their hands the task of defining it doctrinally for the intellect.

By substantial truth we mean this—that in all the great systems of opinion which have had a deep hold on the human mind, over broad spaces and through long periods, there is something suited to man's nature, and corresponding with the facts of the case. The mind of man was made for truth, and not for error. Error is transient: truth only is permanent. Men do not love error for its own sake, but for the sake of something with which it is connected. After a while, errors are eliminated, and the substance retained. The great, universal, abiding convictions of men must, therefore, contain truth. If it were not so, we might well despair; for, if the mind of the race could fall into unmixed error, the only remedy by which the heart can be cured, and the life redeemed from evil, would be taken away. But it is not so. God has made the mind for truth, as he has adapted the taste to its appropriate food. In the main, and in the long run, what men believe *is the truth*; and all catholic beliefs are valid beliefs. Opinions held by all men, everywhere and at all times, must be substantially true.

But error certainly exists, and always has existed. If the human mind is made for truth, how does it fall into error? There never has been any important question upon which men have not taken two sides; and, where they take two sides, one side must be in error. Sometimes these two parties are equally balanced, and that for long periods. With which has the truth been? Is God always with the majority? If so, we must at once renounce our Unitarian belief for the Trinity, as an immense majority of votes are given in its favor. But, then, we must also renounce Protestantism; for Protestantism has only eighty or ninety millions against a hundred and forty millions who are Catholics. And, still further, we must renounce Christianity in favor of Heathenism; since all the different Christian sects and churches united make up but three hundred millions, while the Buddhists alone probably exceed that number. Moreover, truth is always in a minority at first,—usually in a minority of one; and, if men ought to wait until it has a majority on its side before they accept it, it never will have a majority on its side.

These objections lead us to the only possible answer, which consists in distinguishing between the substance and the form. When we assert that all creeds, widely held and long retained, have truth, we mean substantial truth. We do not mean that they are true in their formal statement, which may be an erroneous statement, but that they are true as to their contents. The substance of the belief is the fact inwardly beheld by the mind; the form is the verbal statement which the mind makes of what it has seen. It has seen something real; but, when it attempts to describe what it has seen, it may easily commit errors. Thus there may be, in the same creed, substantial truth and formal error; and all great and widely-extended beliefs, as we assert, must contain substantial truth and formal error. Without substantial truth, there would be nothing in them to feed the mind, and they would not be retained; and, if they were not more or less erroneous in form, it would imply infallibility on the part of those who give them their form.

§ 10. Importance of this Distinction

This distinction is one of immense importance; because, being properly apprehended, it would, by destroying dogmatism, destroy bigotry also. Dogmatism consists in assuming that the essence of truth lies in its formal statement. Correctly assuming that the life of the soul comes from the sight of truth, it falsely infers that the essence of truth is in the verbal formula. Consequently, this formula must necessarily seem of supreme importance, and the very salvation of the soul to depend on holding the correct opinion. With this conviction, one *must and ought* to be bigoted; he ought to cling to the minutest syllable of his creed as the drowning man clings to the floating plank. Holding this view, we cannot blame men for being bigoted: it is their duty to be bigoted. But, when the distinction is recognized, they will cling to the substance, knowing that the vital truth lies there. It is the sight of the fact which is the source of our life, and not the statement which we make, in words, as to what we have seen. Then the sight becomes the thing of immense importance; the creed in which it is expressed, of comparative unimportance.

This distinction would tend to bring the Church to a true unity—the unity of the spirit. All would strive for the same insight, all tolerate variety of expression. Instead of assenting outwardly to the same creed, every man ought, in fact, to make his own creed; and there should be as many different creeds as there are different men. Nor should my creed of to-day be the same as that of yesterday; for, instead of resting on a past experience, I should continually endeavor to obtain new sights of the one unchangeable truth. Seeing more of it to-day than I did yesterday, my yesterday's creed would seem inadequate, and I should wish to make a new one.

Substantial truth means the truth which we see—the inward sight, the radical experience. Formal truth is the verbal statement, and consists in accuracy of expression. And so of error. Substantial error means error in regard to the substance, and is necessarily inadequacy of inward experience. Strictly speaking, there cannot be substantial error; for error, in regard to the substance of truth, is purely negative. It is not-seeing. It is failing to perceive the truth, either from want of opportunity, weakness of vision, or neglect in looking. But formal error is not merely defect: it may also be mistake. We may misstate the truth, and say what is radically false. From this source come contradictions; and, where two statements are contradictory, both cannot be true. Falsehood, therefore, originates with the statement. The errors of insight are merely defects; but the errors of statement may be positive falsehoods.

This leads us to take a special view of theological controversies. In all great controversies, in the conflicts of ages, where the good and wise have stood opposed to each other, century after century, it is probable that there are truth and error on both sides.

Each side may hold some truth which the other has not seen. There is, therefore, also substantial error on both sides; for each may have failed to see some phase of truth which the other has recognized. But there may be formal error, or error of statement, even where there is substantial truth; for the truth may be overstated, or understated, or misstated, and a false expression given to a true observation.

What, then, is the duty of those who stand opposed to each other in these controversies—of Catholics and Protestants, Christians and Deists, Orthodox and Unitarians? They have plainly a twofold duty to themselves as well as to their opponents. They ought to increase their insight, and to improve their statements; to deepen and widen their hold of the substance; to correct and improve their expression of the form. The first is the work of religion; the second, that of theology.

The first is infinitely the most important, because the life of the soul depends on the sight of truth. This is its food, without which it will starve and die. But it is also important that it should improve its theology, because a correct theology is a help to insight, and a ground of mental communion.

§ 11. The Orthodox and Liberal Parties in New England

The Liberal party in New England have carried on a theological controversy for some forty years with the Orthodox. This controversy was inevitable. Calvinism had neglected important truths which the human soul needed, and without which it would starve. Unitarianism came to assert and vindicate those truths. At first, it was inevitable that the statements on either side should be narrow and mutually exclusive. But, as a battle goes on, the position of the opposing armies changes. The points of attack and defence alter. Old positions are abandoned, and new ones occupied. Seldom does it happen to either army to sleep on the field of battle. Nor has it so happened to us. Neither the Unitarians nor the Trinitarians have gained a complete victory: each has taken some important position, and yielded some other. We have a book called "Concessions of Trinitarians:" another might be written containing the "Concessions of Unitarians." Neither side has conceded, or ought to concede, any real truth of experience or of statement; but it is honorable to each to concede its own partial and inadequate statements.

We intend, in this volume, to endeavor, from our own point of view, to gain what sight we can of the radical, vital truth underlying each great Orthodox doctrine. At the same time, we shall freely criticise the forms, especially the more recent ones, in which Orthodox doctrines have been stated.

We assume, at the outset, that each doctrine *does* cover some truth of experience, some real solid fact, which is as important to us as to our opponents. We assume, that, though the doctrines may be false, there may be an experience behind them which is true. We have satisfied ourselves of the formal error of their statements. We consider it impossible for a sound Unitarian intellect to accept the Orthodox theology as a whole, without being untrue to itself; but there is no reason why we should not break this shell of doctrine, and find the vital truths which it contains. And if it be said, "Who made you a judge or a divider on these subjects?" we reply, that only by contributions from all quarters can a final judgment be reached. Meantime, it is the right and duty of every serious thinker to add his own opinion to the common stock; willing to be refuted when wrong, — glad, if right, to be helpful in any degree towards the ultimate result.

This is the object of the present work, which, though written by a Unitarian, and from a Unitarian stand-point, and though published by the American Unitarian Association, will, we trust, be sufficiently unsectarian.

Chapter II
The Principle And Idea Of Orthodoxy
Stated And Examined

§ 1. The Principle of Orthodoxy defined

The principle of Orthodoxy is, that there is one true system of Christian doctrine, and that all others are false; that this system can be, and has been, so stated in words as to distinguish it from all the false systems or heresies; and that this true system of doctrine is the one which is now held, and always has been held, by the majority of Christians; and, finally, that the belief of this system is, as a rule, essential to salvation—so that those who may be saved, while not accepting it, will be saved (if at all) by way of exception, and not according to rule.

§ 2. Logical Genesis of the Principle of Orthodoxy

The principle of Orthodoxy seems to have arisen, and to have maintained itself in the Church, in some such way as this. Jesus Christ, it is assumed, came to save the soul from sin and evil. He saves the soul by the word of truth. In order that this truth shall become saving truth, it must be believed, and so strongly believed as to have a practical influence on life and action. We are therefore saved by believing the truth taught by Christ. But in order to be believed, it must be expressed in some definite statement, or in what we call Christian doctrine. But truth is one, and therefore the doctrine which expresses it must also be one.

Therefore there must be one system of Christian doctrine, containing in itself the substance of Christian truth, and constituting the object of Christian faith. This system, though it may vary in its unessential parts, must in its essence be unchangeable. In proportion as any system of belief varies from it, such system is heterodox and dangerous, while this system alone is orthodox and safe.

Another form of this argument would be as follows: Christ came to *reveal* something to men. If revealed, it must be made known. If made known, it must be capable of being so expressed that there can be no reasonable doubt concerning it. Otherwise, Christianity would not be a revelation. But if expressed so as to enter the human mind, it must be expressed in human language. A verbal revelation, therefore, is essential for the purposes of Christianity. Such a revelation is nothing else than a system of doctrine, or that which can be systematized into doctrine. And this system must be one and the same from age to age, or it is not a permanent divine revelation, but only a transient human seeking for such a revelation.

§ 3. Orthodoxy assumed to be the Belief of the Majority

The natural test of Orthodoxy is assumed to be the belief of the majority of Christians; for if Christianity be a revelation of truth, its essential contents must be easy to apprehend, and when apprehended, they must be generally accepted. The revelations of God in nature are seen and accepted by the human intellect, and so become matters of science. Orthodox science is that which the great majority of scientific men have accepted as such; and Orthodox *Christianity*, in like manner, must be that which the majority of Christian believers accept as such. Hence it is taken for granted, as regards Orthodox doctrine, that it meets the test, "*Quod semper, quod ubique, quod ab omnibus.*"

§ 4. Heterodoxy thus becomes sinful

But if the essential truth of Christianity be thus plain, those who do not receive it must be either stupid or wilful. Its rejection argues a want of intellect or a bad heart. Heretics, therefore, ought logically to become to the Orthodox objects either of contempt or hatred. If they cannot see what is so plain, they must be intellectually imbecile. If they will not see it, they must be morally depraved. Therefore intelligent people who accept and teach heresies ought to be considered wicked people by logical Orthodox minds. Moreover, they are the most dangerous persons in the community, because, by denying that truth by which the soul is to be saved, they endanger not merely the temporal, but also the eternal, welfare of those whom they seduce. And if we have a right to abate a nuisance which only interferes with the earthly comfort and peace of society, how much more one which attacks its spiritual peace and eternal welfare! Have not the majority a right to protect themselves, their children, and society from that which they not merely believe, but know, to be evil? For Orthodoxy assumes to be not merely opinion, but knowledge. Hence Orthodoxy legitimates persecution.5 Persecution is only the judicious repression of criminal attempts to pervert and injure society. Moreover, Orthodoxy, according to its principle, ought to discourage inquiry in relation to its own fundamental principles. For why continue to discuss and debate about that which is known? Progress consists in advancing from the known to the unknown. The unknown, and not the known, is the proper subject for inquiry. The system of Orthodoxy, therefore, according to its own principle, should be withdrawn from further examination. Intellectual advance requires us to take for granted something—to forget that which is behind in order to press forward to that which is before. The doctrines of Orthodoxy therefore, when once established, should afterwards be assumed, and need not be proved. We do not call a scientific man a bigot because he refuses to discuss fundamental principles. If Orthodoxy be science, why accuse it of bigotry when it follows the same course?

§ 5. The Doctrine of Essentials and Non-essentials leads to Rome

If Orthodoxy consists in a statement of opinions the belief of which is essential to salvation, the question arises, Are *all* these opinions essential, or only a part? It is generally admitted that the great system called Orthodoxy contains some things not essential to salvation. How shall these be distinguished? Moreover, some variation of statement is judged allowable. No Orthodox creed is assumed to be inspired as to its language. The same essential truth may be expressed in different terms. How, then, are we to define the limits of expression so as to know what error of opinion is venial, and what vital? Orthodoxy assures us that our salvation depends on accepting its statements. In which particular form, then, must we accept them? In so important a matter as this, where salvation is assumed to depend on accepting the right form of doctrine, one surely ought to be able to know which the right form is. Now, the rule of Orthodoxy, as given above, is, that nothing is Orthodox, as essential doctrine, which has not been believed "always, everywhere, and by all." But this raises an historical question, and one of no little difficulty. For since heresies have always existed, and some one has always been found somewhere to deny the most essential doctrines of Orthodoxy, the question is somewhat intricate who these "all" are who have never disbelieved the Orthodox system. It is plain that the majority of Christians have neither time nor ability for these investigations. The historical inquiry must be conducted for them by others. And here seems to come in the law of Church authority as against private judgment. And so the principle of Orthodoxy, carried out to its legitimate results, appears to land us at last in the Roman Catholic Church, to set aside the right of private judgment, and to justify intolerance and the forcible suppression of heresy. But as these results are not accepted by those who yet accept the principles of Orthodoxy, it is necessary to see if there is a fallacy anywhere in our course of thought, and at what precise point the fallacy has come in.

§ 6. Fallacy in this Orthodox Argument

The fallacy in all this argument lies here—that faith is confounded with belief; knowledge with opinion; the sight of truth with its intellectual statement in the form of doctrine. Undoubtedly there is only one faith, but there may be many ways of stating it in the form of opinion. Moreover, no man, no church, no age, sees the whole of truth. Truth is multilateral, but men's minds are unilateral. They are mirrors which reflect, and that imperfectly, the side of the object which is towards them. Therefore even knowledge in any finite mind is partial, consequently imperfect; and consequently needs other knowledge to complete it.

This, apparently, is what the apostle Paul means (1 Cor. 13:8-12) in his statement concerning the relation between knowledge and love. Knowledge (Gnosis) "shall pass away." The word here used is elsewhere translated by "destroyed," "brought to nought," "abolished," "made of none effect." "Knowledge" here probably refers to definite and systematic statements of real insights. It is something more than opinion, but something less than faith. Faith abides, but knowledge passes away. Faith abides, because it is a positive sight of truth. It is an experience of the soul, by which it opens itself in trust, and becomes receptive of spiritual influence. Faith, therefore, remains, and its results are permanent in the soul. They make the substance of our knowledge as regards the spiritual world. This substance becomes a part of the soul itself, and constitutes a basis of self-consciousness as real as is its experience of the external world. But *Gnosis* is this faith, translated by the intellect into systematic form. Such systems embody real experience, and are necessary for mental and moral progress. They are the bodies of thought. But all bodies must die, sooner or later; and so all systems of knowledge must pass away. The body, at first, helps the growth of thought, helps the growth of the soul; but afterwards it hinders it. The new wine must be put into new bottles. Therefore the apostle Paul, the great teacher of doctrinal theology in the Christian Church, distinctly recognizes here, that every system of doctrine, no matter how much truth it contains, is partial, and therefore transient. He makes no exception in favor even of inspired statements—he does not except his own. All bodies must die; all forms are fugitive; nothing continues but the substance of knowledge, which is faith; the inward sight of God's goodness producing that endless expectation which is called hope; and the large spiritual communion with God and his creatures, here called Agape, or love. The apostle speaks in the first person when he says that knowledge passes away—"*We* know in part, and *we* prophesy [or teach] in part." He speaks for himself and his fellow-apostles.

We see, therefore, that the great master and head of Orthodoxy in the Church has himself declared every form of Orthodoxy to be transient.

We conclude, therefore, that the apostle Paul, in this famous passage, overturns the whole principle of verbal Orthodoxy. He takes away its foundation. Not denying the reality and permanence of religious experience, not denying the saving power of truth, he declares that no expressed system of truth is permanent. The basis of doctrinal Orthodoxy is the assumption that its own particular form of belief is essential to salvation. But the apostle declares that *all* forms are transient, and, therefore, *none* essential. All statement is a limitation, and the moment that we make a definition, we say something which is incomplete. When Paul says, "We know in part," he says the same thing which is said by Kant, by Sir William Hamilton, by Auguste Comte, by Mr. Mansell, and most modern thinkers, when they declare the relativity of knowledge. All thinking is limitation. "To think," says Sir William Hamilton, "is to condition." We only know a thing, says this school, by its being different from something else. The school of Kant declares all knowledge to be phenomenal, and that all phenomenal knowledge consists of two parts—the part given by the thing, and the part added by the mind. Herbert Spencer (in "First Principles") insists on the certainty of the existence of things in themselves, but also on their absolute and eternal unknowableness. According to John Stuart Mill, the same view of the unknowableness of Noumena is taken by M. Auguste Comte.

These modern philosophers, it will be seen, go much farther than Paul, and lay down positions which inaugurate a universal scepticism. According to them there is nothing certain and nothing fixed. Mr. Mansell virtually teaches us that we cannot know anything of God, duty, or immortality; and that faith means, taking for granted on some outward authority. To use a striking expression of President James Walker, "We are not to believe, but to make believe." That is, we are not to believe with our intellect, but with our will. Or, in other words, we are to believe not what is true, but what is expedient. This he calls regulative truth, as opposed to speculative truth.

But this is by no means the doctrine of the apostle Paul. He teaches the certainty of substantive knowledge, but the fallibility of formal knowledge. He thus avoids the two extremes of dogmatism on the one side, and scepticism on the other. The substance of Gnosis, which is the sight of truth, is a reality, and, like all that is real, has its root in God, and shares his eternity. The form of Gnosis is subjective, relative, and transient. Everything which is seen is temporal; only that which is not seen is eternal. All that takes outward, visible form, comes under the law of change; the roots of our knowledge, fixed in God, are unchangeable.

§ 7. The three Tendencies in the Church

The human soul, a unit, indivisible, and without parts, nevertheless acts in three directions—of will, affection, intellect. These are distinguishable, though not divisible. Every one knows the difference between an *act*; an *emotion* of anger, pity, sorrow, love; and a process of logic, or an intellectual argument. These are the three primary states of the mind, evidently distinct. It is impossible to mistake either for the other. I may direct my mind towards action, towards thought, or towards emotion. The first of these, action, is the most within my own power, depends chiefly on myself, lies nearest the will. *Will* passes instantaneously into action. I will to lift my arm, and it is done. On the other hand, feeling or emotion lies the farthest from this centre of will, depends least of all on my own choice, and in it I am most passive. But the sphere of intellect is intermediate. I am more free when I think than when I feel; less free than when I act. In the domain of will, I act upon external things; in the domain of feeling, I am acted upon by external things; in the domain of intellect, I neither act nor am acted upon, but I *see* them. In all thinking, in proportion as it is pure thought, both will and emotion are excluded. We are neither actors nor sufferers, but spectators. Things seen pass into our life through the intellect, and become sources of emotion and action. Love of truth causes us to desire to know it; this desire leads us to put our mind in the presence of truth, but when there, the functions of emotion and will cease, and all we have to do is to look.

Now, there have always been in the Church three parties, or at least three tendencies, in regard to the basis of religion. One of these makes the basis of the religious life to consist in thought, one posits it in feeling, the third in action. With one, the intellect must take the initiative; with the second, the heart; with the third, the will, or power of determination. The three parties in the Church, based on these three tendencies, may be characterized as the Orthodoxists, the Emotionalists, and the party of Works. The first says, "We are saved by faith;" the second says, "We are saved by love;" the third says, "We are saved by obedience." The first assumes that the sight of truth must take the lead in all Christian experience; the second believes that love for goodness is the true basis in religion; the third maintains that the first thing to be done, in order to become a religious man, is to obey the law of duty. It is evidently very important to decide which of these answers is the true one. What are we to do first, if we wish to become Christian men or women? Are we to study, read, reflect, in order to know the truth? Are we to go to church and listen to sermons, join Bible classes and study the

Scriptures, read compends of doctrine and books of Christian evidence? Or are we to seek for emotion, to pray for a change of heart, to put ourselves under exciting influences, to go where a revival is in progress, to attend protracted meetings, to be influenced through sympathy till we are filled full of emotions of anxiety, fear, remorse, followed by emotions of hope, trust, gratitude, pardon, peace, joy? Or are we to do neither of these things, but to begin by obedience, trying to *do* right in order to *be* right, beginning by the performance of the humblest duties, the nearest duties, letting fidelity in the least open the way to more? Shall we *know* the truth in order to love it and do it? Or shall we *love* the truth in order to see it and do it? Or shall we *do* right in order to know it and love it?

Large numbers in the Church have followed each of these three methods, and made each the basis of its action. One has said, "We are saved by works;" a second, "We are saved by faith;" a third, "We are saved by love."

§ 8. The Party of Works

Two tendencies have joined in teaching salvation by works, or, more strictly, in teaching *the initiative of the will in religion*. These are the Church-tendency and the Moral-tendency in Christianity. The Church party in Christianity teaches that the first duty towards a child is to make it a member of the Christian Church by baptism, and that the first duty of every baptized person is to obey the commands of the Church. The Church thus becomes a school, in which baptized persons are educated as Christians. The Church of Rome, and the High Church party in the Church of England and in the Episcopal Church of the United States, teach this doctrine of salvation by works. This system by no means dispenses with Christian belief or Christian feeling, but makes them both subordinate. The Church says to its faithful, We do not require you to believe or to feel, but to obey. If we said, "Believe," or "Feel," you might justly reply, "We cannot believe or feel when we choose, and you have therefore no right to ask us to do so." Therefore the Church only demands obedience, which it is in the power of all to render. It, indeed, requires an assent to its creed, and forbids heresy. But this only means, "Receive the creed as true until you are able to see *how* it is true." The Church also insists greatly on love, and its saints have been filled with the highest raptures of piety. But it never *requires* feeling. It says, "Use the means we put into your hands, and feeling will come. Pray, as we command you to do, whether you feel deeply or not. Feeling will come by and by." Discipline, therefore, and not illumination, has been the method of the Church of Rome, and is also the method of all other Churches, so far as they are ecclesiastical Churches. All such Churches teach that by a faithful conformity to their ritual, methods, sacraments, services, discipline, the Christian life will surely come. The one thing needful and primary with them all is obedience, and the result of obedience is knowledge and love.

Essentially the same view is taken by the Ethical party, or Moralists, in Christianity. Their statement, also, of the foundation of religion is, that it lies in obedience. They differ only from the Church party as regards the authority to be obeyed. With them it is not the Church, but the Moral Law, as made known to men in revelation, or in the natural instincts of conscience. The foundation of all goodness and religion is right doing. This leads to right thinking and right feeling; or, when it does not lead to these, it is still sufficient, and is satisfactory to God. "What doth the Lord require of thee," say they, "but to do justly, and love mercy, and walk humbly with thy God?" At this point the extremes meet, and the Roman Catholic Church, or the extreme right, offers its hand to the Liberal Christians, or the extreme left. This is the point of contact between the two, which sometimes, also, becomes a bridge by which proselytes pass either way, from one to the other. But the practical question is, Is this answer sound? *Does* the will lead the way in religion? Is obedience the first step to be taken at every point of the way? Is the initiative in the religious life always an action? Are we saved by works?

The objection to this view is, that a religious action, without a religious thought and a religious affection behind it, is not in any sense religious. It has in it nothing of the essence of religion. Religion, regarded merely as obedience to God, implies the knowledge of God. We must know God in order to obey him; we must know God in order to love him. Knowledge, therefore, must precede obedience, and not the contrary. Otherwise obedience is an empty form, having no religious character. Unless we see the truth and justice of obedience, we are only yielding to human persuasion, to human authority, and not to the authority of God. It may be well, or it may be ill, to yield to such human authority; but there is no religion in it, or only a religion of dead works.

§ 9. The Party of Emotion in Christianity

There are those, and always have been those, who have placed the substance of religion in love, in which they have, perhaps, not been mistaken. But they have often taken another step, by degrading love into mere emotion. They have considered that feeling was the basis of religion; not thought, nor action. They too have texts to quote in support of their view. They say that "with the *heart* men believe unto righteousness;" that we must "be rooted and grounded in *love*;" that the *first* commandment is to "*love* God with all the heart." As with them religious emotion constitutes the essence of religion, they make use of all means of producing it, and especially the excitement which comes from sympathy. The Methodist Church has, perhaps, gone farther than any other towards making this a principle. This great and noble body has done its vast work for Christianity by making prominent the love-principle in all its operations. If the Church party stands at one extreme, Methodism, in all its forms, stands at the other. The Roman Catholic Church sums up all the inspirations of the past, collects in its large *repertoire* all ancient liturgies, all saintly lives, all sacred customs, and so brings an imposing authority, a reverend antiquity, made up of the best history of man. Methodism drops the past, and finds God in the present—in present inspirations, in the newly-converted soul, born out of darkness into light, by the immediate coming of the Spirit of God. According to the Catholic Church the Christian life commences with an outward act,—that of baptism,—and is carried on by outward sacraments; according to Methodism, the Christian life begins with an inward emotional experience,—the spiritual new birth,—and is carried on by successive emotions of penitence, faith, hope, joy, and pious devotion. According to Catholicism, the one thing needful is the outward sacramental union with the Church; according to Methodism, the one thing needful is the inward emotional union with the Holy Spirit.

§ 10. The Faith Party in Religion

If Churchism and Moralism place the essence of Christianity in action, and Emotionalism puts it in feeling, Orthodoxy places it in something intellectual, which it calls faith. All the sects of Christendom do, indeed, place faith at the root of the Christian life; but some make it essentially an intellectual act, others essentially affectionate, and others an act of will. Orthodoxy makes it, in substance, a sight of faith, or an act of looking at spiritual realities. Sometimes it is called a realizing sense of spiritual things. But, at all events, the sight of truth is considered the beginning and root of religion by the Orthodox party in the Church. We are saved by the word of truth; and the Saviour himself is called "the Word,"—belief in whom constitutes eternal life. Rationally, it is argued that the essential difference between the Christian and the unbeliever, or the unchristian, must lie in seeing Christ or not seeing him. The first step in the religious life always consists in looking at the truth.

§ 11. Truth in the Orthodox Idea

Admitting, then, what all these systems and parties in the Church unite in asserting,—that an act of faith is always at the foundation of every Christian state and of all Christian experience,—we ask, Which is the most essential element in faith—will, intellect, or affection? Is an act of faith chiefly an act of the will, a determination, or is it a loving desire, or a state of knowledge, a looking at truth? Suppose we call it a state of love, for this reason, that in order to be good, the first thing requisite is to wish to be good. A longing for goodness, it may be said, must precede everything else. But what makes us long for goodness, if we *do* desire it? What shall produce that longing, if it does not exist? The only answer must be, The sight of truth. The sight of God's holiness and of God's tenderness, the sight of law and gospel, whatever shows us the beauty of goodness and the meanness of sin, must come first to awaken this desire. Or suppose it be said that the essential thing in faith is the active element, because it is submitting to God's law, trusting in his help, coming to the truth, opening the heart to the Holy Spirit,—all of which are determinations of the will. We must reply, True; but these determinations will never be taken unless we first *see* the will of God to which we submit, see the salvation of God on which we lean, know that there is a truth to which we may come, know that there is a Holy Spirit, in order to ask for it.

So that, on the whole, we may say that Orthodoxy is right in making the sight of truth the beginning of the Christian life, and the beginning of every Christian state, act, or experience. All human goodness is the reflection of God's goodness; it all has its source in the sight of a divine holiness, truth, beauty. This is the fundamental idea of Orthodoxy, and in this Orthodoxy is right.

It is no answer to this to say that man has an instinctive longing for goodness, which causes him to feel after God before he finds him. For what are these instincts themselves, as soon as they begin to act, but the voice of God speaking in the soul, showing it some glimpses of a divine truth? The longing in the soul must be aroused by the sight or knowledge of something better than that which one has or is. Consequently, we say again, that the sight of truth is that which saves the soul, and first creates in it a better life.

If we make Christianity to be essentially obedience, we make of it, at last, an oppressive form. If we consider it as essentially an emotional experience, we destroy its moral character; for emotion is both passive and blind, while the definition of morality is the freely choosing what we see to be right. Ecclesiasticism and Emotionalism both tend to demoralize Christianity. They remove from it the element of moral freedom in the interest either of Church authority or of mystical piety. Then Christianity must come anew, in the form of truth, to purify the air, and renew the moral life of society.

Protestantism arose in this way, to salt the corrupting Church. Ecclesiasticism, in its well-meant efforts at training men, by a complete discipline, to a perfect virtue, had suppressed the individual love of truth to such an extent, that religion had become a mere surface, without substance. Jesuitism abolished the distinction between things right and wrong in themselves, and made right to consist solely in the intention; that is, made it wholly subjective. The Lutheran reformation was the revival of the intellect in regard to religion—the demand for conviction instead of assent; for the sight of God in place of obedience to the Church. It repeated, with an emphasis adapted to the needs of the sixteenth century, the words of Jesus, "This is life eternal, to *know* thee, the only true God, and Jesus Christ whom thou hast sent." In these words is the sufficient defence of Protestantism. It was the cry of the soul to *know* God, and not merely to assent to what the Church taught concerning him; it was the longing to *know* Christ, and not to repeat by rote the creeds of the first centuries, and the definitions of mediæval doctors in regard to him. In a subsequent chapter we shall consider the truth and error in the Protestant principle of justification by faith. Our purpose here is to show that the truth in Orthodoxy is identical with the truth in Protestantism. Both place, as the root of all religion, an individual personal sight of God and truth. To this, freedom of thought is an essential means. Right thinking involves free thinking. If to know the truth makes us free, freedom, again, is the condition of knowing the truth. Protestantism and Orthodoxy have often attempted to limit the application of this principle. Protestants, as well as Catholics, have persecuted heretics. But while Catholics, in doing this, have been faithful to their own idea, and have therefore made of persecution a system, Protestants have been vacillating and undecided persecutors. They have been drawn in opposite directions by antagonist principles. Fundamentally, Protestantism, as such, claims for all the rights of private judgment, and is, therefore, in its whole stress and influence, opposed to persecution, and in favor of religious liberty. It has conquered the Catholic Church on this point so far as to compel it to renounce the practice of persecution, if it has not relinquished the theory. During three centuries Protestantism has been, more and more, emancipating the human mind—making it the duty, and consequently the right, of every human being to see truth for himself. It has been drawn into inconsistencies by its belief in the saving power of certain doctrines, and the supreme importance of believing them. On one hand it has claimed, with a trumpet voice, the freedom of conscience and opinion for all, and then has cried out against those who freely came to opinions differing from its own.

But, notwithstanding these inconsistencies, Protestantism has steadily given freedom of spirit to mankind. And with the awakened and emancipated intellect all the elements of progress have shown themselves in Protestant lands. In 1517, when Luther nailed his theses to the church door, Italy,

Spain, and Portugal were far in advance of Northern Europe in civilization. In commerce, art, and literature, Italy was the queen of Europe. In military force, extent of possessions, and unbounded wealth, Spain was the leading power of the world. The Portuguese mariners had ransacked every sea, and discovered new continents and islands in every zone. How insignificant, in comparison with these great nations, were England, Holland, and Germany! But England, Holland, and Germany became Protestant; Italy, Spain, and Portugal remained Catholic; while France and Austria adopted a half-way Catholicism.

The result has been, in the course of three centuries, a complete reversal of the position. The last have become first, and the first last. What now has become of the terrible power of Spain, the enterprise of Portugal, the art and literature of Italy? When the element of Protestantism was crushed out of these nations by the Inquisition, the principle of national progress was also destroyed. But the northern powers who accepted the Lutheran reform received with it the germs of progress. Holland, Denmark, Norway, Sweden, Prussia, Saxony, England, and Scotland, have, by a steady progress in civilization, wealth, knowledge, and morality, conclusively demonstrated the impulse of progress contained in the Protestant idea.

So far, therefore, as this great experiment, continued during three hundred years, can prove anything, it proves the truth of the central idea of Protestantism and Orthodoxy, namely, that saving faith is essentially not emotional nor volitional, but intellectual.

§ 12. Error in the Orthodox Principle

We are well aware of the reply which might be made, from the standpoint of Ecclesiasticism, to the historical argument just given. The Roman Catholic might answer thus: "We admit that the tree must be known by its fruits; but the tree of true Christianity is known by bearing the fruits of Christianity, not those of worldly civilization. Suppose that England is to-day richer than Italy, more powerful than Spain; is she *better*? Are there more piety and more morality in Protestant than in Catholic countries? In which communities do you find the most humility, simplicity, religious faith, reverence for religious institutions, fear of God? In which do you find most of sympathy, kindliness, good will from man to man? The fierce civilization of Protestantism is hard, cold, and cruel. It tramples under its feet the weak. It accumulates wealth and power; but are these Christianity? Is London or Rome the best model of a Christian city? Is it London, with its terrible contrasts of enormous wealth and naked want, its proud aristocracy and brutalized mob, its empty churches and illuminated gin-shops? or is it not rather Rome, poorer in material wealth and luxury, but rich in grace—

Rome, with its odor of sanctity about it; its numerous churches, on which art has lavished her resources to make them worthy to be the temples of God—Rome, with its priests and monks; its religious houses, the centres of the great religious orders, whose missions have been known in the four quarters of the earth? Protestant countries may have a higher worldly civilization, more education and intelligence, more manufactures and commerce; but Catholic countries have more humility and reverence, a more habitual piety, more gentle manners. If Protestants have more *knowledge*, Catholics have more *love*."

And we, though Protestants of the Protestants, must admit that there is some truth in this. The discipline of Romanism has repressed some amount of evil which the liberty of Protestant lands has allowed to appear. But repressed evil is none the less evil, and often works a greater inward corruption than when it is allowed to show itself as it is. We may also admit that while in Protestantism there is more of truth, and all the virtues which go therewith,—such as honesty, manliness, self-respect, conscientiousness,—in Catholic countries there is more of love, and all the virtues which follow it,—as kindly, genial manners, ready sympathy with suffering, a spirit of dependence and trust. Still, this does not prove that there is more real Christianity among Catholics; for love which does not grow out of the sight of truth is not genuine nor healthy. Its life is weak. Protestant Christianity is an immature fruit, harsh because not quite ripe. Catholic Christianity is a fruit over-ripe, and so rotten.

Therefore we still contend that Protestantism and Orthodoxy are right in making the free and independent sight of truth the root of all religion. But the mistake of Orthodoxy has been in confounding truth with doctrine—the sight of the thing with the theory about that sight. From hence come the hardness and coldness of Orthodoxy. Pure thought is always cold, and ought to be. The sight of spiritual things is truth and love in one; but when we begin to reflect on that sight, the love drops out, and the truth becomes cold.

The defect of the Orthodox principle, therefore, is the confusion of truth with belief. Out of this mistake come dogmatism, bigotry, and all their natural consequences. It is therefore well, before going farther, to explain more fully this distinction and its importance.

§ 13. Faith, Knowledge, Belief, Opinion

Religion originates at every moment, from looking at truth. Now, there are four kinds of looking; *faith*, which is intuitive looking; *knowledge*, which is the intuition itself looked at by reflection, and so brought to consciousness;

third, *belief,* which arranges the products of knowledge in systematic form, and makes them congruous with each other; and lastly comes *opinion,* which does not deal at all with things, but only with thoughts about things. By faith we see God; by knowledge we become conscious that we see God; by belief we arrange in order what we see; and by opinion we feel and grope among our thoughts, seeking what we may find of his works and ways. Every act of faith brings us into the presence of God himself, and makes us partakers of the divine nature. Thus faith is strictly and literally the substance of things hoped for, or the substance of hope.6 Substance here has its etymological sense, and is the same word in Greek and English, meaning basis, foundation, support, or substruction. It is the inward experience by which we come in contact with invisible things, as perception is the experience by which we come in contact with visible things.

These steps of intellectual activity may be called by other names than these. What we (with Jacobi) call faith,7 may be denominated "intuition" (with the transcendentalists), reason (with Coleridge), God-consciousness (with Schleiermacher), or anschauungs-vermögen (with Schelling and others). But, by whatever name we call this power, we say there *is* a power in man by which he can see spiritual facts, as with his earthly senses he can perceive sensible facts. If he has no such power, he is incapable of knowing God, but can only have an opinion that there is a God. But if he can know God, this knowledge rests on something back of reasoning or reflection; it must rest on an intuition or spiritual perception. And this, for our present purpose, we call faith. By means of it we know the spiritual world, just as we know the material world through sight, touch, and hearing. The senses are the organs by which we perceive material things; intuition, or faith, the organ by which we perceive spiritual things. He who denies the existence of such a power in man, falls necessarily into dogmatism on the one hand, or rationalism on the other. But as these words also take a very different sense on different lips, we explain ourselves by saying that he puts either a theory or an inference in the place of God. If orthodox, he puts a theory; if sceptical, an inference. Mr. Mansell does the first, Herbert Spencer the other. Neither of them believes that we can *know* God's existence. So dogmatism and scepticism join hands. All the consequences described in the beginning of this chapter follow as a matter of course when an opinion or theory is put in the place of truth. Then come the inflexible narrowness of bigotry, the hot zeal of the persecutor, the sectarian strife which has torn the Church in twain. The remedy and prevention for these are to recognize that the basis of religion is in faith, in a living sight of God, the soul, duty, immortality, which are always and forever the same.

The best definitions of faith, by theologians of all schools, include the notion of insight, will, and affection. It is an act of the soul by which it looks at truth. But this act implies a desire to see and know the truth. Now, such an act as this lies at the root of all our knowledge, both of the material and spiritual world. How do I know the outward world? The passive exercise of sensation would never give such knowledge. The sights which enter the passive eye, the sounds which fill the passive ear, the feelings which affect the passive sense, give no real knowledge of outward things. That comes, not from sensation merely, but from sensation changed into experience by a voluntary activity. We must not only see, but *look*; not only hear, but *listen*; not only feel, but *touch*, in order to know. *Life*, therefore, the constant synthesis of these three elements,—life which, in every act, at once thinks, feels, and does,—alone gives us knowledge. Divorce *thought* from affection and will, and let it act by itself, and it does not give knowledge; it only gives belief or opinion. Knowledge comes only from experience—and experience means communion. Communion with Nature by thought, desire, and action gives us the knowledge of Nature; communion with God by thought, desire, and act, gives us the knowledge of God. The organ by which we commune with God is faith; it includes the desire of knowing God, and the act of looking to him in order to know him.

Knowledge of God, of immortality, and of spiritual things does not come from any process of reasoning on the one hand, nor from any single intuition of reason. Just so we do not know the material world by a process of reasoning on the one hand, or any single sensible perception on the other. *All knowledge comes from life*; or, as the apostle John expresses it, "Life is the light of man." We become acquainted with outward nature by living processes—by repeated acts of sight, hearing, touch, taste. So we become acquainted with the spiritual world by repeated spiritual acts; by repeated processes of faith; by continued steps of devotion, submission, obedience, trust, love, prayer. In this way we come to *know* God just as certainly, and just in the same way, as we know things visible or things audible.

But knowledge is not belief. Knowledge is the rooted conviction of the reality of certain facts or persons, derived from communing with those facts or persons. Belief is the intellectual assent to a proposition—a proposition formed by analytic and synthetic methods. We analyze our notion concerning any subject, and then arrange the results of this analysis in order, and deduce from them a proposition, a law. This we call our belief, or creed, concerning it. The substance of this belief is given us in life; the form of it comes from thinking or reasoning. But it is evident that such a belief differs in each individual according to his experience, and according to his habits of reasoning, and even according to his facility in expression.

Moreover, knowledge and belief differ also in this, that knowledge places us in the presence of the reality, belief only in the presence of a proposition concerning it.

Thus John and James are friends. John *knows* James through a long intercourse. He is just as certain in regard to the essential character of James as he is about his own. But if he tries to express this knowledge of James in the form of belief, he may evidently express it badly. He may fail from a defective analysis, or from imperfect powers of language.

On the other hand John may not know James at all. He may never have seen him. But he has heard about him from a mutual friend, in whose judgment he trusts, or from several persons, and so he has formed a very decided belief in regard to James. He has a creed about him, though he has never known him.

In the same way those who *know* God truly and well, by the experience of obedience and prayer, may have a very erroneous belief concerning him. Those who do not know him at all, by any personal experience, may have a very correct belief concerning him. But which saves the soul? Which governs the life? Which affects the heart? Evidently not the belief, but the knowledge.

We are not saved by any belief whatsoever concerning God or Christ, concerning sin or salvation, concerning duty or destiny. Belief brings us into contact with the images of things, not the things themselves. Belief has no saving power. But knowledge has. "This is life eternal, to know thee, the only true God, and Jesus Christ, whom thou hast sent."

It is therefore a great mistake when Orthodoxy or Rationalism reverses the axiom of John, and instead of saying, "Life is the light of man," tells us that "Light is the life of man." Knowledge comes from life. Belief comes from knowledge, and not the contrary.

The Principle of Orthodoxy, as stated at the commencement of this chapter (in § 1), is, that there is one true system of Christian doctrine, and that all others are false. The Idea of Orthodoxy, as stated in § 10 of this chapter, is, that the soul is saved by the sight of truth. The idea of Orthodoxy is true—its principle is false. The sight of truth—that is, of the great spiritual realities—saves us, for only by that sight are we lifted above our feeble and imperfect selves, and enabled to partake of the nature of God. But while truth is ever one and the same, doctrine varies from age to age, varies from man to man. Each man's statement is limited by his position, his mode of thought, his power of speech. Nor can any council, assembly, conference, synod escape from similar limitations.

Let the distinction be once clearly recognized between truth as seen and truth as stated,—between knowledge and belief,—and we see the end of dogmatism, bigotry, intolerance, and superstition. We shall then see that religion is one thing and theology quite another, and that the test and evidence of a sound religious experience are not what a man says, but what he is. The sight of truth remains, as always, the source of our moral and spiritual life, but this sight of truth must pass into knowledge, by means of life, in order to renew the soul. Faith, or the act by which the soul, desirous of good, puts itself in the presence of truth, is always the beginning of each spiritual state. Knowledge, born of this faith, through repeated acts of conscience, love, obedience, prayer, is the next step, and that which fixes the truth in the soul. Belief comes afterwards, resulting from the knowledge thus obtained, analyzed, and arranged by the systematizing intellect. And theory, or opinion, goes forward, like the skirmishers before an army, examining the route and opening the way, but incapable of resisting any attack, or holding permanently any position.

Chapter III
The Orthodox Idea Of Natural And Revealed Religion; Or, Naturalism And Supernaturalism

§ 1. Meaning of Natural and Supernatural

Orthodox Christianity claims that Christianity is a supernatural revelation, consisting of truths revealed by God, not according to the method of nature, but outside of it. But not merely the orthodox, the heterodox too, Unitarians, Universalists, Quakers, Swedenborgians, all hold to Christianity as a supernatural faith. What do they mean by this, and why do they insist on it so strongly? This is our first question, and the next will be, "What do those who hold to naturalism mean by *it*, and why do they insist on their view?"

The distinction between the two seems to be this: The naturalists in theology assert that God comes to man through nature, and nature *only*; the supernaturalist declares that God comes to man, not only through nature, but also by other methods outside of nature, or above nature. There is no question between them as to natural religion. Both admit that; supernaturalists believe all that naturalists believe, only they believe something more.

But how is *nature* to be defined? What is meant by nature? Various definitions are given; but we wish for one now which shall really express the issue taken in this controversy. So we may define nature as law. All the nexus or web of existing substances and forces which are under law belong to nature. All that happens outside of these laws is either preternatural, unnatural, subternatural, or supernatural. If it is something *outside of law*, but *not violating* it, *nor coming* from a higher source, we call it *preter*natural; like magic, ghosts, sorcery, fairies, genii, and the like. What *violates* law is *un*natural. What is so low down that it lies below law, as chaos before creation; or nebulous matter not yet beginning to obey the law of gravitation; or intelligences, like Mephistopheles or Satan, who have sunk so low in sin as to have lost the perception of right and wrong, is *subternatural, below* nature. What belongs to a religion above the laws of time and space, above the finite, is supernatural.

Thus brutes, and men like brutes, who are below the moral law, are *subter*natural as regards that law. We do not call it a sin in a tiger to kill a man, for he is *below* law as regards sin. He is *below* the moral law. Again, we can conceive of angels so high up as to be above the moral law, in part of its domain, not capable either of common virtue or of common sin, according to *our* standards of morality, though perhaps under some higher code of ethics. They are supernatural beings as regards *that* law—the moral law of this world. As regards some parts of the moral law, there are, no doubt, multitudes of human beings above it even in this world. There are many persons quite incapable of swearing, lying, stealing, getting drunk, flying into a passion, and to whom, therefore, it is no virtue to avoid these vices. They are simply *above* that part of the moral law. They are *super*natural beings as respects that part of human character.

After these illustrations, we can see what is meant by *supernaturalism*. If there is anything in this world which comes from above the world, and not from the existing laws of being, *that* is supernatural.

§ 2. The Creation Supernatural

In this sense, all but atheists must admit the supernatural. If, for example, you admit the *creation of the world* by God, that was a supernatural act; *that* did not come from the existing laws of the world, because it created those laws. All the order and beauty of the world, its variety and harmony, its infinite adaptation of part to part, and each to all,—these existed in God's mind before they existed in nature. They were supernatural, as ideas, before they appeared in nature as facts. And if, as most geologists suppose, the crust of the earth denotes a long series of creations, successive epochs, at the close of each of which new forms of vegetable and animal life appeared, then each of these was a new creation; that is, a new supernatural act of the Almighty.

The physical world, therefore, shows a power above itself. The natural testifies to the supernatural, the all to the over-all. The existing web of laws gives evidence of mind, outside of itself, above itself, arranging and governing it.

§ 3. The Question stated

This being granted, the question between naturalism and supernaturalism is, whether this superintending mind, which came from above the world into it by acts of creation, when the world was made, has or has not come into it subsequently. We have a series of creations down to the time that man arrived on the earth. When *he* came, he was a supernatural being, and his coming a supernatural event. Unless we assume that he was developed, by existing laws, out of some ape, gorilla, or chimpanzee, his coming was supernatural. Now, did supernatural events cease then, and since that time has the world gone on of itself? or have there been subsequent incursions from a higher sphere—a new influx from above, from time to time, adding something new to nature? Naturalism says no; supernaturalism says yes.

§ 4. Argument of the Supernaturalist from successive Geologic Creations

The supernaturalist says, God comes to us in both ways—through nature; that is, through the order of things already established; and also by new creative impulses, coming in, from time to time, from above. He contends that such a new creative impulse came into the world through Jesus Christ, adding a new substance and new forms to those already existing—a new life not before in the world, proceeding according to new laws. This new creation, as the Scriptures themselves term it, is Christianity. This is also said to be in analogy with the course of events. For, if there has been a series of creations before, bringing animals into the world, and higher forms of physical life,—if these have been created by new supernatural impulses coming in at intervals of hundreds of thousands of years,—why deny that another impulse may have come in four thousand years, or forty thousand years, after man was created, to add a new form of spiritual life to society?

In the world, as it was at first, there was not a living plant or animal; after thousands of years, or millions of years, there came into the broad seas of the lower Silurian epoch, some of the lowest kinds of animals and seaweeds, a few trilobites and mollusks, but no plants save fucoids. Next came, after a long time, a few cartilaginous fishes and corals. A long time passed—thousands of years rolled by: then came real fishes and land plants in what is called the Devonian period, or the old red sandstone. After a great while came the period to which belongs all the coal formation; and in that carboniferous epoch first appears a whole vegetable world of trees and plants, to the number of nine hundred and thirty-four species. Some insects arrived at this time, as beetles, crickets, and cockroaches, which are, therefore, much more venerable than man. More thousands of years go by: then the earth receives a new creation in the form of gigantic frogs, enormous reptiles, and strange fishes. But as yet no mammal has come—not a bird nor a quadruped has been seen on the earth. Then, after another long period, these appear, in what is called the *tertiary* period; until, at last, some remains of man are found, in the diluvium, or gravel. Geology thus, once thought to be atheistic, gives its testimony to a long series of supernatural facts; that is, to the successive creation, after long intervals, of entirely new genera and species of vegetables and animals. As you turn these great stone leaves of that majestic manuscript roll written by God's hand, which we call the earth, you and he has been writing new things on each page, new facts and laws, not on any former leaf. New types of life, not prepared for by any previous one,—by no slow evolution, but by a sudden step,—break in. On the previous rocky page is to be found not one of their species, genus, order, or even class, to point back to any possible progenitor. So that the globe itself says, from these eternal monuments of rock, "Behold the history of supernatural events written on me." Each creation is higher than the last: finally man is created. But still from above, from outside the world, the creative life is ready to be poured in. Only the next creation is to be moral and spiritual, not physical. No new physical forms are now added, but a new moral life is poured into man, making *him* a new creation of God. "For if any man is in Christ, he is a new creature." The analogy was so striking, that the apostles noticed it, and constantly speak of Christ as the medium of a new creation.

§ 5. Supernatural Argument from Human Freedom

But there is another example of the supernatural element in the world. Dr. Bushnell, in his book called "Nature and the Supernatural," contends that man is capable of supernatural acts; that, in fact, every really *free* act is, and must be, a supernatural act. To those who hold the doctrine of necessity, this is, of course, no argument. But they who believe, in the testimony of their own consciousness, that they are free beings; who feel that they are not dragged helplessly by the strongest motive, but can resist it or yield to it; who, therefore, feel themselves responsible for what they do, or omit to do, they can see that in a real sense they create new influences. Their actions are not results of previous causes, but are new causes, not before in the world. Some supernatural power dwells in man's will just as far as it is made free by reason and choice. Man stands between good and evil, right and wrong, truth and error, with the power of choosing either one or the other. If he chooses one, he sends a power into society, life, humanity, to help it forward; if the other, he sends in a power to hold it back. This power is not from man's nature, but from something in him outside his nature. When he acts from habit, impulse, passion, and not from choice, he is simply a natural being; when he acts from choice, he is not a natural being, but either a *super*natural or a *subter*natural being, according as he chooses good or evil. When he chooses good, he rises above the natural man into the sphere of angels; when he chooses evil, he sinks below the natural man into the sphere of brutes or demons.

§ 6. Supernatural Events not necessarily Violations of Law

Now, says the supernaturalist, if we have all this evidence to show that God not only acts through nature, by carrying on existing forces and laws, but also has repeatedly come into nature with new creations, not there before,—and if even man himself has a certain limited but strictly supernatural power, so as to be able to stand outside of the nexus of law, and act upon it,—why deny, as incredible, that God should have made a new moral creation in Christianity? should have created a new class, order, genus, and species of spiritual beings, not represented before by any existing congeners? And why question that what we call miracles—that is, physical interferences with natural laws—should have attended this sudden influx of spiritual life? We do not claim, says the judicious supernaturalist (like Dr. Bushnell, for example), that miracles are suspensions or violations of natural laws; but that they are the natural modification of the agency of such laws by a new and powerful influence. Of this, too, there is ample analogy in nature. The mineral kingdom, for example, is passively subject to mechanical and chemical laws, which are resisted and modified by plants and animals. A stone obeys passively the law of gravitation; a plant resists it, rises into the air in opposition to it. Such a proceeding on the part of a plant must seem to a stone a pure miracle. If a piece of granite should write a book of theology, it would probably say that the plant, in growing up, had violated or suspended a law of nature. But it has not. The force of gravitation has worked on according to its own law; it has been dragging the plant downward all the time, only the vital power in the plant has overcome its force, and modified the result. And, again, a tree, seeing a dog run to and fro, might call that a miracle. The tree, unable to move from its place, could not conceive of the possibility of voluntary motion. But no law of nature is violated; only a higher power comes in—the power of animal life.

To a dog, again, the proceedings of a *man* are strictly miraculous. To plant corn, reap it, thresh it, grind it, and bake bread out of it, is exactly as much a miracle to the dog, as the multiplication of loaves, or turning water into wine, by Christ, is a miracle to us. But no law of nature was violated in either case. Reason in the one case, some profounder spiritual power in the other, may have modified the usual operation of law, and produced these results.

The Orthodox supernaturalist therefore contends that the supernatural is a constant element of life. Higher natures are all supernatural to lower natures, but natural in themselves, because obedient to the laws of their own nature. Nature, without this supernatural element, is only a machine, of which God, standing outside, turns the handle. This is a low conception both of nature and of God. As Goethe says, in one of his immortal lyrics,—

"Not so, outside, doth the Creator linger,

Nor let the all of things run round his finger,

But moves its centre, not its outer rim;

Comes down to nature, draws it up to him;

Moving within, inspiring from above,

With currents ever new of light and love."

§ 7. Life and History contain Supernatural Events

And besides all this, says the supernaturalist, we have continued and constant evidences, in all history and in all human experience, of the existence of this supernatural element. Only a small minority of mankind have ever doubted it; and those are men so immersed in physical science, or so hampered by some logical manacles, or so steeped in purely worldly affairs, as to be incapable of seeing the supernatural facts which are recurrent evermore. Christianity itself has been an uninterrupted series of supernatural events. The physical miracles of Christ are nothing to the spiritual miracles which Christianity is always working. Bad men are made good, weak men strong, cowardly men brave, ignorant and foolish men wise, by a supernatural influence given in answer to prayer, poured down into hearts and minds which open themselves to receive it. The conversion of a bad man by the power of Christianity is a miracle. The power of faith, hope, love, which every Christian has experienced, coming into him, not through any operation of his nature, but simply poured into his soul from some higher sphere,—this makes all argument unnecessary to one who has had ever so little Christian experience.

This is the substance of Orthodox supernaturalism; and this seems to me to be its truth, separated from its errors.

The naturalism of the present time we conceive to be partly directed against a false supernaturalism, and partly to be a mistake arising from a too exclusive attention to the *order* of the universe, as expressed in *law*.

§ 8. The Error of Orthodox Supernaturalism

Supernaturalism has generally disregarded God in nature, and only sees him in revelation. It has allowed a sort of natural religion, but only in the way of an argument to prove the existence of God by what he did a long time ago. But it has not gone habitually to nature to *see* God there, incarnate in sun, moon, and stars; incorporate in spring, summer, autumn, and winter; in day and night; in the human soul, reason, love, will. God has been all around us, never far from us; but theology has only been willing to see him in Jewish history, in sacred books, or on Sundays in church. Let us see him there all we can, but see him also in every rippling brook, in every tender flower, in all beauty, all sublimity, all arrangement and adaptation of this world. No wonder that naturalism should come to do what the Church has left undone—to find its God and Father in this great and wonderful world which he has made for us. The creed says, "God the Father, God the Son, and God the Holy Ghost;" that is, God the *Creator*, seen in Nature and Providence; God the *Redeemer*, seen in Christianity; and God the *Sanctifier*, seen in every righteous and holy soul. But the Church has neglected its own creed, and omitted *God the Creator*, often also God the Sanctifier, and has only seen God in *Christianity*, in its history, its Church, its doctrines, its ceremonies.8 Against this, naturalism comes as a great and needed protest, and calls us to see God also in nature and life.

Then the Church has been too apt to teach a miraculous revelation, in which the miracles are violations of law. But as God is confessedly the author of law, it has made the Deity violate his own laws; that is, has made him inconsistent, arbitrary, irregular, and wilful. Deep in the human mind God has himself rooted a firm faith in the immutability of law; so that when miracles are thus defined, naturalism justly objects to them.

§ 9. No Conflict between Naturalism and Supernaturalism

But between true naturalism and true supernaturalism we do not think there need be any war. We know that there are many men so rooted in their faith in nature, that they cannot see anything outside of it, or beyond it. To them God is law, and law only. Even creation is repugnant to them, because they see that creation is really a supernatural thing. Hence come the theories of development; the "Vestiges of Creation;" the nebular hypothesis; the Darwinian theory of formation of species by natural selection; the notion of man coming out of an ape; pantheistic notions of a God so immersed in nature as to be not its intelligent guide, but only its unconscious soul; the whole universe proceeding according to an order which is just as much above God's knowledge as above ours. Now, the best geologists assure us that there is no evidence in support of the transmutation of species. Mr. Darwin's theory of the formation of species by natural selection is this: In the struggle for life, the strongest and best adapted animal lives, the rest die. This animal transmits to its offspring its own superior qualities; so a higher animal is gradually developed. For example, the giraffe was not made by

God with a long neck in order that it might browse on the leaves of high trees. But when leaves were scarce, the animal who happened to have a neck a little longer than the rest was able to get leaves. So he lived, and the rest died. His children had longer necks by the law of hereditary transmission. So, in the course of ages, animals were gradually found with very long necks. Thus the walrus has a curved horn growing downwards from his lower jaw, by which he climbs on to the floating ice. We must not suppose, however, that God gave him the tusk for that purpose; but the walrus, or seal, who happened to have a little horny bone under his chin, could climb on the ice and get his food more easily, and so he lived, while the rest died; and his descendants in the course of a few hundreds of thousands of years came, by repeating this process, to have horns, and so this species of phoca arrived.

It is certainly possible to believe this theory. But in believing it we have to suppose two things; first, a happy accident, and then a law of transmission of hereditary qualities. Now, the theory substitutes this law of transmission and these happy accidents for the creative design. Is anything gained thereby? The domain of law is extended a little. But extend it as much as you will, you must at last come to something above law. Suppose these laws by which walrus and giraffe came, were all in the original nebula, so that no Creator has been needed since, and nothing supernatural—nature has done it all since. But who put the laws there to begin with? You have to take the supernatural at last, or else suppose an accident to begin with. Accidentally, all these wonderful laws happened to be in a particular nebula. He who shrinks from this supposition accepts the supernatural, all at once, at the beginning, instead of the supernatural all the way along, "What does he gain by it?" He gains merely this, that he puts the Creator out of sight; or rather, puts himself out of sight of the Creator. He worships the great god *Development* instead.

Equally satisfactory to the intellect, to say the least, and much more satisfactory to the best human instincts, is the view of God which sees him coming evermore into nature from above nature. This view says, "God is not only order, but also freedom. He is not only law, but also love. He is in the world as law and order, but he is above the world as thought and love; as Providence, as the heavenly Father. He comes to us to meet our exigencies, to inspire our doubting hearts, to lift us into life and light. He does not set a grand machine going, and then look on and see it work; but he is in the world, and with us always. The supernatural dwells by the side of the natural. Just as a wise and good father has rules and laws by which to govern his children—rewarding and punishing them as they obey or disobey; but besides that, does a thousand things for them, taking the initiative himself; so God governs us by law, but also often takes the initiative, giving us what we never asked for, and knew nothing of."

§ 10. Further Errors of Orthodox Supernaturalism— Gulf between Christianity and all other Religions

Orthodoxy has erred, as it would seem, in placing too great a gulf between Christianity and all other religions. Christianity is sufficiently distinguished from all other religions by being regarded as the perfect, and therefore universal, religion of mankind. It is to all preceding religions what man is to all previous races. These are separated from man by various indelible characters; yet they are his fellow-creatures, proceeding from the same creative mind, according to one creative plan. So the previous religions of our race—Fetichism, Brahmanism, Buddhism, the religion of Confucius, of Zoroaster, of Egypt, of Scandinavia, of Judea, of Greece and Rome—are distinguished from Christianity by indelible characters; but they, too, proceeded from the same creative mind, according to one creative plan. Christianity should regard these humanely, as its fellow-creatures. The other animals prepared man's way on the earth, and since man's arrival we have seen no subsequent creation. So the ethnic religions prepared the way for Christianity, and since Christianity came no new religion has appeared; for Mohammedanism is only a *mélange* drawn from the Old and New Testaments, and may therefore be considered as an outlying Christian sect. So, too, the gigantic abstractions of Gnosticism were hybrid systems, formed of the union between Oriental thought and Christian life. The analogy may be traced still farther. Man is the only animal who possesses the whole earth. Every other race has its habitat in some geographical centre, from which it may emigrate, indeed, to some extent, but where only it thrives. To man, only, the whole earth belongs. So the primitive religions are all *ethnic*; that is, religions of races. The religion of Confucius belongs to China, that of Brahmanism to India, that of Zoroaster to the Persians; the religion of Egypt is only for the Egyptians. Exceptions to this law (like that of Buddhism, for example) are only apparent. The rule is invariable. Christianity alone is a cosmic or universal religion. It only has passed the boundaries of race, so inflexible to all other religions. Born a Semitic religion, it soon took possession of the Indo-European races, converting Romans, Greeks, Teutons, Kelts, and Sclaves. It finds the African mind docile to its influence. Its missionaries have made believers from among the races of America, India, China, and the Pacific Islands. It is evidently destined to be the religion of humanity.

But, if so, why should it be put into antagonism with the religions which preceded it? These are also creations of God, not the work of man. Theologians have found multitudes of types of Christ in Jewish books and Jewish history. But they might also find types of Christianity in the so-called heathen religions. For as coming events cast their shadows before, so coming revelations are seen beforehand in shadowy preludes and homologons. The lofty spiritualism of the Brahmanical books, the moral devotion of the Zendavesta, the law of the soul's progress in Buddhism,—these are all types of what was to appear in a greater fulness and higher development in Christianity. First the natural, afterwards that which is spiritual. But these foregleams of Christian truth, irradiating the night-side of history, are all touching proofs that God never leaves himself without a witness in the world or in human hearts.

Instead, therefore, of placing an impassable gulf between Christianity and other human religions, we should consider these are preparations and stepping-stones to something higher. Nor will they pass away until Christianity has purified itself from the errors which still cling to it. Judaism was not to pass till it was fulfilled in Christianity; and neither will the other religions of the world pass away till they also are fulfilled in Christianity.

Now, the common teaching in our churches and religious books and newspapers tends to depreciate all natural religion in the interest of revealed religion. It is commonly said that the light of nature helps us a very little way in the knowledge of God. "Look at the heathen," it is said; "see their religious ignorance, their awful superstitions, their degrading worship of idols, and their subjection to priestcraft. This is your boasted light of nature, and these are its results—the Fetichism of Africa, the devil-worship of the North American Indians, the cannibalism of the Feejee Islands, the human sacrifices of Mexico and of the ancient Phœnicia." "Then," it is continued, "look at the observations of the wisest intellects apart from revelation! How little they knew with certainty! Their views of the Deity varied from pantheism to idolatry; their views of immortality were wholly vague and indistinct; their ideas of duty confused and false."

To which we might reply, "Is not the same thing true among Christians? Are there no superstitions among them? Were not witches hanged and burned during sixteen centuries in Christendom? If the heathen are ignorant, what multitudes in Catholic countries also do not read the Bible! How many are there even in Protestant churches who can give a reason for their belief? If the heathen worship degrades mankind because it is a superstition, with fear for its motive, how large a part of Christian preaching consists also of an appeal to terror! Is not the fear of everlasting torment in hell the motive power of much which is called Christianity? Consider Catholics eating their God: is that the worship of the Father in spirit and truth? Think of the religious wars, of the religious persecutions: did natural religion ever do anything as bad as this? We cry out against Nero, who covered Christians with pitch, and burned them as torches in the amphitheatre. But how many were thus tortured? Perhaps ten, perhaps twenty, or let us say a hundred. But, according to Llorente, the Holy Office of the Inquisition, in Spain, burned alive, under Torquemada, 8800: under Deza, 1669; under Ximenes, 2536; in all, from 1483 to 1498,—that is, in fifteen years,—it burned alive 31,912 persons for heresy, and subjected to rigorous pains and penalties 291,450 persons."

It is not right to judge of any doctrine by the corrupt practices which have taken place under it, unless it can be shown that these are its legitimate fruits. We maintain that Christianity is not fairly responsible for these persecutions; but let us make the same allowance for the religions which prepared its way.

§ 11. Christianity considered unnatural, as well as supernatural by being made hostile to the Nature of Man

If the nature of man be regarded as wholly evil, then Christianity is not merely a supernatural religion, but an unnatural one. This has been very commonly taught. Man's nature has been declared so totally corrupt and alien from all good, as to be radically opposite to the love of God and man. Christianity, therefore, comes, not to help him attain that which he is seeking after, but to change his whole purpose and aim—to give him a wholly new nature. This is the result of the doctrine of total depravity, so long taught in the Church as Orthodoxy. It has taught that all natural tendencies and desires in man were wholly evil, and to be rooted out. It has thus made Christianity unattractive, and has driven men away from it. But of this it is not necessary to speak here, as we shall discuss this doctrine and its influence hereafter.

Chapter IV
Truths And Errors As Regards Miracles

§ 1. The Subject stated. Four Questions concerning Miracles

In considering the truth and error in the Orthodox doctrine concerning miracles, we must, *first*, find out what this doctrine is; *secondly*, see what objections have been urged against it; and so, lastly, we may come to some conclusion as to where the truth or the error lies. There are, however, four distinct questions in regard to miracles, each of which may be considered separately. There is the philosophic question, or definition of a miracle, which asks, What is a miracle? Then there is the historical question, which asks, Did such facts actually occur? Next is the theological question, What are the value and weight of these facts in determining our Christian belief? And lastly comes the religious question, What are the spiritual meaning of miracles, and their influence on the heart and life?

§ 2. The Definition of a Miracle

As the creeds give no authoritative definition of a miracle, we must examine individual statements, in order to get the Orthodox idea.

To answer the question, *What is a miracle?* is not as easy as it would seem, as will appear from considering the different definitions given by different authorities, taking first those of the dictionary.

Johnson. "*Miracle.* A wonder—something above human power. (In theology.) An effect above human or natural power, performed in attestation of some truth."

Webster. "*Miracle.* (In theology.) An event or effect contrary to the established constitution and course of things, or a deviation from the known laws of nature; a supernatural event."

Robinson's Bible Dictionary. "*Miracle.* A sign, wonder, prodigy. These terms are commonly used in Scripture to denote an action, event, or effect, superior (or contrary) to the general and established laws of nature. And they are given, not only to true miracles, wrought by saints or prophets sent by God, but also to the false miracles of impostors, and to wonders wrought by the wicked, by false prophets or by devils." After giving examples of this from the Scriptures, Robinson adds, "Miracles and prodigies, therefore, are not always sure signs of the sanctity of those who perform them, nor proofs of the truth of the doctrine they deliver, nor certain testimonies of their divine mission."

American Encyclopœdia. *Miracle.* "It is usually defined to be a deviation from the course of nature. But this definition seems to omit one of the elements of a miracle, viz., that it is an event produced by the interposition of an intelligent power for moral purposes; for, otherwise, we must consider every strange phenomenon, which our knowledge will not permit us to explain, as a miraculous event. A revelation is itself a miracle. If one claims to be a teacher from God, he asserts a miraculous communication with God; this communication, however, cannot be visible, and visible miracles may therefore be necessary to give credibility to his pretensions. The use, then, of a miraculous interposition in changing the usual course of nature is to prove the moral government of God, and to explain the character of it."

Theodore Parker. "A miracle is one of three things.

"1. It is a transgression of all law which God has made; or,

"2. A transgression of all known laws, or obedience to a law which we may yet discover; or,

"3. A transgression of all law known or knowable by man, but yet in conformity with some law out of our reach."

He says that a miracle, according to the first definition, is impossible; according to the second it is no miracle at all; but that there is no antecedent objection to a miracle according to the third hypothesis.

Pascal. "A miracle is an effect which exceeds the natural force of the means employed to bring it about."

Hume. "A miracle is a violation of a law of nature."

Dr. Thomas Brown. "A miracle is as little contrary to any law of nature as any other phenomenon. It is only an extraordinary event, the result of extraordinary circumstances; an effect that indicates a power of a higher order than those we are accustomed to trace in phenomena more familiar to us, but whose existence only the atheist denies. It is a new consequent of a new antecedent."

Horne's Introduction to the New Testament. "A miracle defined is an effect or event *different from the established constitution or course of things,* or a *sign obvious to the senses that God has interposed this power to control the established powers of nature* (commonly termed the laws of nature), which effect or sign is wrought either by *the immediate act,* or by the assistance, or by the permission, *of God,* and accompanied with a *previous notice* or *declaration* that it is performed according to the purpose and by the power of God, *for the proof or evidence* of some particular doctrine, or in attestation of the authority or divine mission of some particular person." — Vol. I. p. 203.

"Since, as we already have had occasion to observe, the proper effect of a miracle is *clearly* to mark the divine interposition, it must therefore have characters proper to indicate such interposition; and these *criteria* are six in number.

"1. It is required, then, in the first place, that a fact or event which is stated to be miraculous should have an important end, worthy of its author.

"2. It must be instantaneously and publicly performed.

"3. It must be sensible (that is, obvious to the senses) and easy to be observed; in other words, the fact or event must be such that the senses of mankind can clearly and fully judge of it.

"4. It must be independent of second causes.

"5. Not only public monuments must be kept up, but some outward actions must be constantly performed in memory of the fact thus publicly wrought.

"6. And such monuments must be set up, and such actions and observances be instituted, at the very time when those events took place, and afterwards be continued without interruption." — Vol. I. p. 214 and 215.

From these examples we may see what different definitions have been given of miracles, and that the definition is not so easy a thing as one might at first suppose. All depends on the point of view which we take. If we look only at the outward fact, a miracle is a wonderful event, a portent, something out of the common course of nature, and unparalleled in common human experience. But if we look at it as regards the character of him who works the miracle, it then becomes a supernatural work, or a preternatural work, having a divine or a demoniac origin.

But, on the whole, the Orthodox doctrine of a miracle seems to be this — that it is a wonderful work, contrary to the laws of nature, wrought by the direct agency of God, in proof of the divine commission of him by whom it is done. The two essential points of the definition are, that a miracle is *contrary to the laws of nature*; and that it is *the only logical proof of the divine authority of the miracle-worker*. We call this the orthodox definition, although we must admit that no one in modern times has presented this view more forcibly and decidedly than the Unitarian Andrews Norton, and though many Orthodox men have taken a different view.

§ 3. The different Explanations of the Miracles of the Bible

The four explanations of the miracles of the New Testament (to which we now confine ourselves) are these: —

I. *The Natural Explanation.* — According to this, the miraculous facts of the New Testament are to be explained as resulting from natural causes. They are on the plane of our common human life. They are such events as might easily happen anywhere at the present time. Christ himself was but a natural genius of a high order. His miracles were merely the natural results of his intellect and strength of will, or they were mistakes on the part of the observers and narrators, or myths which have grown up subsequently in the Church. Great ingenuity has been used in attempting to show how each miracle may be explained so as to be nothing very extraordinary, after all. But these explanations are often very forced. Some events which are at first sight seemingly miraculous, are often explained as natural events by the majority of commentators. Thus the account of the angel who went down into the pool and troubled the water is usually interpreted as a natural phenomenon, and no real miracle. Modern travellers have noticed that this pool of Bethesda is an intermittent spring, which may have possessed medicinal qualities.

The old-fashioned naturalism, however, has mostly gone by. Its explanations were too forced and unnatural to continue long. The more common account at present is that which assumes that the narrators were mistaken in the stories which they have given us. Mr. Parker thinks that there is not sufficient evidence of the miracles. If there were more he would believe them. He gives no explanation of their origin farther than this. But Strauss attempts an explanation based upon an unconscious action of the fancy and feelings on the part of the New Testament writers, causing them to create these incidents out of some trifling basis of fact or of history. Renan follows in the same general direction.

II. *The Unnatural Explanation.*—A miracle is a violation or a suspension of a law of nature.

This, until recently, has been the favorite view of miracles among theologians, and is the view of miracles against which the arguments of those who reject them have been chiefly directed.

The arguments in favor of this view are these:—

1. The miracles of the New Testament *seem* to be violations of laws of nature. For example: the turning water into wine; healing by a word or touch; stilling the tempest; feeding five thousand; walking on the sea; transfiguration; raising of Lazarus; Christ's own resurrection. The law of gravitation seems to have been suspended when he walked on the sea, &c.

2. Miracles are appealed to by Christ and his apostles in proof that God was with him. But, unless these miracles had suspended the laws of nature, they would not be proofs of this.

These are the two principal reasons for this view of miracles.

Objections.—On the other hand, it is objected,—

1. That apparent violations may not be real violations of the laws of nature. Examples: The Arab emir in "The Talisman" who was told that water sometimes became solid, so as to support a man on horseback; a steamboat sailing against wind and current; the telegraph; the daguerrotype. In all such cases the laws of nature are not violated or suspended, but new powers come in.

2. Christ appeals to the moral character of his miracles, and not merely to their supernatural character. They are miracles of benevolence.

3. If the proof of Christ's mission depends on this view of miracles, it can never be proved. We can never be sure that the event is a violation of a law of nature.

4. On this view the sceptic's objections to miracles are unanswerable.

So says Dr. Thomas Brown, in an article reprinted by Dr. Noyes, of Cambridge, in the "Theological Essays" published by the American Unitarian Association. He admits the principle of Hume's Essay on Miracles, but says that his error lies in the false definition of the miracle as a violation of the laws of nature. False, because, —

(*a*.) On the principle of continued uniformity of sequence our whole belief of causation, and consequently of the divine Being, is founded.

(*b*.) Gives an air of inconsistency, and almost of absurdity, to a miracle.

(*c*.) Laws of nature are not violated when a new antecedent is followed by a new consequent, but when, the antecedent being exactly the same, a different consequent is the result.

(*d*.) No testimony could prove such a miracle. Suppose testimony so strong that its falsehood would be an absolute miracle; then we should have to believe, in either case, that a law of nature has been violated. No ground of preference between them.

5. A miracle may be supernatural, or above nature, without being unnatural, or against nature.

6. The greatest church teachers have maintained that miracles were not against law or without law, but above common law. Hahn, after mentioning the view of a miracle as a suspension of law, and calling it one neither scriptural nor conceivable, proceeds to quote Augustine and other writers, who held that miracles were by no means opposed to law.9

III. *The Preternatural View of Miracles.* —This view admits the reality of the phenomena, but explains them as resulting from mysterious forces, which are neither divine on the one hand, nor human on the other, but which are outside of nature. This is the demoniacal view, or that which supposes that evil spirits, departed souls, or spirits neither good nor bad, surround the earth, and can be reached by magic, witchcraft, sorcery, magnetism, or what is now called Spiritualism. This theory supposes that the works of Jesus were performed by the aid of spiritual beings. The objections to this view are, —

1. If it is supposed, as it was by the Jews, that Jesus had the aid of evil spirits, the sufficient answer is, that his works were *good* works.

2. If it is argued that he performed his miracles by the aid of departed spirits who were good spirits, the answer is, that he himself never took this view, but always declared, "My Father, who dwelleth in me, he doeth the works." Moreover, the whole character of the miracles of Jesus differs not only from everything ever done by magnetism or spiritualism, but from everything ever claimed to be done.

IV. *The Supernatural View of Miracles.*—This view asserts that the miracles were performed by higher forces, which came into this world from a higher world than this. It asserts that besides the forces which are at work regularly in the world, there are other forces outside of the world, which may from time to time come into it. We call them higher forces not only because they are more powerful than the forces before at work in the world, by overcoming which they produce the extraordinary outward phenomena, but because they always tend to elevate the world nearer to God. They are thus proved to come from a world which is nearer to God than this. The reasons in support of this view are, as before suggested.—

1. Geology teaches it. The rocks show not only an original creation of the world, but successive creations of vegetable and animal life.

2. The creation of the world teaches it. Creation was a miracle in this sense of the word.

3. There seems to be in the constitution of man a faculty provided for recognizing the supernatural element. Phrenologists call it the organ of marvellousness. Such a faculty would argue the existence of an appropriate object on which it might be exercised.

4. The whole life and character of Jesus were supernatural and miraculous in this sense. They cannot be satisfactorily explained as the result of anything existing in the world before.

§ 4. Criticism on these Different Views of Miracles

In attempting to discover the truths and errors contained in these statements it is a great satisfaction to feel that our faith in Christ and Christianity is not depending on them. If we believed with those who consider miracles the only or the principal proof of Christianity, we could hardly hope to be candid and just in examining the arguments of those who deny the marvellous facts of the New Testament. There is no doubt that the number of religious and Christian men who have relinquished all belief in the marvellous part of the Bible has largely increased within a few years. At the present time there is a strong tendency to disbelieve and deny all miracles as incredible and impossible. Renan, in his "Life of Jesus," says, "Miracles never happen except among people disposed to believe them.

We banish miracles from history in the name of a constant experience. No miracle has, as yet, been proved." Renan adds, that "if a commission of men of science should decide that a man had been raised from the dead he would believe it." "Till then," he says, "it is the duty of the historian not to admit a supernatural fact, but to find, if he can, what part credulity and imposition have had in it." Accordingly, Renan writes his "Life of Jesus" in this sense, discarding most of the miracles, or explaining them away, and trying to put together into some kind of shape the fragments which remain. But Renan does not go far enough to satisfy some others. Gerritt Smith, for example, in a recent lecture which he has published, called "Be Natural," says, "Jesus neither performed nor attempted to perform miracles. His wisdom and sincerity forbid the supposition. Am I an unbeliever in the historical Jesus because I hold him innocent of the absurdities which superstition and folly tax him with? No more than I should disbelieve in Shakespeare, by denying that he walked on the Avon, or changed its waters into wine. M. Renan ought to have made no account of these stories of miracles. He should have dropped them entirely, as did Rammohun Roy in his Hindoo translation of the New Testament. Let the credulous feed on these creations of superstition, but let men of sense turn away from them."

The reason why so many intelligent men find it impossible to believe the miracles of the New Testament, while they find it very easy to believe the religious and moral teaching of Jesus is partly due to the spirit of the age. The intellect of this age is more and more scientific. Now, science is the knowledge of facts and laws. A miracle is opposed to all usual observation of facts, and is often called by theologians a violation of the laws of nature. It is not therefore strange that men imbued with the spirit of science should dislike the notion of miracles.

§ 5. Miracles no Proof of Christianity

Now, we should have little objection, on purely theological grounds, to give up the miracles of the New Testament. Theologians have built up the proof of Christianity on miracles. They have declared them the chief evidence of Christianity. They have said, "A miracle is a violation of a law of nature. Now, no one but God can violate a law of nature. If Jesus violated a law of nature, it proved that God was with him. But that he did so we know from the New Testament. That it tells the truth we know, because it was written, by eye-witnesses, who could not have been mistaken, because they saw the miracles with their own eyes, and were not liars, because they laid down their lives in testimony of the truth of what they asserted." Therefore, it is argued, "Christ worked miracles; therefore he had God's help and power; therefore he has God's authority to teach the religion of the New Testament."

Now, for those who hold this view of Christianity, if they renounce miracles, it is evident that the foundation of faith is gone. No wonder, therefore, that they bitterly oppose all attacks of miracles. In defending miracles, they are fighting for their lives.

But we need not hold this view of the foundation of Christianity. Christianity does not rest necessarily on the physical miracles of Christ, but on his moral miracles, which no one has ever doubted, or can doubt. Christianity proceeded from Jesus, and was transmitted by him, not as a philosophy, but as a power, a life, which renewed the old world, and created a new dispensation. This is the great miracle. We do not really believe Christianity on the ground of miracles, but we believe miracles on the ground of Christianity.

Let us explain this. If miracles had been asserted to be wrought by God in order to prove the truth of a doctrine irrational, self-contradictory, odious to the conscience and to the heart,—to prove, for example, the justice of the Spanish Inquisition, the lawfulness of slavery, or that God loves some of his children and hates the rest,—then all the outward evidence in the world would not have convinced us that God had taught such a doctrine and confirmed it by miracles. If we had seen with our own eyes a dead man raised to life, or if M. Renan's committee of scientific men had testified that they had seen it, we should either say they were deceived, or we should say, with the Jews, "It is done by some devilish power, not by a divine power. It is not supernatural, it is preternatural." But Christianity itself is the great miracle of human history. It is more marvellous than raising a dead man, for it was the *resurrection of a dead world*—of a dead humanity. Read Gibbon. He is an infidel writer, but he is a perfect historian. He shows you Christianity, as a living force, coming into history, pouring a tide of life into the decaying civilization of Rome, overflowing upon the German tribes, and changing their whole character, so as to make out of those savage warriors merciful and reverential soldiers, who knew how to pardon and how to spare. Now, there seems something quite as supernatural in this as in the coming of new trees and plants into the world in the carboniferous epoch, or the coming in of mammalia, a hundred thousand years or so after. It seems as if God came near the world, and touched it in Jesus Christ; for the power of one man was wholly inadequate to such results as followed his coming. I believe Christianity a divine religion, a religion from God, because it lifts the soul nearer to God—because it has lifted mankind nearer to God, and enabled men to believe God a friend—not a tyrant, not a stern king—but a father. Christianity is divine, because its truth and love are divine—because it purifies, consoles, and elevates human hearts; because the life of Jesus is, by the testimony of such men as Theodore Parker, Rousseau, and Renan, infinitely superior to all other lives ever lived in this world. Now, believing in Christianity and Christ on such grounds, we may look with much more deference and respect upon the stories of miracles which are intertwined in his life. We should not attend to them at all if we found them told about only common men; but told about Jesus, we are led to examine them more critically, and ask whether it is, or is not, possible for them to have been, in the main, real facts.

The Orthodox doctrine has been, and still is, that Christianity rests on miracles. Our view is, that miracles rest on Christianity. But we close this section with extracts from Luther, Channing, Trench, and Walker, to show that the view for which we contend is not without able supporters in all parts of the Church.

Martin Luther says,—

"People cry it up as a great miracle, that Christ made the blind see, the deaf hear, and the lepers clean; and it is true such works are miraculous signs; but Christ regards his influence on the soul as far more important than that on the body; for as the soul excels the body, so do the miracles wrought on the former excel those wrought on the latter....

"The miracles which Christ wrought on the body are small and almost childish, compared with the high and true miracles which he constantly performs in the Christian world by his divine, almighty power; for instance, that Christianity is preserved on the earth; that the word of God and faith in him can yet hold out; yea, that a Christian can survive on earth against the devil and all his angels; also against so many tyrants and factions; yea, against our own flesh and blood. The fact that the gospel remains and improves the human heart,—this is indeed to cast out the devil, and tread on serpents, and speak with tongues; for those visible miracles were merely signs for the ignorant, unbelieving crowd, and for those who were yet to be brought in; but for us, who know and believe, what need is there of them? For the heathen, indeed, Christ must needs give external signs, which they could see and take hold of; but Christians must needs have far higher signs, compared with which the former are earthly. It was necessary to bring over the ignorant with external miracles, and to throw out such apples and pears to them as children; but we, on the contrary, should boast of the great miracles which Christ daily performs in his church."

In the "Christian Examiner," Dr. James Walker says,—

"Christianity embodies a collection of moral and vital truths, and *these truths,* apart from *all history* or philosophy, constitute Christianity itself. Instead, therefore, of perplexing and confounding the young with what are called the evidences of Christianity, give them Christianity itself. Begin by giving them Christianity itself, as exhibited in the life and character of the Lord Jesus, as illustrated by his simple, beautiful and touching parables, and as it breathes through all his discourses. They will *feel it to be true.* Depend upon it, paradoxical as it may sound, children will be much more likely to believe Christianity without what are called the evidences, than with them; and the remark applies to some who are not children.

"Why talk to one about the argument from prophecy, or the argument from miracles, when these are the very points, and the only points, on which his mind, from some peculiarity in its original constitution, or from limited information, chiefly labors. Give him Christianity itself, by which we mean the body of moral and vital truths which constitute Christianity. Observe it when you will, you will find that the doubts and difficulties suggested by children relate almost exclusively to the *history* of Christianity, or to what are called the *external* evidences of Christianity, and not to the *truth* of Christianity itself. Give them Christianity itself: for if they believe in that, it is enough. Nothing can be more injudicious than to persist in urging the argument from miracles on a mind, that, from any cause, has thus become indifferent, and perhaps impatient of it. How idle to think to convince a person of Christianity by miracles, when it is these very miracles, and not Christianity, that he doubts! The instances, we suspect, are not rare, even of adults, who are *first converted to Christianity itself,* and afterwards, through the moral and spiritual change which

Christianity induces, are brought to believe entirely and devoutly in its *miraculous origin and history.*"

Dr. Channing says, —

"There is another evidence of Christianity still more *internal* than any on which I have yet dwelt; an evidence to be *felt* rather than described, but not less *real* because founded on feeling. I refer to that conviction of the divine original of our religion which springs up and continually gains strength in those who apply it habitually to their tempers and lives, and who imbibe its spirit and hopes. In such men there is a consciousness of the adaptation of Christianity to their noblest faculties; a consciousness of its exalting and consoling influences, of its power to confer the true happiness of human nature, to give that peace which the world cannot give; which assures them that it is not of earthly origin, but a ray from the everlasting Light, a stream from the fountain of heavenly Wisdom and Love. This is the evidence which sustains the faith of thousands, who never read and cannot understand the learned books of Christian apologists, who want, perhaps, words to explain the ground of their belief, but whose faith is of adamantine firmness, who hold the gospel with a conviction more intimate and unwavering than mere arguments ever produced."

And here is an extract from another writer: —

"Doubtless Christ's spiritual glory is in itself as distinguishing, and as plainly showing his divinity, as his outward glory, and a great deal more; for his spiritual glory is that wherein his divinity consists, and the outward glory of his transfiguration showed him to be divine only as it was a remarkable image or representation of that spiritual glory. Doubtless, therefore, he that has had a clear sight of the spiritual glory of Christ may say, 'I have not followed cunningly devised fables, but have been an eye-witness of his majesty,' upon as good grounds as the apostle, when he had respect to the outward glory of Christ that he had seen. A true sense of the divine excellency of the things of God's Word doth more directly and immediately convince of the truth of them; and that because the excellency of these things is so superlative. There is a beauty in them that is so divine and godlike, that is greatly and evidently distinguishing of them from things merely human, or that men are the authors and inventors of,—a glory that is so high and great, that when clearly seen, commands assent to their divinity and reality. The evidence which they who are spiritually enlightened have of the truth of the things of religion, is a kind of intuition and immediate evidence. They believe the doctrines of God's Word to be divine, because they see divinity in them. That is, they see a divine, and transcendent, and most evidently distinguishing glory in them; such a glory as, if clearly seen, does not leave room to doubt of their being of God, and not of men."

Trench, also, denies that the miracle can have absolute authority, since Satanic powers may work evil too. This convinces us, he says, that miracles cannot be appealed to in proof of the doctrine or of the divine mission of him who brings it to pass. The doctrine must first commend itself to the conscience as being good; then the miracle shows it to be a new word from God. But when the mind and conscience reject the doctrine, the miracle must be rejected too. The great act of faith is to believe, in despite of all miracles, what God has revealed to the soul of the holy and the true; not to believe another gospel, though an angel from heaven should bring it. Instead of compelling assent, miracles are *then* rather warnings to us that we keep aloof; for they tell us not merely that lies are here, but that he who utters them is an instrument of Satan.

False miracles, or lying wonders, are distinguished from the true, not by the intellect, but by the moral sense, which finds in them something immoral, or ostentatious, or futile, leading to nothing. Origen says the miracles of Moses issued in a Jewish polity; those of our Lord in a Christian Church. But what fruits have the miracles of Apollonius or Æsculapius to show?

The miracles of Christ are redemptive. Modern writers of evidences make a dangerous omission when they fail to say that the doctrine is to try the miracle, as well as the miracle to seal the doctrine. To teach men to believe in Christ on no other grounds than his wonderful works is to pave the way of Antichrist. Those books of Christian evidences are utterly maimed and imperfect, fraught with the most perilous consequences, which reverence in the miracle only its power.[10]

§ 6. But Orthodoxy is right in maintaining their Reality as Historic Facts

The first thing we notice about the miracles of Jesus is, that they are intertwined inextricably with the whole narrative. It is almost impossible to disentangle them, and to leave any solid historic residuum. There is a story in Goethe of a statue of iron and silver, with veins of gold. The flames licked out the gold veins of the colossus, and it remained standing a little while; but when at last the tenderest filaments had been licked out, the image crashed together, and fell in a shapeless, miserable heap. So when the tongue of criticism shall have eaten out the supernatural elements of the gospel narrative, the heroic figure will fall, as it has already in Renan's construction, into an amorphous mass of unhistoric rubbish.

Then we see that most of these miracles are miracles of healing, which have their analogues in many similar events scattered through history. Many such facts might be collected to show that there is in man a latent power of overcoming disease, in himself and others, by a great exertion of will. If in common men there is such a power, latent, and as yet undeveloped, why should it be an unnatural thing that one so full of a superhuman life as Jesus should be raised to a position where, by his very word or touch, he could cure disease, and that even at a distance?

We see such wonderful discoveries made every day of latent powers in nature, and secrets hidden till now from all men, that we do not know where to put limits to the possibility of the wonderful. To go into a telegraphic office in Boston, and speak to a man in New York or Washington, and have an answer in five minutes; to have your portrait painted in a moment by the rays of the sun,—such things as these would have seemed miracles to us a few years ago. To be able to tell what metals there are in the sun's atmosphere, and what not there; to say, "In the atmosphere of the sun there is silver, but not gold; there are iron, and antimony, and lead, and aluminum, but no copper nor zinc,"—does not this seem incredible? But we know that we *can* now tell just that.

When we read the Gospels, we find everything in them so simple, so unpretending, so little of an attempt at making out a consistent story, such a harmony in the character of the works attributed to Jesus (with one or two exceptions), that we are irresistibly inclined to say, "These stories must be simple facts. Delusion never spoke in this tone,—so clear, so luminous,—in language so honest and sincere."

I do not deny that some mistakes or misapprehensions may have crept into the records. Occasionally we can see signs of something being mistaken for a miracle which was really not one. For example, the finding of a piece of money in the fish's mouth may have been the mistake of a proverbial expression, common among fishermen, and used by Matthew in his original Hebrew Gospel, but which the Greek translator, ignorant of the popular phrase, considered to be meant for a miracle.

The most natural supposition is, that a wonderful power dwelt in Jesus, which enabled him to heal the sick, cure the insane, and sometimes even bring back life to the dead. What do we know about death? The last breath has been drawn. The heart has ceased to beat, the lungs to move. We say, "He is dead." But people have lain two or three days in this state, declared dead by the physicians, and then have come to life again by natural causes. A drowned man has all the marks of death; but after lying in this state half an hour, he is brought to life again. What, then, might not have been done by that supernatural power of life which, as history shows, dwelt in Jesus of Nazareth?

§ 7. Analogy with other Similar Events recorded in History

It may very properly be asked whether miracles have occurred since the Bible record was closed; and if not, why not. Since we have regarded the miracles of the New Testament as no violations of law, but the coming in of higher laws or forces than those usually at work in the world, why may they not have taken place in our own time? If Christ's miracles differ only from other miracles in being higher and more perfect, what are the miracles of a lower class? Can we point out any events belonging to the same class of phenomena which have happened during the last thousand years?

In reply to this question, we will proceed to mention certain phenomena which seem to belong to the same order as the works of Jesus. The *distinction* between the miracles of Christ and all those portents will be pointed out hereafter.

In the "Atlantic Monthly" for February and March, 1864, there appeared an account (written, we believe, by R. Dale Owen), of the Convulsionists of St. Médard. The facts therein stated *seem* to contradict all the known laws of physiology. The lower side of miracles, namely, their apparent violation of physical laws, here appears as fully developed and as fully attested as the most careful sceptic could desire. If, therefore, any one objects to believing the miracles of Jesus on the ground that they *seem* to be violations of physical laws, we ask what they mean to do with these facts, so extraordinary, and yet so fully attested. If believed, there is no reason, based on the abnormal character of Christ's works, for rejecting those. But if disbelieved, it can be done only by setting aside all the ordinary rules of evidence, and all the laws of belief, in favor of a negative prepossession of a purely empirical character.

Phenomena somewhat similar to these have occurred elsewhere, among Protestants as well as Catholics, during periods of great religious excitement. The beginnings of most religious systems—Methodism, Quakerism, &c.— have stories like these of supernatural influences. They have usually been disbelieved because their friends have claimed too much: they have claimed that such phenomena were divine attestations to the truth of the doctrine preached. What *is* proved by them is the simple fact that the soul of man is capable, under high excitement, of suspending, or rather overcoming, all common physiological laws. We have seen similar results follow often from such causes, only in ordinary ways. A sick person is made well in a moment by some moral influence; a weak and sickly mother will nurse a sick child, night after night, without rest or sleep, and keep well, where a strong man would break down. Mesmerism brings forward multitudes of like facts. There are, for example, the well-attested facts concerning the transfer of the senses: that people under the influence of animal magnetism can read with their forehead, the pit of their stomach, or the back of their head. We have seen a weak boy, some thirteen years old, when magnetized, lift a chair with three heavy men standing on it. Clairvoyance, or seeing things at a distance, though not so well proved, is confirmed by a vast number of facts. We come, then, to our final statement concerning miracles, which is this:—

I. There is in man a power, as yet undeveloped, and only occasionally seen in exceptional conditions, of overcoming the common laws of nature by force of will; and this is sometimes voluntary, and sometimes involuntary.

II. This phenomenon takes these forms:—

A. *Power of the soul over the body (a.) to resist pain*, as in the case of martyrs, who are burned alive without any appearance of suffering; *(b.) to resist physical injury*, as in the case of the Convulsionists; *(c.) to dispense with the usual service of the senses*, as in the case of the girl at Worcester Insane Asylum, Massachusetts, under the care of Dr. Woodward, who could read a book in a perfectly dark room and with bandaged eyes; *(d.) to give a preternatural energy and strength to the body.*

B. *Preternatural knowledge*—such cases as that narrated by Dr. Bushnell, of Yonnt, in California; or *knowledge through dreams*, waking presentiments; cases of *foresight*, or prophecy; of *insight*, or knowledge of what is passing in other minds; of *clairvoyance*, or knowledge of what is happening at a distance, of which multitudes of facts are narrated in such books as the "Seeress of Provorst," Mrs. Crowe's "Night Side of Nature," Robert Dale Owen's "Footfalls from the Boundary of the Unseen World," which, after being sifted by a fair criticism, will leave a large residuum of irresolvable facts.

C. Higher than these is a preternatural elevation of the whole character, as in such cases as that of Joan of Arc, where a young girl, ignorant, a peasant, destitute of all common means of influencing any one, by the simple power of faith, because she believed herself inspired and commissioned, succeeded in gaining the command of the armies of France, and then of achieving a series of victories, equal, on the whole, as mere military exploits, to those of the first captains of the world.

In all these cases we see manifestations of a power in the soul over nature, body, men, and the laws of time and space. So we say, *secondly,*—

III. This power was possessed in the highest degree known in this world by Jesus of Nazareth, and it differed in him from these other cases in these points:—

1. It was always voluntary in its exercise, never involuntary. He was not possessed by it, he possessed it. He used it just when and where he chose to use it. It was always at his command; he never appears to have tried to work a miracle, and failed. So,—

2. It was in him constant, and not occasional. In other cases where the miraculous element appears, it seems to come and go; but to Jesus the spirit was not given by measure. He had it always.

3. This power in him was total, and not partial. It was therefore harmonious—in harmony with all his other qualities. He had power over diseases of the body, and also those of the soul. He knew what was in man, and what was in nature—in the present, and in the future. There was nothing ecstatic, enthusiastic, nothing of excitement, about him; but everything denoted a fulness, a pleroma, of this spiritual life.

4. The exercise of this power in Christ was always eminently moral, never wilful. The one or two seeming exceptions, as, for example, the cursing the fig tree, and the causing the evil spirits to go into the swine, ought to be explained in harmony with the vast majority of his actions, which always are guided by love, and justice, and a holy sense of what is true and good.

5thly, and lastly. The miracle power of Jesus reached a higher point of development than in any one else. The raising of the dead to life, and the mysterious power over nature indicated by the turning of water into wine, by the miracle of the loaves and fishes, calming the storm, if facts, are facts unparalleled in any other biography, but seem possible, however unintelligible, when considered as emanating from such a masterly and commanding spirit as that of Jesus.

And this finally brings us to the miracle of the resurrection, concerning which we will first quote from an article in a late number of the "Westminster

Review," to show the most recent ideas of the critical and negative school on this point.

§ 8. Miracle of the Resurrection. Sceptical Objections

In an article in the "Westminster Review," in "The Life of Christ, by Strauss," occurs the following passage:—

"For of the two alternatives open to free inquiry, that if Jesus died he never reappeared, or if he reappeared he never died, Strauss considers the former not only preferable, but the only tenable one; for he cannot persuade himself that a feeble sufferer, who at first had scarcely strength to leave the tomb, and in the end succumbed to death, could have contrived to inspire his followers with the conviction that he was the Prince of life, the Conqueror of the grave. Strauss thus admits that faith in the supernatural revival of the buried Nazarene was undoubtedly the profession of the Christian Church, the unconditional antecedent without which Christianity could have had no existence. If, then, we refuse to assume the resurrection to be an historical fact, we have to explain the origin of the Church's belief in it. The solution which satisfies Strauss, and which seems to us also an adequate interpretation of the problem, is dependent on the two following positions: 1. The appearance of Jesus was literally an appearance, an hallucination, a psychological phenomenon. 2. It was also a sort of practical fallacy of confusion, a case of mistaken identity.

"But it will be said that this natural solution of the problem implies a foregone conclusion—the rejection of the Orthodox or supernatural solution. Of course it does; and accordingly Strauss has been accused of dogmatical or unphilosophical assumption. But the rejection of the theological solution is not the result of ignorant prejudice, but of enlightened investigation. Anti-supernaturalism is the final irreversible sentence of scientific philosophy, and the real dogmatist and hypothesis-maker is the theologian. That the world is governed by uniform laws is the first article in the creed of science, and to disbelieve whatever is at variance with those uniform laws, whatever contradicts a complete induction, is an imperative, intellectual duty.

A particular miracle is credible to him alone who already believes in supernatural agency. Its credibility rests on an assumption—the existence of such agency. But our most comprehensive scientific experience has detected no such agency. There is no miracle in nature; there is no evidence of any miracle-working energy in nature; there is no fact in nature to justify the expectation of miracle. Rightly has it been said by an English *savant* and divine, that testimony is a second-hand assurance, a blind guide, that can avail nothing against reason; and that to have any evidence of a Deity working miracles, we must go out of nature and beyond reason.

"Strauss's prepossession, therefore, is justifiable. It is the prepossession of the rational theist, who does not believe in a God who changes his mind and improves with practice— the prentice maker of the world; it is the prepossession of the pantheist, in whose theory of the perfect government of an immanent God, miracle is an extravagance and absurdity; it is the prepossession of the philosophical naturalist, whose experience of the operations of nature recognizes no extra-mundane interventionalism."

We have quoted this passage as containing the most distinct statement of an extreme anti-supernaturalism. Admitting the death of Jesus as a fact, it denies his resurrection as a fact, and that on doctrinal and theoretic grounds. Declaring anti-supernaturalism to be the final irreversible sentence of scientific philosophy, it assumes supernaturalism to be a denial that the world is governed by uniform laws. It assumes the resurrection of Christ to be at variance with those uniform laws. It denies the existence of any supernatural agency in the affairs of this world. It denies that there ever has been a miracle in nature, or any extra-mundane intervention in the history of nature or man.

This is what claims to be science, at the present time. We deny that it is science, and assert it to be pure dogmatism and theory, contradicted by numerous facts. It is pure theory to assume the resurrection of Jesus to be a violation of law. It is pure theory to define a miracle to be something opposed to law. It is pure theory to assume that the miraculous facts ascribed to Jesus in the Gospels must have been, if they occurred, violations of law. It is an assumption, contradicted by geology, that there is nothing in the experience of the naturalist of the operations of nature to show any extra-mundane intervention.

We have admitted, indeed, that these same assumptions have been made by Orthodox theology. Orthodox theologians have also assumed the miracles of Christ to be violations of the laws of nature. But some of the most distinguished theologians, in all ages of the Church, have not so defined them. And there is no reason why the man of science should deny the possibility of fact because an unscientific explanation has been given of that fact by others. This writer virtually says, "I will not believe that Christ appeared after his death, on any amount of testimony, because some persons have defined such appearances as being opposed to the laws of nature." It is certainly true that we cannot fully believe in the reality of any phenomenon which seems to us to be a violation of law. It is also true that the reported facts concerning the appearances of Jesus *seem* like a violation of law. But the scientific course is neither to deny the facts, nor to explain them away, but to study them, in order to see whether, after all, they may not lead us to some new laws, before unknown.

The resurrection of Jesus deserves this study, since, according to the confession of science itself, the Christian Church rests upon that belief. Strauss admits that Christianity could not have existed without it. But, hastily assuming that the real appearance of Jesus himself would be a violation of a law of nature, he supposes this immense fact of Christendom to rest on an hallucination and a case of mistaken identity.

But perhaps, after all, the resurrection may have been an example of a universal law. Like other miracles, which are sporadic instances, in this world, of laws which may be the nature of other worlds, so the resurrection may have been as natural an event as any other in the life of Jesus. Perhaps it is a law of nature that all souls shall become disengaged from the earthly body on the third day after death. Perhaps they all rise in a spiritual body, substantial and real, but not usually perceptible by the senses. Perhaps, in the case of Jesus, that same superior command of miraculous force, which appeared during his life, enabled him to show himself easily and freely whenever he would. What became of the earthly body we do not know; it may have been removed by the priests or soldiers to prevent the disciples from getting possession of it. The body in which Christ appeared differed evidently from the earthly body in various ways. It came and went mysteriously; it was sometimes recognized, and sometimes not; and it ascended into the spiritual world instead of passing again to death and the grave. Perhaps, therefore, it may be a universal law that souls rise out of the material body into a higher state, clothed in another body, substantial and real, but not material. The essence of the resurrection is this: Resurrection is not coming to life again with the same body, but ascent into a higher life with a new body.

It may be said that all this is only a *perhaps*. Very well; it *is* only a *perhaps*, but that is all we want in order to refute the logic of the article just quoted. The scientific sceptic says, "I will not believe that Jesus was really seen after death, because that would be a violation of a law of nature." We reply, "No, not necessarily. It might *perhaps* have been thus and so." That will do; for if we can show that it is not *necessarily* a violation of a law of nature, we wholly remove the objection.

But we may go farther, and assert that such a supposition as we have made not only accords with the story in the Gospels, but also with the whole spirit of Christianity, and with all the analogies of nature. The resurrection of Jesus, so regarded, becomes the most *natural* thing in the world. If souls live after death, as even natural instinct teaches, they live somewhere. As by the analogy of nature we see an ascending scale of bodily existence up to man, whose body is superior to that of all other animals, because fitted for the very highest uses, so if man is to live hereafter and elsewhere, and not in this earthly body, analogy would anticipate that he should live in a body still, but in a higher form. If Jesus, therefore, rose in this higher body, and appeared to his disciples, it was to lift them above fear of death by showing that this corruptible must put on incorruption. So his resurrection was not merely coming to life again in the same body, but rising up into a higher body and a higher state, to show us how we are to be, to give us a glimpse of the hereafter, to bridge over the gulf between this life and that to come.

§ 9. Final Result of this Examination

We have thus examined, as thoroughly as our limited space will allow, the questions at issue, on the subject of miracles, between the old Orthodox and recent heterodox views; and the result to which we have arrived may be thus stated:—

1. We may believe, on the testimony of history, that through Jesus of Nazareth there entered the world a great impulse of creative moral life, which has been, and is now, renewing society. This new impulse of life may be regarded as miraculous or supernatural.

2. We may believe, though perhaps less strongly, but still decidedly, that during the stay of Jesus on earth many extraordinary phenomena took place, such as the sudden healing of the sick, the raising of the dead to life, a display of miraculous insight and foresight, or knowledge of the present and the future, and some influence over organic and material life, and over the lifeless forces of nature. The precise limits of this we do not know, and need not pretend to define. We need not think it essential to fix the boundary. It may be interesting as speculation, but it is not important as religion.

3. For, in the third place, we may say that these miracles of Jesus have very little direct bearing on our *religion*. As they illustrate his character, they are valuable, and also as they help us to believe that the laws of nature are not stiff and rigid, like the movement of a machine, but that there is force above force, a vortex of living powers, in the universe, rising higher and higher towards the fountain of all force and life in God. All portents and wonders are useful, as they shake us out of the mechanical view of things, and show that even the outward, sensible world is full of spiritual power.

4. We may also believe the miracles of Jesus to be *natural* in this sense— that under the same conditions they could have been done by others, and that they are probably prophetic of a time in which they *shall* be done by others. Looked at as mere *signs* or *portents*, he himself discouraged any attention being paid to them. Looked at as logical proofs to convince an unbeliever, he never brought them forward. His object in miracles, as stated by Mr. Furness, was simply to express his character. Some, indeed, were symbolical, as the cursing of the fig tree. It is the custom in the East for teachers to speak in symbolic language.

Miracles were at first believed, on low grounds, as violations of law by a God outside of the world. Now they are disbelieved on scientific grounds. They may possibly be believed again on grounds of philosophy and historic evidence, not as portents, not as violations of law, not as the basis of a logical argument, but as the natural effluence and outcome of a soul like that of Jesus, into which a supernatural influx of light and life had descended. They are not more wonderful than nature; they are not *so* wonderful as the change of heart by which a bad man becomes a good man. But they will find their proper place as evidence how plastic the lower laws are to the influence of a higher life.

Chapter V
Orthodox Idea Of The Inspiration And Authority Of The Bible

§ 1. Subject of this Chapter. Three Views concerning the Bible

The subject of this chapter is the Orthodox idea concerning the inspiration and authority of the Bible. We shall consider the conflict of opinion between those who believe in the full inspiration of every word of Scripture, and those who treat it like a common book, and endeavor to see how far we ought to believe a fact or a doctrine, because it is asserted, or seems to be asserted, by some writer in the Bible.

Such questions are certainly of great importance to us all at the present time, when opinions on these subjects are unsettled, and few people know exactly what to believe. Especially in regard to the Old Testament, not many persons have any distinct notions. They do not know what is its inspiration or its authority; they do not know whether they are to believe the account of the creation and of the deluge in the book of Genesis, in opposition to the geologists, or believe the geologists, in opposition to Genesis. Certainly it is desirable, if we can, to have some clear and distinct opinions on these points.

And, first, in regard to Inspiration: there are three main and leading views of the inspiration of the Bible. There cannot be a fourth. There may be modifications of these, but nothing essentially different. These three views are,—

(*a.*) *Plenary Inspiration.*—That is, that everything in the Bible is the word of God. All the canonical books are inspired by God, so as to make them infallible guides to faith and practice. Every word which really belongs to these books is God's truth, and to be received without question as truth, no matter how much it may seem opposed to reason, to the facts of nature, to common sense, and common morality.

This is *the Orthodox theory* even at the present time. Any variation from this is considered a deviation into heresy. No doubt, in practice it *is* deviated from, by very Orthodox people; but all Protestant sects, claiming to be Orthodox, profess to hold to the plenary inspiration of the Bible.

(*b.*) *The Rationalist or Naturalistic View of the Bible.*—The Bible is not inspired at all, or at least in no way differing from any other book. Its authors were inspired, perhaps, just as Homer, or Thucydides, or Cicero were inspired, but not differently. It has no *authority*, therefore, over any other book, and is just as liable to be in error as any other. If you should bind in one volume the histories of Herodotus, Tacitus, Gibbon, and Mr. Bancroft, the poems of Horace, Hafiz, and Dante, and the letters of Cicero and Horace Walpole, this collection would have to the Naturalist just as much authority as the Bible.

(*c.*) The *mediatorial* view of the Bible, or the view which *mediates* between the others. This view endeavors to *reconcile* the others, by accepting the truths in each, and eliminating their errors or defects.

To this third division of opinions belong those of a large class, who are not prepared to accept either the first or the second. They cannot believe every word in the Bible to be the word of God, for they find things in it contradicting the evidence of history and the intuitions of reason, and also contradicting other teachings of the same book. They cannot see why, as Christians, they should believe everything in the Jewish Scriptures. As Christians, they go to the New Testament as a main source of faith and practice, but do not see why they should go to the Old Testament for Christian truth. On the other hand, they cannot look upon the Bible as a common book. They remember that it has been a light to the world for thousands of years, that it has been the means of awakening the human intellect and heart, of reforming society, and purifying life. Even in the Old Testament they find the noblest truth and the tenderest piety. The Bible has been the litany, prayer-book, inspirer, comforter of nations and centuries. They cannot and would not emancipate themselves from the traditions in which they were born, nor cut off history behind them. The Christian Church is their mother; she has taught them out of this book to know God, and out of this book to pray to him, and they cannot regard it without a certain prepossession.

To this third class I myself belong. I would not be unjust to the past or to the future. I would be loyal to truth, and not shut my eyes to what God reveals which is new; and I would not be unfaithful to what has already been taught me, or ungrateful for the love which has taught the world by the mouths of past prophets and apostles.

§ 2. The Difficulty. Antiquity of the World, and Age of Mankind

Let us then see, first, what the problem before us is; and this can perhaps be best understood by means of an example.

The common opinion among Christians is, that the world was made four thousand and four years before Christ, and that all mankind are descended from Adam and Eve. These opinions are derived from the book of Genesis, which tells us that after God had made the world and other things in five days, on the sixth day he made man in his own image; and that, when the first man, Adam, was a hundred and thirty years old, he had a son, named Seth; and from Seth, according to Genesis, are descended, by a genealogy given in the fifth chapter of Genesis, Noah and his sons; and the ages being given from Adam down to Abraham, and from Abraham to Christ, the age of the world and the age of the human race have been computed.

As long as there was no reason for supposing any different period for the antiquity of the world, these numbers were quietly accepted. But various new facts have been noticed, and new sciences have arisen, within the past fifty years, which have thrown doubt upon this chronology. In the first place the great science of geology has examined the rocky leaves which envelop the surface of the earth, and has found written upon them proofs of an immense antiquity. It is found that the earth, instead of being created four thousand years ago, must have existed for myriads of years, in order to have given time for the changes which have taken place in its structure. This evidence was long doubted and resisted by theologians, as they supposed in the interest of Scripture; but the evidence was too strong to be denied, and no intelligent theologian, however Orthodox, now believes the world to have been made in six days, or to have been created only six thousand years ago. With some, the six days stand for immense periods of time; with others, the whole story is considered a vision, or a symbolical account of geological events; but no one takes it literally. This result has come from the overwhelming amount of evidence for the antiquity of the earth, derived mainly from the fossil rocks. Of these fossiliferous rocks there are over thirty distinct strata, lying superimposed, in a regular series, each filled with the remains of distinct varieties of animals or of plants. These rocks must each have been an immense period of time in being formed, for the shells which they contain, although very delicate, are unbroken, and could only be slowly deposited in the quiet depths of a great ocean. There are also evidences that after those strata were formed, violent and sudden upheavals took place, throwing them into new positions, then slow uprisings of the bottom of the sea, or slow subsidings of the land. At one time the northern parts of Europe and America were covered with ice. Great glaciers extended over the whole of Switzerland, and icebergs floated from the mountains of Berkshire in Massachusetts upon a sea which filled the valley of the Connecticut River, dropping erratic blocks of stone, taken from those mountains, in straight lines, parallel with each other, half way across the valley, where they still lie. Similar icebergs floated from Snowdon, in Wales, and Ben Lomond, in Scotland, over the submerged islands of Great Britain. At one time the whole surface of the earth, instead of being covered with icy glaciers, was filled with a hot, damp atmosphere, laden with carbonic gas, which no creature could breathe, but in which grew great forests of a strange tropical vegetation. Then came another period, in which all these forests were submerged and buried, and at last turned into coal. Long after this hot period had passed, and long after the cold, glacial period, which followed it, had departed, came a time when the elephant, the rhinoceros, and the hippopotamus covered the whole of Europe, and the mammoth roamed in North America. Such facts as these, incontestably established by the amplest evidence, have made it impossible for any reasonable man to believe that the earth was made in six days, or that it was made only six thousand years ago.

But this question being thus disposed of, other questions arise in their turn. Are all mankind descended from one pair, or from many? Has the human race existed on the earth only six thousand years, or during a longer period? Was the deluge of Noah a real event? and if so, was it universal or partial? Did the sun stand still at the command of Joshua? or is that only a poetic image taken from an ancient book of poems—the book of Jasher? Is there any truth in the story of the passage of the Red Sea by the Israelites? of the passage of the Jordan? of the walls of Jericho falling when the trumpets were blown? of the story of Samson? If we once begin to doubt and disbelieve the accounts in the Bible, where shall we stop? What rule shall we have by which to distinguish the true from the false? Is it safe to begin to question and deny? Is it not safer to accept the whole book as the word of God, and to let everything in it stand unexamined?

No! "It is never safe," said Luther, "to do anything against the truth!" Truth alone is safe; and his soul only is safe who loves and honors truth more than human approbation—more than ease, comfort, or life. It is not safe to pretend to believe what we do not. And in this instance, half of the infidelity of the age and country has come from the teaching that everything in the Bible is the word of God. Sincere men have been disgusted when told they must believe things contrary to their common sense and reason.

Another question, which is now being investigated, is the age of mankind—the antiquity of the human race. The Bible gives the list of generations from Adam to Abraham; and the length of each, and other data, given in Scripture, make six thousand years for the life of man on this earth. Greek history only goes back some twenty-three hundred years; the Egyptian monuments go back fifteen hundred or two thousand years earlier—to 2000 B.C., or 3000 B.C. The "Vedas," in India, may have been written 1500 B.C.; the "Kings," in China, before that. But recently we have been carried back to a yet earlier period,—to a time when man existed on the earth, before any written monument or sculptured stone which now exists. *Two* different sources have been discovered within a few years,—one of them by philology, the other by geology.

It has been found that the languages spoken by Europeans, in their airy sounds, are more permanent monuments than granite or enduring brass. Stamped on these light, imponderable words are marks of a gray antiquity going back to times before Herodotus, before Moses and the book of Genesis, before the Vedas in India, before the Zendavesta in Persia. It has been proved, first, that nearly all the languages of Europe belong to one linguistic family, and therefore that those who speak them were originally of one race. These different languages—seven sister languages, daughters of a language now wholly gone—are the Sanscrit or ancient Hindoo, the Zend or ancient Persian, the Greek, the Latin, the Keltic, the German, and the Slavic languages. By a comparison of these, it has been found that originally there lived, east of the Caspian, a race of shepherds and hunters, calling themselves *Aryan*; that one branch descended into India at least five thousand years ago, and drove out the aboriginal inhabitants, a second branch went into Persia, a third into Italy, a fourth into Greece, a fifth vast immigration filled Northern Europe with the Kelts, a sixth with Scandinavians and Germans, and a seventh with the Slaves. But long ago as this immigration was,—before all history,—it found aboriginal inhabitants everywhere, whose descendants remain. The Lapps and Finns in Northern, Europe, the Basques in Spain, and Magyars in Hungary, are probably descended from this earlier European race. It is difficult to suppose mankind only six thousand years old, when we find such great movements taking place four or five thousand years ago.

But now come the geologists, and tell us that they find evidence of three different races existing in Europe in three distinct periods of civilization, some of which probably preceded the immigration of these Indo-European races. These three belong to what they call the Stone, the Bronze, and the Iron Age. In the gravel and drift, from ten to twenty feet below the surface, along with the bones of the elephant and the rhinoceros, and other animals long since extinct, are found hundreds of flint instruments, axes, arrow-heads, and tools, indicating that men lived in Europe in great numbers, contemporaries with these extinct animals. If this should be proved, we should then be brought to admit, with respect to the antiquity of man, what we have already admitted with regard to the antiquity of the world, that the account in Genesis is not to be understood as theologians have hitherto taught; that is, that we must not go to Genesis, but to philology and geology, for our knowledge of the most ancient history.

In this case, then, it will be evident that the old notion of a literal inspiration cannot be maintained. God certainly did not inspire men to teach anything about the creation which was adapted to mislead and deceive men for two thousand years. We shall be obliged to say, then, that Moses was not inspired to teach geology or history; that what he taught on these subjects he taught from such sources as were available to him, and that he was liable to error.

The old Orthodox theory of plenary inspiration has received very damaging blows from such scientific researches as these which we have been describing. The letter of the Bible seems, in such cases, to be at war with the facts of nature.

§ 3. Basis of the Orthodox Theory of Inspiration

Why, then, should the Orthodox doctrine be so stoutly maintained? What are the reasons used in its defence? What its arguments? What is its basis? On what does it rest? Do the writers of the Bible say that they were inspired by God to write these books? Not at all. Do they claim infallibility? Nowhere. Do they lay down any doctrine of plenary, verbal, literal inspiration? No. We do not even know who wrote many of these books. We do not know who collected them, or why just these books were put into the collection, and no others. The Orthodox theory rests on few facts, but is mainly an assumption. It seemed necessary that there should be *authority* somewhere; and when Protestants rejected the authority of the Church, they took the Bible in its place. The doctrine of inspiration, therefore, was adopted as a basis for the authority of the Bible.

The principal reason given by those who believe in the plenary inspiration of the Bible, for holding to this doctrine, is the necessity of *some* authority. The argument is this: Unless every part of the Bible is believed to be fully inspired, some part of it may be believed to be erroneous; and if we admit error in any part, the Bible loses its authority, and we do not know what to believe. The doctrine of literal and plenary inspiration rests, therefore, in the last analysis, on no basis of fact, but on a purely *a priori* argument. Let us therefore examine this argument, and see what is its force.

Revelation, it is said, is a communication of truth with authority. It is truth shown to us by God, not truth reasoned out by man. Its value is, that we can rely upon it entirely, live by it, die by it, without doubt or hesitation. We do not want speculation, opinion, probability; we want certainty; otherwise religion ceases to be a power, and becomes a mere intellectual amusement.

The only religion, it is added, which is of any real value, is that which carries with it this authority. The outward world, with its influences and its temptations, is so strong, that we shall be swept away by it unless we can oppose to it some inward conviction as solid and real. Amid the temptations of the senses, the allurements of pleasure, the deceitfulness of riches, will it enable a man to hold fast to honesty, temperance, purity, generosity— to believe that in all probability these things are right, and that there is something to be said in favor of the opinion that God approves of them?

Will it help him, to think that unless the writer of the Gospel is mistaken, or his words mistranslated, Christ may have said that goodness leads to heaven, and sin to hell? No. We need authority in order to have certainty; and we need certainty in our convictions in order that they should influence us deeply and permanently.

This is the chief argument in favor of the plenary inspiration[11] of the Bible. We see it amounts to this—that it is very desirable, for practical purposes, that we should believe everything in the Bible to be true.[12]

In reply to this, we ought first to say, that the question in all these cases is not, What is desirable? but, What is true? We should begin by investigating the facts. We should ask, Does the Bible anywhere say of itself that it is inspired in this sense? Do any of the writers of the Bible declare themselves to be thus inspired, so that all that they say is absolutely true in every particular? Does Christ say that those who are to write the Gospels or the Epistles of the New Testament shall be thus guarded against every possible error? Or is there any evidence in the books themselves that the writers were thus protected? Do they never contradict each other or themselves? Do they never contradict facts of nature or facts of history?

Now, to all these questions, we are obliged to say, No. The Bible claims no such absolute inspiration for itself. It says that "holy men of old spake as they were moved by the Holy Spirit," but it does not say that the Holy Spirit made them infallible. It says, "All Scripture is given by inspiration, and is profitable for doctrine," but it does not say what are the limits of Scripture; and to be profitable or useful for doctrine is surely not the same thing as to have infallible authority over belief. Besides, if those who wrote certain Scriptures were infallibly inspired, those who collected the present books of the Old and New Testament, and made our canon, were *not* so inspired. Those who transcribed their autographic manuscripts were not inspired. The manuscripts of the Gospels and Epistles, written by their authors, have long since perished. There were no autograph collectors in ancient times. There was no such reverence then paid to the letter of religion, to cause the original manuscript of an apostle to be kept in a church as a sacred relic. We have plenty of pieces of wood claiming to be parts of the true cross, but not a manuscript claiming to be the original writing of an apostle. The earliest manuscript goes only to the fourth century, and that contains the Epistle of Barnabas. If, then, the writers of the New Testament were inspired, those who collected their writings were not inspired, and may have left out the right books, and put in the wrong ones. Those who copied their manuscripts were not inspired, and may have left out the right words, and put in wrong ones. Those who translated their manuscripts were not inspired, and may have made mistakes in their translating. So that, after all, the plenary inspiration of the apostles does not bestow that infallibility upon our English Bible which this theory demands in order to give it authority.

And yet we admit the importance of having some authority. Truth which does not come with authority is *not* truth; it is only speculation; it cannot influence life. Revelation and philosophy differ in this, that philosophy tells us what men think about God, revelation what God thinks about men. Revelation is the drawing aside of the veil which hides God, duty, immortality. It does not give us speculations about them, but shows us the things themselves.

If, therefore, we can show that the Bible can be authority *without being* plenarily inspired, very possibly Orthodoxy would no longer cling to this doctrine with such remarkable tenacity. This point of authority we shall consider in another section of this chapter, and so we will say no more about it now. We shall try to show, then, that the Bible may be, and is authority, without being inspired as regards every page and word, and that inspiration is one thing and infallibility another. At present we desire to see the truth there is in the Orthodox doctrine of inspiration.

§ 4. Inspiration in general, or Natural Inspiration

There is a foundation for inspiration in human nature, a capacity for inspiration which all possess. Were it not so, Christian inspiration would be something unnatural, and not in the order of providence. Moreover, we commonly speak of the inspiration of the poet, the painter, the inventor, the man of genius. The man of genius is he who has more of this capacity for inspiration than other men. But all men have it in a greater or a less degree. All men have their hours or moments of inspiration. By these experiences of their own, they understand the larger inspirations of genius. If we distribute the thoughts we possess according to their source, we shall find that we have obtained them all, either *from other persons*, or by means of *mental effort*, or by *inspiration*. The largest part of our thoughts and opinions we have taken in ready made, and reproduced them just as we received them. We suppose ourselves thinking, when we utter them, but we are only remembering. A much smaller proportion of our thoughts we have obtained reflectively, by personal efforts of the active intellect. Another part are those which have come to us in some happy moments, when the inner eye was unclouded, and when we seem to see at a glance truth and beauty. These inspired moments give us the most solid knowledge we have. They are mental experiences, which are the master lights of all our being. They give direction and unity to all our other thoughts and opinions. They constitute mental originality. The peculiarity of inspiration, in this general sense, does not lie in the subjects of the thoughts, but in the manner of their coming. Ideas and thoughts of very different kinds may all be inspired thoughts. The poet, the artist, have their inspirations. But the scholar, the thinker, has his also. The man who invents a machine often has the idea come to him by an inspiration. The man who discovers a continent has seen it in idea before he sees it in reality. If Shakespeare was an inspired man, so was Newton, so was Columbus, so was Lord Bacon, so was Faust when he discovered printing, Watt when he improved the steam engine, and Daguerre when he found out photographic pictures; for, in all great discoveries and inventions, and in small ones too, the original idea is an inspiration, though it has to be worked out mechanically by hard thinking.

It will be seen, then, what we understand by inspiration, in this general sense. It is a mental sight, corresponding as nearly as anything can to physical sight. It seems, in the inspired moment, as if we looked into another world, and saw new truths and facts there. We do not bring them up out of our memory; we see them in all their own fresh life and reality. We do not think them out by an effort of the will; we stand still and see them. All that our will has to do with it is negative rather than positive. It is to keep off disturbing influences of memory and sense, to hold the mind still, attentive, receptive, and ready. If we believe in these inspirations, we can thus prepare the way for them, but nothing more. We can wait and look, till the vision is presented, and then we shall see it; but this is all. The man of genius is he who believes in these inspirations, and so looks for them. *What* he shall see will depend on what he looks for. The man whose taste is in the world of imagination looks for forms of poetic or artistic beauty, and so sees these. Every man looks for that which he is most interested in, whether he be metaphysician or mechanic. The world of ideal beauty and truth, which overhangs ours, has a thousand portals, and we can pass in through one or another, and see that which suits our various tastes and desires. Memory, reflection, and sight,—these are the three sources of our thoughts. The inspired man is a seer—he has insight and foresight; and these objects of mental sight are to him more real and certain than any others. But he is unable to prove their reality or justify them to the sceptic. And hence his fate is often that of Cassandra,—to be a true prophet, but not to be believed, until by and by the strength of his own conviction wins its way, and produces faith in others.

There are, therefore, two principal intellectual states of the mind—the one receptive, the other plastic; the one by which it takes in truth, the other by which it works it up into shape. By the one it obtains the substance of thought, by the other the form of thought. The one may be called the perceptive state, the other the reflective state. Thus, too, we see that the perceptive faculty may be exercised in two directions, outwardly and inwardly. It is the same intellectual faculty which, through the senses, looks at and perceives the outward material universe, and through the mind itself, the inward world of thought. It is this power of looking inward which gives us all that we call inspiration. We have, thus, outsight and insight.

There is, then, a *universal inspiration*, on which the special inspiration of the Old and New Testament rests. There are inspired men and uninspired men. There are inspired writings and uninspired writings. There is a general inspiration, out of which the particular inspiration of Bible writers grew. Universal inspiration is a genus, of which this is a species. We cannot understand the inspiration of the writers of the Bible till we understand this universal inspiration on which it rests. We can best explain the special inspiration of Scripture by first knowing the general inspirations of mankind.

Mr. Emerson, in one of his poems, called the "Problem," describes this universal inspiration. He describes Phidias as being inspired to make his Jupiter, as well as the prophets to write their burdens. He says the architect that made St. Peter's was guided by some divine instinct in his heart—he wrought in a sad sincerity. He says we cannot tell how such buildings as the Parthenon and St. Peter's were built, any more than how the bird builds its nest; they were formed by a natural architecture; they grew as the grass grows; they came out of thought's interior sphere, just as the pine tree adds a myriad of new leaves to its old arms every year.

"The passive master lent his hand
To the vast soul that o'er him planned;
And the same power that reared the shrine
Bestrode the tribes that knelt within."

§ 5. Christian or Supernatural Inspiration

Having thus spoken of inspiration in general, we proceed to speak of Christian inspiration in particular.

Christian inspiration is the work of the Holy Spirit on the heart. It is that influence which came to the apostles, and to all Christians after Jesus had left the earth, to unite them inwardly with Christ, and to show them the true Christ. It is that of which Paul speaks, when he says, It pleased God to reveal his Son in me. All Christians were baptized with the Holy Ghost; had the spirit of Christ dwelling in them; were led by the spirit of God; received the spirit of adoption, which bore witness that they were the sons of God; which helped their infirmities; helped them to pray; enabled them to mortify the deeds of the body, and produced many gifts and graces. It is quite certain that all Christians were expected to partake of this Christian inspiration. This enabled them inwardly to see and know Christ—the true Christ. And only thus could they become truly his.

Now, the Christian inspiration, so necessary at first, is equally necessary now, for its object is, as it was then, to turn nominal Christians into living Christians; to turn historical Christianity into vital Christianity; to enable those who already know Christ after the flesh, also to know him after the spirit. What is it which we need for comfort, improvement, usefulness? We need a living, practical faith in God's truth and love. We need to see it as we now see the outward world. We believe in the inevitable retribution of God's laws. We need to see this; to see that selfishness is death, and generosity life; to see that humility is exaltation, and that pride is abasement. Having seen law, we need also to see grace, the reality of forgiveness, the reality of a Father's love. We need to see immortality and eternity, while we are yet surrounded with the world of sense and time; to see that the two worlds are not two, but one, all temporal things having their roots in spiritual things. This is what we need for comfort, for no hardship would seem hard while we were thus looking at the things which are eternal, and knowing that every light affliction works out an eternal weight of glory. This is what we need for improvement. For no efforts at improvement can accomplish that which this inward inspiration can do. It is a tide which bears us on. It takes from us the weight of years. It is the sap which rises into every branch, penetrates every twig, swells the buds, expands the leaves, opens the blossoms, ripens the fruit, and causes universal growth. And it is what we need for usefulness. For how mechanical and lifeless are efforts at usefulness which proceed merely from the sense of duty! How blessed are those which proceed from a heart filled with love and peace!

Christian inspiration, then, reveals inwardly the spirit of Christ, and so gives us a new heart, and makes of us new creatures. It is the most essential and vital part of Christianity, yet it is that part of Christianity which is the least known and prized. How many dogmatists there are fighting for doctrines; how many ceremonialists earnest about forms; how many conscientious Christians trying hard to do their duties;—to one spiritual Christian, whose Christianity consists in living in the spirit, that he may walk in the spirit!

One reason for this seems to be the prevalence of false views concerning the nature of Christian inspiration. It has been regarded as wholly different in its laws from other inspiration, as an arbitrary influence without laws or conditions. Now, in fact, the inspiration of the Christian, while it differs in its subject from that of the poet, rests on the same mental faculty, and has analogous conditions. The condition of the poet's inspiration is, that loving the outward beauty of the natural world, and faithfully studying its truth, he should then hold himself ready, in strong desire, to see, inwardly, ideal truth and ideal beauty. And so the Christian, believing in the outward Christ, and loving him, holds himself expectant of an inward revelation of that same Jesus in his glorified and higher influence. All inspiration has its conditions and laws. The poet's eye, in its fine frenzy, must look from heaven to earth, and from earth to heaven. His inward inspiration is in strict accordance with his outward occupation and his outward fidelity. Every man is inwardly inspired, according to the nature of his outward work. Shakespeare cannot discover America, nor Columbus write Hamlet. And it is only he who believes in Christ, and so endeavors to obey and serve him, who receives an inward sight of his essential spirit. Christian inspiration is not arbitrary, is not unnatural, is not limited. It is the life of Christ, flowing steadily and constantly into all hearts which are prepared for it, which long for it, and which hold themselves ready to receive it.

We are thus prepared to state more distinctly the difference between inspiration in general and Christian inspiration in particular.

(a.) These two inspirations *resemble* each other in resulting from the exercise of the same mental faculties, since the state of mind in both cases is not that of reflection, but perception; and the perception is inward perception. Newton fixes his mind steadily upon the confused mathematical thought within till it becomes clear. Milton fixes his mind upon the inward image of ideal truth and beauty till it grows so distinct that he can put it into corresponding words. Columbus meditates upon the thought of a Western Continent till it seems so plain to him that he is ready to set sail for it. And so Paul and John look steadily at the Christ formed within them till they see clearly what is Christ's thought concerning every question, every subject.

(*b.*) The two inspirations also are alike in this, that the truth seen is in both cases, as to its substance, given to us by God. For the truths seen by Newton, Milton, Descartes, and Columbus were not inventions of theirs, but divine realities shown to them by God.

(*c.*) In both cases the form of the truth seen comes from the exercise of the human faculties of each individual upon the substance thus given. For Paul and John, no less than Newton and Milton, worked up in their own minds the truth seen. This is evident from the fact, that, while their writings agree in contents and substance with each other, they differ from each other in form and style. Each writer of the New Testament has his own distinctly marked style, not only of expression, but also of thought.

(*d.*) They are alike also in combining truth of substance with fallibility of statement. The substance of every inspired man's thought is truth, because it is the reality shown to him by God. The form in which he expresses it varies more or less from this truth, because that comes from the exercise of his own finite faculties. Newton and Milton looked at God's truths, and uttered them as well as they were able. So did Paul and John. That these last were liable to err in matters of statement appears from the fact that they did err in some matters, as, for example, in regard to the speedy coming of Christ.

These being the resemblances between natural and supernatural inspiration, what are *differences*?

(*a.*) The first difference is in the *kind of truths seen*. The truths seen by Newton and Milton belong to the natural world, those seen by Paul and John to the supernatural world. The substance of the inspiration in the one case is nature, in the other case it is Christ. Intercourse with nature had fed the minds of Newton and Milton with the truth, forming the material upon which their inspiration could work. Intercourse with Christ, in the flesh and in the spirit, had filled the minds of Paul and John with the material on which their inspiration could be exercised. Christ had come to them outwardly and inwardly, and this was the substance of their inspiration.

(*b.*) The inspiration of Newton and Milton implies genius; that is, a special faculty in each individual. This possession of genius, or special faculty, is a condition *sine qua non*, of natural inspiration. It is solitary, it is individual. But the inspiration of the writers of the New Testament does not imply genius. Of the eight writers of the New Testament, only one, viz., Paul, appears to have been a man of natural genius. He was great by endowment, the others were made great by their inspiration. In the one case the uncommon man finds wonderful things in the common world; in the other case the uncommon world shows wonderful things to the common man.

(c.) Natural and supernatural inspiration differ also in their occasion. A miraculous event, namely, the coming of Christ inwardly to their souls on the day of Pentecost, was the occasion of the apostolic inspiration. This coming of the Holy Ghost was the second of the two supernatural events of Christianity, of which the other was the birth of Christ. The miraculous events in the life of Jesus may have been the natural results of the coming of such a being into the world. The miracles of Christ's life, including his resurrection, may have been natural to a supernatural being. They are the evidence of a break in the series of causation in the outward world. In like manner the inward coming of Christ to the hearts of his disciples in what is called the influence of the Holy Spirit, is another supernatural event, the natural result of which is the founding of the Church, the writing of the New Testament, and the newly created life in individual souls.

These two inspirations, therefore, differ in their substance, source, and method. The substance of one consists of truths of the natural order, the other of the supernatural order. The source of one is the world of nature, the source of the other is the inward Christ. And the method of the one is that of individual genius, which is solitary, while the method of the other is that of love or communion.

§ 6. Inspiration of the Scriptures, especially of the New Testament Scriptures

We now pass on to ask, What is the inspiration of the New Testament, or of its writers?

The writers of the New Testament had no different inspiration from that of all other Christians. We nowhere hear of any one receiving an inspiration to enable him to write a Gospel or an Epistle. They distinctly repel the idea of any such special or distinct inspiration. "By one spirit we have all been baptized into one body, and have been all made to drink into one spirit." Gifts are different, but the spirit is one and the same in all. But even among these diversities of gifts, nothing is said of any gift for writing Gospels or Epistles. Probably, therefore, the inspiration by which these were written was precisely the same as that by which they preached to the Gentiles or taught in the Church. It was an inward sight of Christ, an inward sight of his truth and love, which enabled them to speak and write with authority — the authority of those who saw what they said, and knew it to be true. "We speak what we know, and testify what we have seen." Hence it is that we find in their writings so much substance, so much comprehensiveness, so much insight. They are in constant communion with an invisible world of truth. They describe what is before their eyes.

A book given by inspiration is not a book made perfect by miracle, but a book, the writer of which was in a state open to influences from a higher sphere. All books which the human race has accepted as inspired — Vedas, Koran, Zendavesta — are sacred scriptures; all that *lasts* is inspired. Perpetuity, not infallibility, is the sign of inspiration.

"The word unto the prophet spoken

Was writ on tables yet unbroken;

The word by seers or sibyls told

In groves of oak or fanes of gold

Still floats upon the morning wind,

Still whispers to the willing mind.

One accent of the Holy Ghost

The heedless world has never lost."

The famous proof-text on this subject is that in the Second Epistle of Paul to Timothy: "All Scripture is given by inspiration of God, and is profitable for doctrine, reproof, correction, and instruction in righteousness." To what Scripture did Paul refer? Some say to the Jewish Scripture. Some say to the Jewish and Christian writings. But the Christian writings were not then all written, and were not collected into what we call the New Testament. The apostle does not limit himself to these. He says, "*All* Scripture is inspired" — not merely Jewish or Christian Scripture, but all sacred writing. All the writings of every age which are looked upon as Scripture, which men from age to age reverence and honor as such, were *not* of man's invention, not of man's device, but came from some irrepressible influence acting on the soul from within. The poet before quoted says truly, —

"Out from the heart of nature rolled

The burdens of the Bible old.

The litanies of nations came,

Like the volcano's tongue of flame,

Up from the burning cone below,

The canticles of love and woe.

The hand that rounded Peter's dome,

And groined the aisles of Christian Rome,

Wrought in a sad sincerity.

Himself from God he could not free;

He builded better than he knew;

The conscious stone to beauty grew."

There is a truth in this—a profound truth. The Bible is not an exceptional book in this, that it has no parallels in nature to its method of production. It is true that Phidias was inspired to make his statue and to build the Parthenon.

"Such and so grew those holy piles,

While love and terror laid the tiles.

Earth proudly wears the Parthenon

As the best gem upon her zone,

And morning opes in haste her lids

To gaze upon the Pyramids;

O'er England's abbeys bends the sky

As on its friends with kindred eye;

For out of thought's interior sphere

These wonders rose to upper air."

When Mr. Emerson and Theodore Parker compare in this way the Bible with the Vedas or the Parthenon, we often feel that it degrades the Bible, and takes away its special sanctity. But this is not necessarily the case. There may be a wide gulf between the inspiration of the Bible and that of the Vedas, or of Homer or Plato; and yet they may all belong to the same class of works. There is a wide gulf between *man* and the highest of the inferior animals; and yet we put man into the class Mammalia, along with oxen, whales, and cats, and into the same Order with apes and bats. We do not think that man is degraded by being thus classified. He occupies a distinct species in this order and class. So the New Testament and Old Testament constitute two distinct species, of which they are the sole representatives of one genus of inspired books; but that *genus* belongs to the same *order* as the Vedas, Edda, Zendavesta, and Koran, and that order belongs to the same *class* as the poems of Homer and Dante, the architecture of the Parthenon and the Strasburg Minster, the discovery of America by Columbus, and of the law of gravitation by Newton.

The *class* of works which we call inspired comprehends, as we have before said, all which come to man by a certain influx into his soul—not by looking out of himself, but by looking into himself. Sometimes we go and search and find thoughts; sometimes thoughts come and find us. "They flash upon our inner eye;" they haunt us, and pursue us, and take possession of us. So Columbus was haunted by the idea of a continent in the west; so Newton was haunted by his discovery long before he made it; so the "Paradise Lost" pursued Milton long before it was written. Every really great work must have in it more or less of this element which we call inspiration.

But while the great works of genius belong to the class of inspired works, we make a distinct order out of the great religious works which have been the sacred Scriptures of races of men. They evidently came from a higher inspiration than the works of science and the works of art. They have ruled men's souls for thousands of years. These, then, we place in an *Order* by themselves, and it is no discredit to the Bible to be ranked with the works of Confucius, which have kept the Chinese orderly, peaceful, industrious, and happy for almost twenty-six centuries.

But still, among these sacred books the Bible may be said to constitute a distinct *genus*, because it differs from all the rest in two ways—in teaching the holiness of God and the unity of God. The writer has been a careful reader of all these sacred books for twenty years; he has read them with respect; in no captious spirit; wishing to find in them all the truth he could. He has found in them much truth—much in accordance with Christianity. But he sees a wide difference between them all and the Bible. They are all *profitable* for doctrine, for reproof, for instruction; but they are not Holy Scriptures in the sense in which we ascribe that word to the Bible. The Old Testament, though having in it many harsh and hard features, belonging to the Jewish mind, has strains which rise into a higher region than anything in the Vedas or the Zendavesta. The Proverbs of Solomon are about on a level with the books of Confucius. But nowhere in all these Ethnic Scriptures are strains like some of the Psalms—like passages in Isaiah and Jeremiah. The laws of Menu are low compared with the Pentateuch.

But if the Old and New Testament make a genus by themselves, they divide again into two species. There is a specific difference between the New Testament and the Old. The New Testament inspiration is of a far deeper, higher, and broader character than the other. In fact, we ought, perhaps, to make a special order by itself from the New Testament writings. They are so full of life, light, and love—they are so strong yet so tender—so pure yet so free! They have no cant of piety, no formalism, but breathe throughout a heavenly atmosphere. Their inspiration is of the highest kind of all.

But what is this Holy Spirit? What does it teach? Scientific truth? No. Scientific truth has been taught the world by other channels. Bacon and

Newton, La Place and Cuvier, Linnæus and De Candolle, have been inspired to teach science. Their knowledge came, not only by observation, not only by study, but by patiently opening their minds to receive impressions from above. Were the writers of the Bible inspired to teach history? We think not. There are histories of the Jews in the Bible, and they are likely to be as authentic, as histories, as are those of Herodotus and Livy, and other painstaking and sincere historians. But the special inspiration of the Bible does not appear in the historic books.

But are not *all* parts of the Bible equally inspired by this Holy Spirit? By no means. We can easily see that they are not. It is evident that there is nothing spiritually edifying in a large part of the history of the Old Testament—the account of Samson, the story of Gideon, large parts of the books of Judges and Chronicles, the Song of Solomon, the book of Esther. The book of Ecclesiastes is full, throughout, of a dark and terrible scepticism. Now, all these books are valuable, exceedingly so, as history, but not as proceeding from the Holy Spirit.

But it may be said, "If the history of the Bible is not inspired, it may be erroneous." Certainly it may. We have seen that the account of creation in the book of Genesis is probably erroneous. It contains one great faith, luminous throughout—namely, that there is one God, Creator of all worlds and of mankind. But as to the *order* of creation,—the six days, the garden of Eden,—all we can say is, that there may be some way by which Moses could, in vision, have seen these things, represented in picture, as they happened long before. There may be such a kind of unveiling of the past before the inner eye of the soul. We do not deny it, for it is not wise to deny where we know nothing. But we can assert that Christianity does not require us to believe those chapters of Genesis to contain historic truth. It may be allegorical truth. It may be a parable, representing how every little child comes into an Eden of innocence, and is tempted by that wily serpent, the sophistical understanding, and is betrayed by desire, his Eve, and goes out of his garden of childhood, where all life proceeds spontaneously and by impulse, into a world of work and labor. If it be such an allegory as that, it teaches us quite as much as if it were history.

§ 7. Authority of the Scriptures

We have seen that the Bible, though inspired, is not infallible. But, it is said, unless the Bible is infallible it has no authority. This we deny. Inspiration is not infallibility, but inspiration *is* authority. The inspired man is always an authority. Phidias and Michael Angelo are authorities in sculpture; Titian and Rafaelle are authorities in painting; Mozart and Beethoven in music; and Paul, John, Peter, in religion.

Authority without infallibility is the problem before us. It is evident that authority is desirable; it is equally evident that infallibility is impossible. Can there, therefore, be the one without the other? Can God reveal himself to man through a fallible medium? Can the writers of the New Testament be so inspired as to be able to communicate truth, and yet so inspired as not to be infallible? To all these questions we answer, *Yes*; and will try to show it to be so.

Suppose that you are going through a forest in company with others. You have lost your way. No one knows which way to go; dangers are around you—dangers from cold, hunger, wild beasts, enemies. If you go the wrong way, you may all perish; if you go the right way, you will reach your destination and be safe. Under these circumstances, one of the party climbs a tree, and when he has reached the top he cries out with joy, "I see the way we ought to go. We must go to the right. I see the ocean in that direction, and the spires of the city to which we are bound." You all immediately go the way that he directs. He has become an authority to you. You follow his guidance implicitly, and put your lives into his hands, depending upon the truth of what he says. Why? Because he has been where you have not been, and has seen what you have not seen, and you believe him honest and true. He has no motive to deceive you. This is his authority.

But is it equivalent to infallibility? By no means. No one supposes him to be infallible. If, after following his direction for a while, you see no signs to show that you are in the right way, you begin to think that he may have been mistaken, and some one else climbs a tree to verify his judgment, or to correct it. But if, instead, signs begin to appear to show that you are in the right way, your faith in your guide is confirmed, and his authority is practically increased.

What gives a man authority as a guide, teacher, counsellor, is not our belief in his infallibility, but our belief in his knowledge; if we believe that he knows something we do not know, he becomes thereby an authority to us. If he has been where we have not been, and seen what we have not seen, he is an authority. A man who has just come from Europe or from California, who has been in the midst of a great battle, who has studied a subject which others have not studied, and made himself familiar with it, such a man is an authority to others. Observe men listening to him. All defer to him while he is speaking on this subject. He may be much more ignorant than they are in regard to other things, but, if he has had superior opportunities in regard to this subject, he is an authority. Yet they do not believe him infallible; for if, in the course of his conversation, he says anything which seems contradictory, incredible, absurd, they begin to withdraw their confidence, and may withdraw it wholly. But if, on the other hand, what he says is clear, consistent, solid with information, his authority is increased continually, and his bearers defer to him more and more.

Now, the authority of the writers of the New Testament is exactly of this kind. The authority of inspiration everywhere is of this kind. An inspired man is one who is believed to have been where we have not been, and to have seen what we have not seen.

In Cooper's novels there is a character whom he calls Leatherstocking, familiar with the woods, knowing all their signs, acquainted with the habits of bird, beast, and Indian. He guides the travellers through the wilderness, and, by his superior knowledge, saves them from the Indian ambush and the pursuing savage. They commit themselves implicitly to his guidance, trust their lives to him. Why? Because they confide in his knowledge of woodcraft and in his fidelity. As regards all matters pertaining to the forest, he is an authority; their teacher if they want information, their guide if they are ignorant of the way, their saviour in imminent peril from savage beasts and savage men. He is an authority to them, a perfect authority; for they confide in him entirely, without a shade of doubt. But no one thinks him infallible, nor supposes it necessary to believe him infallible, in order to trust him entirely.

Just so a ship on a lee shore, in the midst of a driving storm, throws up signal rockets or fires a gun for a pilot. A white sail emerges from the mist; it is the pilot-boat. A man climbs on board, and the captain gives to him the command of the ship. All his orders are obeyed implicitly. The ship, laden with a precious cargo and hundreds of lives, is confided to a rough-looking man whom no one ever saw before, who is to guide them through a narrow channel, where to vary a few fathoms to the right or left will be utter destruction. The pilot is invested with absolute authority as regards bringing the vessel into port.

When Columbus came back from his first voyage, and reported the discovery of America, was he not an *authority*? Did not men throng around him, to hear of what he had seen and done? Yet who believed him infallible. He who has been where I have not been, and seen what I have not seen, is an *authority* to me. If I believe him honest, and no impostor, then I learn from him, and depend on his testimony. Now, the writers of the New Testament have been where we have not been. They have ascended heights, and sounded depths in the spiritual world unknown to us. So they are authorities to us, provided we have enough of their spirit in us to enable us to see and know their inspiration. For, unless I have some musical spirit in me, I cannot discern the inspiration of Mozart; unless I have some mathematical spirit in me, I cannot discern the mathematical inspiration of Newton and Kepler.

So the natural man (the man who has nothing in him corresponding to the Christian inspiration) cannot discern the things of the Spirit of God; for they are foolishness to him, for they are spiritually discerned or judged. He lives in external things, as babes do. The authority of the Spirit in the Bible is that it awakens and appeals to whatever spiritual element exists in our soul, and compels it to feel and admit its truth.

Jesus, it is said, in giving the Sermon on the Mount, taught as one having authority, and not as the Scribes. What was his authority, then? Not official authority, for he was not yet known to be the Christ, hardly yet known to be a prophet. Not merely the *authority* coming from an imposing manner; not an authoritative air, or tone, or manner, certainly. That was precisely the tone and manner which the Scribes *did* have in *their* teaching. But the authority is in the Sermon itself. Its truths are so wonderfully distinct and self-evident, they carry conviction with them. Jesus sees so plainly all that he says—there is no hesitation, no obscurity, no perhapses in his language. He is like one describing what is before his eyes, what he knows to be true because he sees it while he is saying it. It is, in short, the authority which always attends knowledge. He who knows anything, and can speak with certainty, carries conviction with him, though we do not suppose him to be infallible, nor is it thought necessary to believe him so, in order to give to him this authority.

By such examples, we see that in earthly matters of the very highest importance we ascribe authority without supposing infallibility. Now, if we analyze the source of this authority, we shall find that it comes, first, from the testimony of others, and, secondly, from our own experience. Leatherstocking comes recommended to the travellers as a skilful and faithful guide, and they trust him, at first, on the simple ground of that recommendation. But they do not trust him entirely or fully on that ground. They watch him while they trust him,—perhaps we ought rather to say, they *try* him, than that they *trust* him. But, after they have tried him day by day, week by week, and find him always skilful, always faithful, they come to place a more and more implicit trust in his guidance; he becomes more and more an authority.

So the pilot comes at first recommended only by his office. His office implies the testimony of those who ought to know that he is able to guide the vessel into the harbor. But if, besides this, there is some one on board who knows his ability and fidelity by previous experience, and says, "We are all safe now; this is the famous John Smith or William Brown, the best pilot in the harbor," then everybody is ready to trust him more entirely.

Knowledge and fidelity, *not* infallibility, these make a man an authority to others in things pertaining to this life—knowledge and fidelity, evidenced to us, first by the testimony of others, and secondly by our own experience. Testimony leads us to *try* a man and trust him partially, trust him, but watch him. Add to this our own experience of his knowledge and fidelity, and we trust him wholly.

There are two worlds of knowledge—outward and inward. Knowledge of the outward world comes to us through the senses, by observation; knowledge of the inward world comes to us through the consciousness, by insight or inspiration. Every man's knowledge has come to him by both of these methods. The soul has a perceptive power with which it can look either way. It looks outward through the senses, and perceives an external world; it looks inward through the consciousness, and perceives an internal world. It looks outward, and perceives forms, hears sounds, becomes acquainted with external nature. It looks inward, and becomes acquainted with justice, holiness, love, freedom, duty, sin, immortality, the infinite, the eternal, God.

But just as it depends on various conditions as to what a man shall see through the senses in time and space, so it depends on other conditions as to what a man shall see beyond time and space in the spiritual world. The conditions in the first instance are, good perceptive organs, a genius for observation, educated powers for observation, knowledge of what to observe, and finally opportunities for observation, or being able to go where the things are which are to be seen. A blind man standing in front of the Parthenon would be no authority to us as to its architecture; neither would the most sharp-sighted person who should happen in be in America, instead of Greece. So an Indian, with the finest perceptive faculty, and standing directly in front of this majestic temple, would give a very poor account of it, from want of previous knowledge. He, only, would be an authority to us in regard to such a building, who should combine with good perceptive organs, and some knowledge of the subject, an opportunity for looking at it.

When we speak of inspiration, we mean, in regard to the inward world, exactly the same thing. We mean that a man has his spiritual organs in a healthy condition, that he has some knowledge of spiritual things, and that he has been placed by divine Providence where he is able to see them. Some men are lifted into a world of spiritual perception, when they see things not seen by other men. They become prophets, apostles, lawgivers to the human race. They are invested with authority. Men believe what they say, and do what they command, and put their souls into their hands, just as they trust their bodies to the guide of the pilot.

These are the inspired men—the men to whom revelations have been made. They have authority, because they have been where we have not been, and seen what we have not seen. But they have not infallibility, because, as the apostle says, they have this treasure in earthen vessels. This divine knowledge is contained in a finite, and therefore fallible mind. But we see by means of our former illustrations that to grant their fallibility does not detract at all from their authority.

And again, their authority is certified to us exactly as in the other instances. They come recommended by external testimony, and on the strength of that testimony we confide in them and try them. If we find that they are not able to teach us, they cease to be authorities to us. But if we find that they are full of truth, they become our guides and teachers, and their authority is more and more confirmed; that they are good and true guides, is evidenced by their being able to guide us. They lead us into deeper depths of truth and love. They become the teachers of their race. The centuries which pass add more and more weight to their authority. They inspire us, therefore they are themselves inspired. It is no more necessary, after this, to prove their inspiration, in the sense which I have given, than to prove that the sun shines.

One remarkable illustration of this process, by which the test of Scripture, as inspired, is that it should be profitable for doctrine, reproof, and instruction, is to be found in the Epistle of Barnabas. Barnabas introduced Paul to the apostles at Jerusalem, and is called, in the book of Acts, a good man, and full of the Holy Ghost. He was sent on a mission to Antioch by the apostles; afterwards was specially pointed out by the Holy Ghost to go with Paul on his mission. (Acts 13:2.) He is styled a prophet in this place, and we read that the Holy Spirit said, "Separate me Barnabas and Saul for the work whereunto I have called them."

During this mission Barnabas seems to have been the more important of the two, for at Lystra the people called *him* Jupiter, and Paul Mercury. Barnabas and Paul appeared before the first council at Jerusalem; and the apostles, in their letter, say, "Our beloved Barnabas, and a man that has hazarded his life for the name of the Lord Jesus." Now, this Barnabas, called an apostle in the book of Acts, companion of Paul, sent on a mission by the Holy Spirit, and commended by the apostles at Jerusalem, was believed by the early Church to have written an Epistle. It is quoted as his, seven times by Clement of Alexandria, in the second century, three times by Origen, and by other writers.

Accordingly, it was originally included in the New Testament, and for nearly four hundred years made a part of it. The oldest manuscript of the

New Testament in the world, supposed to have been written in the fourth century, contains the Epistle of Barnabas; and one reason for believing the manuscript so old, is that it *does* contain it. This manuscript was found by the celebrated German critic Tischendorf, in 1859, in the convent of St. Catharine, at Mount Sinai. Why, then, is not this Epistle of Barnabas printed in our New Testament? Whoever reads it will easily see the reason. It is because it does not deserve to be there; it does not have the marks of a high inspiration; it is made up in a great degree of quotations from the Old Testament, of imitations of St. Paul, and of allegories. It evidently dropped out of the Bible by its own weight. It had every opportunity offered it to become a part of sacred Scripture; but being tried by Paul's test, it was found not to be profitable for doctrine, reproof, or anything else, and so the copyists saved their time, labor, and vellum by leaving it out. It was received on testimony, and discarded after experience. It had authority at first, because of its supposed author; it lost it afterwards, by means of its empty self.

This, then, is the authority of the writers of the Bible. It is the authority of inspired men—men who have been into spiritual regions where most men have not gone, and seen what most men have not seen. It is not infallibility. They are capable of mistakes and error. Their being in the Bible is only so far a proof that they are inspired, as it gives the testimony of the Church that it has found the proofs of inspiration in their writings. The Christian community has followed the apostolic direction, and tried the spirits whether they were of God or not, and has come to the conclusion that these New Testament writers have the marks of inspiration. For you will observe that the present code of the New Testament was gradually formed, and that not by the votes of councils or the decisions of bishops, but by the feelings of the Christian community. An inward instinct, and no external authority, presided over the collection of the Scriptures, gradually dropping out some books (like Barnabas, Hermas, and the Revelation of Peter), and taking in others.

So the Christian Church says to us, of the New Testament, "Here is a book concerning which we testify that the writings in it are profitable for doctrine; that its writers have superior knowledge in regard to spiritual things; that they are inspired men, who have been taken up into a region where most men have never gone, and seen what most men have never seen, and therefore *know* more than most of us about spiritual truth."

But you may say, "If inspiration gives *knowledge*, and these writers are inspired, then they do more than believe or think what they say about God, duty, and immortality. They *know*; and if they *know*, does not that mean that they are infallible?" No, knowledge is not infallibility. It is true that inspiration gives knowledge, while speculation only gives opinion. This is the reason why inspired men speak with authority, and philosophers without it. But knowledge, though it gives authority, does not give infallibility.

A Frenchman *knows* the French language; still he may make mistakes in speaking it. The man from California knows that country, but he may be mistaken about it. Thus, if these writers are not infallible, they may make mistakes; and if so, how are we to distinguish between their truth and their error? This is a fair question: let us try to answer it.

Let us return to our former comparison of travellers and their guide. How are you to distinguish between your guide's knowledge and his errors?

Probably, when your guide begins to be uncertain as to the way, he will show his uncertainty in his behavior. He will become doubtful, hesitating, undecided; he will, by and by, supposing him honest, begin to express his uncertainty, and say, "I am not quite sure of this path."

It is just so with inspired writers. While their inspiration runs in a full tide, they speak confidently; they are distinct in their statements.

Again, if your guide begins to speak of things outside of his province, he does not carry much authority. If Leatherstocking discusses Shakespeare, or the pilot begins to talk about politics, his opinions carry no weight except what is inherent to them.

So when the writers of the Bible, leaving themes of religion and morals, describe natural objects, as the leviathan or behemoth, we give no more credit to their descriptions than we should to those of any other writer of their day.

A question would arise here whether history was a subject of inspiration or not; that is, whether an inspired writer, when he comes to speak of historic facts, has any more authority than another. There may be some way by which past events might be presented by inspiration to the mind of one caught up by the spirit into another world. But the writers of the Old and New Testament are careless about dates and numbers, and do not seem to be made accurate by any special gift. I should, therefore, incline to the opinion that the historic books of the Bible have no authority except that of their reasonableness and conformity to what we might believe on other grounds. As fragments of history, coming from so remote a past, they are invaluable, when we treat them as simple, honest records of what was then believed or known.

Take, for instance, the story of the deluge, and compare it with similar stories in other mythologies. We find it so corroborated by these, that we may believe that there is a basis of reality in it.

§ 8. The Christian Prepossession

It is a great thing to read a book with expectation instead of distrust. Expectation opens the mind to light, and makes it easy to see. Distrust closes it. If I have read Shakespeare till I feel sure of his poetic inspiration, then I read with expectation all he writes; I am looking for truth and beauty, and so I find it. If I had never read Shakespeare, nor heard of him, and Hamlet were put into my hand, I should probably be displeased with something or other, and throw it aside, and so lose the deepness and loveliness of that wonderful creation. How much we find in the words of Jesus and Paul, because we read them with expectation and hope! because we read them always looking for what is deep and high!

Nevertheless many persons recommend a contrary course. They say that we ought to forget all that has been told us about the Book, and read it as if we had never seen it before. But this method is neither practicable nor desirable. It is impossible to look at the Bible as though it were an unknown book; impossible to forget that it is the text book of Christianity; regarded as sacred by millions of our fellow-men; the source of spiritual and moral life to the world for the last fifteen hundred years; that our parents and friends have found in it strength for duty, comfort in trial, hope in the hour of death. You might as well tell the child who begins to study geography to forget that he lives in America, or when he studies the history of the United States, to forget that it is the history of his own land. Nor would it be desirable to study the New Testament thus. For it is this grand belief concerning it which makes us desire to study it at all. Were it not for this belief it might be occasionally read by a student in the interest of science, but never by the mass of the community. Faith in its divine origin and divine purpose, causes it to be read in families, schools, churches, to be used as a manual of prayer in the closet, and to grow familiar in every home. The Book is surrounded by a traditional halo of wonder, reverence, and hope, and this gives us motive and power with which to read it. If a cold criticism, a sceptical spirit, shall ever succeed in causing the New Testament to be regarded as a common book, on the natural plane of human thought, full of errors and imperfections, inspired only as Plato is inspired, then it will be read as Plato is read, that is, by one man in a million. It is not desirable to lose the reverence which causes us to expect extraordinary truth and good in certain books, men, and institutions; for so we lose the best motive power of the soul; so life becomes tame, the day empty, and events unmeaning.

It is, therefore, perfectly right for the Church to surround Christ and Christianity with this divine aureola of reverence and wonder, not exaggerating it, but neither understating it. For this wonder and reverence, when legitimate, is a great treasure of spiritual life, animating and elevating, which the Church possesses in order that it may communicate it. It is continually proclaiming its good news; constantly asserting that through Christ God has given it a divine peace; that in Christ there is a marvellous truth and beauty; and that the Gospels and Epistles, which contain his life and truth, have a strange power of raising us above ourselves, and bringing us into communion with an eternal world. When this is said, not by rote, or as a mere form, but from sincere conviction, the spirit of faith creates faith, and faith is the great motive which leads to action.

As it is the duty of the Church to excite our interest in the New Testament, by declaring its own love and respect for it, so it is right for the student of the New Testament to give a certain preliminary weight to this testimony of the Church in commencing his study. This is what we call the Christian prepossession. And it regards the New Testament exactly as when a friend whose judgment we respect earnestly recommends to us some book which he has read, and which has done him good. He recommends it to us as a good book, and he recommends it with enthusiasm. His enthusiasm produces in us a desire to become acquainted with the book, and a certain hope that we shall find in it what our friend has found. This hope leads on towards fruition, and is one of its conditions. It ought not, therefore, to be relinquished; but neither should it lead us to accept blindly everything which we are told. We must look with our own eyes, think with our own mind, feel with our own heart.

To wish to come to the study of the Bible without prepossession in its favor is, therefore, a foolish wish; for, without prepossession in its favor, we should have little motive for studying it at all. It is our faith in the Bible that leads us to read it; and faith here, as everywhere, is the motive power which reason has only to guide and restrain. Faith is the brave steed which carries us forward, full of fire and full of pride. Reason is the bridle by which he is guided, supported, and restrained. There is a story of a thief so skilful that he could steal a man's horse from under him without his knowing it, and so leave him holding the bridle in his hand, and supposing himself to be still on horseback. So are those deceived who think to live by reason without faith. The motive power of their life has been taken away from them, and they do not know it; they suppose that they can ride with a bridle and saddle, without a horse.

To read the New Testament to any purpose, we must, therefore, read with the faith that there is some great good to be got from it. But what is the true foundation of this faith? Is it legitimate, or is it an illusion? The basis of this faith is to be found in the fact that the Bible has done so much, and is doing so much, for the world—a fact which cannot be stated better than in these words of one who is not commonly supposed to have too high a reverence for the Bible:—

"This collection of books has taken such a hold on the world as no other. The literature of Greece, which goes up like incense from that land of temples and heroic deeds, has not half the influence of this book from a nation alike despised in ancient and modern times. It is read of a Sabbath in all the ten thousand pulpits of our land. In all the temples of Christendom is its voice lifted up week by week. The sun never sets on its gleaming page. It goes equally to the cottage of the plain man and the palace of the king. It is woven into the literature of the scholar, and colors the talk of the street. The bark of the merchant cannot sail the sea without it, no ship of war go to the conflict but the Bible is there. It enters men's closets; mingles in all the grief and cheerfulness of life. The affianced maiden prays God in Scripture for strength in her new duties; men are married by Scripture. The Bible attends them in their sickness; when the fever of the world is on them. The aching head finds a softer pillow when the Bible lies underneath. The mariner, escaping from shipwreck, clutches this first of his treasures, and keeps it sacred to God. It goes with the pedler in his crowded pack; cheers him at eventide, when he sits down dusty and fatigued; brightens the freshness of his morning face. It blesses us when we are born; gives names to half Christendom; rejoices with us; has sympathy for our mourning; tempers our grief to finer issues. It is the better part of our sermons. It lifts man above himself; our best of uttered prayers are in its storied speech, wherewith our fathers and the patriarchs prayed. The timid man, about awaking from this dream of life, looks through the glass of Scripture, and his eye grows bright; he does not fear to stand alone, to tread the way unknown and distant, to take the death-angel by the hand, and bid farewell to wife, and babes, and home. Men rest on this their dearest hopes. It tells them of God, and of his blessed Son; of earthly duties and of heavenly rest. Foolish men find it the source of Plato's wisdom, and the science of Newton, and the art of Raphael. Men who believe nothing else that is spiritual believe the Bible all through; without this they would not confess, say they, even that there was a God." — *Theodore Parker, Discourse of Religion.*

A book which exercises this great influence over our fellow-men ought to be approached with reverence. It is for the same reason that we approach with faith and expectation the writings of Shakespeare and Milton. We read them expecting to find in them great truths, and this expectation enables us to find them. "Seek and ye shall find" is the law. How often we should have been disappointed and dissatisfied with such books, and have thrown them aside impatiently, had we not remembered the great universal testimony to their surpassing excellence!

This Christian prepossession is, however, only a general confidence that there is something exceedingly good in the New Testament; that it is a book containing in some way a divine revelation, in some way or other inspired, in some way likely to be a great help and comfort to our spiritual nature, and the best guide we can have for this life and towards the next. It is an expectation of all this, an expectation based on the testimony of mankind. So far it is a reasonable expectation. So far it is right and just to entertain it. It is the natural inheritance to which we were born, by being born Christians. To throw it away, or to try to throw it away, would be as though one should try to throw away the habits of civilization which he inherits by being born in a civilized community, and try to go back and start as a savage. It is neither more futile nor more foolish in the one case than in the other.

But, though this Christian prepossession is a perfectly legitimate one with which to begin, it is not a legitimate one in which to remain. It is our business, by the free action of our intellect, to change this general and vague expectation into a distinct opinion of one kind or another. Protestantism allows us to take our faith in the Bible from the Church, but not to take from the Church our opinions about the Bible. Faith may, and ought to be, received, but opinions are to be formed. An opinion or belief received from another man is his opinion, and not ours.

With regard to any other book this would be self-evident. For example, suppose that I have never read the play of Hamlet. I hear it universally spoken of as one of the greatest works of the human intellect. That naturally and properly creates in my mind the expectation of finding it so. It produces the general belief that it is a great work of genius. But suppose that, besides this general expectation, I should also accept from my neighbors their particular opinions concerning the play. I hear them say that it is more philosophical, but less dramatic, than Macbeth; that the character of Hamlet is overcharged with intellect, and the like. If, now, I adopt and repeat these opinions, without having read the play, it is evident that I am only a parrot or an echo. It is evident that they are not *my* opinions at all, and that they indeed interfere with my having any opinions. Fifty thousand echoes of a voice leave us only one voice and fifty thousand echoes.

This distinction between faith and opinion, which we have already spoken of, is of the utmost practical importance. We may add here that, for want of it, intellectual people try to go to the study of the Bible without faith in the Bible, and religious people think they must accept all their opinions from others, and take them in ready made. It is not absolutely essential to have opinions; but if we do have them, they ought to be our own. Faith must be received, opinions must be formed.

All persons, therefore, ought to form opinions for themselves about the New Testament. They may bring to the work a faith in the New Testament, as being in some sense or other a revelation, as being written in some way or other by inspired men, as being somehow or other a holy book, the legitimate source of spiritual life, moral goodness, and inward peace.

§ 9. Conclusion

If the views given in this chapter are reasonable, we shall conclude that Orthodoxy is right in maintaining the supreme excellence and value of the Christian Scriptures, but wrong in claiming for them infallible accuracy. It is right in saying that they are written by inspired men, but wrong in considering this inspiration a guarantee against all possible error or mistake. It is right in calling the Bible "The Holy Scripture," but wrong in denying to the scriptures of other religious some divine influx and some religious life. It is right in asking that the Bible be read with faith and expectation; wrong in demanding for it unreasoning, uncritical submission. Let reverence for its spirit and criticism of its letter go hand in hand; for reverence and criticism, faith and reason, docility to great masters and freedom in seeking for ourselves, are antagonist, indeed, but not contradictory. They are not hostile, but helpful, though acting in opposite directions—like the opposition of the thumb and fingers in the human hand, which makes of it such a wonderful servant of the thought. They belong to the group of sisterly powers which the Creator has placed in the human soul—varied, complex, like and unlike.

"Facies non omnibus una,

Nec diversa tamen, qualis decet esse sororum."

Chapter VI
Orthodox Idea Of Sin, As
Depravity And As Guilt

§ 1. The Question stated

We now approach the orthodoxy of Orthodoxy—the system of sin and redemption, which constitutes its most essential character. The questions hitherto treated—the natural and supernatural, miracles, the Scriptures—belong to universal religion. On these points heretics and the Orthodox may agree. But the essence of heresy, in the eyes of an Orthodox man, is to vary from the standards of belief in regard to sin and salvation.

We commence with the subject of human sinfulness; in other words, with the character of man in relation to Orthodoxy. The theology of the East asked, "What is God?" and entered on its course from the specially theological side. It began with ontology, and proceeded to psychology. In this, Oriental theology followed in the path of Oriental philosophy. But Occidental theology, originating strictly with Augustine, followed the practical and experimental method of European thought, and, instead of asking, "What is God?" asked, instead, "What is man?"

We begin, therefore, with the great question, "What is man?" This is the radical question in practical, experimental theology, as the question, "What is God?" is the radical question in speculative theology. But we are now concerned in the theology of experience and of life. We are seeking for human wants. Knowing what man is, we can next ask what he needs.

§ 2. The four Moments or Characters of Evil. The Fall, Natural Depravity, Total Depravity, Inability

Orthodoxy answers the question, "What is man?" by saying, "Man is a sinner;" and this answer has these four moments:—

1. Man was created at first righteous and good.

2. Man fell, in and with Adam, and became a sinner.

3. All now born are born totally corrupt and evil;—

4. And are utterly disabled to all good, so as not to have the power of repenting, or even of wishing to repent.

These four ideas are,—

First, that of The Fall, or Inherited Evil.

Second, of Natural Depravity.

Third, of Total Depravity.

Fourth, of Inability.

These points are fully stated in the following passage from the "Assembly's Confession of Faith," chap. 6:—

"1. Our first parents, being seduced by the subtlety and temptation of Satan, sinned in eating the forbidden fruit. This their sin God was pleased, according to his wise and holy counsel, to permit; having purposed to order it to his own glory.

"2. By this sin they fell from their original righteousness, and communion with God; and so became dead in sin, and wholly defiled in all the faculties and parts of soul and body.

"3. They being the root of all mankind, the *guilt* of this sin was imputed, and the same *death in sin, and corrupted nature*, conveyed, to all their posterity, descending from them by ordinary generation.

"4. From this original corruption, whereby we are utterly indisposed, disabled, and made opposite to all good, and wholly inclined to all evil, do proceed all actual transgressions.

"5. This corruption of nature during this life doth remain in those that are regenerated; and although it be, through Christ, pardoned and mortified, yet both itself and all the motions thereof are truly and properly sin.

"6. Every sin, both original and actual, being a transgression of the righteous law of God, and contrary thereunto, doth in its own nature bring guilt upon the sinner, whereby he is bound over to the wrath of God and curse of the law, and so made subject to death, with all miseries, spiritual, temporal, and eternal."13

We assume the "Assembly's Catechism" as almost *the* standard of Orthodoxy. It was prepared with the concurrence of the best minds in England, in an age when theological discussion had sharpened all wits in that direction. Thoroughly Calvinistic, it is also a wonderfully clear and precise statement of Calvinism. Framed after long controversies, it had the advantage of all the distinctions which are made only during controversy. It is a fortress made defensible at all points, because it has been attacked so often that all its weak places have been seen and marked. It is a masterpiece of statement.

Now, it is very easy, and what has often been done, *to stand on the outside* and show the actual error and logical absurdity of this creed; to show that men are not by nature totally depraved, and that, if they were, this would not be guilt; that, if they have no power to repent, they are not to blame for not repenting; and that God, as a God of justice even (to say nothing of mercy, of love, of a heavenly Father), cannot condemn and punish us for a depraved nature inherited from Adam.

It is easy to say all this. But it has often been said; and with what result? Unitarians have been, by such arguments, confirmed in their Unitarianism; but the Orthodox have not, by such arguments, been convinced of the falsity of their creed. Let us see, then, if we cannot find some truth in this system, — some vital, experimental truth, — for the sake of which the Orthodox cling to these immense and incredible inconsistencies. Let us take an *inside* view of Orthodoxy, and see why, being unreasonable, it yet commends itself to so many minds of the highest order of reason.

§ 3. Orthodox and Liberal View of Man, as morally diseased or otherwise

Let us begin with the substance of Orthodoxy (neglecting, at present, its form), and say, in general, that it regards human nature as being in an abnormal or diseased condition. The first thing to be done with man, according to Calvinism, is to cure him. Many systems, differing from each other in name, agree in this — that they do not believe in any such diseased condition of man. According to them, he is not to be cured, but to be educated. The Church is not a hospital, but an academy. Man needs, mainly, instruction. His purposes, in the main, are right; but he errs as to what he has to do. What he requires is precept and example.

As Orthodoxy believes man to be diseased, its object is twofold, and the truths which it employs are of two kinds. First, it seeks to convince man that he really has a dangerous disease; and then to convince him, that, by using the right means, he can be cured. It therefore constantly dwells upon two classes of truths: first, those which reveal man's sinfulness and his ruined condition; and, secondly, those which reveal the plan of saving him from this condition—a plan which has been devised by the Almighty, and which is accomplished in Christianity. Orthodoxy dwells upon sin and salvation: these are its two pivotal doctrines.

On the other hand, all the systems which may be associated under the term "Liberal Christianity" regard man, not as in a state of disease, and needing medicine, but as in a state of health, needing diet, exercise, and favorable circumstances, in order that he may grow up a well-developed individual. It regards sin, not as a radical disease with which all are born, but as a temporary malady to which all are liable. It does not, therefore, mainly dwell on sin and salvation, but on duty and improvement. Man's nature it regards, not as radically evil, but as radically good; and even as divine, because made by God.

Here, then, in the doctrine of evil, lies the essential distinction between the two great schools of thought which have divided the Church. What is evil? and how is it to be regarded? This is, perhaps, the most radical question in Christian theology. Is evil positive, or only negative? Is it a reality, or only a form? What is it? Whence comes it? Until these questions are exhaustively discussed, there is little hope of union in theology.

§ 4. Sin as Disease

We regard Orthodoxy as substantially right in its views of sin as being a deep and radical disease. Our Saviour says, "I came not to call the righteous, but sinners, to repentance." "The Son of man came to seek and to save that which is lost."

But the question recurs, Is there only one kind of sin,—namely, voluntary and conscious transgression of God's law, originating with the individual himself, and in the moment of committing it, by means of his free will, which is its only seat? or is there sin which is a tendency in man's nature, something permanent, involuntary, of which he is not conscious, and which has its seat not merely in the will, but in the desires and affections. To this question Liberal Christianity has commonly said, "No," and Orthodoxy has said, "Yes."

And on this point I concur with Orthodoxy. Besides the sin which consists in free choice, and which is essentially transient, there is also the sin which consists in wrong desire, and which is essentially permanent, because it is a habit of the mind. If it were not so, there could be no such thing as a bad character, and no such thing as a vicious habit.

If we attempt to analyze evil, we shall find that it may be conveniently distributed into these divisions:—

1. Physical Evil.

(*a*.) Pain.

(*b*.) Weakness.

(*c*.) Physical disease.

2. Intellectual or Mental Evil.

(*a*.) Ignorance.

(*b*.) Error, or mistake.

(*c*.) Sophism, or falsehood.

3. Moral Evil. Disobedience to the Moral Law.

(*a*.) Ignorant and accidental, or transgression.

(*b*.) Habitual disobedience, or vice.

(*c*.) Wilful violation of human law; crime.

(*d*.) Diseased moral state, as selfishness, bad temper, &c.

4. Spiritual Evil.

(*a*.) Wilful alienation from God, or perverse choice.

(*b*.) Spiritual inability.

Now, we see that in all these divisions of evil,—physical, intellectual, moral, and spiritual,—it is found in the two forms of active and passive evil. In the latter form it is disease, and independent of the will.

Returning, then, to the Orthodox view of evil, which it is our business to examine, we find already that it has the advantage of the Liberal theology in recognizing this passive side of evil, which we may call *disease*. It is true that Orthodoxy has not yet succeeded in coming to any clearness on this question, and has not yet any firm, intellectual hold of the main points of its argument. Examples of this confusion are quite common. Not to go back to the Calvinistic and Arminian controversies, which were but a revival of the Augustinian and Pelagian dispute; not to recur even to the Hopkinsian and Edwardian discussions,—we have only to refer to the differences between new and old school theology in the Presbyterian Church; to the trial of Dr. Beecher; to the book of his son Edward; to the divergence of Andover from New Haven, and Princeton from Andover. Unsettled, because superficial, views of evil are at the roots of all these controversies.

§ 5. Doctrine of the Fall in Adam, and Natural Depravity. Their Truth and Error

The first point of the doctrine of evil regards the Fall, including the doctrine of depravity.

Modern French philosophers have dwelt much on what they call the solidarity of the human race. By this they mean that two individuals are not independent of each other, like two trees standing side by side, but like two buds on the same tree or bough. There is a common life-sap flowing through them all. Let the life of the tree be attacked anywhere,—in its roots, its trunk, its limbs,—and all these individual buds feel it. Yet each bud has also a life of its own, and develops its own stalk, leaves, blossom, fruit. It can be taken from its own tree, and put into another tree, and grow. So it is with separate men grafted into the great tree of mankind. No one lives to himself, nor dies to himself. If one suffers, all suffer. The life of mankind, becoming diseased, pours disease into all individual men.

Now, is there not something in this doctrine to which our instincts assent? Do not we feel it true that we inherit not our own life merely, but that of our race? and is not this the essential truth in the doctrine of the fall?

It is true that we fell in Adam. It is also true that we fell in every act of sin, in every weakness and folly, of any subsequent child of Adam. We are all drawn downward by every sin; we are lifted upward, too, by every act of heroic virtue, not by example only, but also by that mysterious influence, that subtle contagion, finer than anything visible, ponderable, or tangible,—that effluence from eye, voice, tone, manner, which, according to the character which is behind, communicates an impulse of faith and courage, or an impulse of cowardice and untruth; which may be transmitted onward, forward, on every side, like the widening circles in a disturbed lake,—circles which meet and cross each other without disturbance, and whose influence may be strictly illimitable and infinite.

No doubt, sin began with the historical Adam—the first man who lived. "By one man sin entered into the world, and death by sin." But still more true is it that we fell in the typical Adam—Adam who stands for innocent, ignorant human nature before temptation; truest of all, that we *fall* in Adam, because we are, each of us, at first an Adam.

We are all in the garden; we are at first placed in paradise; and each has in himself all the four *dramatis personæ*—Adam, Eve, the Serpent, and the Voice of God. Adam is the will, the power of choice, the masculine element, in man; Eve is the affection, the desire, the feminine element, in man; the Voice of God is the higher reason in the soul, through which infinite truth commands,—i.e., the higher law; and the Serpent, the lower reason in the soul, the cunning element, the sophistical understanding, which can put evil for good, and good for evil. The garden is our early innocence, where there is no struggle, no remorse, no anxiety; where goodness is not labor, but impulse. But, when we go out of the garden, we enter a life of trial, till we reach the higher paradise, the kingdom of heaven; and then joy and duty become one again. Then—

"Love is an unerring light,
And joy its own security."

From paradise, through the world, to heaven; from Egypt, through the wilderness, to Canaan; from innocence, through temptation, sin, repentance, faith, to regeneration,—such is the progress of man.

To me, the belief that I fell in Adam is not an opinion fraught only with sadness. This tide of life which comes pouring through me comes from ten thousand ancestors. All *their* sorrows and joys, temptations and struggles, sins and virtues, have helped to make it what it is. I am a member of a great body. I am willing to be so—to bear the fortunes and misfortunes of my race.

It is true that I find evil tendencies in me, which I did not cause; but I know, that, for whatever part I am not the cause, I am not accountable. For this part of my life I do not dread the wrath, but rather claim the pity, of my God. My nature I find to be diseased—not well; needing cure, and not merely food and exercise. I can, therefore, the more easily believe that God has sent me a physician, and that I shall be cured by him. I can believe in a future emancipation from these tendencies to vanity, sensuality, indolence, anger, wilfulness, impatience, obstinacy—tendencies which are, in me, not crime, but disease; and I can see how to say with Paul, "Now, then, it is no more *I* that do it, but sin that dwelleth in me."

If, now, we return to the consideration of the Orthodox doctrine of the fall, as set forth by the Westminster Assembly, we shall find it to be half true and half false. It states *truly* (chap. 6, § 1) that our first parents sinned, and also (§ 2) that by this sin they fell from their original righteousness; for this only means that the first conscious act of disobedience by man produced alienation from God, and degeneracy of nature. This was no arbitrary punishment, but the natural consequence. The creed also says *truly* (§ 3) that this corrupted nature was conveyed to all their posterity; for this only means, that, by the laws of descent, good and evil qualities are transmitted; which all wise observers of human nature knew to be the fact. It is also *true* (§ 5) that this corrupt nature does remain (to some extent at least), even in the regenerate, in this life.

So far, so true. Sin, as disease, began with the first man, in his first sin, and has been transmitted, by physical, moral, and spiritual influences, from him to us all.

But now we find complicated with these truths other statements, which we must need regard as falsehoods. Tried either by reason or Scripture, they are palpably untrue, and are very dangerous errors.

The first error of Orthodoxy is in declaring transmitted or inherited evil to be total. It declares that our first parents "were *wholly* defiled in all faculties and parts of soul and body," and that *we*, in consequence, "are utterly indisposed, disabled, and made opposite to all good, and wholly inclined to all evil." This statement is indefensible. But we shall consider this in another section on "Total Depravity," and only allude to it now in passing.

Another error, however, and a very important one, is to attribute the *guilt* of Adam and Eve to their descendants. This is the famous doctrine of *imputation*, which is now rejected by all the leading schools of modern Orthodoxy. That we can be *guilty* of Adam's sin, either by imputation or in any other way, seems too absurd and immoral a statement to be now received.

But though many intelligent Orthodox teachers and believers do now reject the imputation of Adam's sin, they admit what is just as false and just as immoral a doctrine. They make us *guilty* for that part of sin which is *depravity*, as well as for that which is *wilful*.

Whatever, either of moral good or moral evil, proceeds from our nature, and not from our will, has no character of merit or demerit. The reason is evident, and is stated by the apostle Paul. We are only guilty for what we do ourselves, we are only meritorious for what we do ourselves: but what our nature does, we do not do. "Now, then, it is no more *I* that do it, but sin that dwelleth in me."

Professor Shedd, late of Andover, some years ago published a very able essay in the "Christian Review," the title of which was, "Sin a Nature, and that Nature Guilt." This title is a sufficient refutation of the essay. A man could not utter a more palpable contradiction, if he said, "The sun solid, and that solid fluid," or, "The earth black, and that black white."14

There are two kinds of moral good and two kinds of moral evil, which are essentially different. The two kinds of moral good may be named *moral virtue* and *moral beauty*; the two kinds of moral evil may be named *guilt* and *depravity*. Now, so far as goodness proceeds from a beautiful nature, it is not virtuous, and so far as sin proceeds from a depraved nature, it is not guilty.

We can conceive of an angelic nature with no capacity of virtue, because incapable of guilt.

We can also conceive of a nature so depraved as to be incapable of guilt, because incapable of virtue.

§ 6. Examination of Romans, 5:12-21

The famous passage in Paul (Rom. 5:12-21), which is the direct scriptural foundation claimed for the doctrine of Adam's fall producing guilt in his posterity, is in reality a support of our view. The only other passage (1 Cor. 15:22) where Adam is referred to, declares that we all *die* in him, but by no means asserts that we *sin* in him.

The passage referred to runs thus (Rom. 5:12-18):—

Verse 12: "As by one man sin entered into the world,"—

(Paul here refers to the fact that sin began with the first man.)

"And death by sin;"—

(By means of the sin of one man, *death* entered.)

"And so death passed upon all men, for that all have sinned."

(Rather "death *came upon* all men, *because* all have sinned." The Vulgate has here *in quo*, "in whom;" that is, in Adam. So Augustine. But even those who, like Olshausen, contend for Augustine's views, admit that ἐφ᾽ ᾧ here is a conjunction, equivalent to *because*, and not a relative.)

The next five verses (13, 14, 15, 16, 17) constitute a parenthesis, and refer to an objection which is not stated. Some one might say, "How could all sin, from Adam to Moses, when there was no law till Moses? and you, Paul, have said (Rom. 4:15), that 'where there is no law there is no transgression.' "

Paul replies that "sin is not *imputed* without law;" that is, as I think evident, it is not regarded as *guilt*. A man who sins ignorantly is not *guilty*; but he *suffers* the consequences of his sin, which are depravity of his nature, or moral death. "Sin is not imputed," says Paul; "but death reigns." Those who do not sin "after the similitude of Adam's transgression,"—that is, who do not violate a positive command,—nevertheless are depraved morally, and are dead spiritually. The Hottentots and Fejee Islanders violate no positive law given them by God, and consequently are not guilty of that; but because they violate (even ignorantly) the laws of their moral nature, they are depraved morally.

We see, then, that Paul distinctly recognizes the distinction made above between *sin as guilt* and *sin as depravity*.

He distinguishes between sin as sinfulness, or unconscious transgression (ἡ ἁμαρτία), and sin as conscious transgression of a known command (παράβασις).

The consequence of the first is death, or moral and spiritual depravity; the consequence of the second is condemnation, or a sense of guilt.

Sinfulness, bringing with it depravity (the general demoralization of human nature), began with Adam. All became involved in sinfulness, and consequently all partook of the depravity which belongs to it as its wages.

It should, however, be observed that it is not the purpose of Paul to teach anything about Adam. His intention is to teach something about Christ. He refers to Adam's case as something they all are acquainted with; he compares Christ's case with it both by contrast and resemblance. But his object is not to instruct us about Adam, but about Christ. He uses Adam as an example to enforce his doctrine about Christ. Through Christ, goodness and happiness were to come into the world. He illustrated this fact, and made it appear probable, by the fact which they already knew—that through Adam sin and death had entered the world. If it seemed strange, in an age in which men were so disunited, that one man should be the medium of communicating goodness to the whole human race, they might remember that Adam also had been the medium of introducing sin to the whole human race. If the Jews wondered that Christ should bring salvation to those who were not under the law, they might remember that Adam had brought death to those not under the law, and who did not sin as he did. If they doubted how Christ's goodness could help to make men righteous, they might remember that in some way Adam's transgression had helped to make men sinners. Yet, after all, the main fact which he states is in the twelfth verse, chapter five—"that by one man sin *entered into* the world, and death by sin." This amounts to saying that sin *began* with Adam. Then he adds, in the same verse, "that death has passed upon all men, *because all have sinned.*" He therefore distinctly declares that every man is punished for his own sin, and not for the sin of Adam.

In the other passage (1 Cor. 15:22), Paul says, "As in Adam all die, even so, in Christ, shall all be made alive." He does not say here, either that "all sinned in Adam," or that "all fell in Adam," or that "all died in Adam." It is the present tense, "all die in Adam."

What he means by this, he explains himself afterwards. He tells us that as "souls" descended from Adam, we are liable to death; as spirits quickened by Christ, we are filled with spiritual and immortal life.

In the forty-fourth verse he gives the explanation. The body "is *sown* a natural body" (σῶμα ψυχικὸν)—literally a soul-body, a body vitalized by the soul. "It is raised a spiritual body"—literally spirit-body (σῶμα πνευματικὸν), a body vitalized by the spirit. "There is a soul-body, and there in a spirit-body." "And so it is written, The first man, Adam, was made a living soul" (which is a quotation from Genesis 2:7—"and man became a living soul"), "but the last Adam," says Paul (meaning Christ), "became a life-making spirit." But, continues Paul, the soul-man (psychical man) comes first; the spiritual-man afterwards, according to a regular order. "The first man is of the earth, earthy; the second is the Lord from heaven." And then he adds,—and this is the key to the whole passage,—"As we have borne the image of the earthy, we shall also bear the image of the heavenly." The doctrine, then, is plainly this: that we have two natures—a soul-nature, which we derive from Adam, and share with all mankind, which nature is liable to weakness, sin, and death; and a spirit-nature, which we derive from God, which Christ comes to quicken and vitalize, and the life of which constitutes our true immortality.

The apostle Paul, therefore, does not by any means teach Calvinism. The Catechism says that "our first parents being the root of all mankind, the guilt of their sin was imputed to all their posterity." But Paul says, "So death passed upon all men, because all have sinned." The Catechism says that "this same death in sin, and corrupted nature, being conveyed to their posterity, makes us utterly indisposed and opposite to all good," and that "from this original corruption do proceed all actual transgressions."

But if this is so, there has been no such thing in the world as guilt since Adam fell. If all actual transgressions proceed from original corruption, and original corruption comes from the first transgression of Adam, it logically follows that there has been but one sin committed in the world since it was made, namely, the sin of Adam. All other sins have been pure misfortunes; his alone was guilt. His transgression alone came from a free choice; all others have come from an involuntary necessity of nature.

Nothing can be more certain from reason and Scripture than this—that transgressions which come from a corrupt nature are just so far done in us, and not done by us. This the apostle distinctly affirms when he says (7:17), "Now, then, it is no more I that do it, but sin that dwelleth in me." No man is responsible for disease, when he has not brought that disease on himself, but inherited it from his ancestors. The disease may make him very odious, very disagreeable, but cannot make him blamable. Therefore, when Calvin says that hereditary depravity "renders us obnoxious to the divine wrath," he utters an absurdity. This confusion of ideas runs through all Orthodox statements on the subject, and the only cure is, that we should learn how to make this distinction between natural evil and moral evil, or the evil which proceeds from a corrupt nature and the evil which comes from a free will.

If we were to sum up the doctrine of the apostle Paul on this subject, it would be thus:—

1. The first man, Adam, consisted, as we all consist, of nature and will. His nature consisted of innocent tendencies and appetites. None were excessive; all were well balanced. His nature inclined him no more to evil than to good, but each faculty was in proper poise. The first sin, therefore, could not have been a gross one; it was a simple transgression; but its effect was to introduce what the apostle calls *death*; that is, a diseased or corrupt nature. The process is this: With the first conscious and free transgression there arises a sense of guilt. This sense of guilt leads the soul away from God. Adam and Eve hide in the garden. Every act of sin tends to create a habit, and so destroys the moral equipoise. There hence arises a tendency *towards* evil, and *from* good; and this is called death, because it takes us away from God, who is the source of life.

2. A tendency towards evil is thus introduced into the world by the transgression of the first man. His descendants are now born with a nature which is not in equipoise, but which leans more towards evil than towards good. Their will remains free as before; but they cannot perform the same amount of good as before. These corrupt tendencies tempt to greater sin than the pure tendencies did, and, whenever yielded to, bring a greater amount of moral evil into the race.

3. Things, therefore, are thus growing worse continually; for every new act of sin makes it easier to sin again. And this tendency to death, or estrangement from God, must go on increasing, unless some antagonist principle can be communicated to the race. This is actually done by Jesus Christ. The principle of life which Christ introduces consists in reconciliation to God. Sin separates us from God, and therefore tends to death. Christ reconciles us to God, and so gives life. The way in which Christ reconciles us to God is by manifesting God's pardoning and saving love to the sinful soul. In his own life, but especially by his death, he communicates this pardoning love, and so produces the atonement. This is the central, Pauline view of the relation of Adam and Christ to the race. Adam introduces death into the world: Christ introduces life. He does not speak at all of *imputation*, or transfer of guilt; but he speaks of an *actual communication* of death and life. Adam and Christ both stand in actual, and not merely ideal, connection with the whole race of man. Adam is a living soul; Christ, a life-giving spirit. By inheritance, we receive a depraved life of the soul from Adam; by communion, we receive an eternal or spiritual life from Christ. And, in regard to both of these acts, the notion of blame or merit is entirely excluded. We are not to blame for our inherited depravity derived from Adam. We deserve no credit for the salvation which comes to us from Christ. The

compensation for the misfortune of inherited evil is the free gift of divine goodness in Jesus.

We have thus considered the truth and the error contained in the Orthodox doctrine of the fall. The truth of it is in its assertion of a depravity of nature, to which we are liable in consequence of ancestral sins: the error is in imputing guilt to us in consequence of them.

§ 7. Orthodox View of Total Depravity and Inability

In speaking of the fall of man, we necessarily anticipated somewhat the doctrine of total depravity. Still, we must say something further on this doctrine, because it is so important in the Church system: it is, indeed, at its foundation. Those who accept, in its strictness, the doctrine of total depravity cannot avoid any point of the severest Calvinism. Schleiermacher has shown, in his "Essay on Election," that this latter doctrine necessarily follows the doctrine of total depravity; for, if man is wholly depraved, he has no power to do anything for his own conversion; therefore God must do it. And if some are converted, and not others, it must be because God chooses to convert some, and does not choose to convert others.

Let us look, then, at what Orthodoxy says of the *extent* of human depravity. In all the principal creeds, this is stated to be unlimited. Man's sin is total and entire. There is nothing good in him. The Westminster Confession and the Confession of the New England Congregational churches describe him as "dead in sin, and wholly defiled in all the faculties and parts of soul and body." Other creeds use similar language.

In considering this theory, we are struck at first by the circumstance, that the Bible gives it very little support. The Bible continually speaks of man as a sinner; but there are very few texts which can, without straining, be made to *seem* to teach that he is totally depraved. Let us examine a few of them.

§ 8. Proof Texts

1. A text often cited is Genesis 6:5,—the reason given for destroying the human race, in the time of Noah, by the deluge: "And God saw that the wickedness of man was great in the earth, and that every imagination of the thoughts of his heart was only evil continually." But this seems to be a description of the state of the world at that particular time, not of its character in all ages. It is not a description of man's natural condition, but of an extremely degenerate condition. If the state of the world here described was its natural state, it would rather be a reason for not having created the race at first; or, if it was a reason for destroying it, it would, at best,

seem to be as strong a one against creating it again. If a man plants a tree in his garden, whose nature he knows is to produce a certain kind of fruit, it would seem hardly a good reason for cutting it down, that it produced that kind of fruit: certainly it would not be a good reason for cutting it down, and planting another of precisely the same kind in its place. The reason why the race of men was destroyed was, that it had *degenerated*. But there were some good even then; for in the ninth verse we are told that "Noah was a just man, and perfect in his generation, and walked with God."

2. There is another passage, in the fourteenth Psalm which is quoted by Paul in Rom. 3: "There is none righteous; no, not one: there is none that understandeth, none that seeketh after God. They have all gone out of the way, they are together become unprofitable: there is none that doeth good; no, not one. There is no fear of God before their eyes."

This passage is relied on to prove total depravity. But we may reply, that—

This also is a degenerate condition, not a natural one. It was a condition into which men had fallen, not one in which they were born. "They have all *gone* out of the way; they are together *become* unprofitable." It does not, therefore, apply to men *universally*, but to men in those particular times.

It was not true of *all*, even at that particular time. It was not true of David himself, that he did not seek after God, or have the fear of God before his eyes; or else other passages in the same book are not true, in which he says the contrary. "O God! early will I seek thee: my soul thirsteth for thee; my flesh longeth for thee." He also frequently speaks of and to those who fear the Lord, and says, "I am a companion to all those that fear thee."

The "all" is not to be taken strictly. It means people generally at that time. Just so it is said, "There went out to him Jerusalem and *all* Judea, and *all* the region round about Jordan;" which does not imply that *no one* staid at home.

"But," it may be said, "does not Paul teach that this is to be taken universally, when he quotes it, and adds, 'Now we know that what the law saith, it saith to those under the law, that every mouth be stopped, and all the world guilty before God' "? We think he means to say, that, as this is said to Jews, it proves that *Jews*, as well as Gentiles, are very guilty. He is addressing the Jews, who boasted of their knowledge of the law. Chap. 2: "Behold, thou art called a Jew," &c.

3. Jer. 17:9. "The heart is deceitful above all things, and desperately wicked."

If we suppose that we are to take this as an unlimited expression, and not merely a strong declaration of the wickedness of the Jews, it still does not prove total depravity of the nature, but merely that of the affections, or "the heart." Man's nature has other things besides desire: it has conscience, reason, and will; and it does not follow that these are also depraved.

4. Rom. 8:7. "The carnal mind is enmity against God."

This does not intend that the mind of man, in its *natural* state, is enmity, but in its *carnal* state; that is, when subject to fleshly desires. Nearly the same phrase is used in the verse before, and is translated, "To be carnally minded is death."

5. There is one famous passage, however, which seems to say that God is angry with us on account of our nature. This is a passage very much quoted, and we hear it so often that it seems as if the Bible was full of such texts. It is in Eph. 2:3. "We were by nature *children of wrath*, even as others." This is quoted to prove that God is angry with men for their natures, and hates them for being born evil—just as we may hate a snake, a scorpion, or spider, for its nature. But, as it happens, the very next verses show that this is impossible, unless God can be hating one of his creatures and loving it at the very same moment.

For, in the next verse Paul says that God loved us with a great love *when we were dead in trespasses and sins*, and children *of wrath*. It is therefore evident that *"children of wrath"* must mean something else. It may mean that men outside of Christianity—Jews and Gentiles—were afraid of God; living under a constant sense of his displeasure; that God seemed to them a terrible being, always disposed to punish them with severity. This was the fact. Jews and Gentiles were afraid of their gods, before Christ came, and so were "children of wrath." Or it may mean that men are exposed to the consequences of sin; for, in Scripture language,—

"God's wrathful said to be, when he doth do

That *without wrath* which wrath doth force us to."

Moreover, "nature," in Scripture usage, does not necessarily mean, "as human beings." It often intends external position, origin, and race. So (in Gal. 2:15) we read, "Jews by nature;" and so (in Rom. 2:27) "uncircumcision, which is by nature."

The same word is used twice in James 3:7, and is translated *kind*. "Every *kind* of beasts, birds, serpents, things in the sea, is tamed of man-*kind*:" literally, "the whole animal *race* is tamed by the human *race*."

If φυσις here meant "constitutional depravity," the same word in Rom. 2:14 must mean *constitutional goodness*, where we are told that some "do *by nature* the things contained in the law." So, too, we read of the olive tree, wild by nature, in Rom. 11:24.

"By nature," here, plainly means the original condition, not the original constitution. Just so we say that wild animals are in a state of nature, and call savages the children of nature.

These five texts are the strongest in the Bible to support the doctrine of total depravity, and, as such, are constantly quoted. They have very little weight, and not one of them is from the words of Jesus.

On the other hand, there are many passages which seem to declare that there is something good in man in his unconverted or natural state, and that even in that state he may turn towards the light, and struggle against evil.

John 3:20, 21. "Every one that doeth truth cometh to the light."

Matt. 26:41. "... The spirit is willing, the flesh is weak."

Rom. 2:24. "Gentiles, who have not the law, do by nature the things contained in the law, and show the work of that law which is written in the heart."

Acts 10:35. "In every nation, he that feareth God, and worketh righteousness, is accepted of him."

But the passage most strikingly and thoroughly opposed to the doctrine of total depravity, is the description, in the seventh chapter of Romans, of the conflict between the law in the members and the law of the mind. Paul, speaking evidently from his own experience in his unconverted state, describes the condition of one morally depraved, who is trying to do right, but is prevented by evil habits which have become a part of himself. He describes this as moral death, but *not* guilt. He says, "It is no more I that do it, but sin that dwelleth in me." He describes himself as morally impotent— *wishing* to do right, but unable to do it. He says *he delights in the law of God after the inner man.* The inmost is right, but outside of that are evil habits, in the body, which drag down the soul and enslave it. Paul therefore distinctly says that a man in such a condition is not himself a sinner, because he does not commit the sin. Thus he makes clear and strong the distinction we referred to above, between depravity and guilt—between *natural evil* and *moral evil.*

Paul teaches that man is not totally depraved, but that even in the carnal man there is a good principle, only that it is conquered by the evil. If the mind delights in the law of God, and the will to do right is present with us, we evidently are not *totally* depraved; but the total depravity, if anywhere, is in the flesh only, as Paul plainly says: "I know that in me (that is, in *my flesh*) dwelleth no good thing;" that is, the depravity is physical, not moral. But physical depravity is not guilt, but only disease.

§ 9. Truth in the Doctrine of Total Depravity

Nevertheless there is a sense in which man may be said to be often totally sinful; but this is only in a total alienation of the will from God. It is not a total depravity, but a total alienation. There is a natural depravity, but it is not total. But the choice may be totally perverted, when it chooses darkness instead of light, evil instead of good.

Let us see what there is of this in man.

The gospel of Christ, as we understand it, undertakes to effect an entire change, a radical reformation, in human character. It proposes to reform the life by changing the heart, by giving new aims, new affections, new aspirations, new objects of love and pursuit. Jesus does not endeavor to alter and improve, a little here and a little there, on the outside of the character, to improve a little our modes of action in this and the other particular; but he alters the conduct and character by altering the fundamental ideas, and inspiring an inward life. This wonderful change, which takes place in the profoundest depth of our nature, under the influence of the Gospel, — this great event of life, which forms the turning-point of our being and history, — is called in the New Testament "the new birth," "regeneration," "to be born again," "conversion," "a new creation," "to be born of God," "to be baptized with the Holy Ghost and with fire," "to put off the old man," "to have Christ formed within us." It is a very superficial view which explains away the meaning of all these profound expressions, and supposes that they only signify a little outward improvement and reformation. We need just such a change as is here described—a radical one, not a superficial one. All need it. Those who are the most pure in heart and most blameless in character (spotless children, as they seem to us, of a heavenly world) feel their own need of this change no less than do the profligate and openly vicious. Parents and friends say, "We have no fault to find with them." They do not say they have no fault to find with themselves. They feel they have all kinds of fault to find with themselves, and nothing is so painful to them as this commendation. They say, "Outwardly we may seem innocent, but we feel an inward want that weighs on our heart like a frost."

"This is a true saying, and worthy of all acceptation, that Christ Jesus came into the world to save sinners." It is because we are sinners that we need to experience this great change. We do not wish to exaggerate the amount of human sinfulness. Theologians have carried their attacks on human nature quite too far, and the result has often been that men have looked on sin as a sort of theological matter, which has nothing to do with actual life. They have cheerfully admitted that they were totally depraved by nature, and could not think or will a good thing, and then have thought no worse of themselves than before. We know that there is something good in man, something which God loves, some pure aspiration even in the natural heart, some throbs of generosity, some warnings of conscience, some pure love, some courageous virtue, in the humblest, the most depraved, the most abandoned. There are some flowers of sweetest perfume which spring up in the uncultivated soil of the natural heart on which God and his angels smile, for the seeds of those flowers God himself planted. We have seen harebells, graceful and lovely as the sweetest greenhouse plant, growing out of a sand-heap; and we have seen some disinterested, generous benevolence in the mind of a hardened profligate. It is not, therefore, because there is nothing good in man that he needs a change of heart, but because he is destitute of a deep-rooted and living goodness till this change has taken place.

Look at the *actual sins* of men. The majority of men, in a civilized community like ours, do not commit great crimes, or fall into flagrant vices, because they have little to attract them to such a course, and much to deter them from it. They are aiming at those objects which they need the countenance, aid, and good opinion of their fellow-men to obtain, to be glaringly vicious would make it impossible. Also, there is a certain amount of conscience which restrains them—the influence of good education and good habits which preserves a certain uprightness and purity of character. But is it a deep principle? If so, why do the vast majority of men allow themselves in many small violations of the same laws which they would not break on a large scale? They would not steal; yet they commit every day some slight acts not perfectly honest; they take advantage of others in little things. They would not lie; yet they exaggerate, and conceal part of the truth, and color their statements to produce an effect. They would not kill; but they are willing to injure one who has interfered with their interests. With these tendencies and feelings, why would they not, under different influences, commit greater crimes? How often do we feel, in talking with the criminal and abandoned, that, in their circumstances and with their temptations, we might have been as bad as they!

Does not all this show that there is a deep and hidden fountain of evil within our hearts which is restrained by external influences, by checks and barriers with which God has kindly surrounded us? and if these were taken away, it would break out into something far worse than now appears. How much there is of evil under the smooth surface of refined society! How many thoughts of sin pass to and fro in the heart while the countenance seems pure and calm! Who ever looked into the interior depths of our most moral community, and saw all the secret sins and pollutions which are hidden there? Every now and then there occurs in the midst of the most refined classes some startling revelation of long-concealed wickedness which makes men look each other in the face and draw a long breath, as though they should say, "Which of us will next fall?" So in the midst of a fruitful country, of lakes, and valleys, and vine-clad hills, the earth will sometimes open, and a river of melted lava pour forth, desolating all around. We hear of this with wonder, and do not think that right beneath our own feet, a few miles down, under these smooth fields and gentle plains, that same fiery ocean is rolling its red billows. God has laid his hand upon our heart, and restrains its lawless passions as he restrains the tornadoes, and earthquakes, and volcanic fires; else they might easily hurry us to swift destruction.

Still, if this were all, no radical change might be necessary. It might be enough that by effort, and self-discipline, and direction of the thoughts, we gradually overcome our evil habits and tendencies; but when we resolve to do so, and make the effort, we meet with an unexpected resistance. "The spirit is willing, but the flesh is weak." "I find a law in my members warring against the law of my mind, and bringing me into captivity to the law of sin in my members." The Church has long asserted the doctrine of an hereditary depravity; and we have seen that there is more truth in it than we have sometimes supposed. It is not total, but it is real. Besides the sins of our own committing, there are the sins which our ancestors have committed, which have made themselves part of our bone and flesh. We are not exactly balanced in our natural state; there is a preponderating tendency towards evil in one or another direction.

This forms too fearful an alliance with circumstances, the moment they become powerful to draw us away from good. A friend of ours, some years since, was making a trip up the Lakes, late in the season. As they entered Lake Huron from the River St. Clair in the noble steamer, the skies were serene, and she ploughed her way on towards the north, so that by night the land had sunk almost out of sight. But then the wind began to freshen, the sea rose, and as the night advanced, and the wind blew harder and harder, the boat strained and staggered along, occasionally struck hard by a heavier sea, till at last one of her wheels was carried away, and the fires were put out by the water. How long and anxious was that night! How many prayed then who never prayed before! When morning came, the boat was found to be drifting before the wind and waves, directly upon a rocky shore on the south-east side of the lake. There was no help in man; but a gracious

Providence all at once caused the storm to lull, so that a fire could be built, and with one wheel the boat got into a harbor. Man seems a powerful being when he is surrounded by favorable circumstances, and is going with a fair wind and fair weather; but let the wind change, and his weakness becomes apparent. He who just now breasted the tide, is now drifting helplessly before it.

But there is a difficulty far worse than any we have mentioned. We might conquer the sin which most easily besets us, we might conquer our inherent evil tendencies, and outgrow them, if we really wished to do so; but the deepest of all evils is a want of love for God and for goodness. We know that we ought to love and obey God; but our heart is alienated from him. The great mass of men are living away from God. They are not conscious of his presence, though they know that he is near to them. Though they know that his eye is upon them, it does not restrain them from sin. Though they know that their heavenly Father and best Friend is close at hand, how seldom do they pray! how seldom look up with gratitude for all their mercies and joys! This shows a terrible estrangement of soul from God. The veil is on their *hearts*, not on their minds.

The question is sometimes asked, "whether sin is a positive or merely a negative evil." Now, whatever may be the case with other kinds of sin, this alienation of the heart seems to us a very positive evil; for it is an antagonism, and resistance of goodness. If the supreme goodness of God does not attract us, does not excite our affection, does not irresistibly draw us to him, then it repels us; it makes the thought of his presence a restraint and burden; it makes us wish to go away from God. The goodness of God is so very positive a thing, that we cannot be indifferent to it; we cannot be neutral in regard to it. If we do not love it, it is disagreeable, and we are uncomfortable in the thought of it. Swedenborg relates that certain wicked persons were allowed to enter heaven on a certain occasion; but they immediately became almost lifeless, and, from the torment and pain in their head and body, prostrated themselves on the ground, and writhed like worms; but, being taken and carried into hell, became comparatively comfortable. What can be more terrible than the idea thus conveyed of our aversion to goodness, which makes heaven intolerable, and the presence of God insufferable torture! Can anything express, more than this, the need of a change of heart?

Jesus, we think, asserts a similar view when he says, "He that is not with me is against me." "No man can serve two masters; for he will either love the first and hate the last, or love the last and hate the first." He will not be indifferent to either, if their characters and commands are of an opposite kind.

We do not mean to say that we *hate* God; but we mean that there is something within us, while our hearts are not wholly his, which makes it unpleasant and burdensome to think of God and pray to him. We feel a certain repugnance to a familiar and happy intercourse with our heavenly Father. Our prayers, if we pray, are formal and cold; our hearts are hard, and their affections do not flow easily upward.

Now, if there be such a thing as a change of heart, which will make it a pleasure to pray, a joy to think of God; which will make it natural to us to approach him, and dwell on the thought of his goodness; which will enable us to see him in the majesty and sweetness of nature, in the rise of empires or the death of an infant, in the coming of Christ, and in every good thought which swells in our souls,—then it is evident that this is what we need. Let us dig deep, and build our house upon a rock.

We shall see in another section that there is such a change of heart as we have described. Jesus saves sinners by taking away the heart of stone, and giving a heart of flesh. He saw the whole depth and extent of the disease which he came to cure. There are some preachers who do not know how great an evil sin is, and would not know what to do for a penitent and anxious soul which really saw the greatness of its needs. Thus, when George Fox went to the rector of his church to ask advice for the distress of his soul, he was told to amuse himself and divert his mind. But Jesus saw all the extent of sin, and yet was ready to encourage and help the sinner. He knew that his remedy was equal to the emergency. The gospel of Christ can give to us love to God and love to man; can soften our hearts in humility, can enable us to fight with and conquer even the hereditary evil of our organization; can ultimately redeem us from all evil. This is the depravity we are to conquer; not of nature, but of will, and aim, and purpose.

§ 10. Ability and Inability

One of the pivotal points in the Orthodox theory of evil is that of *moral inability*. Indeed, the doctrine of total depravity seems to be taught for the sake of this. Total depravity resolves itself, in the mind of the Orthodox teacher, into total inability, and means that man, unable to do right by any power in himself, must throw himself wholly and absolutely on the divine grace. The secret motive of the whole Orthodox doctrine of evil is to lead through a sense of sin to humility, and at last to dependence. Orthodoxy here becomes intelligible, so soon as we perceive that its purpose is not speculative, but practical. As religion consists so greatly in the sentiment of dependence, it is a leading purpose in the Orthodox system to produce this sense of dependence. That group of graces—reverence, humility, submission, trust, prayer—which lend such an ineffable charm to the moral nature, which purify and refine it to its inmost depths,—these spring almost wholly from the sense of dependence on a higher and better being than ourselves. These being absent, the elevating principle is wanting; the man cannot rise above himself. There may be truth, courage, conscience, purity, but they are all stoical and self-relying. It is only he who relies on a higher power, clings to a higher being, and draws his moral life from above, who can ascend. He who humbles himself, and he only, shall be exalted. But humility does not consist in looking down, but in looking up. It does not come from looking at our own meanness, but at something higher and better than ourselves. The sense of sin is only elevating when connected with the sight of a higher beauty and holiness.

It is, therefore, in order to produce a conviction of absolute dependence that Orthodoxy urges so strongly the doctrines of total depravity and total inability. A man will not pray, says the Orthodox system, till he feels himself helpless. He will not seek a Saviour so long as he hopes to save himself. He must see that he can do nothing more for himself; and then, for the first time, he exercises a real faith in God, and casts himself on the divine mercy.

Reasoning in this way, consciously or unconsciously, Orthodoxy has built up its doctrine of human inability, which we will proceed to state,— first, however, indicating the scriptural view of this subject.

Scripture teaches that man is able to choose the right, but not always able to perform it. He is free in his spirit, but bound by circumstances of position, and by bodily organization. He is free to choose, but not free to do. His freedom is in effort, not necessarily in accomplishment. He can always try; he cannot always effect what he tries.

Thus Jesus says (Matt. 26:41), "Watch and pray, that ye enter not into temptation; the spirit indeed is willing, but the flesh is weak." And so Paul says, in the passage on this subject before referred to (Rom. 7:18), "To will is present with me, but how to perform that which I will, I find not."

Without attempting here to enter into the tormented question of fate and freedom, of necessity so irrefragably demonstrated by the logic of Edwards and others,—of free-will perpetually reasserted by the intuitive reason in the soul,—we may say this: Whether there be such a thing as metaphysical freedom or not, there is such a thing as moral freedom. In proportion as man sinks into the domain of nature, he is bound by irresistible laws. In proportion as he rises into the sphere of reason, justice, truth, love, he is emancipated, and can direct his own course. "Ye shall know the truth, and the truth shall make you free." "If the Son, therefore, shall make you free, ye shall be free indeed." (John 8:32, 36.) "Stand fast in the liberty wherewith Christ hath made us free." (Gal. 5:1.) It is therefore true that only as we direct our course by eternal laws, we rise above the controlling influence of habit, prejudice, public opinion, inherited and original tendencies of the blood and brain. According to Paul (Rom. 6:16-22), man must be either the servant of sin or the servant of God. He must serve, willingly or unwillingly. He must be the degraded slave of desire and selfishness, or the willing, loyal subject of truth and right. Paradoxically enough, however, he only feels free in these two cases. For in these two states he is doing what he chooses to do. When he is blindly and willingly following his lower instincts he feels free. When he is rationally and freely choosing right, and doing it, he also feels free. But when half way between these two states, when his conscience is pulling one way and his desires drawing him the other, when he is choosing right and doing wrong, he feels himself a slave.

There are therefore these three conditions of the will, corresponding to the Pauline division of man into spirit, soul, and body (1 Tim. 5:23)—a view of man which was held throughout antiquity. The carnal man (σαρκικος) is one in whom the earthly appetites are supreme, and the soul, (ψυχη) and spirit (πνευμα) subordinate. The natural man (ψυχικος ανθρωπος, 1 Cor. 2:14) is one in whom the soul, or central principle, the finite will, is supreme. The spiritual man (πνευματικος, 1 Cor. 2:15) is he in whom the infinite principle, the sense of eternal truth and right, is supreme. In the first condition—that of the carnal man—one is the slave of sin, but without knowing it, because there is no wish to become anything different. In the second state—that of the natural man (or psychical man)—the soul chooses the good, but is drawn down by the evil. The law of the mind is warring against the law of the members, and the man is torn asunder by this conflict. He tries to do right, and does wrong. He now first feels himself a slave; yet he is in reality *less* a slave than before, for now he is endeavoring to escape. His *will* is emancipated, though his habits of conduct, his habits of thought, his habits of feeling, still bind him fast. In the third condition, that of the spiritual man, he has broken these chains. He not only wills to do right, but does it. His body shares in the new life of his soul. He now is made free by the truth and the spirit from the service of evil, and shares in "the glorious liberty of the children of God."

In all these conditions the human being has some freedom, but differing in degree in each. In the lowest state he has freedom of action, for he does what he wishes to do; but he has not freedom of choice, for he does not choose at all. He acts not by intelligent choice, but by blind instinct, habit or custom. In the middle state he has freedom of choice, but not of action. He chooses the good, but performs the evil. This is the condition described by Ovid, and other profane writers, before Paul described it in the seventh chapter of Romans.15 But in the highest state—a spiritual condition—he has both freedoms; he can both choose and perform. The carnal man seems to be free, but is most thoroughly enslaved of all. The psychical man seems to himself to be enslaved, but has begun to be free. The spiritual man both seems to be free and is so. The apparent freedom of the carnal man differs from the real freedom of the spiritual man in this—the spiritual man could do wrong if he chose to do so, but chooses to do right. But the carnal man could not do right if he should choose. A good man, if he chose to do so, might lie, and steal, and drink, and be profane; but a bad man could not, by choosing, become temperate, pure, truthful, and honest.

Scripture and experience give, therefore, the same account of human ability and inability. In the lowest state man is the servant of sense, and can neither will nor do right. In the higher condition he can will, but cannot perform; for his ideal aim is above his actual power. In the highest, or regenerate, state he can both will and do. Body, as well as soul, serve the spirit.

These are the truths which lie at the basis of the Orthodox doctrine of inability. But Orthodoxy, in its desire to awaken a sense of dependence, has pushed them to an unreasonable extreme. It asserts that man, in his natural state, before he is regenerated, has *no* power to will or to do right. It is evident, however, that all men have power to will and to do *many* right things. Even in the lowest condition, a man wills and does much that is right. Though the governing principle be the lowest one, he can yet perform many good actions. In the second condition also, the psychical man, though not able *always* to do right, *often* succeeds in doing so. And in this state the apostle declares that *he* does not do the evil, but "sin that dwells in him." So long as his *purpose* is right, he is right.

§ 11. Orthodox Doctrine of Inability

Let us see what Orthodoxy says of the inability of the unregenerate man. The Assembly's Confession declares (chap. 6, § 4), that by our corrupt nature "we are utterly indisposed, disabled, and made opposite to all good, and wholly inclined to all evil." In chap. 9, § 3, it says that "man, by his fall into a state of sin, hath wholly lost all ability of will to any spiritual good accompanying salvation."

This seems plain enough. It would justify the charge made by Dr. Cox, that there are those who teach that "a man has no ability to do his duty,"[16] and "that, where the means of grace are abundantly vouchsafed, a man can do nothing for, but can only counteract, his own salvation." It would also seem to lay a fit foundation for that kind of Calvinistic preaching which, according to Professor Finney, of Oberlin (see "Revival Lectures"), virtually amounts to saying,

"You can, and you can't;
You shall, and you shan't;
You will, and you won't;
You'll be damned if you don't."

These charges, it must be noticed, are brought against Calvinism, not by us, but by Presbyterian divines, themselves holding to this same Westminster Confession.

But let us look at some of the expositions given to this doctrine of inability by modern Orthodox authorities.

(a.) The Old School Presbyterians. — As stated by one of their own number (Professor Atwater, of Princeton College, Bibliotheca Sacra, January, 1864), they hold an inability "moral, sinful, and real," "irremovable by the sinner's own power." He sets aside the objection that we are not bound to do what we are unable to do, by saying that this applies to actions only, not to sinful dispositions. He illustrates this by saying that an irrepressible disposition to slander would be only so much more culpable. But in this he is evidently wrong. Such a habit has become a disease, and the unfortunate victim is no longer accountable for what he does.

(b.) The New School Presbyterians. — (Rev. George Duffield, in Bibliotheca Sacra, July, 1863.) Although Dr. Duffield objects to the language of the Old School Presbyterians in denying "free agency," and regarding man "as destitute of ability as a block of marble," he yet declares that the New School, as well as the Old, believe that in the unconverted state "man can do nothing morally good." Still, he adds, men can accept the offers of salvation made by Jesus Christ. But he positively denies that "man, in his natural state, independent of the gospel and Spirit of Christ, has ability *perfectly* to obey *all* the commandments of God." We suppose that most persons would agree with him in this statement.

(c.) The Old School in New England Theology. — (Bibliotheca Sacra, April, 1863. Article by Professor Lawrence, East Windsor, Connecticut.) This writer contends that human inability is moral, and not natural — a distinction much dwelt upon by the Hopkinsians, but rejected by the Old School Presbyterians. This system differs from the Arminian or Methodist view in insisting that man has power enough to sin, though not enough to obey.

(d.) Hopkinsianism. — (Bibliotheca Sacra, July, 1862.) The Hopkinsians profess to contend for free agency, in order to save responsibility. They adopt the ideas of Edwards on free agency. But freedom, with them, consists only in choice. Whatever we choose, we choose freely. The carnal man is as free in choosing evil as the spiritual man in choosing good. All real freedom in this system disappears in a juggle of words.

The result of this examination will show that the great body of the Orthodox, of all schools, continues to deny any real ability in the unregenerate man to do the will of God. They do not *say* that "man has no power to do his duty," but that is the impression left by their teaching. The distinction between natural and moral inability is insufficient; for it is as absurd to say that a man is unable not to sin, when you only mean that he chooses to sin, as it would he to say, when invited to eat your dinner, "I am unable to eat," meaning only that you were unwilling. Besides, if inability is moral, it is in the will, and not in the nature, and so is not natural depravity at all. It is also making God unjust to teach that he considers us guilty for a misfortune. If we derive a corrupted nature from Adam, that is our misfortune, and not our fault, and God owes us not anger, but pity. Instead of punishing us, he should compensate us for this disaster.

Therefore the unreason, the want of logic, and the absence of any just view of God, appear, more or less, throughout these statements. For where there is no ability, there can be no guilt. Just as soon as man ceases to have the power to do right, he ceases to have the power to do wrong. Inability and guilt, which are connected by all these creeds, logically exclude each other. If our nature is incapable of doing good, then it is incapable of committing sin. One or the other must be given up. Keep which you will, but you cannot keep both. We may be totally depraved by our nature; but then we cease to be sinners, and cease to be guilty. Or we may be going wholly wrong, and so be sinful, but then we have the power of going right.

This is the inconsistency in almost all Orthodox systems. By dwelling so much on human weakness, they destroy at last the sense of responsibility.

§ 12. Some further Features of Orthodox Theology concerning Human Sinfulness

In the article in the Bibliotheca Sacra before referred to (April, 1863), by Edward A. Lawrence, D. D., Professor at East Windsor, Connecticut, on "The Old School in New England Theology," the writer gives the following account of the doctrines of this body concerning sin:—

"God created man a holy being. He was not merely innocent, as not having committed sin, not merely pure, as not inheriting any derived evil, but was positively holy in his very being." This, we suppose, must mean that he was inclined by nature to do right, rather than wrong. It was as natural for him to love God as for a fish to swim or a bird to fly. Nothing less than this, certainly, would deserve to be called "holiness of being."

"The first man," says Professor Lawrence, "was the federal head of this race, representatively and by covenant, as no other father has been or can be with his children." This is illustrated by the fact of a legal corporation, whose members are responsible in law for the actions of their agent.

Professor Lawrence explains the belief of the Old School in the imputation of Adam's sin thus: It was not the personal guilt of Adam which was imputed to his descendants, but "certain disastrous consequences." They, as well as he, became "subject to temporal and eternal death." The next consequence of Adam's sin we must give in Professor Lawrence's own language, in order not to misrepresent him. "The first evil disposition which led to the evil choice was not only confirmed in him as an individual, but also as a quality of human nature, and it reappears, successively, in each one of them." Imputation, therefore, means not the transfer of guilt, but of a corrupt nature. "It is not a sin to be born sinful; but the sin with which men are born is nevertheless sinful." Then follows this statement: "We are strictly guilty only for our own sin; but the sinfulness with which we are born is as really ours as if it originated in our own act."

This, again, is explained by defining guilt as liability to punishment on account of the acts of another, "as when the members of a corporation suffer from the ill management of its agent." This he calls corporate guilt.

The Old School doctrine, according to this writer, concerning sin, makes it a state rather than an act. It is not merely the act of disobedience, but the wrong bias of the will, out of which the act proceeds. He thinks it wrong to call "sin a nature," for neither the substance of the soul, nor its faculties, are sinful. The depravity of nature is not choice, so much as tendency which leads to choice. It is hereditary, being transmitted from father to son.

The old theology, therefore, predicates sinfulness of human nature; affirms sin to be a wrong state or bias of will; considers it to be hereditary; regards new-born infants as depraved, but thinks that those of them who die in infancy, before actual transgression, are renewed and saved by the blood of Christ; and considers temporal death as a part of the penalty of sin.

Upon this statement of the Old School doctrine, the following criticisms naturally occur:—

First. If original righteousness was holiness of nature, and not mere innocence; if it was a positive tendency to good, and not merely a state of indifference between good and evil; then, we ask, What produced the fall? What motive led to the commission of the first sin? If the nature of the first man was holy, there was nothing in it which could lead him to sin, and any external temptation addressed to such a nature must fall powerless before it. It would be like trying to tempt a fish to fly in the air, or like tempting a bird to go into the water. Even if the first man could have been induced by any deception or external influence to commit a wrong act, this would not be sinful, because there would be no sinful motive behind it. A wrong act proceeding from a holy nature is either an impossibility or a mere innocent mistake. Our first criticism, therefore, on the Old School doctrine of sin, is, that it makes Adam's fall an impossibility.

Second. As regards Adam's federal headship and the illustration of a corporation, we say, that the members of a corporation are not considered guilty in consequence of the acts of their agent, although they may suffer in consequence of these acts. If he commits forgery they may lose money thereby, but no one would think of calling them forgers. The sin of a parent may be visited upon his children to the third or fourth generation, but in their case it is neither punishment nor guilt, but only misfortune. When Professor Lawrence, therefore, says, that "we are guilty for the sinfulness with which we are born, because it is really ours," he utters a moral absurdity, and strikes at the root of all moral distinctions. He says, "The sinfulness with which we are born is really ours;" but in what sense ours? Only as any congenital disease may be called *ours*. If a man is born with a tendency to consumption, blindness, lameness, he may say, "my lameness, my near-sightedness." But no one would suppose that he meant thereby to hold himself responsible for them, or to consider himself guilty because of them. It is absurd to speak of "corporate guilt." The corporate guilt, for example, of the stockholders of a bank, because of the crime of an absconding teller!

The natural objection to this illustration of a corporation is, that those who enter into a corporation do it by a free act, and make themselves voluntarily responsible. But *we* did not consent that Adam should be our agent. We did not agree that if Adam should commit a single act of disobedience we should be born totally depraved, and liable to everlasting torments in consequence. Professor Lawrence replies, that it would have been impossible for God to ask our consent, and therefore, apparently he supposes that God took for granted that we would consent. This seems to be no answer to the objection. If it was impossible for God to obtain our consent, before we were born, to incur this awful danger, he was not compelled to expose us to it. It is an insult to the justice of the Almighty to assume that he could have done so.

Third. Professor Lawrence does not think it correct to say that "sin is a nature." But why not, if it be a universal and constant element, an original and permanent state of the soul? To say that human nature is sinful, but deny that sin is a nature, seems to be making a distinction without a difference. It is a disposition to sin born with the child. Now, say what we will, such a disposition to sin thus born with us is not guilt but misfortune. A just God will not hold us responsible for it, but will hold himself responsible to help us out of it. As a faithful Creator, he is bound to do so, and will do so.

It is common for theologians to deny all such assertions as these last. They hold it irreverent to say that God owes anything to his creatures. They accumulate responsibility upon man, but deny responsibility to God. But in doing this they take from the Almighty all moral character. Calvinism, especially, makes of the Deity infinite power and infinite will. But no blasphemy is worse than that which, though with the best intentions, virtually destroys the moral character of the Almighty, reducing him to an infinite will: that is, making of him an infinite tyrant. For the essence of tyranny is the union of power and will in a ruler, who recognizes no obligations towards his subjects.

The book of Job seems to have been written partly to refute this sort of Calvinism. The friends of Job were Calvinists in this sense. The sum of their argument was that, since God was all-powerful, therefore whatever he did must be right; and, since he punished Job, Job must be a sinner, and ought to confess his sin whether he saw it or not. This has been, in all ages, the substance of Calvinism—Jewish Calvinism, Mohammedan Calvinism, Christian Calvinism. It declares that we are bound to submit to God, not because he is good, but because he is powerful. But the answer of Job to his friends is a rebuke to the same spirit wherever shown. He asks them "if they will speak with unfairness for God," and "speak deceitfully for him," and "accept his person." He declares that if he could find God he would go before his throne and defend his own cause. "Would he contend with me with his mighty power? No! he would have regard unto me."

This is the sin of Calvinism, that it "accepts the person of the Almighty," assuming that he has a right to do as he pleases with his creatures, and that they have no rights which he is bound to respect, except that of being punished. Thus it destroys the moral character of the Almighty.

Fourth. Professor Lawrence says, "It is the general belief of the Old School that those who die in infancy before actual transgression, are renewed and saved by the blood of Christ."

The power of infancy is wonderful. It can even break down the logic of Calvinism. Wordsworth was right in calling the infant—

"Mighty prophet! Seer blest!

On whom those truths do rest

Which we are toiling all our lives to find."

Every kind of theology, however savage and bitter it may be against adult sinners, sending them into an eternal hell without the least hesitation or remorse, hesitates and stammers when it comes to speak of little children. Even the idolatrous Jews, sacrificing their children to Moloch in the valley of Hinnom, beat drums to drown their cries, which they could not bear to hear. Both schools of theology, Old and New, hasten to say that infants are not to be damned. But *why* not, if they are born with a depraved nature, and die without being converted? Both the great schools of Presbyterian theology hold to the doctrine of the Assembly's Catechism, which declares (chap. 6, § 6), that "every sin, both original and actual, being a transgression of the righteous law of God, and contrary thereunto, doth, in its own nature, bring guilt upon the sinner, whereby he is bound over to the wrath of God." Therefore the infant who dies before he has exercised repentance and faith in Christ, is under the wrath of God. Orthodoxy does not allow of repentance in the other life: how, then, can infants be saved according to Orthodoxy? Professor Lawrence can only reply, that it is *a general belief* that they will be saved. The Catechism declares, less decidedly, that "elect infants" will be saved. Dr. Whedon (Bibliotheca Sacra, April, 1862), on behalf of the Methodists, says, "That the dying infant is saved, and saved by the atonement, all agree." But *how* he is saved, or what reason they have to think him saved, except their wish to believe it, no one can tell. Death, in fact, becomes to the infant a saving sacrament. As long as he lives he is believed unregenerate and unconverted. As soon as he dies he is considered ready for heaven. But he cannot be ready for heaven until he is regenerate; and after death there is no such thing as obtaining a new heart, and no opportunity for repentance. Logically, therefore, the infant is converted by the mere act of dying. We presume that no Orthodox theologians would assert this; and yet we really do not see how they can avoid the conclusion.

But why is it any worse for children to be damned in consequence of Adam's sin than for adults to be damned? Orthodoxy assures us that in consequence of Adam's sin we are born depraved. Dr. Duffield, stating and defending the doctrines of the New School Presbyterian Church (Bibliotheca Sacra, July, 1863), says that Adam subjected his posterity to such a loss that they are born without any righteousness, are exposed to the consequences of his transgression, and all become sinners as soon as they are capable of it. He quotes with approbation from a protest of the New School minority, in the General Assembly of 1837 (which he calls a document of great historic value), an assertion that "by reason of the sin of Adam, the race are treated as if they had sinned;" and from another document of the same school which says, that "we are all born with a tendency to sin, which makes it morally certain that we shall do so." Now, we do not see why it is any worse to send infants to hell because of this depraved nature, than to send grown persons there who have sinned in consequence of possessing such a depraved nature. If it be said that adults have had an opportunity to repent, and have not accepted it, we reply, that to the mass of mankind no such opportunity is offered; that, where it is offered, no one has the power to accept it, except he be one of the elect; and that at all events, since infants are sure to be saved, and a very large proportion of adults are very likely to be lost, *death in infancy is the most desirable thing possible*. According to this doctrine, child-murder becomes almost a virtue.

The radical difficulty in all these theories consists in refusing to apply to God the same rules of justice which we apply to man. To do so implies no irreverence, but the highest reverence. There is nothing more honorable to the Almighty than to believe him to be actuated by the same great principles of right which he has written in our conscience and heart. Those laws of eternal justice, so deeply engraven on the fleshly tables of the heart, are a revelation of the character of God himself. If we think to honor him by rejecting these intuitions of the reason, and by substituting for this divine idea of a God of justice that of a being of arbitrary will, who is under no obligations to his creatures, we deeply dishonor the Almighty and fatally injure our own character. From this perverted view of God comes a cynical view of man. When we make *will* supreme in God, we legitimate all tyranny and contempt from man to man. Then comes the state of things described by Shakespeare: —

"Force should be right, or, rather, right and wrong
(Between whose endless jar justice resides)
Should lose their names, and so should justice too.
Then everything includes itself in power,
Power into will, will into appetite;
And appetite, a universal wolf,
So doubly seconded with will and power,
Must make perforce a universal prey,
And, last, eat up himself."

Shakespeare, Troilus and Cressida.

Chapter VII
Conversion And Regeneration

§ 1. Orthodoxy recognizes only two Conditions in which Man can be found

Orthodoxy knows only two states in which man can be found. Man is either in the natural state, and then he is totally depraved; or he is in the supernatural state, in which the chain of sin has been broken. He is either impenitent or penitent, either unregenerated or regenerate, unconverted or converted, a sinner or a saint.

There is no gradation, no shading off, no twilight between this midnight gloom and midday splendor. To the common eye, and in the judgment of their friends and neighbors, the people who enter a church seem of all degrees of goodness; and every one has good and bad qualities mixed up together in his character. But, as the Orthodox minister looks at them from the pulpit, they instantly fall into two classes, and become "my impenitent hearers," and "my penitent hearers."

Moreover, it is assumed that the distinction between these two classes is so marked and plain, that it can be recognized by any one who will. Orthodox people inquire, "*Is he pious?*" just as they would ask, "*Is he married?*"

Again, the change from one state to the other is assumed to be so distinct and marked, that he who runs can read. One may say to another, "*Where were you converted?*" just as they may say, "*Where did you go to college?*" "Where were you born?" said an English bishop to Summerfield, the Methodist preacher. "In Dublin and Liverpool," he answered. "Were you born in *two* places?" said the bishop. " 'Art thou a master in Israel, and knowest not these things?' " replied Summerfield.

On the other hand, it is quite common among Liberal Christians to doubt the reality, or deny the importance, of such changes altogether. With them the Christian life consists, not in change, but in progress. In the Christian source, Orthodoxy lays the main stress on the commencement; Liberal Christianity, on the progress. The one wishes you to begin the journey, without seeming to care whether you go forward: the other urges you to go forward, without inquiring whether you have begun to go. According to one, Christianity is nothing but a crisis; according to the other, nothing but a development.

§ 2. Crisis and Development

Is there any truth in this Orthodox view of man? anything essential, substantial, vital? And is there any formal error? If there is, what is it? Is Christianity crisis or development, or both?

Common sense and the analogies of common life must answer, "Both." If Christianity is a life, it must begin with a birth; if a journey, it cannot be taken except we set out; if an education, we must determine to commence the education; if labor in God's vineyard, we must go into the vineyard, and begin. There are only two classes—those who are alive, and those who are not alive; those who are taking the journey, and those who have not yet set out; those who are studying, and those who have not yet begun to study; those who are at work for God, and those who are standing idle. The distinction into two classes seems, therefore, substantial and real. It does not follow, to be sure, that these two classes can be distinguished so easily by the eye of man; but they certainly can be by the eye of God. Nor does this primary distinction interfere with other distinctions and many degrees of difference—greater or less differences and degrees of progress, usefulness, goodness. Nor does it follow that those who are now on the right side may not change again to the wrong, and again to the right. There may be conversion, and re-conversion; but that, at any moment, every person must be either endeavoring to do right, or not so endeavoring, is evident. This view is confirmed by the New Testament: "No man can serve two masters."

That in the religious life there should be both crisis and development, accords with the analogies of nature. The seed lies in the ground in a dormant state, perhaps for a long period. After a time comes a crisis; thrills of life vibrate through it; the germ is stirred; it sends its roots downward; its stalk pierces the mould, moving upward into light and air. After this great change, there comes a period of progress and development. The plant grows; its roots multiply; its stalk ascends, and divides into leaves. Then there comes a second crisis. The plant blossoms. In the course of a few hours, after weeks of growth, the bud bursts into beautiful petals, surrounding the delicate stamens and precious pistil. Then there comes a second long period of slow development. The petals fall, and the fruit slowly swells through many weeks of growth. At last there comes a day when the fruit is ripe. Yesterday it was not ripe; to-day it is. This is the third crisis. And so, in human life, long periods of development terminate in critical hours—the seeds of another long growth. So it is in other things; so also in religion.

§ 3. Nature of the Change

The next position of Orthodoxy is, that man, in the second or regenerate state, is a new creature. It asserts the change to be entire and radical, and the difference immense. Not only the whole direction of the life is changed, but the motive power is different, and the spirit different. Instead of ambition, there is content; in the place of sensitive vanity, there comes humility; instead of anxiety, trust in God. The burden of sin is taken away; the sense of our unworthiness no longer torments us: for God has forgiven our sins. Duty no longer seems arduous and difficult; for there is joy in doing anything for the sake of God. The law is written in the heart. We are born into a new life, the principle of which is faith. "The life I now live in the flesh, I live by faith in the Son of God." This faith enables us to see God as he is, not as a stern King, or a distant Power, or an abstract Law, but as a Friend, Father, watchful Providence, surrounding Love, inflowing Life; Source from which we are always coming, and towards which we are always tending. This life of faith makes all things new. Old things have passed away, and the outward world is fresh as on the first morning of creation. Our inward and outward life are both new. We have new convictions, new affections, new aims, new hopes, new joys. Nature is new, life is new, the Bible is new, the future world is new. Such and so great is the change which Orthodoxy assumes as the result of conversion.

§ 4. Its Reality and Importance

And the experience of the whole Church, the biographies of the saints in every denomination, assure us of the substantial truth of this description. Even in churches which are not Orthodox,—churches like our own, which insist more upon development than upon crisis,—observation verifies this description. Even those who do not expect such a change, nor believe in it, often come to it unexpectedly. In the course of each one's experience as a Christian minister, though he may never have insisted on the importance of sudden changes, and though he may be no revival preacher, he must have known numerous instances of those who seem to have passed from death to life in the course of a day or an hour. And is not this change, either sudden or gradual, that which makes Christianity a gospel? It is the good news, not of a future and distant heaven, but of a present heaven,—a heaven not outward, but inward; a present salvation from the power of sin; a present relief from the sense of guilt; a present joy and peace in believing; happiness in serving God; sympathy and good-will to man, instead of envy and uncharitableness; peace with God, with man, with ourselves, with our condition and circumstances.

That such a state is possible for every human being who desires it, is the good news which Christ brings; and the experience of ten thousand times ten thousand grateful hearts declares that it is a reality.

§ 5. Is it the Work of God, or of the Man himself? Orthodox Difficulty

But now comes a difficulty in the Orthodox statement. Orthodoxy declares that this regenerate state is the result of faith, not of works; and that faith is the gift of God; and herein Orthodoxy follows the Scripture. Yet Orthodoxy calls upon us to repent and be converted, that our sins may be blotted out; and herein likewise Orthodoxy follows the Scripture. Is, then, conversion an experience, or is it an action? Is it something God gives, or something which he commands? Is it a duty to be done, or a gift to be received? Is it submission to his will, or joy in his love? a new life of obedience, or a new heart of faith? If it is submission, then we can all change our hearts at once, and make ourselves love God and love man. But who can love by an effort of the will? Yet, if the new life is a gift, then we have no power to procure it, and can only wait till God sees fit to send it; and how, then, can we be called upon to be converted?

Here is a difficulty which it seems to us Orthodoxy does not solve; and yet we think that a solution is to be found in a very simple distinction, which, like all other true and real distinctions, throws light on many other difficulties.

§ 6. Solved by the Distinction between Conversion and Regeneration

The distinction of which we speak is between repentance or conversion on the one side, and regeneration or a new life on the other side. Repentance or conversion consists in renouncing all sin, and resolving to forsake it; in turning to God, with the purpose of submitting to his will and obeying his law. This conversion or repentance is an act proceeding from the will, and in obedience to the conscience. This is what God commands, and what we can and ought to do. Every conscientious person, every person who is endeavoring to do right and is ready to act up to his light, is a converted person. Every one who hates his sins, resists temptation, watches and prays against it, is a penitent person. This is the great, broad distinction between man and man. This divides all men into two classes—those who, in their will and purpose, are for God, truth, and right; and those who, because they are not *for* God, are really *against* him.

But, besides this broad distinction, there is another secondary distinction—a distinction among those who are conscientiously endeavoring to do God's will. Among the *converted* there are two classes—the regenerate and the unregenerate. A man may be converted, and not be regenerate; for a man may repent of his sin and turn towards God, and yet not have the life of love and joy which we have described.

He is under law, not under grace. He is struggling to do right, but is not borne forward on a joyful tide-wave of love.

§ 7. Men may be divided, religiously, into three Classes, not two

If this be so, we may divide men into three classes, and not into two. The first class is of those who are neither converted nor regenerate; the second, who are converted, but not regenerate; the third, who are converted, and also regenerate. The first are like the prodigal in the parable,—living without God; the second, like the hired servants in the same story,—serving God for wages; the third are sons, serving from love, ever with their Father, and all that he has is theirs. The motive of the first class is selfish will, selfish pleasure; the motive of the second is duty; that of the third, love. The first are without law, the second under law, the third under grace. And so we might multiply distinctions. But is it not clear to common observation, that this threefold classification meets the facts of life better than the other? There are three degrees of character. There is the worldly man, who is just as good or bad as society around him leads him to be; whose virtues result merely from a happy organization, or fortunate influences, but who has no principle of goodness, no purpose of righteousness, no serious aim in life. Then there is the conscientious man, who means to live, and does live, by a standard of morality; who has a serious aim, but who is not yet deeply and joyfully religious; whose religion, at any rate, is hard work, not confiding, child-like faith. And then there is the Christian believer, who has begun to live from faith; who begins to feel a higher life pouring into his heart from on high; who has help and strength from above. From his heart the burden has been lifted, and he has become again as a little child. He knows how to pray the prayer of faith. He may not be so very much better than the other in outward character; but he has the principle within him which will make all things new, sooner or later.

The New Testament confirms this view of a threefold division. We saw, in our last chapter, that the apostle Paul, who considers human nature to consist of three elements,—spirit, soul, and body,—divides mankind into the carnal man, the natural (psychical or soulish) man, and the spiritual man. The carnal man is he in whom the bodily instincts and appetites are supreme. "He is not subject to the law of God, neither indeed can be." The natural man is he in whom the *soul* is supreme: he is neither carnal on one side, nor spiritual on the other. "He cannot receive the things of the Spirit of God;" yet he is not in opposition and hostility to them, like the carnal man, whose mind is enmity against God.

Still more plainly does the apostle indicate the distinction when speaking of those who are without law, those who are under law, and those who are free from law and above it. The first state he describes in such words as these: "I was alive without the law once"—the glad, natural life and freedom before conscience is developed. But conscience does awake in all: "The commandment came, sin revived, and I died." When man sees that he ought to serve God, yet continues to serve the flesh and the world, he is spoken of as dead in sin; for all the principle of progress ceases. But if he does endeavor to do right, then Paul speaks of him as *under law*, and on his way to a higher state. That higher state he speaks of as being "delivered from the law, to serve in newness of spirit, and not in oldness of letter."

Thus we see that all religious experiences coincide. The experience of the apostle Paul is exactly the same, in its essentials, with that of every soul, however humble, that begins and goes forward in the Christian life.

If this distinction between conversion and regeneration be correct, it removes the difficulty in the Orthodox statement.

§ 8. Difference between Conversion and Regeneration

Conversion is an act, regeneration an experience. "Turn ye, turn ye; for why will ye die?" is the command of the Old Testament. "Repent, and be converted, that your sins may be blotted out;" "Repent, and be baptized, and ye shall receive the gift of the Holy Ghost," is the command of the New Testament. It is a duty to repent; but to become regenerate is not a duty: *that* is a gift, to be received afterwards. God commands conversion: he bestows regeneration. Submission is an act of our own: faith is the gift of God. A change of outward life and conduct we can accomplish ourselves; at least, we can endeavor to accomplish it; but the change of heart God himself will bestow.

Conversion, a turning round, is necessarily instantaneous: it is a change. But regeneration, or reception of divine Love, is a state, not sudden, but passing by gradations into a deeper and deeper life of faith and joy.

So, too, conversion may be repeated: we may often find that we have again turned round, and are going the wrong way. But the inflow of life, when begun, cannot be begun again. When God has touched the heart with his love, it is forever lifted by that divine experience beyond the region of mere law. We can never forget it. These are the:

"Truths which wake

To perish never;

Which neither listlessness nor mad endeavor,

Nor man nor boy,

Nor aught that is at enmity with joy,

Can utterly abolish or destroy."

And herein lies the basis of the truth in the doctrine of the "perseverance of saints."

§ 9. Unsatisfactory Attitude of the Orthodox Church

We cannot but think the attitude of Orthodoxy towards this part of Christianity to be singularly unsatisfactory and inefficient. The work of the Church, all admit, is to convert the world to God, and so save it from the power and evil of sin. But if this is a work which the Church has to do, it ought surely to have some fixed method or rule by which to act. It should not be a matter of accident whether it can do its work or not. It should not be in doubt, every day, as to the success to come from its efforts. If its work is to make men Christians, it ought to know how to do it, be able to do it, and know when it is done. Such is the case with all other work. If a man is to build a house, he does not bring together his materials, hire his carpenters and masons, and, when all are on the ground, sit down with them, and wait for some emotion or interior change by which they will be enabled to go on and do their work. If we are mechanics, merchants, lawyers, physicians, teachers, we do not wait for a revival before we can properly fulfil our engagements. It is only in the work of converting the world to God—the greatest and most important of all—that such a strange system is adopted. We are told to put ourselves in the proper place, namely, the Church; collect our materials, that is, the means of grace; and then we are to wait until, somehow or other, we may be able *to get religion*. Religion is made a spasm, a struggle, an agony—not a regular work, not a steady growth. Everything about it is uncertain and tentative. No one knows when he will become a Christian, but hopes, some time or other, that he shall be made one. The common thought, produced by the common Orthodox system of preaching, was expressed once in a public meeting by Henry Clay. "I am not," he said, "a Christian. I am sorry I am not. I wish I were. I hope that, some day, I shall be." He did not mean by this to say that he was an unbeliever; but he had adopted the helpless, passive system by which he was taught that he had nothing to do but wait till some great change should take place in his soul.

Out of this way of thought comes the revival system, which is a curious blending of machinery and expectation, of adroit and careful management with reliance on some great inspiration. Crisis and development are to be expected, no doubt; but we do not set a trap to catch the Spring. It is ours to plant and to water, but it is God's to give the increase. That, therefore, should be left to him.

The revival system is Arminianism grafted on Calvinism. It is an attempt to unite the belief that man is wholly passive in conversion, and is not able to prepare himself thereunto, with the opposite doctrine that by a use of means he can become a Christian. It is an attempt to unite the Calvinistic article that God, when he chooses, calls those he has predestined to eternal life, with the attempt to make him choose our time and way. Such a system, disjointed at its centre, must necessarily work badly, and result in an alternation of feverish heats and aguish chills. To carry on the work of the Church by revivals is as unreasonable as it would be to carry on a school, or a cotton factory, by a revival system—alternations of violent study and work, followed by relapses into indolence and sloth.

The Church of Rome has a great advantage over Protestant Orthodoxy in this respect. It, too, admits revivals, and has its periods of extraordinary attention to religion. But there is this great difference. It does not depend on them for creating Christianity in the soul; it uses them only for increasing its warmth and power. In the Roman Church every baptized person is a Christian so long as he does not continue in mortal sin, but by the regular use of the sacraments preserves his Christian life. The essential work of the Church is done by its regular methods—by baptism, confession, and its ritual service. In the Church of Rome, all connected with it are Christians, and in the way of salvation. In Protestant Orthodox churches, if any of those born and brought up in it are Christians, it is, so far as they are concerned, a happy accident.

All this shows something wrong in the common theory of conversion. Every one in a Christian community who desires to be a Christian ought to be able to become one. Christianity is a gospel, because it opens the kingdom of heaven to all. The call of the Church at the beginning was to *follow Christ*. Any one who was willing to follow Christ was baptized at once, and became a Christian. No one waited till he should experience some remarkable interior change, or some influence of the Holy Ghost. The promise at first was, that whosoever became a Christian *should* receive the Holy Ghost afterwards. Spiritual influences were not the condition of Christianity, but the result of Christianity.

One bad consequence of the Orthodox idea is discouragement on the one side, and spiritual pride on the other. Those who are not converted are discouraged, and deprived of the comforts of Christian faith. Those who think they have been converted are satisfied with this past experience, and believe themselves Christians on the strength of it. Because some spiritual commotion took place in their souls at a certain time and place, they consider themselves children of God and heirs of his favor, though in their daily lives they may show little proof of practical Christianity. And the result of this, again, is a professed distrust, by the majority of sensible men, of such conversions. Men of the world do not find that professed Christians are better than themselves. Often, indeed, church members are not so just, honest, manly, or truthful as those who make no claim to religion. And the reason is simply this—that they have been taught to believe that the essence of Christianity does not consist in righteousness, but in certain religious experiences.

§ 10. The Essential Thing for Man is to repent and be converted; that is, to make it his Purpose to obey God in all Things

As far as man is concerned, repentance is the one thing needful. But by repentance we do not mean sorrow or contrition, but simply turning round whenever we are going wrong, and beginning at once to go right. This is something in every man's power, and this makes him a Christian; this gives him a claim to all the promises and hopes of the gospel here and hereafter. It would seem that there need be no doubt as to the nature of repentance while the parable of the prodigal son stands in the Bible. That divine story gives us the whole theory of repentance and regeneration—repentance being that which comes from man, regeneration that which is given by God. When the prodigal son was aware of his sin and sorrow, and said, "I will arise, and go to my father;" and when he arose, and went to his father, and confessed his sin and need, then he had repented. It was simply going to his father with the purpose of obedience. And when the father received him, not with reproach, but with pardon and joy, then he was born again, introduced into a new life, into the peace, and love, and freedom of his own home.

"One thing is needful," said Jesus; that is, to sit at the feet of the Master, to follow him, to become his disciple. That is all we have to do; then we are safe. We can trust God to do his part if we do ours. He will give us his Holy Spirit; he will give us a new heart; he will put his peace and strength into our souls. It is not necessary to be anxious, or to be inspecting our feelings to see if we are feeling right. All such introspection is unnecessary if we have faith in God and his promises. We are Christians just as long as we are obeying

God and following Christ. When we find ourselves disobedient, selfish, going wrong, then the one thing needful is to repent and be converted. We are to come back to our duty.

The general impression in Orthodox churches, resulting from the preaching, is, that not much is gained by doing one's duty unless one is regenerate. Doing our duty does not make us Christians, does not save the soul; so, why be particular in doing more than others, or being better than others? Orthodox congregations believe in the new life, but not in obedience as its necessary antecedent.

Unitarians, on the other hand, believe in obedience, but have little faith in a higher life as attainable here. Hence a Unitarian congregation usually consists of intelligent, virtuous, well-meaning people, but destitute of enthusiasm, and with little confidence in the new birth or religious life.

Unitarians believe in obedience as the one thing needful; and in this they are right. But they are wrong in not expecting the influences which God is always ready to give, which change the heart, and fill it with a peace passing understanding, which make duties easy, which fill life with joy, and take the sting from death. The Orthodox believe in all these higher emotions and states of the soul, but unfortunately do not believe in obedience as the one thing needful. They think that some emotional transaction in the soul is the one thing needful.

§ 11. Regeneration is God's Work in the Soul. Examination of the Classical Passage, or conversation of Jesus with Nicodemus

In the third chapter of John we have the conversation which has been made the basis of the doctrine of the new birth.

In this conversation of Jesus with Nicodemus we have the old argument, which is always being renewed, between the letter and the spirit, between knowledge and insight, between routine and genius, ceremony and inspiration, the past and the future, the goodness of habit and the holiness born out of the living vision of good. In fact this little dialogue may be considered as a renewal, on a higher plane, of the picture given us by Luke of the boy Jesus in the temple talking with the doctors.

The common doctrine of the Orthodox churches about this chapter is, that Jesus teaches here that no man can be a Christian or a good man unless he passes through some mysterious experience, usually sudden, of which he must be conscious, which gives him a certain definite series of very deep feelings. First, he must feel very deeply that he is a sinner; then that he cannot by any effort of his own become different; thirdly, that, unless God makes him different, he never can be saved; and, lastly, he must feel that God will change his heart, and save him. Having passed through this kind of experience, it is assumed that he is "born again;" that he is a Christian; that he is a new creature; that he has a new heart; that if he dies now he will go to heaven; whereas, if he had died before, he would have gone to hell. It is also Orthodox to believe that a man can do nothing himself to produce this change of heart, or facilitate it.

A very interesting book was published not long ago, written by Miss Catherine Beecher, in which she describes the sufferings caused in her own experience by this theory of regeneration. Her father fully believed in it, and thought it necessary to carry all his children through it somehow or other. Their conversions, to be sure, were not all quite in rule; especially that of Henry seems to have been a little abnormal, if we may trust an account given by himself in an article on the dissolution of the Bowdoin Street Church and congregation, Boston, of which his father was the first minister. The description is so suggestive that we will quote the passage:—

"If somebody will look in the old records of Hanover Street Church about 1829, they will find a name there of a boy about fifteen years old, who was brought into the Church on a sympathetic wave, and who well remembers how cold and almost paralyzed he felt while the committee questioned him about his 'hope' and 'evidences,' which upon review amounted to this—that the son of such a father ought to be a good and pious boy. Being tender-hearted and quick to respond to moral sympathy, he had been caught and inflamed in a school excitement, but was just getting over it when summoned to Boston to join the church! On the morning of *the* day, he went to church without seeing anything he looked at. He heard his name called from the pulpit among many others, and trembled; rose up with every emotion petrified; counted the spots on the carpet; looked piteously up at the cornice; heard the fans creak in the pews near him; felt thankful to a fly that lit on his face, as if something familiar at last had come to break an awful trance; heard faintly a reading of the articles of faith; wondered whether he should be struck dead for not feeling more—whether he should go to hell for touching the bread and wine that he did not dare to take nor to refuse; spent the morning service uncertain whether dreaming, or out of the body, or in a trance; and at last walked home crying, and wishing he knew what, now that he was a Christian, he should do, and how he was to do it. Ah, well; there is a world of things in children's minds that grown-up people do not imagine, though they, too, once were young!"

Now, if his state of mind, thus described, had been at that time exposed and told, it would not have been thought a very sound Orthodox experience.

But in reality the boy was at that very time as good a Christian for a boy as he is now for a man. But Miss Beecher, in the book referred to, tells us that when one of her other brothers was striving in prayer for this change of heart, with groans and struggles, the house was like a tomb. The poor young man was in his chamber alone, and his groans and cries were heard through the whole house. All the other members of the family staid in their own rooms in silence, until at last, by some natural reaction of feeling, there came a sense of rest and peace to his mind, which they believed to be the new birth. She also describes the way in which Dr. Payson, of Portland, tortured his little daughter, three years old, by a torture as well meant, as conscientious, and more terrible than that of the Holy Inquisition. He told his little daughter that she hated God; that she must have a change of heart, but that she could not get it for herself; and that even her prayers, until she was converted, were only making her worse. The poor little girl denied that she hated God; she said she was sure she loved him. Then the misguided father brought up all her little childish faults as a proof that she hated God; for if she loved him she would never do wrong. And so, from three years of age till she was thirteen, this poor, infatuated parent tormented this little child by keeping her on this spiritual rack—all because of a false view of the passages concerning regeneration in the Bible. And when we think of the twenty thousand pulpits which to-day are teaching in this country this same sort of belief, it is evident that it is our duty to see what the Master really meant to teach us by this passage.

Nicodemus is the type of a class of men common in all times. We have seen Nicodemus very often. He is a good man whose goodness has no life in it. His goodness is a sort of an automaton—all machinery and no soul. He is so thoroughly right in all he does; everything about him is so proper; he is so perfectly *en règle* in his own eyes,—that we sometimes wish that he might be betrayed into some impropriety, commit some not too great folly, have some *escapade* of rash enthusiasm. You respect him so much, you wonder why you do not love him more. It is because he is not open to influence. His goodness is so rigid, his opinions so declared, his character so pronounced, that there is no crack anywhere by which God or man can reach him. He has a whole armor of opinions all round him, and you cannot get through it. He has narrowed himself, and shut himself in, so that he feels no influence of sympathy coming from the wide ocean of humanity around, no influence of love from the deep heaven of God above. He is a sort of good rhinoceros, with a skin so thick that nothing can pierce it.

Nicodemus was such a man, and he came to Jesus with all his opinions cut and dried, ready for an argument. He begins in a very formal and precise way. "Rabbi, we know thou art a teacher come from God, for no man can do these miracles that thou doest except God be with him." He observes all proprieties; he calls Jesus Doctor,—"Rabbi,"—but takes good care *not* to call him Christ. He gives his reason for thinking Jesus a teacher come from God, namely, his miracles. Not his holiness, not his inspiration, not his supreme sweetness, not that he is a channel through which God's tenderness runs down into our hearts. No; he sees no such spiritual proof as this, but a merely logical one, expressed almost in the form of a syllogism. Major proposition—"No man can work miracles without God's help." Minor proposition—"Jesus works miracles." Conclusion—"Therefore Jesus has God's help."

Now, what does Jesus reply? Evidently much of the conversation has been omitted. We have only the substance of it here. "You believe in the kingdom of heaven, Nicodemus." "Certainly." "How do you expect to know it when you see it?" "By some great outward signs; something which shall shake heaven and earth; the Messiah coming in the sky, with angels." "Nicodemus, you cannot even see the kingdom when it is here, if you look for it so; you must be born again yourself; you must be changed, and become as a little child, in order to enter the kingdom." We remember that Peter, who was probably not half as good as Nicodemus, an impulsive soul, was nevertheless enough of a little child, in openness of heart, to see that this was the kingdom of heaven,—this teaching and life of Jesus,—and that Jesus was the Messiah.

But Nicodemus says, "No. A Gentile, a heathen, ought, no doubt, to begin at the beginning, give up all his old opinions, and be born of water by being baptized. He should begin by a recantation. I suppose that is what you mean by being born again. But *I* ought not, for I am a Jew, grown up in the true knowledge of God, learned from Moses and the prophets. So I need not begin *my* life again."

Jesus then replies, "The form is nothing. You must be born not only of water, but of the Spirit, in order to enter the kingdom of God. You need not only to wash off all your old opinions and conduct, as the Gentiles must do; but also you must be made a little child by laying your heart open to God's Spirit, and letting it lead your thoughts into new ways, your heart into new love, and your life into new action. You must be willing to follow me, not by night only, but in the day. If they turn you out of the Sanhedrim, you must not mind that; you must find your happiness in getting good and doing good; receiving God's love into your soul, and letting it go out again. You must give yourself up to this divine influence."

Then Nicodemus says, "*How* can these things be?" He wishes to see the way, to have it all marked out; to have a creed with all its articles of belief fixed; a programme of what he is to do arranged. The spirit he does not quite understand. Give it to him in the letter, and he can do it. He wants a map of the operations of the Holy Spirit.

"Are you a teacher of Israel, and do not know this?" replies Jesus. "The whole Old Testament is full of this inspiration; full of the Spirit of God coming and going, in a thousand ways, and not by any special rule or method; going as the wind comes and goes in the sky, we do not know whence or how." It is well that some things cannot be arranged beforehand—well that no almanac can tell if the wind to-morrow is to be east or west, north or south.

I sit in the sweet autumn woods. I see the squirrel leap from branch to branch. I hear the woodpecker tapping the trunk with sagacious beak, watching when the sound shall indicate that a worm has hidden himself below the bark. All else is calm and still. I look up and see the white clouds drifting through the deep ocean of blue above. Then there comes a sudden shiver through the tree-tops, a sprinkling of dry leaves on the grass, a whisper, a rush of air; and now every tree is swinging its branches in the breeze.

So is every one that is born of the Spirit! God comes to us all in these uncalculated, incalculable ways. He moves our conscience by the light of loyalty and fidelity in another soul. There comes through all the land a fresh breeze of justice and right, and all at once we feel that we ought to lead better lives, more manly, more true. There comes a revival of honesty, as well as of piety. Yesterday you did not care for it; now you do. God's holy air of truth and right is sweeping through the land. We all arise and say, "No matter what our fathers consented to; no matter what we have consented to in past times; we will have no more compromises with evil and sin, no more concessions to tyranny and cruelty." When this spirit comes to a nation, or to a community, it is as much a revival sent by God, as the reformation of Luther, or the reformation of Wesley.

Jesus means to teach us here that the Spirit of God comes in a great many different ways, comes unexpected and unforeseen, comes unapparent as the invisible air. So came the reformation of Luther. Luther did not mean to make a reformation, or to build a new Church.17

All recollect the story of the Quaker, George Fox, how he went from Church to Church, and got no good, and at last opened his soul to God, and was led by the Spirit into new and strange thoughts and purposes, and became a reformer, and founder of a denomination, unintentionally. And so the Quaker movement came—the most radical reform which ever sprang up in the Christian Church. It abolished the ministry and sacraments, baptism, and the Lord's supper. It reformed the theology of Christendom, putting the inner light above the written words. It reformed life, opposing war, oaths, slavery, and fashion. And as it came, so is it passing away, having done its work. As the breeze dies softly, and the leaves cease to glitter in the sunlight, and the red leaf on the top-most twig, far up in the sky, leaves off its airy dance, and at last hangs motionless, so the wild air which stirred in the depths of all hearts dies away in silence, and old opinions and old customs resume their places, yet all purified and changed. Only those which were so wholly dead that the wind blew them entirely away, are gone forever.

So are the changes which come in human hearts, we know not whence or how. It is a great mistake in the Church to have a stereotyped experience, to which all must conform. Procrustes only lopped the limbs to suit the measure of his bed; but these rules and moulds for the spiritual life, cut down the new man, who is made by God's Spirit, to the earthly standard of some narrow stunted experience of other times. This it is "to grieve the Spirit," and to "quench the Spirit." For God's Spirit goes everywhere, and where it goes it produces the best evidence of Christianity in sweet, holy, Christian lives. It is the wind which blows where it will, which does not run on a railroad through the sky, or stop at any particular stations in the clouds, or go by any time-table. God's Spirit comes and goes not according to any rules of ours. The publicans and sinners have it, and show it, sometimes, instead of the Scribes and Pharisees. For so the apostle declares that there are "differences of operation, but the same Spirit."

Sometimes you see a hard man, a man of the world, who has been fighting his way through life, till he has come to rely wholly on himself, and feels like some of those rocky reefs which stand out in the sea on our New England coast, and have borne the onset of a thousand storms. Yet at last he is softened. We see it, we feel it. There is a strange softness in his tone, a gentleness in his manner, a suspicion of moisture in his eye. The good God has been moving in his heart; perhaps it was by some trial or disappointment, or the loss of some curly-headed darling, who went up to heaven, and left the doors open behind, so that the joyful music which welcomed her came down to his ears and touched his soul.

When men see that, they say, "Well, there is something in religion, after all, if it can touch such a heart as his."

Sometimes we see a Christian who is at first all conscience, all work. Religion means to him, doing his duty. He intends to be a Christian, and wishes others to be so. But it is a piece of hard work. His Christianity reminds one of the poor woman who thought it "a chore to live." But after a while, we see a change—very gradual, but still very certain. He is beginning to get acquainted with the gospel side of Christianity. He learns to forgive himself his own sins, and so he can forgive others. His face begins to reflect more and more of heaven. It is the change which comes to the grapes in October. Perhaps you have some Catawba grapes on the south side of your house, and they grow very nicely all through the summer. They are good, large grapes well formed, good clusters, but very sour. But by and by there comes the final change; the juice grows sweet within the berry. There is but a very little difference in its appearance, but a very great change *within*.

When we see this alteration in a man, we say, "There is surely something in Christianity to produce such a change. Why, what a very sweet Christian he has grown to be!" It took all the summer and part of the fall to do the work; but no matter. God is not in a hurry. Some fruit ripens sooner, and some later; that is all.

I looked up from my table as I wrote these words, and saw from my window a tulip tree and a maple, each dressed in its royal robes of beauty— the gift of the declining year; the green leaves of the one touched with gold, and the other with its crimson and scarlet glories. They were full of sunlight, and made the whole landscape glad and gay. No Tyrian loom could rival the purple splendors and deep crimson of these trees. Why does God give all this varied beauty to the October woods, so that Solomon in all his glory was not arrayed like one of these oaks or maples? Is not this also to touch our hearts with a sense of his love? An autumn ride is also a means of grace; quite as much so, perhaps, as a tract or sermon. If we see God in nature, then nature may also be the source of a new birth to us.

"One impulse from the autumn wood

May teach us more of man,

Of moral evil and of good,

Than all the sages can."

What I understand Jesus, then, to teach in this passage, is, that we must become as little children, in order to see heavenly things; that, like new-born babes, we must receive meekly the milk of the word of God; that spiritual influences are all around us, invisible—incalculable: that not by the regular outward means of religion alone, but by a thousand other ways, God comes to us. He means that we should believe in the presence and nearness of God's Spirit always; that we should open our hearts and minds to be led by it into truth and love. He meant the very opposite of what he has been made to mean. He did not mean that all souls must pass through one and the same religions experience, but that, as the wind blows a thousand ways, so God's Spirit comes to the heart by a thousand ways. So coming, it makes the hard heart tender, the rude will gentle, the selfish soul generous, gives the reckless a new sense of responsibility. Jesus means that we should not be discouraged because we find it hard to correct our faults, or to enter into God's love. God's Spirit comes to us when we cannot go to find it. God's love comes into our hearts when we long for it, look for it, wait for it.

Look up, then, poor trembling heart; look up, and see God near. Look up, hard heart, and feel the soft showers of divine grace coming down to make everything tender. Look up, and be made new creatures, become as little children, be born anew, every day, into a fresh inspiration, faith, and hope; and so enter every day the kingdom of heaven!

§ 12. Evidences of Regeneration

The common Orthodox method is to require and expect evidence of the Christian change. As we have already said, a Christian is expected to know and to be able to tell when, where, and under what circumstances he entered into the new life.

But, perhaps, the preliminary question is, Ought we to have, and can we have, any evidence at all of the new life? And to this question many reply in the negative, and with very good reason.

The new life is a hidden life; a "life hid with Christ in God." Its essence is love, and love is an inward sentiment, not an outward act. Conviction demands utterance; actions speak louder than words; but love is accustomed to hide itself away in the heart, and to be known only to its object, and that indirectly. *Evidences of love!* What should we think of asking of young people coming to be married, the evidences that they loved each other; obliging them to give an account of their experience; to say when, where, and how they began first to care for each other; and then, if the evidence was satisfactory, allowing them to be married! Why, then, ask of the soul wishing to be united with God and Christ in a Christian covenant, to tear open the folded bud of this tender affection, analyze it metaphysically, measure it mathematically, and cross-examine it as a witness suspected of falsehood is questioned by lawyers before a jury?

What do we know of this new life? what can we tell of it? Almost always it comes to us gradually and unconsciously. It is veiled in shadows, misty lights, and neutral tints. The second life comes like the first. The child is born, and knows not of the awful change from not being to being—the immense event of passage from unconscious existence to conscious life. For consciousness dawns slowly, imperceptibly. The infant is long immersed in outward things. Years pass before it becomes aware of the fact that it exists, before it begins to look in and see itself in the mirror of reflection. So, probably, will it also be, when we pass from this life into the next. We shall, perhaps, awaken very gradually, in the future life, to the knowledge that we are in another state. As the little child becomes quite at home in this world before he thinks to ask how he came here, so probably in the other world we shall become quite at home with the angels, before we shall begin to say, "I am in heaven."

All the births of time partake of this quality. They do not reflect on themselves, are not surprised at themselves, but come as a matter of course. Years after, when the early heat of the new life has grown cold, the historians and biographers arrive to examine it in the crucible of their painful analysis, and to tell us how wonderful it is.

How can any man *prove that he is alive*? Why *should* he prove it? Let his life show itself, but not try to prove itself. Let its light shine, and those who see its good and joy will glorify the Father in heaven who has sent it.

The mistake here, as before, is in confounding conversion and regeneration.

Including in the terms "conversion" and "repentance" the whole activity of the will, the religious purpose, the aim of life, it is, no doubt, of the utmost importance to see, continually, what it is. "Know thyself" is a heaven-descended maxim, if we understand by it that we are to watch ourselves always, and see whither we are going. We need continually to know the direction of our life, whether it is *to* God or *from* him; whether it is upward or downward; whether we are following truth, and justice, and love, or following our own selfish desires and will. In this sense self-examination is both possible and necessary.

When the great ocean steamer is in the midst of the mighty Atlantic, it is necessary to watch continually its direction, and keep it always heading the right way. Day and night, therefore, the man stands sleepless at the helm, his eye always turning from the compass to the ship's head, with unfailing vigilance. But it is not thought necessary to inspect the interior of the boilers, or to examine the quality of the fire. If steam enough is made, and the wheels revolve, that is enough.

The new life into which we enter by the new birth has this one character—that it gives us for a motive, not fear, but hope; not law, but love; not constraint, but joy. Prayer is not a duty, but the spontaneous impulse of the child, to seek and find its father. Work is not drudgery but satisfaction, when the motive is to serve the great cause of Christ. The only real evidence, therefore, that we are born of God, is, that we have the fruits of the Spirit, love, joy, and peace. The tree is known by its fruits, and these are the appropriate fruits of the new life. When we find them, let us gladly receive them; but if we do not find them, let us at least be glad that if not yet new-born, we are, nevertheless, converted; if not sons, at least servants. We have the one thing needful when we have the right purpose; sooner or later, we shall also have the happy life. When we do right, we sow to the Spirit, and we shall, in due season, reap life everlasting.

As regards the evidence of the new life, too much stress, we think, has been laid on outward profession, ceremonies, religious language, religious acts. Because a man professes religion, it is no evidence that he is religious. Because he partakes of the Lord's supper, or prays openly, or speaks in the habitual religious language of his sect, it is no evidence of his religious life. Many persons are quite comforted if one who has led an immoral life says on his death-bed that he "trusts in the atoning blood of Christ." But this may be a mere word.

All ceremonies and prayers are means, but none of them are evidence, of a state. The only evidences are the fruits of the Spirit. "The tree is known by its fruits." "The fruits of the Spirit are love, joy, peace, long-suffering, gentleness, goodness, faith, meekness, temperance."

Let us remember that though a man may be converted, and not as yet be regenerate, he cannot be regenerate unless he is converted; that is, there can be no true piety, no love, no faith, no spiritual religion, except there be a sincere and determined purpose of righteousness beneath it. There may be true morality without piety, but there cannot be a true piety without a true morality. The law must precede the gospel. Conscientiousness must go before love, to prepare its way. "That is not first which is spiritual, but that which is natural, and *afterwards* that which is spiritual."

The *first* question, therefore, to ask ourselves, is not, "Do I love God?" but, "Do I obey God?" Every man's own soul, if sincere, can answer that question. "If our heart condemn us, God is greater than our heart." "If our heart condemn us not, then have we confidence towards God."

But if we are obeying God, then let us believe in a higher life which God has to bestow, and believing, seek for it. It is not earned, it is not a reward, it is not by works; but it is very nigh and close at hand; it is ready to be given to those who believe in it and look for it.

So, if the question be asked, "Is man active or passive in this process?" the answer is, that he is active in conversion, receptive in regeneration.

So in regard to faith and works. "We are justified by faith;" but justification is the sense of God's forgiving love which is received into an open heart. Justification is not salvation; it is only a step in that direction, and a preparation for it.

And now we ask, "Why is it, if this new life is a gift, do not all good men receive it?" The answer is, "There are conditions. All good men do not believe in it. Some believe that duty is every thing; that Christianity consists *wholly* in obedience. They know nothing higher, and therefore seek for nothing higher. Regeneration they hear of, but think it something mystical, miraculous, unnatural, and, to say the truth, not very attractive. If they believed in a life of love and trust, a life free from the burden of anxiety, they would surely desire it."

Those also who believe in it do not always believe it is for themselves. They think it not meant for common people in the midst of common life, but for some special saintship. They do not believe in this divine life flowing into every heart and soul, high and low, wise and ignorant, be it only sincere, honest, and believing.

Yet it is like the life of nature, which in the abounding spring-time comes down from the skies, and flows not only into the majestic tree, swelling at once its myriad buds, but also into every seed, and root, and weed, awakening them all.

This is what we need for peace, for real progress, for present comfort, for future joy.

It is communion with God, it is receiving his love, it is accepting his forgiveness, and living day by day as his beloved children.

Chapter VIII
The Orthodox Idea Of The Son Of God

§ 1. Orthodox Doctrine stated

Having considered the Orthodox idea of man in his natural state, and of man in his supernatural state, we next pass to consider the Orthodox idea of Christ's person and of Christ's work. In this chapter we shall consider the Orthodox view of the person of Christ, and ask what is its substantial truth, and what its formal error.

The Orthodox opinion concerning Christ is thus stated in the Assembly's Confession of Faith: "The Son of God, the second person in the Trinity, being very and eternal God, of one substance and equal with the Father, did, when the fulness of time was come, take upon him man's nature, with all the essential properties and common infirmities thereof, yet without sin; so that two whole, perfect, and distinct natures—the Godhead and the Manhood—were inseparably joined together in one person, which person is very God and very Man."

Christ, therefore, was perfectly God and perfectly man. The formula is, *"two natures, but one person."* The Orthodox doctrine is not of God dwelling in a human body as its soul (which seems to be the view of Swedenborg), but it is of God united with a human soul and body as one person or one consciousness.

§ 2. This Doctrine gradually developed

This idea of Christ, as we know, was gradually formed in the Christian Church, and did not become Orthodox until after many struggles. First came the question whether the Deity of Christ was equal or subordinate to that of the Father. Hardly had the Orthodox doctrine triumphed over that of subordination, against those who denied the equal Deity, than it was obliged to turn round and contend against those on the other side, who denied the humanity of Christ altogether. The Ebionites considered Jesus as a mere man. Theodotus, in the year 200, taught the same, with Artemon and Praxeas. In the next century the Arians and Sabellians opposed Orthodoxy from opposite sides,—the one confounding the persons of the Godhead, and the other dividing the substance. So for several centuries the pendulum of opinion swung from one side to the other before it rested in the golden mean of Orthodoxy.

The Nestorians separated the two natures of Christ, and maintained that his Divinity consisted only in the indwelling of God. But scarcely had Nestorius been banished for separating the two natures than Eutyches plunged into heresy on the other side, by confounding them together. This was the Monophysite heresy; and no sooner was this overthrown, and it was decided to be wrong to say that Christ had only one nature, than others began to contend that he had only one will. These were the Monothelites. But through all these controversies, the main doctrine of Orthodoxy continues to shine out luminous and distinct, asserting that Christ combines the fulness of Deity and the fulness of Humanity.

§ 3. Unitarian Objections

As this view of the Deity of Christ has been stated, it seems, in its doctrinal form, contradictory to Scripture as well as to reason. That the infinite God, who fills the universe, and sustains it; present in the smallest insect; present in the most distant nebula, whose light just arriving at our eye has been a million of years on its journey,—that this infinite Being should have been born in Palestine, seems to confute itself by its very statement. Who took care of the universe when God was an infant in the arms of the Virgin Mary? Jesus was born, and died; but God cannot be born, and cannot die. Jesus suffered from hunger, fatigue, and pain; but God cannot suffer. Jesus was seen by human eyes, and touched by human hands; but no man hath seen God at any time. Jesus had a finite body; but God is Spirit. Jesus was tempted; but God cannot be tempted with evil. Jesus prayed; but God cannot pray. Jesus said, "My Father is greater than I;" but God has no one greater than himself. Jesus said, "I can of mine own self do nothing;" but God can of his own self do everything. Jesus said "that he came down from heaven not to do his own will;" but God always does his own will. Jesus said that there were some things he did not know; but God knows everything. He declared that all power was *given* to him in heaven and earth; but God's power cannot be given to him. Scripture, therefore, as well as common sense, seems to deny the Orthodox doctrine of the Deity of Christ.

The common Trinitarian answer to these texts is, that Christ is speaking in his human nature when he asserts these limitations. But this answer, as Dr. Bushnell has well shown, is no answer; for, as he says, "it not only does an affront to the plain language of Scripture, but virtually denies any real unity between the human and the divine." Jesus does not say, "All power in heaven and earth is given *to my human nature*," but "to *me*;" and when the

Trinitarian himself declares that in Christ, with two natures, there is but *one person*, the question is concerning that one person, whether *that* is finite or infinite, absolute or dependent, omniscient or not so, omnipresent or not so, omnipotent or not so. The question does not concern his nature, but himself. The one person must be either finite or infinite: it cannot be both.

§ 4. Substantial Truth in this Doctrine

But now we ask, What substantial truth underlies this formal error? What truth of life underlies this error of doctrine? Let us remember how empty the world was of God at the time of Christ's coming. The wisest men could speak thus with Pliny: "All religion is the offspring of necessity, weakness, and fear. What God is,—if in truth he be anything distinct from the world,—it is beyond the power of man's understanding to know." All intelligent men agreed that if God existed he could not possibly take any interest in the affairs of the world or of individuals. Phariseeism on the one hand, and Sadduceeism on the other,—a religion hardened into forms, and an empty scepticism, cold and dead,—divided the world between them. But men cannot live without God, and be satisfied. They were feeling after him, if haply they might find him, who is not far from any one of us.

Then Christ came; and in all that he said and did, he spoke from the knowledge of God; he acted from the life of God. Here was one, then, at last, to whom God was not an opinion, but a reality; through whose life flowed the life of God in a steady current. We see that all sincere souls who came near Jesus received from him the same sight of God which he possessed; for faith in a living and present God is so congenial to the nature of man, that it carries conviction with it wherever it is not a mere opinion, but a state of the soul.

Those, therefore, who could find God nowhere else, found him in Christ. Those who saw *him*, saw the Father. As when through a window we behold the heavens, as when in a mirror we see an image of the sun, we do not speak of the window or the mirror, but say that we see the sun and the heavens, so those who looked at Christ said that they saw God.

The apostle said that God was in Christ; and this was wholly true. Christians afterwards said that Christ was God; and they thought they were only saying the same thing. They said that Christ had a divine nature as well as a human nature; and in this also there was no essential falsehood, for when we speak of our nature, we intend merely by it those elements of character which are original and permanent, which are not acquired, do not alter, and are never lost. God dwelt in the soul of Christ thus constantly, thus permanently. The Word thus "became flesh, and dwelt among us."

The word of the Lord *came* to the prophets, but it *dwelt* in Christ. He and his Father were one. The vital truth of all this was that men were now able to see God manifested in man as a living, present reality. "*Here,*" they said, "is God. We have found God. He is in Christ. We can see him there."

Is it any wonder that men should have called Jesus God? that they should call him so still? In him truly "dwelt the fulness of the Godhead bodily;" and this indwelling Spirit expressed itself in what he said and what he did. When Jesus speaks, it is as if God speaks. When Jesus does anything, it is as if we saw God do it. It becomes to us an expression of the divine character. When Jesus says to the sinner, "Go and sin no more," we see in this a manifestation not merely of his own compassion, but of God's forgiving love; and when he dies, although God cannot die, yet he dies according to the divine will, and thus expresses God's willingness to suffer for the redemption of the world.

§ 5. Formal Error of the Orthodox Statement

When we look at Christ's Divinity from this point of view, the distinction between the Trinitarian and Unitarian seems almost to disappear. Still the question remains, Is it right to call him God? The distinction remains between saying, "God was in Christ," and saying, "Christ was God." In short, was the *person* of Christ human or divine? We agree with the Orthodox in saying that Christ had two natures—a divine nature and a human nature. We also maintain with them that he had one person. But the question comes, Was that one person divine or human, finite or infinite, dependent or absolute? The consciousness of the one person is a single consciousness. Christ could not at the same time have been conscious of knowing all things and of not knowing all things, of having all power and of not having it, of depending on God for all things and of not depending for anything. One of two things alone is possible. Either Christ was God united with a human soul, or he was a human soul united with God. When Christ uses the personal pronoun "I," he must mean by that "*I*" either the finite man or the infinite God. I believe the Unitarian is right in saying that this personal pronoun "I" always refers to the finite being and consciousness, and not to the infinite Being. For example: "*I am not alone, but I and the Father that sent me.*" "*I proceeded forth and came from God; neither came I of myself, but he sent me.*" God cannot proceed from God; God cannot send God. Again: "If I honor myself, my honor is nothing; it is my Father that honoreth me." This cannot mean, "If God honors God, his honor is nothing; but it is God that honors him." It must mean that the human being, Christ, receives his honor from the divine Being. This view—that the person of Christ is human, but is intimately united and in perfect union with the indwelling God—makes all Scripture intelligible. Any other view is either unintelligible or contradictory. This view of the divine nature of Christ united with the human person, of God dwelling in the flesh, does not confound the mind like the common Trinitarian view, and yet has a value for the heart of paramount importance. If Christ is really a man like ourselves, made in all respects like his brethren, and yet is thus at one with God, thus full of God, it shows us that sin and separation from God are accidental things, and not anything necessary. If Jesus is truly a man, he redeems and exalts humanity. What he has been is a type of what all men may be. Thus the apostle Paul speaks when he says that all things were created in Christ, who is the beginning, the first-born from the dead, that he might go before us, or be our leader in all things; which is a much higher view than the common understanding of the passage, which merely supposes him to have been God's instrument in creating the physical universe. He is the image of the invisible God—the first-born of the whole creation. This creation is the new creation—that which is intended in Revelation (3:14), where Christ is spoken of as the Amen, the faithful and true Witness, the Beginning of the creation of God, and that which Paul means when he says that in Christ Jesus neither circumcision nor uncircumcision is worth anything, "but the new creation."

All such passages refer, as it seems to us, not to a past natural creation, but to a supernatural creation—a creation of life eternal, which, beginning in Christ, is to embrace the whole of humanity.

§ 6. Errors of Arianism and Naturalism

And we cannot but think this doctrine far truer, as well as more Orthodox, than the Arianism which so long struggled in the Church for supremacy. That view which supposed that Christ was neither truly man nor truly God, but some high, preëxisting being between the two, appears to us to be the falsest and most unsatisfactory of all the doctrines concerning Christ's person. It separates him more entirely from our sympathies than either of the others. It destroys both his divinity and his humanity, and, by giving us something intermediate, gives us really nothing. It makes his apparent human life a delusion, his temptation unreal, his human sympathies and sorrows deceptive. We think, therefore, that the Church was right in rejecting the Arian doctrine.

We think it was also right in rejecting the Humanitarian doctrine, or that of mere Naturalism. Christ was something more than mere man,—

something more than Moses and Elijah,—something more than a man of great religious genius. The peculiarity of Christ was, that he was chosen by God's wisdom, and prepared by God's providence, to be the typical man of the race,—the God-man, in whom the divine Spirit and human soul become one in a perfect union. He was, perhaps, placed, by an exceptional birth, where the first Adam stood,—rescued from inherited depravity, made in the image of God. Then the Spirit was given him without measure. The word of God *dwelt* in him, and did not merely come to him as a transient influence for a special purpose. Add to this a freely chosen aim of life, and a fidelity which was always about his Father's business, and aiming to finish the work which was given him to do, and we have a being in whom we can see either a manifestation of God or a manifestation of man. The Spirit in Christ was one with God; the soul and body were human.

Chapter IX
Justification By Faith

§ 1. This Doctrine of Paul not obsolete

That portion of the New Testament which speaks so earnestly of justification by faith is by many supposed to have become obsolete for all useful purposes at the present time. The doctrine that "we are justified by faith, and not by works," it is supposed, was intended for the benefit of the Jews alone, and to amount to this—that admittance to the privileges of the gospel is to be obtained, not by practising the ceremonies and external ritual of the Jewish law, but by a simple belief in Jesus Christ. Accordingly, as no one nowadays endeavors to become a Christian by practising the Jewish ceremonies, we suppose that there is no present need of this doctrine; and when we come upon it in the Scripture, we turn over the pages in search of something more practical and profitable. As, in the book of Acts, we read, that, "when Paul was about to open his mouth, Gallio said unto the Jews, If it were a matter of wrong or wicked lewdness, O Jews, reason would that I should bear with you; but if it be a question of words and names, and of your law, look ye to it; for I will be no judge of such matters," so we, when Paul is about to open his mouth to speak to us of this doctrine, think it a mere question of words and names, and of the Jewish law, and interrupt him to ask him for something *practical*. If he has anything to say to us of wrong-doing or wicked conduct, it would be reasonable to hear him; but we will be no judge of such matters as this.

There are also many persons, who, while they can understand the Gospels and enjoy them, find it difficult to understand and enjoy the writings of the apostle Paul. Among these writings, the most difficult is the Epistle to the Romans, and especially that part of it which treats of this doctrine of justification by faith. Anything which can be done to remove this difficulty will do good; for the writings of Paul are so intimately connected with the rest of the New Testament, that it is not easy to reject them, and yet to believe the rest. It can be done, no doubt; but it is done with difficulty. It is as if one part of the foundation of the house had given way: perhaps the house will not fall; but it has become unsafe. It is as if a part of the wall of a city had been battered down: the breach may be defensible from within; but it is also practicable from without. At all events, we miss the satisfaction of a complete faith, perfect and entire, round and full.

Besides, may there not be something important for us to know in this part of the New Testament? Are we quite sure we do not need these very doctrines, and that they will do us good?

We have said that it is sometimes thought that the questions discussed by Paul were only Jewish questions,—not human questions; that they belonged only to that time, not to all time. But, though the form which they assumed was temporary and local, there is reason to believe that the substance of the question is one belonging to human nature in every age; that it is the question of the spirit and the letter, the substance and the form, the root and the branches, the inside of religion and the outside. While contending against a particular Jewish error, the apostle unfolded principles by which similar errors may be opposed and refuted in every age.

At all events, it is a matter of fact, that there seldom has been in the Church any great religious movement which has not immediately gone back to the apostle Paul, and planted itself on his doctrine of justification by faith. This was the watchword of Luther, and the soul of the reformation. Luther and his companions armed themselves with this doctrine to contend against the great power of the Papacy and the Romish Church.

Let us, then, endeavor to see what we can of the truth there may be in this doctrine.

§ 2. Its Meaning and Importance

And, first, let us see what the doctrine does not mean, and what it does mean.

To be justified by faith does not mean that we are to be saved by our opinions. To say that a man can be saved by holding certain opinions, instead of certain other opinions, is to say what is contradicted by all experience; for experience shows us that there are good men holding every variety of opinion, and bad men holding every variety of opinion. But God saves men by making them good: therefore men are not saved by their opinions. Let us suppose that men are to be saved by the opinion that Jesus is the Christ: then we ought to find that all men holding that opinion are on the way of salvation; that is, are becoming good men. But this is far from being the case. In fact, the connection between mere opinion of any kind, and goodness, is very distant and indirect. No doubt, in the long run, opinion affects character; but it is only in the long run that it does so. And, at all events, the doctrine of the New Testament is very distinct and decided, that men may hold very sound opinions, and yet not be in the way of salvation. The Scribes and Pharisees held very sound opinions; and Jesus told his disciples to do whatever they said, but not to imitate their works; for their doctrine was much better than their lives.

Nor does the apostle mean to say that one can be saved without morality. He certainly does not mean to undervalue goodness; for, in that case, he would contradict his own teachings, which uniformly declare, as all the rest of the Bible declares, that without holiness no man can see the Lord. It is certainly a very superficial view which is satisfied with supposing that an earnest man, as the apostle certainly was, devoting his life, as he certainly did, to the teaching of Christianity, with such a grand intellect as he certainly possessed, could assert with so much energy a doctrine plainly contradicting common sense, daily observation, the plain teachings of Jesus, and his own uniform doctrine elsewhere.

Some persons have a short method of getting over the difficulty by saying that Paul did not himself know what he meant. They assume that he was talking at random. It would be about as wise, when we open Newton's "Principia," and cannot understand it, to say that Newton was talking at random; or, when we cannot understand Plato or some other profound metaphysician, to declare directly that he did not himself know what he was talking about. No doubt, this is the shortest and easiest way of getting out of such difficulties, but perhaps not the most modest, nor the most wise.

When an earnest man, a profound man, a man in the highest degree practical, a man who has done the greatest work for Christianity which has been done since its foundation, sums up his doctrine in a comprehensive maxim like this, it is, perhaps, wise to admit, at once, that he had a meaning, and probably an important one.

"No doubt he *had* a meaning," it may be said; "but has he any meaning *now*? His formula meant something for the Jews; but does it mean anything for us? Is not this merely a Jewish question, with which we have nothing to do?"

This is another easy way of getting over difficulties. In reading the New Testament, when we come to a place where we are stopped by something which looks deep and is dark, we are often told, "That darkness is not depth: it is the shadow of a Jewish error which lies across the path."

Have we not often felt dissatisfied, when, approaching some great saying of Christ and his apostles from which we hoped to gain new insight, we have been told, "That has nothing to do with *us*. The Jews had such and such an opinion, and this was meant to show them their mistake"? So the great and earnest words of the Bible, which we thought to be full of spirit and life, are found to be only fossil remains of old opinions, of opinions long since passed away—good for nothing but to be put into the museums of antiquaries, and paraded by scholastic pedants.

But, after all, take it on the lowest ground, were not the Jews men? Did they not, as a race, represent some element, common, in a less degree, to the rest of mankind? and therefore is there not in each of us something of that Jewish element? Are not we also sometimes Jews, therefore liable to Jewish errors, and needing to have them corrected? The Jews did not live in vain: their struggles, errors, hopes, were for the benefit of humanity. We were to learn something by their mistakes, and to be taught something by their experience.

Another way of treating such a passage is to translate it into some trivial, insignificant commonplace. Thus, we are told, our doctrine only means that *"God does not approve a man merely for going through a routine of outward, formal ceremonies, but for a thoroughly religious life."* This explanation assumes that the apostle is here talking to simpletons, and that what he says is no more worth listening to by us than the prattle of a nurse to her infant.

There are, therefore, four ways of explaining this passage, none of which are satisfactory. These are, that Paul,—

1. Was teaching a self-evident absurdity;

2. Was teaching a self-evident truism;

3. Was teaching nothing, and only talking at random;

4. Was correcting a Jewish error, which only the Jews ever had, or are ever likely to have.

If these views are not satisfactory to us, the simplest way would seem to be, first, to endeavor to understand precisely what the Jewish error was, and then to see if there is anything like it in ourselves, and if there be anything which we can learn from this old argument which will be, not old, but new for our time and for all time, because a part of the tendencies of man. Let us translate these old terms—*justification, faith, works*—into their modern equivalents, and see what they mean for us at the present time.

We have shown that we may be mistaken in supposing this Orthodox doctrine of justification to be of merely local and temporary interest, having no permanent value. It is not likely that a man like Paul, of so large, so deep, so philosophic a mind, should have devoted himself so earnestly, and returned so fondly, to a theme involving no universal and eternal principles, whose interest was to perish with the hour. It is not probable that, in this small volume of writings of the new covenant,—this precious gift of God to the world in all ages and in every nation,—so large a portion should be devoted to a wholly temporary argument; and, more than all, it is a most remarkable fact, that whenever there arises a man uniting a deeper spirit of piety with a larger sense of liberty than other men,—a man commissioned by God to give a new religious impulse to his age, and to help Christianity to shake itself free from the cumbrous mass of human forms and traditions which have crushed it, and to go forth in its native grace and loveliness again,—some profound instinct should always lead him to this doctrine as to a weapon effectual for pulling down the strongholds of bigotry, scepticism, and spiritual death. Sir James Mackintosh somewhere says, that the great movement which shook Christendom to its centre, and did more to change and reform society than the political revolutions and wars of a thousand years, originated with an obscure Augustinian monk preaching the doctrine of justification by faith. This acute Scotchman saw, what all must see who read Luther's writings with any attention, that it was no accident, no temporal interest, which led him to lay such stress on this doctrine. It was the soul of his preaching, the essence of his doctrine, the secret of his strength, the life of his life. And so, when Wesley and the early Methodists were called upon to pour new religious life into the English Church, they fell back on this doctrine—this ancient sword of the Spirit. And so we may believe that it has a value for all ages; that it did not relate merely to Jewish usages, but is a principle of vital and everlasting application.

No doubt that if by faith we understand intellectual belief, or the assent to opinions, and if by works we understand true obedience, and by justification final salvation or actual goodness, there can scarcely be a greater absurdity than to say that a man is justified by faith, and not by works. To say that goodness, in the sight of God, consists in receiving certain opinions, rather than in true obedience, is a most unscriptural and irrational doctrine.

But none of the great reformers of whom I have spoken, and no profound theologians of any sect or school, have ever held the doctrines of justification by faith in this way. Neither Luther nor Wesley ever made faith synonymous with intellectual belief or opinion. "What is faith?" said Wesley. "Not an opinion, nor any number of opinions put together, be they ever so true. A string of opinions is no more Christian faith than a string of beads is Christian holiness. It is not an assent to any opinion, or any number of opinions. A man may assent to three or three and twenty creeds, he may assent to all the Old and New Testament, and yet have no Christian faith at all."

But what is the true doctrine of justification by faith, as taught in the Scriptures, and as inspiring these great reformers? This is naturally our next inquiry.

§ 3. Need of Justification for the Conscience

There is nothing in the nature of man more paradoxical than conscience. It is that which lifts him to God; and yet it is that which makes him capable of sin, and without which he could not be a sinner. It gives him the sense of right, but at the same time makes him conscious of wrong. It makes him capable of duty, but thereby also capable of disobedience. It shows us what we ought to do, without giving us the least strength wherewith to do it. It condemns us for not doing right, even when we have no power to do anything but what is wrong. It shows us a great ideal of goodness to which we ought to aspire, and discourages us by the very loftiness of the standard. It tells us in the same breath that we are sinners, and that we ought to be angels. It seems at the same time to elevate and degrade us. It elevates us by giving a great object to life, and making it serious and earnest; but it degrades us by making us constantly ashamed of ourselves, and keeping us in a perpetual state of humiliation. Now, one of the chief peculiarities of the conscience is, that beyond a certain point, the more we try to obey it, the less satisfaction we have. We know that this is not the usual theory. We are commonly told that the conscientious man is always contented and happy,—satisfied with himself, and at peace with God. But facts contradict this theory. The conscientious man is apt to be very much dissatisfied with himself,—much, more so than the man whose conscience is torpid and indifferent. There is comfort in faithful work; no doubt there is great content in the steady performance of regular duties; but here conscience is subordinate to work. It is *work* which gives contentment; but conscience, when thoroughly roused by the strong meat of a divine law, is the source of much self-dissatisfaction. How can it be otherwise? It shows us that we ought to *love God and love man with all our heart, soul, mind, strength*. Which of us does it? Do you? Do I? How large a part of our life have we given to the service of God? how large a part to the service of our neighbor? How often do we thank God for his goodness? How often do we pray to him? how often *think* of him? If we do not think of him, of course we do not love him.

Love makes us very thoughtful of another's wishes. When people love each other, they joy in thinking of each other; they treasure souvenirs of each other; they like to make each other presents of things they think will please; they steal an hour from daily cares or nightly rest to write letters to each other. Our heavenly Father's arms are around us all day,—his infinite bounty blessing us, his careful providence making for us home, friends, all; yet we do not think of him, or wish to do anything to please him.

Conscience tells us that our heart is hard and cold to our best Friend; and that is by no means a pleasant piece of information.

Moreover, it is evident that this condition of self-dissatisfaction is not a good one. *Self-reproach may be a wholesome medicine, but it is a bad food.* We cannot do our work while we are finding fault with ourselves. The man whose conscience is always tormenting him is in a morbid state. He is a spiritually sick man,—sick of too much medicine. What must be done? He is always looking at his sins, and that disqualifies him for doing his duties. What shall he do?

This question in its Jewish form is stated thus: How shall he be justified before God? If God can excuse him, he can excuse himself. How, then, can he know that God looks at him not as a sinner, but as a just man, so that he can look on himself not as a sinner, but as a just man? This is the problem. What are its solutions?

In the Jewish mind, the Jewish law had brought the conscience into an extremely irritable state. The same effect, in a less degree, is produced by the Catholic confessional.

§ 4. Reaction of Sin on the Soul

Now, the consequences of sin are these: First, every act of sin brings after it natural evil consequences. It weakens the strength of the soul, it darkens the spiritual eye, it hardens the heart, it adds a new link to the chain of evil habit. By a result as inevitable as the law of gravitation, every act of sin pollutes, darkens, weakens the spiritual principle in man. "He who sows to the flesh shall of the flesh reap corruption." We may call these results the *external* consequences of sin, because they change our spiritual relation and position in God's external universe. But there is another more awful and as inevitable consequence of sin. It alienates us from God himself. It turns our face from the Source of life and love. It makes us at war with him. It fills us with the sense of his displeasure, and burdens us with the consciousness of guilt. To escape the dreadful sense of his anger, we hide ourselves from him, as Adam did. It is a law of the human mind that we dread the sight of any one whom we have wronged, because it condemns us. Perhaps he may be perfectly willing to forgive us; perhaps he does not even know that we have wronged him; but we cannot bear to see him, notwithstanding. It was a profound feeling of this law which led an ancient historian to say, "He hated him because he had injured him." Thus an active conscience, if it does not make a man better, will make him worse: to escape its torture he will plunge into new crimes. Some of the darkest crimes which stain the page of history may be traced to this source,—to the operation of a conscience strong enough to produce the sense of guilt, but not strong enough to produce the determination to reform. It is related that when the mother of Charles IX. of France and his uncles were urging the young king to consent to the execution of some of the principal Protestants to whom he was strongly attached, after a long resistance, when he at last gave way, it was with these remarkable words: "I consent, then, but only on one condition,—that you do not leave a Huguenot in France to reproach me with it."18 And hence the Bartholomew Massacre, which its authors had intended before only to include a few individuals. So sin takes occasion by the law, and the commandment ordained for life becomes death.

The same principle operates with respect to God. We have broken his law. We feel that he must be displeased with us; we therefore hide ourselves from him, turn away from him, avoid the thought of him, are alienated from him. This is the greatest evil of sin, and this we may call the inward consequence of sin, because it affects our inward relation to God rather than our outward relation to the universe.

And now, how are we to be reconciled to God? How are we to be freed from this sense of guilt which falls on us in his presence, and makes us fear and shun him?

§ 5. Different Methods of obtaining Forgiveness

There are two ways in which, when we have injured our brother, and so have become estranged from him, we may become reconciled again, and freed from a sense of shame in his presence. One is by endeavoring to atone for the evil we have done by acts of kindness, by expressions of penitence. So at last we may feel that we have done him far more good than evil; and though he may not forgive us or be reconciled to *us*, we, on our part, may feel freed from any shame in his presence, and be reconciled to *him*. The other way is by *his* coming to *us*, and *proving* to us, by his conduct and words, that he is not estranged from us by our bad conduct; that he loves us as ever. So he will overcome our evil by his good, and reconcile us to him.

The pagan nations in all ages and lands have taken the first way of being reconciled to God. Oppressed by a guilty fear of their terrible idols, they have brought as gifts to their altars what they had most valuable; they have hung their gold, their jewels, in the temple; they have slain their cattle on the shrine. Still unable to pacify their trembling hearts, they have gone farther, and sought to prove the sincerity at least of their repentance by self-inflicted tortures, and by giving even their children's lives to the bloody power whom they worshipped. Hence sacrifices: they originated in the very same feeling which induces a man to give a present to one whom he has wronged, to appease him.

Pagan religions are founded, therefore, wholly on the first mode of reconciliation. The offending party comes to him whom he has injured, and does something to pacify him. But these religions never brought peace to the heart of the worshipper. After the wretched mother had dropped her infant into the burning arms of Moloch, she still had no evidence that his wrath was turned away.

In the religion of Moses, the first mode of reconciliation was united with the second. Pitying the weakness of man, the law allowed him to bring his sacrifice of birds or beasts or the fruits of the soil, and place it on God's altar as an expiation and atoning offering for his sin; and then, the suppliant, having faith in the permanent presence of God in the holy of holies, was received again to favor and assured of pardon. The Jew, who had broken any of the laws of Jehovah, knew exactly what to do in order to be reconciled to his national God and King. God had pointed out the way which he would accept. By certain acts of sacrifice and restitution, the Jew became once more worthy of living under the protecting care of Jehovah.

This mode of reconciliation under the law was far superior to that in pagan religions. It gave temporary peace to the conscience, though not permanent. It prevented the sinner from going farther from God, though it did not unite him with God in unbroken union. It kept the conscience awake, and prevented it from being hardened. It was a schoolmaster to bring the Jews to Christ. It was a preparation for a more excellent way. In the Epistle to the Hebrews, the writer declares that the law was but the shadow of that which was to come; that it could not, "by the sacrifices offered year by year, make the comers thereunto perfect; for then would they have ceased to have been offered, because the worshippers, once purged, would have had no more conscience of sin." The sacrifice made no revelation of God's character and love, planted no root of piety in the heart: it relieved the conscience only for this once, only with respect to this one sin; and there its influence ended. And therefore was a new covenant necessary, and promised by the prophets, and looked forward to by holy men, when they should be reconciled not by works, but by faith.

We have seen that there are two modes by which alienation may be removed: first, by the offending party doing something to atone for his offence; second, by the injured one showing that he has forgiven the offence, and is ready to be reconciled without an atonement. The first mode is the way of reconciliation in pagan religions; the first and second are united in the Jewish religion; the second is the mode in the Christian religion.

§ 6. Method in Christianity

In Christianity, in the gospel of grace, God offers pardon freely to those who are willing to accept it. He is ready now to receive those who are ready to come to him. It is only necessary to believe this in order to be reconciled. We are, therefore, reconciled by faith.

But we are said to be reconciled by the death and blood of Christ. How is this? We have seen the source of our alienation: it lay not in God, but in ourselves. God had not gone away from *us*; we went away from him. He had not ceased to love us; but by a terrible reaction from our sinfulness, we had ceased to believe in his love. "God's hand," says the prophet (Isa. 59:2), "is not shortened, that he cannot save, nor is *his* ear grown dull, that he cannot hear; but *your* iniquities have separated you from your God, and your sins have hidden his face from you, that he doth not hear." By an immutable law of our mind, God's wrath abides on us, and we cannot believe in his love. Here is the source of our alienation. Now, merely to be told that God is merciful does not wholly help the matter. True, we say, He *is* merciful, but not to *us*; we have sinned too long and deeply. Something must be done, then, to *convince* us that God is ready to forgive and receive us freely. The death of Christ is the fact which produces this conviction. The death of Christ, therefore, is not merely an *emblem* of God's love, but an *act* of God's love. It draws us to him. It changes our hearts. It melts our doubt, our distrust. It reveals to us our Father's love. The blood of Christ makes those who were afar off nigh. This all experience teaches as a *matter of fact*. It is the cross of Christ, borne by the simple missionary, preached by the devout Moravian, which, amid the ice of Greenland or beneath the burning sun of the tropic, reconciles the sinner to God.

And if one asks *how* the death of Christ does this, we will briefly indicate what we believe to be the way in which it operates. We look at Christ, and see the brightness of God's glory and express image of his person. We see a holiness pure and perfect, a character infinitely beautiful and lovely. We see how dear and near such a one must have been to God; and we hear God say, "This is my beloved Son, in whom I am well pleased;" and we hear him say of God, "My Father has not left me alone; for I do *always* the things which please him."

And now we look at the world, and see it "lying in wickedness;" we see men trampling on God's law, polluting his image, cruelly oppressing each other, and boldly defying and mocking at the Almighty. What does he then? For the sake of these miserable, weak, and wretched sinners, who seem scarcely worth the saving, he sends his holy child among them; he sends this pure being to have his heart rent with the sight and knowledge of human sin; he sends him to be cruelly and shamefully killed by a death of agony, in order that *we*, sinful and miserable, may be reconciled. We say, in the view of all this, "He who spared not his own Son, but delivered him up for us, how shall he not *with* him freely give us all things?" We say, "God commended his love towards us, in that, while we were sinners, Christ died for us." "Herein is love; not that we loved God, but that he loved us." Christ, "being lifted up, draws all men unto him." Thus, in the midst of the gloom of that horrible scene on Calvary, when the power of darkness was at its height,—that crisis of the world, when human sin stood at the flood,—the heavens were opened, and a new ray of divine love poured into the world.

§ 7. Result

Let us sum up, then, the doctrine of justification by faith, as we have now explained it.

1. Justification is not the doing away with all the consequences of sin, but only the consequence which consists in present alienation from God. It is objectively, as a divine act, what *forgiveness* is subjectively, as a human experience. It relates to *present* acceptance with God; it is not the cancelling of the results of our past sins on the character, nor is it the hope of future salvation. It relates to the *present*.

The following passages show that justification is equivalent to reconciliation or forgiveness. Rom. 5:8-10: "But God commendeth his love toward us, in that, while we were yet sinners, Christ died for us. Much more then, being now justified by his blood, we shall be saved from wrath through him. For if, when we were enemies, we were reconciled to God by the death of his Son, much more, being reconciled, we shall be saved by his life." Rom. 4:6-8: "David also describeth the blessedness of the man unto whom God imputeth righteousness without works; saying, Blessed are they whose iniquities are forgiven, and whose sins are covered. Blessed is the man to whom the Lord will not impute sin."

2. Faith is not mere intellectual belief or opinion; nor is it mere feeling, nor a mystical emotion in which we are wholly passive; but a sentiment, in which belief, feeling, and determination are blended together. The belief is that Christ is the Son of God; the feeling is trust and joy in the love of God seen in him; and the determination is to rely on him as a Mediator and Saviour.

That faith is not a mere intellectual belief, but involves also a feeling of trust, appears from such passages as these: "If thou believe in thy heart;" "An evil *heart* of unbelief."

That faith is not a mere emotion, in which we are wholly passive, appears from such cases as those where men are exhorted to believe, as a thing in their own power.

3. Works, in this doctrine, include every effort to reconcile God by offering him anything in expiation of our sin, whether sacrifices, sacraments, the assent to creeds, the struggle after feelings and experiences, or reformation of character.

And the whole doctrine of justification by faith may be thus expressed:—

If you are burdened with a sense of unworthiness and guilt; if something seems to separate your heart from God; if you want confidence to come to him boldly in prayer,—do not try to remove this difficulty by any effort to do something different, or become something different; but simply look at Jesus in his sufferings and death, and see your heavenly Father calling you to him *now* to be forgiven. Go at once to God through Christ. Repose on that love that will cleanse you, that will save you; and nevermore doubt, even in your darkest hour, that your Father is ready to hear, to forgive, and bless you.

§ 8. Its History in the Church

We have seen the origin, nature, and value of this doctrine. Let us now look at its history.

The apostolic Church was founded on the simple doctrine of faith in Christ. It was not founded on any theory or speculation *about* Christ, or about his plan of salvation, but on *Christ himself* as the Saviour. All that the first Christians professed was faith in Jesus as the Son of God. They had been reconciled to God by him; they were at peace with God; they were washed in the blood of the Lamb; and they were happy. A deep and wonderful joy brooded over the early church. A hurricane of persecution and war raged around them: within the Church, all was security and peace. How beautiful are the expressions by which the apostles describe the serenity and joy of the Church! "They ate their meat in gladness and singleness of heart, praising God, and having favor with all the people." New converts "gladly received the word, and were baptized" by thousands, in the face of the bitterest persecution. "The multitude of them that believed were of one heart and one soul; neither said any of them, that aught of the things that he possessed was his own." Whence came all this peace and union in the early Church? Was it because they had attained to such clear views of truth, and all held the same opinions? So far from it, some had not heard that there was a Holy Ghost; others did not believe in a resurrection of the dead; and many thought the whole Jewish ritual essential to salvation. Was it that they had become suddenly pure in heart, and holy in life, and freed from sin? So far from it, we find the apostles exhorting them against very great vices,—against murder, theft, and licentiousness,—and condemning them for having practised gross immoralities. It came from the simplicity of their faith. They looked to Jesus, and their faces were lightened. They *saw* the love of God in him; they felt it in their hearts; they reposed on it undoubtingly. In quietness and confidence was their strength. O, happy days! in which men's minds had not yet been harassed by thousands of vain controversies and empty verbal disputes; by questions, and strifes of words; by most profound theological discussions, ending in nothing but weariness; but were satisfied, that, if men would go to Christ, they would find truth. O, happy time! in which men had not learned to dissect their own hearts, and pry curiously into their feelings, and torture themselves by anxious efforts to *feel* right, and tormenting doubts as to whether their inward experiences were as they ought to be, but believed that all good feelings would come in their own time out of Christian faith. O, happy, golden hour! when love, and joy, and duty were all one; when men did not prescribe for themselves and others a task-work, an outward routine of duties; but had confidence, that, if they lived in the Spirit, they would also walk in the Spirit.

That hour of simple, child-like faith passed away. Its decay appeared in a return to the old mode of justification. Instead of simply relying on what God had done, men must do something themselves to atone for their sins; they must do penance, and have priests, and sacraments, and masses, and countless ceremonies to come between them and God; they must pile up a cumbrous fabric of religious and moral works, by which to climb up to God; until, at last, though the doctrine of justification by faith was never given up, it was made of none effect by the rubbish of human ceremonies heaped before it. And then came Luther, armed with the old doctrine, to sweep these all away, and call men back to the simple faith in the Saviour. The pure word of faith went forth through all lands, conquering and to conquer.

But there is a continual tendency to fall back again from faith upon works. Ever as the life of religion weakens, ever as the strength of holy confidence decays, men betake themselves to some outward forms or efforts. When they cease to lean on the love of God, they begin to lean on sacraments and ceremonies, on opinions and doctrines, on feelings and experiences, on morality and works of duty. Ever, as the cold winter of worldliness and sin causes the stream of holy faith to shrink back into its channel, the ice of forms accumulates along its shores; and then, as the inevitable consequence and sign of the decay of faith, we find the Church becoming anxious and troubled, confidence giving way to anxiety, cheerfulness to gloom, hope to fear. Everything terrifies the unbelieving Church; new opinions terrify it; new measures terrify it. It has ashes instead of beauty, mourning for joy, the spirit of heaviness instead of the garment of praise.

§ 9. Orthodox Errors, at the present Time, in Regard to Justification by Faith

We have said that there is a constant tendency to fall back from faith to works of some kind or other. The important question comes, How is it with us *now*? Does this tendency show itself in our present churches? And the answer we am compelled to make is, that *it does*, certainly to some extent, and in all the churches. Orthodox churches have fallen away, more or less, from the doctrine of justification by faith. They have fallen back from the central point of Christianity, faith in Jesus, in different directions, and seek to be justified by a law,—some upon a law of belief, and others on a law of emotion.

Do not understand us as saying that any of the churches have denied, or that they do not constantly teach, the doctrine of justification by faith. This is not the point. The Romish Church never denied, nor ceased to teach, this doctrine; but she virtually abolished it, and made it of none effect by teaching other things also. Is not this, to some degree, the case now?

Are there not many Orthodox Christians, at the present time, who seek to make their peace with God, not by relying on Jesus himself, but on some theory with respect to his nature or person; not on his death, but on some speculation *about* his death,—some theory, scheme, or plan? Is it not the idea of many, that they are to be brought to God, not by faith in Jesus and his death, but by assenting to the correct doctrine about it? and accordingly they anxiously labor, and make it a work, to believe in the true theory, in order that they may be brought to God. We do not say that correct opinions on these points are unimportant; but we say that the faith in Christ which justifies us does not come from believing right opinions, but that right opinions come from the justifying faith. Are religious teachers now willing to do as Paul did, and say simply, *"Believe on the Lord Jesus Christ"*? or do they not rather find it necessary to say, "Believe this, that, and the other thing, about Jesus Christ"?

And again: is it not thought by Orthodox people, that, in order to be justified and have peace with God through Jesus Christ, it is necessary that a person should experience certain feelings, beginning with a sense of guilt, a fear of punishment, and passing into a state of hope and assurance? And, accordingly, men make it a work, and labor, to have these feelings in the precise order and manner, and, until they can experience these feelings, believe that they can have no access to God. As before, we do not mean that these feelings are unimportant, but only that we should not try to work ourselves up into certain feelings in order to be just before God. It is faith in Jesus which is the *source*, not the *result*, of piety as well as of holiness. It is faith in God's love to us which enables us to love him. The sense of pardon produces both the feeling of gratitude and of unworthiness. God does not forgive us because we have had the right feelings, but that we may have them. Those love much to whom much is forgiven; but to whom little is forgiven, the same love little.

Were we ever struck with the remarkable contrast between the conversions to God in the apostolic time and those which we hear of now? How much more *simple* they were! A man is riding in a chariot, reading his Bible, and trying in vain to comprehend it. An apostle comes, and explains to him the prophecy, and applies it to Jesus. Presently they come to water, and he says, "See, here is water;" he is baptized, and goes on his way rejoicing. We fear there are not many churches now who would receive that Ethiopian as a member, if he could give no further account of his religious experience than is recorded in the book of Acts.

But is it not, we say again, remarkable, that not only in this case, but in all the cases of conversion recorded and described in the Acts, there should be nothing of the descriptions which we read every week in our religious newspapers? In the case of the three thousand baptized on the day of Pentecost, we only read that they were cut to the heart; said, "What shall we do?" were told to repent and be baptized; joyfully received the word, and were baptized. Even the remarkable conversion of Paul was nothing like what we now have. How is this—that now we are not willing to trust to a simple act of faith in Jesus Christ, and in turning to God; but we have a scale and rule of religious experience—a work which all must go through in order to be justified?

And what is the result of thus substituting for justification by faith, justification by belief in opinions, and by processes of feeling? Look at the churches where this has been carried farthest, and see the result. Religion becomes gloomy, anxious, and austere; it ceases to breathe cheerfulness and joy around; the gentler graces die before it; fear treads fast in the footsteps of hope; a stiff formality introduces cant in the place of what is natural and artless; the heart is stretched on a rack of self-torturing doubts and anxieties. The biographies and private journals of many eminent saints show us how little happiness they had in their religion,—how they were tortured by spiritual doubts, perplexities, and anxieties. The reason is, that they rely on their *own* feelings, instead of relying on Christ.

And with the reliance placed on theory and opinion vanishes the union of the Church. There are five sects in this country, all holding to the Assembly's Catechism—a large and minute compendium of opinions,— and yet which often do not allow each other to commune at the Lord's table.

The New School Presbyterians might permit the others to commune with *them*, but are themselves excluded. The Old School Presbyterians would commune with all but the New, but are not permitted. Nay, the Associate Reformed, the Covenanters, and the Seceders carry it so far as to discipline and excommunicate their members for what is called *occasional hearing*; i.e., attending worship at other churches than their own. There was in the State of Indiana an Old School preacher, and president of a college, who refused to allow a Unitarian to give a literary address which the students had asked him to give, and which he had gone to deliver, and, in defending himself for this, called him a "public propagator of infidelity;" and within a mile or two of his college there was a society of Seceders, or Covenanters, holding, like himself, the Assembly's Confession, who would excommunicate any of their members who should go to hear him preach.

There is, then, a tendency among the Orthodox to rely on their own opinion and their own feelings, rather than on Jesus Christ.

§ 10. Errors of Liberal Christians

Liberal Christians have fallen into error of a different sort. They seek to be justified, not by opinion nor by feeling, but by action; by works of righteousness, honesty, charity; by the faithful performance of social duties; by an active obedience to the law of God. Looking at the Scriptures, and seeing in how many places we are plainly taught that we are to work out our own salvation; to be rewarded and punished according to our active goodness; to be judged by our works,—they say that a man is forgiven when he has corrected his fault, and not before; that repentance and reformation are the only means of atonement with God; that, if we wish to be forgiven, we must reform our conduct and change our character. Accordingly, they lay great stress on duty, and are continually exhorting men to the performance of their duties in order to be forgiven.

But there is a mistake here also, which arises from confounding two very different things; namely, justification and final salvation. We have seen that the consequences of sin are twofold—external and internal. The inward consequence of sin is separation from God; the external is the weakening and debasing of the soul. The first consequence is removed by faith; the second, by obedience. Every act of sin pollutes, darkens, and ruins the soul; every act of obedience strengthens, elevates, and saves it. Obedience, persevered in to the end, insures the salvation of the soul. But, in order that we may obey, we must first be justified; for what is to give us the strength and the heart to obey, except the pardoning love of God? It is this sense of reconciliation,—it is this spirit of adoption, whereby we cry, "Abba, Father,"—which gives us the power to obey. We do not obey God to be forgiven; but we are forgiven that we may obey. Have we read the Gospels, and have we forgotten all the instances in which Jesus said, "Thy sins are forgiven thee," before there had been any change of conduct, or reform of character? and have we forgotten the memorable passage in which he explains to the captious Pharisee why he does this (Luke 7:36-50),—on the principle that the one to whom the most is forgiven will love the most?

To point out to men their duties, and tell them to do them, does not enable them to do them; but the sight of God's love in Jesus Christ *does* create in them new strength. That true follower of Jesus, the first of our Ministers at Large, Dr. Tuckerman, did not say to the poor victim of sin, that when he reformed his conduct, he would be his friend. No: like his Master, he showed himself his friend while he was yet a sinner, and so gave him hope and courage to break away from his sin. He has left on record one of the most touching instances of the power of love to melt down the impenitent heart, in the case of a convict whom he persisted in visiting, though he was perfectly hardened, and filled with bitterness and rage. He persisted in patient attempts to soften his heart, till he succeeded, by the irresistible power of love, in making him humble as a little child. Suppose he had sent him word, that if he repented, and showed the proper spirit, he would come and visit him. He had not so learned God or Christ. He knew that he must overcome evil with good. Exactly so does God overcome our evil with good.

To tell men to do their duties that they may be forgiven, is to tell them to do what they have no power to do. A confident reliance on God's love, and steadfast communion with him, are the only source of real improvement. When we feel these, we are one with God; when we can go to him confidently, as children to a father; when we can betake ourselves to his love in every emergency of life,—we have a source of real strength, and growth, and improvement within us. But, without this feeling of peace with God, the effort to do our duties only harasses and irritates our conscience: it produces weariness of heart, a constant feeling of unworthiness and failure, a constant sense of obligations and responsibilities which we do not and cannot fulfil. Duty is a weary task, a heavy burden; and our life is crushed down by constant anxiety and care. But if we begin right, and come to God first, and lean on his love, and rely on his promise, then we are filled with hope and joyful assurance, and failure does not dismay us, for we say, "God's truth is pledged for our success; and if, while we were enemies, we were reconciled to God by the death of his Son, much more, being reconciled, we shall be saved by his life."

It may be objected that it is dangerous to religion to admit that we can be justified before we have believed certain important doctrines or experienced certain peculiar feelings. It may also be objected, on the other hand, that it is dangerous to morality to suppose that pardon can precede reformation. But the more we read the Scriptures, the more we look into our own heart, and the more we become acquainted with our fellow-men, the deeper is our conviction, that there is but one source of true piety and sound morality—a heart reconciled to God, and at peace with him. We do not undervalue correct belief, deep feeling, or active obedience; but we place them where they belong. They are the fruit of the tree, not the root of the tree. The root and source and beginning of all piety and holiness is simple faith in God through Christ. We must ask ourselves, therefore, first of all, "Are we reconciled to God, or are we not? Are we living in filial communion with him, or living without him in the world?" If unreconciled, we must not think to work ourselves up into a degree of goodness or pious feeling without God. There is no strength where there is no confidence, where there is nothing to lean on, where there is hollowness within. We ought to come at once to God. We ought to lift our hearts to him, not saying, "Who shall go up to heaven for us, to bring him to us? Who shall go over the sea for us?" For his word is very nigh, in our mouth and heart.

The above discussion will show what we consider to be the truths, and what the errors, in the Orthodox view of justification by faith.

Chapter X
Orthodox Idea Of The Atonement

§ 1. Confusion in the Orthodox Statement

The subject of this chapter is the Orthodox doctrine of the work of Christ, and especially of the atonement.

No doctrine of Orthodoxy is more difficult to state to the satisfaction of the Orthodox than this. The reason is, that there is no doctrine concerning which the Orthodox differ so much among themselves. There is no difficulty in stating the Orthodox doctrine of the Trinity; for this is the same, or nearly the same, in the symbols of all the Orthodox sects. The Roman Catholic doctrine of the Trinity is essentially the same with that of the Presbyterian, Lutheran, Methodist, and Episcopal Churches. But not so with the doctrine of Christ's reconciling and atoning work. This has taken every form in past history, and is altogether unsettled at the present time. Usually, many views are mingled together in modern Orthodoxy; and while all Orthodox teachers use the same language, speaking of the death of Christ as "atonement," "expiation," "vicarious sacrifice," "sin-offering," "substitution," "satisfaction," yet they connect with these words very different ideas. Such is the testimony of an eminent Orthodox divine, who speaks thus:—

"There is a general concurrence in the words *vicarious, expiation, offering, substitute,* and the like, but no agreement as to the manner in which they are to get their meaning. Sometimes the analogy of criminal law is taken; and then our sins are spoken of as being transferred to Christ, or he as having accepted them to bear their penalty. Sometimes the civil or commercial law furnishes the analogy; and then, our sins being taken as a debt, Christ offers himself as a ransom for us. Or the analogy of the ceremonial law is accepted; and then Christ is set forth as a propitiatory or expiatory offering to obtain remission of sins for us. Regarding Christ as suffering for us in one or another of these Scripture forms or figures taken as the literal dogmatic truth, we have as many distinct theories. Then, again, different as these figures are from each other, they will yet be used interchangeably, all in the sense of one or another of them. And then, again, to double the confusion yet once more, we have two sets of representations produced under each, accordingly as Christ is conceived to offer himself to Jehovah's justice, or as Jehovah is conceived himself to prepare the offering out of his own mercy.

"On the whole, I know of no definite and fixed point on which the Orthodox view, so called, may be said to hang, unless it be this, viz., that Christ suffers evil as evil, or in direct and simple substitution for evil that was to be suffered by us; so that God accepts one evil in place of the other, and, being satisfied in this manner, is able to justify or pardon.

"As to the measure of this evil, there are different opinions. Calvin maintained the truly horrible doctrine, that Christ descended into hell when crucified, and suffered the pains of the damned for three days. A very great number of the Christian teachers, even at this day, maintain that Christ suffered exactly as much pain as all the redeemed would have suffered under the penalties of eternal justice. But this penal view of Christ's death has been gradually giving way, till now, under its most modern, most mitigated, and least objectionable form, he is only said to have suffered under a law of *expression*.

"Thus God would have expressed a certain abhorrence of sin by the punishment of the world. Christ now suffers only as much pain as will express the same amount of abhorrence. And considering the dignity of the Sufferer, and his relations to the Father, there was no need of suffering the same, or even any proximate amount of pain, to make an expression of abhorrence to sin, that is, of justice, equal to that produced by the literal punishment of the race. Still, it will be seen to be a part of this more mitigated view, that Christ suffers evil as evil; which evil suffered is accepted as a compensative expression of God's indignation against sin. Accordingly, in the agony of Gethsemane, and when the Saviour exclaims in his passion, 'My God, my God, why hast thou forsaken me?' it will be taken for literal truth, that the frown of God, or divine justice, rested on his soul.

"It will probably be right, then, to distribute the views of those who are accepted now as Orthodox teachers, into two classes—one who consider the death of Christ as availing by what it *is*; the other, by force of what it *expresses*; the former holding it as a literal substitution of evil endured for evil that was to be endured; the latter holding it as an expression of abhorrence to sin, made, through the suffering of one, in place of the same expression that was to be made by the suffering of many.

"As regards the former class of representations, we may say, comprehensively, that they are capable, one and all, of no light in which they do not even offend some right moral sentiment of our being. Indeed, they raise up moral objections with such marvellous fecundity, that we can hardly state them as fast as they occur to us."19

§ 2. Great Importance attributed to this Doctrine

But, notwithstanding the fact that there is such confusion in the minds of the Orthodox about this doctrine, there is, nevertheless, no doctrine the belief in which is regarded as so important. With respect to other doctrines,—the Trinity, for example,—dogmatic Christianity declares our salvation to depend upon our belief of it; but in regard to the atonement, it goes farther, and makes our salvation depend on using the phraseology of the doctrine. Other doctrines will save us, on the condition of believing them; this, on the condition of using the language. If a man shall lead a life of purity and goodness, but expresses doubts concerning this doctrine, his Orthodox friends will have scarcely any hope of his salvation; but if the most depraved criminal, after a life steeped in wickedness, shall merely say on his death-bed, that he hopes "to be saved by the atoning blood of Christ," he is thought immediately to be on the fair way to heaven. No matter how good a man is, if he does not accept the Orthodox language on this point, his friends *fear* for him: no matter how bad he is, if he does accept it, they *hope* for him. There is a sort of magical power attributed to the very words. They are almost supposed to act like a talisman or a charm.

Now, while we reject all such superstitious views of the power of mere words, while we reject all false meaning and all no meaning, it is proper to think that there may be some substantial truth in these Orthodox opinions concerning the atonement. Let us endeavor to find what this vital truth really is, and why this doctrine is so dear to the heart of Orthodoxy.

§ 3. Stress laid on the Death of Jesus in the Scripture

Consider the stress laid on the sufferings of Jesus in the New Testament. Notice what our Saviour says himself: "This is my blood of the New Covenant, which is shed for many for the remission of sins." "The bread that I will give is my flesh, which I will give for the life of the world." "For as Moses lifted up the serpent in the wilderness, even so must the Son of man be lifted up, that whosoever believeth in him should not perish, but have eternal life." "I am the good shepherd: the good shepherd giveth his life for the sheep."

Consider, again, what is said on this subject in the Epistles. "Jesus Christ, whom God hath set forth as a mercy seat through faith in his blood."

"When we were enemies we were reconciled to God by the death of his Son." "He died for our sins." "He is sacrificed for us." "He gave himself for our sins." "We have redemption through his blood, even the forgiveness of sin." "Having made peace through the blood of his cross." "He gave himself a ransom for all." "He washed us from our sins through his blood." "By whose stripes we are healed." "Though he were a Son, yet learned he obedience by the things which he suffered, and being made perfect, became the author of eternal salvation unto all them that obey him." Again: "But we see Jesus, who was made a little lower than the angels, for the suffering of death, crowned with glory and honor, that he, by the grace of God, should taste death for every man. For it became him, for whom are all things, and by whom are all things, in bringing many sons unto glory, to make the Captain of their salvation perfect through sufferings." "Wherefore in all things it behooved him to be made like unto his brethren, that he might be a merciful and faithful high priest in things pertaining to God, to make reconciliation for the sins of the people. For in that he himself hath suffered, being tempted, he is able to succor them that are tempted."

These are some of the passages which connect the sufferings of Jesus Christ with sin on the one hand, and salvation on the other.

§ 4. Difficulty in interpreting these Scripture Passages

There is a difficulty, however, in understanding the meaning and feeling the force of such texts as these. This difficulty consists in the fact that these passages are constantly quoted as proof texts. From our childhood up we have heard them brought forward to prove the truth of some particular doctrine or theory of atonement, and when we read these verses, we immediately associate them with some doctrine which we like or dislike. Our feelings and prejudices are involved in interpreting the passage one way or the other, so that we are unable to look at it fairly. In order to overcome this difficulty, we must make this obvious distinction. We must distinguish between the statement of a fact and the theory concerning it. The fact which the Bible states is simply this—that the sins of man were the occasion of Christ's death, and that by his death he saves us from our sin. This is the fact which the Scriptures assert. The way in which he saves us is a matter of theory. Why it was that human sin made it necessary for Christ to die, how it is that his death reconciles us to God,—this belongs to the theory.

Now, while the Scriptures say a great deal about the fact that Christ's sufferings save us from our sins, they say very little as regards the way in which they save us from our sins.

§ 5. Theological Theories based on the Figurative Language of the New Testament

The Scriptures state the fact; the theologians have supplied the explanations. Innumerable have been the theories devised by theology to show in what way the sufferings of Christ have availed for the salvation of men—theories of imputation, theories of substitution, theories of satisfaction. He was punished in our place; he paid our debt; he was our federal head and representative; he satisfied the justice of God; he appeased the wrath of God. But especially are the figures and metaphors of the New Testament pressed into the service of theology, and made the basis of grave theories. Thus are metaphors turned into metaphysics, and rhetoric changed to logic. The images of the New Testament were naturally taken from familiar objects and transactions, especially from war, from slavery, and from the Jewish ritual. Sin is our enemy, who has conquered us in battle, and made us his prisoners. Christ redeems us from this captivity, and pays our ransom. Sin is a cruel master, and we are his slaves. He is about to torture us with the rod. Christ comes and takes our punishment on himself. He bears our stripes. According to the Jewish ritual the paschal feast was a commemoration of God's mercy. It was to the Jews what Thanksgiving Day is to the people of New England. So the Christians said Christ is our Passover. In the Jewish ritual God was believed to manifest himself over the mercy seat in the inner sanctuary of the temple. The Christians said, Christ is our mercy seat. All this was natural; but these images have been turned into elaborate theories by the theologians who have argued that Christ's death was a literal ransom, a literal mercy seat, and a literal passover.

These theories have mostly passed by. The common Orthodox theory in New England now is much more reasonable, but unfortunately much less scriptural. It is founded on the analogy of human government. God is compared to a wise and kind ruler, who governs by law, and who wishes to pardon the penitent criminal, but fears that if he does so, he will impair the respect felt for his law, and therefore thinks it necessary to do something to show the evil of disobedience before he can pardon. Christ is willing to die in order to make this impression on the minds of men. And this he accordingly does. But unfortunately, as we said, there is nothing in the Scripture, not even a metaphorical expression, to support this theory. The apostles did not have recourse for their figures and images to such usage of government, and that for the simple reason that no such usage or necessity then existed. The governments were all despotic, and no despot, wishing to pardon, had any difficulty on the ground that the sanctity of his laws might be impaired.

War, slavery, and the Jewish ritual, and household usages existed. Their images were taken from these. They spoke of ransom, of stripes, of the passover, and the mercy seat, of washing and healing, but not of governments and laws.

Sin is our conqueror, and Christ redeems us. Sin is a slavery, and Christ ransoms us. Sin is defilement, and Christ washes us. Sin is a disease, and Christ heals us. All this occurs again and again, but nothing occurs about constitutional governments, or conflicts between the claims of justice and mercy.

§ 6. The three principal Views of the Atonement— warlike, legal, and governmental

Three principal views on this subject have prevailed in the Christian Church as Orthodox. The first may be called the *warlike* view of Christ's work, the second may be called the *legal* view, and the third the *governmental* view. The first was the prevailing Orthodox view from the earliest times till the middle ages, and is based on the idea of a conflict or war between Christ and the Devil for the soul of man. The Devil had gained possession of the human race in consequence of its sin. The right of the Devil over men was fully admitted. Augustine considered it as the right of property, Leo the Great as the right of a conqueror. Christ gave his own life to the Devil as a ransom, which was adequate to redeem the whole race. This theory rested on the literal interpretation of the words "ransom" and "redemption." If Christ's death was a *ransom*, if he came "to give his life a ransom for many," the question naturally arose, "*From* whose power were men redeemed, and to whom was the ransom paid?" Certainly, men were not redeemed from the power of God. The ransom could not have been paid to God, but to some enemy who held us as his prisoners. The only possible answer, therefore, is, that the ransom was paid to the Devil. The Devil was the cruel tyrant who had enslaved us. He had a right to do so; for we had become his slaves through our sin. But he had no right over Christ, for Christ had committed no sin; so that the death of Christ was a free offering to the Devil to redeem the race. According to this view, therefore, the atonement was made to the Devil.

But in the middle ages another view of the atonement became Orthodox, founded not upon the idea of a ransom, but on that of a *debt*. According to this view the divine law requires that the debt which man owes to God, which is perfect obedience, shall be paid, either by himself or by some one else. Anselm, the founder of this theory, defined sin "as not giving to God his due." Man cannot pay this debt himself, and therefore Christ pays it for him. This is the legal view of the atonement, or perhaps we might rather call it the commercial view.

But this theory, after having endured as Orthodox for some five hundred years, gave place to a third, based not on the idea of a ransom or of a debt, but of a state necessity. It would not do for God, as a moral Governor, to forgive sin, unless by some great example an impression could be made of the evil of sin. This impression is produced by the death of Christ, who therefore died not to atone for past sin, but to prevent future sin, or, in other words, to make a moral impression on the human mind. This is the popular theory of the atonement held by the Orthodox at the present time. But it is very much mixed up with the others. The different views held by modern Orthodoxy range all the way from the old Calvinism of Princeton, through the various shades of New England theology, to the latest form expressed by Dr. Horace Bushnell in his recent work on "Vicarious Sacrifice."

§ 7. Impression made by Christ's Death on the Minds of his Disciples. First Theory on the Subject in the Epistle to the Hebrews

The sufferings of Jesus produced a wonderful impression on the minds of his disciples. This impression was compounded of astonishment, tenderness, and gratitude. That a man so divine in character, in wisdom, in a command over nature, should submit willingly to such labor, ignominy, and anguish, was a wonder to them. But there was a mystery of sorrow beneath the visible sorrow, a pain within the pain, a depth of grief felt not for himself, but for others, an anguish on account of the sin of the world, which especially awed and touched them. Christ plunged into the midst of sin to save souls, as a hero rushes into the midst of burning flames to save lives. No man like Jesus had ever felt such anguish and horror at the sight of sin; but instead of flying from it, he came into the midst of it to save the sinner. This was the secret of his agony, the bitterness of his cup. Martyrs at the stake are borne up by their own triumphant self-approval. But Jesus, in his anguish, did not think of his own triumph, but the sin and sorrow of those who afflicted him. "Daughters of Jerusalem, weep not for me, but weep for yourselves and your children." "Father, forgive them; they know not what they do." This is the secret of Christ's anguish—this infinite horror of sin joined to an infinite love for the sinner.

Through this depth of sorrow there came to the minds of the apostles a revelation of the evil of sin and the infinite compassion of God, which produced penitence, hope, and love. The dying Christ reconciled them to God. This they felt and declared; they did not attempt to explain how, but by images and metaphors drawn from all familiar objects, they declared that Christ's sorrows more than his glory, his patience rather than his power, his death more than his life, had withdrawn their hearts from sin, and given them peace with God.

One writer alone in the New Testament attempts an explanation of this influence. It is only an attempt, a mere hint, the germ of a theology: it is found in the Epistle to the Hebrews.20

According to these passages Christ suffered,—1. To learn obedience; 2. That he might thus become perfect; 3. By an entire cultivation of his sympathies with the tempted; 4. So as to become to them the author of eternal salvation by reconciling them to God.

This, we may observe, so far as it goes, is really a theory of atonement, and not a mere statement of the fact. Moreover, it seems to us to contain the germ of a far nobler and deeper theory than any in which the Church has hitherto believed. It is more human, more rational, connected more with real experience and the solid facts of life.

§ 8. Value of Suffering as a Means of Education

The sufferings of Christ were necessary for his own perfection, and suffering in some form or other is necessary for all perfection. It is often said that suffering in this world is casual, an accidental thing, arising from human mistakes, and that the time will come in which man will grow up into perfection without suffering. A perpetual sunlight is thought to be the best condition for the human plant. Pain and want stunt its growth, winter storms arrest its development; and so it is supposed that if we can get rid of this element of suffering, human beings will soon become all they ought to be. But the poet speaks more wisely who says,—

> "To each their sufferings: all are men
>
> Condemned alike to groan;
>
> The feeling for another's woe,
>
> The unfeeling for his own."

For suppose that we could remove from the world all outward evil— get rid of sickness, pain, poverty, death. Would not the worst part of evil still remain? Would not discontent, selfishness, envy, wilfulness, cruelty, self-indulgence continue? All these exist—perhaps exist most frequently— where there is the least of outward evil; and the outward evil is the bitter medicine which comes by and by as a cure.

§ 9. The Human Conscience suggests the Need of some Satisfaction in order to our Forgiveness

The central idea of the atonement is, that Christ has done something which enables God to forgive us our sin; and the reason why this doctrine of atonement seems so precious is, that we feel that there is a real difficulty in the way of forgiveness,—as if something else were necessary besides repentance,—as if some compensation or reparation should be made somehow to the offended law of God, or to the aggrieved holiness of God. We do not say that this feeling is a true feeling: that question we must consider afterwards. But it is, at any rate, a natural feeling, whether it be founded on our knowledge of God or our ignorance of God. It is hard to believe that a *man* whom we have injured will forgive us that injury merely because we ask him to do so, and are sorry for what we have done. We feel that we must make some reparation before he can or ought to forgive us. Unquestionably, the conscience is the source of this feeling. It led Zaccheus to say, "If I have done any man wrong, I restore him four-fold." A full reparation for an injury, accompanied with sorrow for having done it, the expression of which sorrow is confession, satisfies the conscience. Having done this, we feel that we have a right to be forgiven.

But it is very seldom that such full reparation can be made. The consequences of our wrong acts cannot usually be removed or effaced. Wrong-doing is like the gate of hell—easy to open, but difficult, if not impossible, to close again. "She opened, *but to shut* excelled her power." Instead of reparation, therefore, the conscience substitutes retribution—either reparation or the penalty; and the natural form of the penalty is an equivalent. Natural justice says, "An eye for an eye, a tooth for a tooth." This the conscience thinks right; this is justice. All less than this is mercy; all more than this is revenge.

We think that if we analyze the feeling which the conscience gives us concerning the consequences of wrong-doing, it is this: First, conscience demands reparation to the injured party; second, it demands punishment as a satisfaction to be made to the law of right, and this suffering to be accepted as just by the guilty party; and thirdly, it declares that guilt should produce an alienation or separation between the guilty party and those who are not guilty.

To illustrate all this, let us suppose a case. A man, hitherto respected and trusted by society commits some great breach of trust, and robs the community. What does the conscience in such a case demand? First, that he should give up his property, and make, if he can, full restitution; second, that he should endure some suffering—that he should not continue to enjoy, as before, all his accustomed privileges; and third, that he should not retain his standing in society, and receive, as before, the countenance and esteem of honorable persons. Conscience requires that he should make atonement to those he has injured by restitution; to the law of right, which he has offended, by suffering some punishment; and to honorable men by keeping out of their way.

This, which the conscience teaches of an injury done to man, it also teaches of an injury done to God. The offence against man is *a crime*; the offence against God is *a sin*. For a crime, the conscience requires restitution, punishment with confession, and alienation from the good, which is shame. For a sin, the conscience requires, in like manner, restitution, punishment, and alienation. It merely transfers to God's justice the ideas of atonement which human justice has given to it.

But God's justice is not like man's. The ideas of atonement so abstracted are essentially false; and to convince us of their falsehood is one of the objects of Christ's death. It is to show us that God does *not* demand this full restitution, does *not* intend to inflict this punishment, and is *not* alienated from the penitent sinner. The death of Christ has done this.

§ 10. How the Death of Jesus brings Men to God

As a matter of fact, the death of Christ has enabled men to come to God. "They who were afar off are made nigh by the blood of Christ." As a matter of fact, it has lifted men above the fear of God into the love of God. And this must be a divine work. Not the mere death of the human being could have done this; but the God who dwelt in him has uttered his tender love, his forgiving grace, from the cross. "God was in Christ, reconciling the world unto himself." The death of Christ is an expression of God's free grace. If we regard Christ, in his life and character, as a manifestation of God's will, then his pathetic and tender death reveals to us that God loves us even when we are sinners, before reparation or repentance; "for, while we were sinners, Christ died for us."

There is, however, a difficulty in *believing* that we can be forgiven. This difficulty is in the conscience; and,—

(*a.*) To say *there is no difficulty*, will not remove it.

(*b.*) To say that *repentance and good works* are enough, will not remove it.

(*c.*) To say that *God is merciful*, will not remove it; for the difficulty lies in the *conscience*, which declares that every sin is,—

1. An injury done to God.

2. An injury to the moral universe; inasmuch as it is an example of evil, and a defiance of right.

3. An injury to ourselves, by putting us away from God, the source of life, and alienating us from him.

Now, it is true that the New Testament says, "Repent, and be converted, and your sins shall be blotted out;" "Believe, and be saved." It is true that if we will believe ourselves forgiven, we shall be forgiven. But how can we believe it, when the inward voice of conscience is always saying that God ought not to forgive us without some reparation made for the injury done to himself, to the universe, and to ourselves?

We need something to believe in—some manifestation, some object. Something we need done by God to assure us that he is in earnest in desiring us to come and be reconciled to him.

Now, the *sufferings and death* of Christ seem to be this object: they enable us to believe in forgiveness, and so to be forgiven; they meet the difficulty of the conscience, and relieve it of its threefold embarrassment. For, in regard to the injury done to God, Christ's sufferings are substitution, or vicarious suffering. I do not say vicarious *punishment*. The innocent cannot be *punished* in the place of the guilty; but he can suffer, and constantly *does* suffer, in the place of the guilty. These two laws are announced in the Old Testament: "The soul that sinneth, it shall die;" "The wickedness of parents shall be on the children." If a man is alone, he must bear *all* the consequences of his sins; but if he have friends and children, they will relieve him of some by their self-sacrificing kindness: their *sufferings* take the place of his *punishment*. How often a wife does this!—interposing her sufferings between her husband's sins and their penalty. And what a profound impression is made by it of the evil of sin! It torments innocent women and children; it shipwrecks the peace of a family. What an effect is produced on the man himself! What a reproach and tender rebuke to him is this! The sufferings of Christ are *substituted* in this way for ours, according to this law; and this divine substitution is continued in the sacrifices of Christians. Missionaries and martyrs, by their zeal, patience, and generosity, carry out the sacrifice of Christ. This is God in Christ working in us and in the Church, and working for sinners.

Then, as to the *injury to the world* by the contempt sin does to the law, the sufferings of Christ are *satisfaction*: they satisfy the divine law; they make an impression of the importance of the law. But here, again, it is not merely Christ alone who does it, but God in Christ, and Christ in the Church, who honor the divine law by the respect produced for it. They bring us to repentance; they make us feel the sinfulness of sin; show us the misery it causes to those who love us,—how it pains God, pains Christ, pains the good, and pains our friends. So we feel it, and show it by true penitence, and so honor the law. The law is *satisfied* when the sufferings of Christ and his followers, caused by sin, lead men to abhor sin, and love righteousness.

As to the injury which *sin does to a man himself* by separating him from God's love, and making him at enmity with God, and God's wrath on him, the sufferings of Christ are *reconciliation*. "God was in Christ, reconciling the world to himself." Why was God alienated from man? Because he is holy. How can an unholy person be at one with a holy God? The answer is this: God comes into his heart by Christ, to form Christ within him, and to make him holy as Christ was holy. He sees that when united with Christ his sinfulness is killed in its roots, and a seed of perfect purity is planted in his soul; and so God is able to be at one with him through his union with Christ: "I in them, and thou in me, that we may be perfectly at one." A love for Christ in the heart forms Christ within us. He is our life, our motive power, our aim; and so he casts out the root of our sin, and brings us to God.

Thus we see that, even though we should reject all the Orthodox theories about atonement, we may accept the fact. We can believe that God in Christ *does* reconcile the world to himself,—*does* create a sense of pardoned sin,—*does* remove the weight of transgression,—*does* take away the obstacle in our conscience,—*does* help us into a living faith, hope, peace, and joy.

Moreover, Christ is really a sacrifice for sin—a real and true sin-offering. For what were the sin-offerings under the law? How did they remove sin? Not by themselves (it was impossible for the blood of bulls and goats to remove sin), but because they were an appointment of God, and so showed God's disposition. They showed that his holiness was displeased with evil; they showed that he loved the sinner, and wished to make him holy. So the death of Christ is a true sacrifice in exactly the same way, but in a higher degree, convincing us of the evil of sin and the love of God.

The experience of the whole Church teaches the power of this faith to create in our souls a new life of love. Seeing God coming to us in Christ to reconcile us to himself, and freely forgiving our sins, removes from our hearts doubt, anxiety, and the burden of hard responsibility, and fills the soul with a deep peace and joy in believing. So felt the apostle Peter when the Master forgave him his denial. From the fountain of that forgiveness flowed forth a river of devotion. So felt Paul when forgiven by Jesus; so felt Augustine, so Ambrose, so Luther, so Wesley: because they had been forgiven much, they loved much; for to whom little is forgiven, the same loveth little.

The practical conclusion is, that it is less important to speculate as to the *how*, than to endeavor to see the fact. What we need is faith in God's pardoning, redeeming, saving love in Christ Jesus—faith that our sins are blotted out; that we can come at once to our Father; that we can come boldly to the throne of grace; that the infinite Father looks at us with love when we are a great way off, and says, "This my son was dead, and is alive again; was lost, and is found."

We may therefore, when we are conscious of going wrong and of doing wrong, instead of trying to reform ourselves alone by our own strength, go first to God, and be forgiven through faith in the great sacrifice of Christ: "When God hath set forth to be a propitiation (or mercy seat), through faith in his blood, to declare his righteousness for the remission of sins that are past, through the forbearance of God, that he might be just, and the justifier of him which believeth in Jesus."

§ 11. This Law of Vicarious Suffering universal

Orthodoxy, in all its theories concerning the influence of the death of Jesus, has supposed his case exceptional and his work peculiar. It would be very shocking to most Orthodox minds to suppose that the same law of vicarious sacrifice applies to others; that the sufferings and death of the good, in all ages, have helped to atone for evil; have enabled sinners to obtain pardon. But such, we believe, is the fact.

Jesus Christ came, providentially, as the typical and perfect man—the one who was sent by God, in his providence, to illustrate what humanity is to be and to do. If this is so, then Christ did essentially nothing but that which is finally to be done by *all*, in some degree, or some way. He is a channel, a mediator, through whom God's life flows into ours; but then he makes us also mediators, by whom *his* life shall flow to others. He is the image of God; but every true Christian is, again, the image of Christ. For what Christ did, and was, was no afterthought, no exception, but a part of the plan of the universe. He was "foreordained before the foundation of the world, but manifest in these last times." He was the "Lamb of God, slain from the foundation of the world." That is, his coming, his character, his death, his resurrection, his miracles, were all a part of a divine law. And all God's laws are the same "yesterday, to-day, and forever."

If this were not so, we could not understand Christ, nor sympathize with him. His life would be, not only supernatural, which it is, but unnatural, which it is not. His miracles would be, not what they truly are,—God's higher life flowing into nature, and the Spirit overcoming the material resistance of things,—but they would be magical; they would be like sorcery and enchantment—violations of the course of events.

All of Christ's life, then, is typical of our future lives, in this world or in some other world. It would be easy to prove this out of Scripture. Everything asserted of Christ is, somewhere and in some way, asserted also of his disciples, and of all Christians. Is he said to be one with God? "I and my Father are one." They also are said to be one with God: "That they all may be one, as we are one; I in them, and thou in me. As thou, Father, art in me, and I in thee, that they also may be one in us."

Was Christ said to know all things? It is also said of his disciples, "Ye have an unction from the Holy Ghost, and know all things."

Did Christ work miracles? He says to his disciples, "Greater works than these shall ye do?"

Did God give to Christ glory which he had before the world was? He himself says of his disciples, "The glory thou gavest me I have given them."

Did Christ rise from the dead into a higher life? We shall do the same. "As we have borne the image of the earthly, we shall also bear the image of the heavenly."

Christ, in his high and perfect life, may be regarded as a prophecy of what man is to become: we may look on him as a revelation of the higher laws of human nature, as a type of all humanity.

As regards his atoning death, his reconciling sufferings, the same thing is true. As he died for man, so must we die for each other. Thus says the apostle John: "Herein is love; not that we loved God, but that he loved us, and sent his Son to be the propitiation for our sins. Beloved, if God so loved us, we ought also to love one another." And again, "Because he laid down his life for us, we ought also to lay down our lives for the brethren."

And Paul, after having spoken of "Christ's having made peace by the blood of the cross," says of himself that he rejoices in his own sufferings for their sake—rejoices to "fill up that which is behind of the afflictions of Christ;" that is, make up any deficiency in Christ's sufferings for them. "Christ's sufferings," he says elsewhere, "abound in us," his disciples. "We are partakers of his sufferings," says the apostle Peter. If he thought Christ's sufferings entirely different in their nature and meaning from all other sufferings, he would scarcely have said that he "partook" of them.

§ 12. This Law illustrated from History—in the Death of Socrates, Joan of Arc, Savonarola, and Abraham Lincoln

The death of Jesus, therefore, manifested in a higher degree the same law which is illustrated in the deaths of all good and great souls, martyrs to a principle, or to an idea. In proportion to the greatness and universality

soul became the leader of the armies of the Union, going before them to victory.

And how much, also, was Abraham Lincoln glorified by his martyr death! How he rose at once into a great figure in history—a monumental form before which enmity was silenced! All men forgot their hostility, their criticisms, their sneers—forgot that they had ever done anything but honor him. The assassin, who thought to revenge the wrongs of the southern slaveholders on Lincoln, gave to him a lasting niche in the temple of fame.

Now, we are not by any means *comparing* the work of these persons with that of our great Master, Jesus Christ. Such is not our object. We are only pointing out the law by which a person who has devoted himself to a great cause, when he comes to die in its service, gives to that cause an immense help, and seems to sanctify and glorify the cause and himself. There is a mystery about it which we do not fully understand, —which is not accounted for by saying that death proves a man's sincerity, and makes him a more competent witness, or that death conciliates his enemies, and puts an end to personal dislike. No; there is something more than this. When men live for a cause outside of themselves, when they labor for public objects, they are not *seen* while they live. Those whose interests are interfered with by their action, misrepresent them, and surround them with a cloud of suspicion, jealousy, and slander. When they go to death for their cause, all these slanderous voices are hushed, and they emerge from this cloud of prejudice, and are seen as they are. They are glorified then in their cause, and their cause is glorified in them. The cause for which Socrates lived was the education of the people of Athens to truth and justice. All the Sophists were his enemies. Aristophanes ridiculed him as no other reformer has ever been ridiculed, holding him up, by his inimitable wit, to the scorn of the crowded theatre. When he died, and died in the faith, all this ended. Socrates and his great cause of justice rose at once, and drew all men to them. So Savonarola, who lived only with the purpose of helping on the triumph of pure religion in the Church, and pure liberty in the state, was mocked and abused in his life; but his death made him an undying power, and being dead, he spoke across the rapid years to Martin Luther and the reformers who came after. John Brown lived and died for universal freedom; Abraham Lincoln lived and died for the existence and deliverance of the nation. Of them, exactly as of Christ, we may say that when they died the hour came for them to be glorified. They died, and they rose again. The resurrection, in these instances, came close after the crucifixion; not seen in their cases, as is that of Jesus, by the visible eye, but essentially the same thing inwardly as his. They and their cause went *up*, instead of going down, by their death. When they were lifted up, they drew all men to them. In all such deaths, also, there is a certain atoning, reconciling influence. Death brings together, in harmony, conflicting interests; it silences hatreds, and breaks down many a partition wall of separation.21

The difference between Christ's death and all of these is, that Christ lived and died not merely for popular education, for patriotism, for philanthropy, but to be the power of God for the salvation of the world; to found a universal religion of love to God and man; to reveal God as a Father, not a King; to show man to man as brother. But the effect of his death, as in all these other cases, was simply to glorify his life and his cause. The same law worked in his case and in theirs, only on a higher plane, and for a vastly greater object.

We may observe that most of the passages concerning the effect of Christ's death are from the apostle Paul. They are written thirty years after that death by one who probably had never seen him, at least never knew him. But Paul had seen the actual effect of the death of Jesus on the minds and hearts of the people. It was a reconciling effect; it did away with their hatred to his religion, and enabled them to see it, and be led by it to God. It made "those who were afar off, nigh." It made peace between man and God,—between man and man. When Jesus died, men's eyes seemed at once to open, and they saw for the first time the beauty and holiness of his life. His death, therefore, did what his life had not done. We, misled by a false theology, imagine Paul to be speaking of some transcendental transaction in the spiritual world by which the death of Jesus acted on God's mind to make him placable; whereas, in truth, he is speaking of the simple historic fact that the death of Christ did draw men to his religion, and so to God; did, therefore, bring them to see God's forgiving love; did unite them with each other. So Paul says that he "is not ashamed of the cross of Christ,"—not ashamed of the fact that Christ was hanged as a malefactor, since that very death was the power of God to bring man to salvation. It made men just, and kind, and true, and so was the power of God.

§ 13. Dr. Bushnell's View of the Atonement

In his book, lately published, Dr. Bushnell teaches that the vicarious sacrifice of Jesus consists in his sympathy with sinners. He suffers with them and for them, as a friend suffers for a friend, or a mother for a child,—in the same way, and in no exceptional or uncommon way. He did not die officially, but naturally. He did not come here to die, but he died because he was here.

We are persuaded that this is the right view. We are sure that one day we shall all see that Christ's sufferings and death, and their influence, are as simple, as natural, as wholly in accordance with human nature, as that of any other saint or martyr; that the difference is of degree, not of kind; and Christ will go before the world, its great Redeemer and Leader, all the more certainly because one of us,—educated, as we are, by trial and sorrow; tempted as we are, but without sin; crying out, as we do, from the depths of our despair, "My God! why hast thou forsaken me?" and rising, as we do, through death to a higher life, through sorrow to a completer joy, through the pains of earth to the glories of heaven. "For it became him for whom are all things, and by whom are all things, in bringing many sons unto glory, to make the Captain of their salvation perfect through suffering; wherefore in all things it behooved him to be made like unto his brethren, that he might be a merciful High Priest; for in that he himself hath suffered, being tempted, he is able also to succor those who are tempted. For we have not a High Priest who cannot be touched with the feeling of our infirmities, but was in all points tempted as we are, yet without sin; who can have compassion on the ignorant, as he also himself is compassed with infirmity, and though a Son, yet learned obedience by the things he suffered."

§ 14. Results of this Discussion

The Orthodox doctrine of the atonement contains a fact and a theory which ought to be carefully discriminated. *The fact* asserted by Orthodoxy is, that Jesus Christ has done something by means of which we obtain God's forgiveness for our sins. *The theory* attempts to explain what is the difficulty in the way of our forgiveness, and how Christ removes it. Thus Orthodoxy attempts to answer three questions: "What?" "Why?" and "How?" The first of these regards the fact. "*What* has Christ done?" And the answer is, that he has brought to man forgiveness of sin. The second and third questions regard the theory. "*Why* was it necessary for Christ to do and suffer what he did?" and, "*How* did he accomplish his work?"

Now, as concerns the matter of fact, Orthodoxy is in full accordance with the Scriptures, which everywhere teach that through Christ we have redemption, through his blood, even the forgiveness of our sins. But the Scriptures are perfectly silent concerning the theory. They do not tell us *why* it was necessary for Jesus to die, nor *how* his death procured forgiveness. The only exception is, as we have seen, in the statement, in the Epistle to the Hebrews, that the sufferings of Christ were necessary to make him perfect, and to enable him to be touched with a feeling of our infirmities.

Of the three theories which in turn have been regarded as Orthodox in the Church, two have completely broken down, and the third rests on such an insecure foundation that we may be very sure that it will follow the others as soon as any better one comes to take its place. The warlike theory and the legal theory of the atonement have gone to their place, and are no more believed by men. The governmental theory must soon follow.

Nevertheless, in each of these three theories there is one constant element. And it is due to Orthodoxy to state it. This element is, that the necessity of the death of Christ lay in the divine attribute of justice. According to the first theory, Christ died to satisfy what was due by God to the Devil; according to the second, he died to satisfy what was due by God to himself; according to the third, he died to satisfy what was due by God to the moral universe. Divine justice, in the first theory, owed a ransom to the Devil, which Christ paid; in the second, it owed a debt to the divine honor, which Christ paid; in the third, it owed protection to the universe from the danger of evil example.

The difficulty to be removed before God can forgive sin, lay, according to all of these theories, in the divine justice. Christ died to reconcile justice and mercy, so as to make justice merciful, and mercy just.

But, in opposition to this view, the Unitarian argument is so formidable as to seem quite unanswerable. On grounds of reason, the Unitarian maintains that there can be no such conflict among the divine attributes, waiting till an event should occur in human history by which they should be reconciled. That God's justice and mercy should have been in a state of antagonism down to A.M. 4034, when Jesus died, is an incredible supposition. No event taking place in time and space can be the condition *sine quâ non* of divine perfection. And any struggle or conflict like that supposed implies imperfection.

Moreover, the Unitarian truly maintains that the Orthodox theory that men cannot be forgiven on the simple condition of repentance, is wholly unscriptural. The Scriptures plainly teach that forgiveness follows repentance. In the classic passage of the Old Testament (Ezek. 18:20-32), the Jews were taught, unequivocally, that the death which is the wages of sin, is always removed by the simple act of repentance. If the modern doctrine of Orthodoxy be true, that in order to be saved it is necessary not only to repent, but also to believe in the atoning sacrifice, the Jews were fatally misled by this teaching of the prophet.

And so in the New Testament, the parable of the prodigal son teaches us plainly that when we repent and return to God, we shall be received, and that without any reference to belief in the atonement.

Moreover, the Unitarians are fully justified in saying that the New Testament nowhere asserts that the primary and immediate influence of the death of Jesus is upon the divine attributes. In every instance Christ is said to reconcile us to God, never to reconcile God to us. (See Rom. 5:10, 11; 11:15. 2 Cor. 5:18, 19, 20. Eph. 2:13, 16. Coloss. 1:20, 21. 1 Peter 3:18.) It is we "who were afar off, and have been made nigh, by the blood of Christ." It is *we*, "who, when we were enemies, were reconciled to God by the death of his Son;" not God, who was afar off, who has been brought nigh to us; not God, who has been reconciled to us. It is "*we*, who have received the atonement." Christ has suffered for sins, "to bring *us* to God," not to bring God to us. All this is plain, positive, and unequivocal.

And yet, notwithstanding that the Old and New Testaments declare the forgiveness of sin to the penitent, we nevertheless find a difficulty in believing it. It seems as if God *ought* not to forgive us our sins on so simple a condition. And it is on this very feeling that the whole Orthodox theory of the atonement rests.

The explanation of this is, that man is obliged to understand God by himself. Since man was made in the image of God, he can know God only by understanding the moral and spiritual laws of his own soul. Now, in himself, he finds the constant antagonism of truth and love, justice and mercy, conscience and desire. From this essential original antagonism of truth and love spring all the moral conflicts which make cases of conscience. Whenever we see before us a divided duty, on being analyzed, it resolves itself into this conflict between truth and love. We naturally, and almost necessarily, transfer this same conflict to the mind of God. Whenever we wish to forgive an offender, but feel as if we ought not to do so, we teach ourselves to regard God as feeling the same difficulty. Conscience tells us that we are not fit to be forgiven, that it would be wrong for God to forgive us. Orthodoxy plants itself on this instinct, and elaborates its various theories, which men accept for a time as a sufficient explanation of their difficulty, and then reject when their inconsistencies appear. The deep-lying difficulty is the sense of our want of holiness, and the instinctive feeling of the eternal mutual repulsion of good and evil. Since God is good, and we are evil, how can he forgive us? If forgiveness merely meant the remitting of penalty, it might be done after sufficient expiation. If forgiveness meant laying aside of anger, we can well believe that God cannot retain wrath against his children. But forgiveness means communion, the mutual love of father and child, the being always in the presence of God. And for this, even after we have repented, and are endeavoring to do right, we do not feel ourselves qualified.

This is the real difficulty. Christ did not die to pay a debt to God, or to appease his wrath, but "to bring us to God," and to put the Spirit into our heart by which we can say, "Abba, Father!" The atonement is made to the divine justice—but not to distributive justice, which rewards and punishes, but to divine justice in its highest form, as holiness. And this consists in making us fit to appear before God, notwithstanding our sinfulness, because we have received a principle of holiness which will ultimately cast out all our sin. When we have faith in Christ, we have Christ formed within us, the hope of glory. God, looking on us, sees us not as we are now, but as we shall be when we are changed into that same image from glory to greater glory.

This suggests the theory which may replace the rest, and reconcile all those who believe in Christ as the Saviour and Redeemer of men. Christ saves us by pouring into us his own life, which is love. When Christian love is formed within us, it has killed the roots of sin in the soul, and fitted us to be forgiven, and to enter the presence of God.

In conclusion, we may say that Orthodoxy is right in maintaining that Jesus has by his sufferings and death brought forgiveness to mankind—not by propitiating God or appeasing his anger, not by paying our debt or removing a difficulty in the divine mind, but by helping us to see that the love of God is able to lift us out of our sin, and present us spotless in the presence of his glory with exceeding joy. The way in which his death produces this result is the sympathy with human sinfulness and sorrow, which finds in it its highest expression. Those whom men cannot forgive, and who cannot forgive themselves, see that God, speaking through the sufferings of Jesus, is able to forgive them. So the love of God brings them to repentance, and those who were afar off are made nigh by the blood of Christ.

Chapter XI
Calling, Election, And Reprobation

§ 1. Orthodox Doctrine

The Assembly's Catechism, with its usual frankness, states this doctrine thus:—(chap. 3).

I. "God, from all eternity, did, by the most wise and holy counsel of his own will, freely and unchangeably ordain whatsoever cometh to pass, yet so that neither is God the author of sin, nor is violence offered to the will of the creatures, nor is the liberty or contingency of second causes taken away, but rather established.

II. "Although God knows whatsoever may or can come to pass upon all supposed conditions, yet hath he not decreed anything because he foresaw it as future, or as that which would come to pass upon such conditions.

III. "By the decree of God, for the manifestation of his glory, some men and angels are predestinated unto everlasting life, and others foreordained to everlasting death.

IV. "These angels and men, thus predestinated and foreordained, are particularly and unchangeably designed, and their number is so certain and definite, that it cannot be either increased or diminished.

V. "Those of mankind that are predestinated unto life, God, before the foundation of the world was laid, according to his eternal and immutable purpose, and the secret counsel and good pleasure of his will, hath chosen in Christ unto everlasting glory, out of his mere free grace and love, without any foresight of faith or good works, or perseverance in either of them, or any other thing in the creature, as conditions or causes moving him thereunto, and all to the praise of his glorious grace.

VI. "As God hath appointed the elect unto glory, so hath he, by the eternal and most free purpose of his will, foreordained all the means thereunto. Wherefore they who are elected, being fallen in Adam, are redeemed by Christ; are effectually called unto faith in Christ, by his Spirit working in due season; are justified, adopted, sanctified, and kept by his power through faith unto salvation. Neither are any other redeemed by Christ, effectually called, justified, adopted, sanctified, and saved, but the elect only.

VII. "The rest of mankind God was pleased, according to the unsearchable counsel of his own will, whereby he extendeth or withholdeth mercy as he pleaseth, for the glory of his sovereign power over his creatures, to pass by, and to ordain them to dishonor and wrath for their sin, to the praise of his glorious justice."

This statement is contained in the creed of more than three thousand churches in the United States. So far as it is believed by those who profess it, it conveys the idea of a God who is pure will — a God, in short, who does as he pleases, saving some of his creatures and damning others, without reason or justice. He does not reward virtue nor punish sin, but scatters the joys of heaven and the torments of hell out of a mere caprice, as an Eastern despot gives a man a purse of gold, or inflicts the bastinado, without reason, simply to gratify his sense of power. The essential character of such a Being is arbitrary will, and this creed of Calvinism places an infinite caprice on the throne of the universe, instead of the Being whom the Gospels call "Our Father."

Let us see how far this view of God is mitigated by modern explanations.

The Old School Presbyterianism, or Princeton Orthodoxy, accepts it in its entireness. They simply deny the consequences supposed to be drawn from it. They deny that it makes God the author of sin, or that sinful dispositions are created by God. They deny that this doctrine interferes with freedom of will in man. But they are obliged to admit that, according to their creed, God decrees things which he forbids; for, "inasmuch as many things occur contrary to his commands, while yet he foreordains all things, it must be that in these cases he purposes one thing and commands another."22 In other words, God sends his prophets, and apostles, and Son, to command men to do justly and love mercy, when he has already determined that they shall commit sin. This school rejects the Arminian doctrine that God's decree is founded on his foreknowledge, and asserts that his foreknowledge is based on his decree.

The Old School in New England do not go quite so far as Princeton. They say, decidedly, that God foreordains sin only by permitting it. Still, they reject, as stoutly as their sterner *confrères*, the Arminian view, and insist that God's decrees are not based on his foreknowledge.23

According to Dr. Duffield, of Detroit, the New School Presbyterians escape the pinch of this conflict by taking refuge in their ignorance. They are not "Ultra-Calvinists," and they are not "Arminians," and especially they "do not wish to be wise above what is written."24 Dr. D. asserts that the Old School makes the decree in election to be wholly arbitrary, while the New School believes that it has a reason, though one wholly unknown. But the Hopkinsians25 say that "the sovereignty of God belongs to him as the Supreme Disposer, and consists in his perfect right and perfect ability to do us he pleases." Of course, having made the will of God wholly arbitrary, they proceed to deny that it is arbitrary, or that wilfulness in God can possibly be wilful. But all this is using "words of wind for the Almighty," and "accepting his person."

Methodism, on the contrary, denies that God foreordains whatsoever comes to pass, holding foreordination to be a causative act.26 It also denies that man is guilty for inherited sin, or is any way responsible for his depraved nature. He only becomes responsible when he begins to act freely. He may suffer for inherited evil, but cannot justly be punished for it. Thus Methodism avoids the rude injustice of the Calvinistic system. And yet, as Schleiermacher has shown,27 if it accepts total depravity, it must also consistently accept the Calvinistic doctrine of election. For if man is totally depraved, he cannot take a single step towards his own salvation. God must, in every case, take the initiative, and begin the conversion of each man who is converted. Therefore, if we ask why one man is converted, and another not, the only answer possible is this—that God chose to convert one, and not the other. Schleiermacher accepts and defends the doctrine of election, but by connecting it with that of universal restoration, which reduces it to the statement that God saves all, but in a certain order, which order is determined by himself, without regard to any foresight of merit or demerit in man.

§ 2. Scripture Basis for this Doctrine

The principal passages relied upon for the doctrine of absolute decrees are found in Rom. 8:30, and 9:8-24. In these passages, Paul is, no doubt, speaking of an unconditional election. In the first, he declares that the gift of Christianity to those who received it was no accident. God had known them long ago as individuals, known them before they were born, known the character they were to have. He had foreordained them to become Christians, to be made into the likeness of Christ. He had called them to be Christians by his providence; he had forgiven them their sins; he had glorified them, filling them with the glory of the new life of faith and love. In the other passage, Paul shows the Jews that God selects races and families, not according to any merit of theirs, but for reasons of his own, to do his work. Ishmael as well as Isaac was a child of Abraham, but Isaac was selected. Esau as well as Jacob was a child of Isaac, but Jacob was selected. It is no merit of the man which causes him to be chosen, no fault which causes him to be rejected, but that one is made for the work, and the other not. One is influenced to obey and serve; one is allowed to resist God's will; and yet both of them—he who obeys and he who resists—serve the divine purpose. The Jewish Christians, therefore, may believe that their nation, in resisting Christ, is blindly serving the providential designs of God, and making way for the Gentiles to come in; and then, the Gentiles, in turn, will help *them* to come in, "and so all Israel shall be saved." But in neither of these passages is any reference to final salvation or damnation. All that is spoken of is the predestined and divinely arranged order, the providential method, in which gifts are bestowed and opportunities offered. In fact, in Rom. 11:28, election is formally opposed to the gospel. As regards the gospel, or the reception of Christianity, the Jews are *enemies*; that is, are left out of the circle of God's gifts, in order that the Gentiles may come in. But as regards the election, they are still the chosen people, inheriting all the qualities, powers, position, which their fathers had before them, since God never takes back his gifts.28 So also in Ephesians 1:5, 11, Paul says that we, Christians, have been chosen in Christ before the foundation of the world, and predestined to be adopted as children, and obtained an inheritance in Christianity. But neither here is anything intended concerning final salvation. It all refers to their having received the gift of Christian faith, in the plan of God, by a wise providence of his, and not by accident. So also, in Timothy (2 Tim. 1:9), Paul says that God hath saved us out of the world, and called us to be Christians, not because of any merit of ours, but simply according to a gracious purpose which he always had, that the Gentiles should come into his kingdom with the Jews. In none of these passages is any final doom or destiny hereafter intended: *all of them* refer to the gift of Christianity in this world. The apostle softens the exultation of the Gentiles, and consoles the sorrow of the Jewish Christians, by telling them that the acceptance of the Gentiles and rejection of the majority of the Jews is part of a great plan of Providence, which will finally redound to the good of both.

§ 3. Relation of the Divine Decree to Human Freedom

In order that God shall be the Ruler of the world, and its providence, he must know the course of events, and determine them. In order that man shall be responsible, and a moral being, he must be free to choose, at every moment, between right and wrong, good and evil. In part of his nature and life, man is a creature of destiny; in part, he is the creator of destiny. Every man's character is the result of three factors—organization, education, and freedom. The character he has now has come to him, partly from the organization with which he was born, partly from the influences by which he has been educated, and partly from what he has done or omitted to do at every moment of his life. Now, the two first of these factors are out of his power. A man born in Africa, or descended from Chinese parents, cannot, by any choice or effort, become what a man born of French or German parents may become. A man born among the Turks or Arabs, and educated by the circumstances surrounding him there, *must* be a wholly different man from one born in New England. Man's freedom, therefore, may be likened to the power of the helmsman to direct a vessel. He cannot determine what sort of a vessel he shall be in, nor what sort of weather or currents shall come: all he can do at any moment is to steer it to the right or left. If, now, in steering, he guides himself by a compass turning to a fixed point, and by a chart giving the true position of continents and islands, then this power enables him, in spite of storms and calms, to take the vessel round the world, to the harbor he seeks. But if he has no chart and compass, but steers as he chooses from moment to moment, he goes nowhere. His vessel will then drift before the steady winds and constant currents. So is human freedom a great power when it guides itself by eternal truths and fixed laws. But if it does not, then it is not freedom, but only wilfulness, and it accomplishes nothing. Man's freedom is thus surrounded by divine providence. God determines the original organization of every human being; God determines the circumstances which educate him; and God has fixed the laws by which he must guide himself in order to become really free. He cannot therefore resist the divine will, except temporarily. He can postpone the *time* when God's kingdom shall come, and his will be done; but that is all.

§ 4. History of the Doctrine of Election and Predestination

Before Augustine, all the Greek and Latin Fathers of the Church taught the concurrence of free will and grace in human conversion. They taught that man must begin the work, and that God would aid him. God and man must work together.

Then came the controversy between Augustine and Pelagius. The latter, being at Rome, heard this sentence read from the writings of the former: "*Da quod jubes, et jube quod vis*" —Give what thou commandest, and command what thou willest. Pelagius objected to this formula. He said, "Since man ought to be without sin, he can be without sin." "There is," said he, "in man, a '*Can Do*,' a '*Will Do*,' and a '*Do*.' " The first is from God; in the others God and man unite.

Augustine objected that God worked in us both to will and to do. He had first taught that God sends motives which we can obey or resist; but he saw that if God works in us to will, he must also conquer our resistance, and work the power by which we consent.

But to this Pelagius replied, "Then there is no freedom in man."

Augustine answered, "God does not move us as we move a stone, but rationally; he makes us *will* what is good, and does not force us against our will. He frees the will from its proclivity to evil, by 'preparing grace,' and determines it to good by 'effecting grace.' That some do not yield to this, is not because of their greater resistance, but because God does not choose to conquer their resistance."

This is the point where grace passes into predestination.

The Old Church had maintained that God predestined to life those whom he *foresaw* would repent and obey him. His foreknowledge did not cause this to happen, but he foreknew it because it would happen. It did not take place because he foresaw it, but he foresaw it because it would take place.

Election, according to the early Fathers, was nothing arbitrary. It depended on man to be saved or lost. So taught Justin Martyr, Origen, Basil, Hilary.

Basil said, "God hardened Pharaoh's heart by his judgments, which were sent to show how hard it was, because he saw he would not repent."

Origen adds, "Like a wise physician, God did not cure Pharaoh too soon, for fear of a relapse. He let him drink the cup of sin to the bottom in this life, so as to cure him more thoroughly hereafter."

Pelagius (and Augustine at first) took the same view. They said that God foresees and permits evil, and decrees the consequence of it.

Augustine said, "God has chosen some men in Christ, not because he foresaw they would be good, but because he determined to make them so." The reason of this choice, therefore, lay not in man, but in God's arbitrary will.

Pelagius said, "This is fatalism, under the name of grace, and is saying that God accepts the persons of men."

Augustine answered, "All men in Adam are in ruin. God saves some of them. If he let *all* die, we could not blame him: how much less for saving some!"

But why does he *not* save all? The answer is, —

Because the elect see in the fate of the non-elect what they have escaped, and God's justice is revealed with his goodness.

None of the elect perish, though they may die unbaptized, and be ever so bad in their lives; but they will be all converted before they die.

The non-elect may be often better men than the elect; but they will not be saved.

The only place where Augustine allows freedom is in Adam, who might have turned either way.

Semi-Pelagianism consists essentially in saying, "Man begins the work; God aids him."

Augustine's view was carried out afterwards thus: "If God does all, it is no use to preach, exhort, or read Scripture, or use any means of grace."

Augustine had said that reprobation was not a decree to sin, but to punishment.

But Gottschalk, his follower, said it was a decree to *sin*. The Church rejected this statement, and softened the doctrine. Thomas Aquinas revived it again.

Luther and Calvin both maintained that there is no good in man after the fall. Flacius said that original sin is the substance of human nature, and human nature now bears the image of the devil.

Luther made freedom of the will to consist in doing evil with pleasure, and not by constraint.

Calvin denied that there is any free will. "Why give it such a lofty title?" he said. He seemed to think that all the power left to men is so much taken from God.

When God says, "Do this and live," it is, says Luther, merely irony on his part, as though he had said, "See if you can do it! Try it."

Luther actually taught that God's will in revealed Scripture was, that all should be saved, but his real and secret will was, that *not all* should be saved.

Melancthon said, "Man has no power by himself to do right; but when grace is offered, he can receive it or reject it."

Calvin went beyond Augustine. He taught that,—

1. The decree of predestination was not merely a decree to punishment, but to sin. He rejects with scorn the distinction between permitting and causing, between foreknowledge and predestination. He says it is improper to have God's decree waiting on men's choice.

2. He taught that Adam's sin was decreed by God. The Infralapsarian taught that God foresaw that Adam would sin, and so decreed some men to life, and others to death. The Supralapsarian taught that God determined to

reveal his majesty, and mercy, and justice. He created men, and made them miserable to show his mercy, and made them sinful to show his justice.

3. If men complain that God has so created them, Calvin answers, God has the same right that the potter has over the clay. If they complain that God has chosen some, and not others, to life, he replies, that so oxen, horses, and sheep might complain that they were not men.

4. God causes the sin which he forbids. This is not a contradiction in him, for his nature is different from ours.

God created all for his own glory, and sinners to glorify his justice.

Finally, Calvin himself admits that this is "a horrible decree."

§ 5. Election is to Work and Opportunity here, not to Heaven hereafter. How Jacob was elected, and how the Jews were a Chosen People

This *reductio ad absurdum* disproves the common idea of election. If a man were elected by God to heaven, and so could not help going to heaven, it would not be worth his while to give diligence to make his calling and election sure. It is sure already, without any diligence.

The common Orthodox idea of election is, therefore, a false one. God does not elect, or choose us, for passive enjoyment, but for active duty. He elects us to opportunities. He elects, or, as we may say, selects, us for certain special work, gives us certain special privileges, and holds us to an accountability for the use of them.

In the parable of the talents, God elected, or selected, one man to the possession of five talents, another to the possession of two, and another one. Each was elected; but each was elected to opportunities, and each to a different opportunity; but they all had to give diligence to make their calling and election sure.

The word "elect" was first applied to the Jews. They were an elect or chosen people. They were selected from among all nations for a great duty and opportunity. They were taught the *unity of God* and his *holiness*. They were a city set on a hill, a light shining in the darkness of the world, to proclaim these truths. That was their opportunity. It was not happiness, or heaven, or even goodness, that they were chosen for, but work. As long as they continued to do this work, they continued to be God's chosen or selected people. But when they hardened into the bigotry of Phariseeism, and froze into the scepticism of Sadduceeism, when they ceased to do the work, then they ceased to be the elect people. While they were diligent to make their election sure, they were the elect, but no longer.

God selected Jacob and rejected Esau. "Jacob have I loved, and Esau have I hated." But how did God love Jacob? He loved him by giving him opportunity. And why? Not because he was better than Esau, but because he was different. Jacob was selected to be father of the chosen people because he had the qualities required for his work. Esau was wild, reckless, martial. Jacob was industrious, money-making, fond of small trade; pastoral, rather than warlike; tenacious of his ideas even to obstinacy. These were the qualities required in a people who were so few that if they had been warlike they would have been swept from the earth. They never fought for the pleasure of fighting, but only when they could not help it, or when a political necessity compelled it. Though surrounded by nations much more powerful than themselves,—the Assyrians on the north-east at Nineveh, the Egyptians on the south-west, the Babylonians on the east, the Tyrians on the west, and the Greeks on the north-west,—they saw the fall of all these great nations and empires, but they continued. Many waves of war swept over their Syrian hills, and left them still there, peaceful, industrious, worshipping Jehovah in their sacred city, offering no motive for conquest, too poor to tempt invasion, too far from the sea to grow rich by commerce, like the Phœnicians. Their obscurity, poverty, and unheroic qualities were their salvation, and these they derived apparently from Jacob, their ancestor.

Thus we see that the Jews were a chosen people, and we see what they were chosen for, and also that they were chosen not because of superior virtue, but for superior capacity.

§ 6. How other Nations were elected and called

Other nations were chosen, too, for other purposes. The Greeks also were a chosen people—chosen to develop the idea of beauty, as the Jews that of religion. Their mission was beauty in art and in literature. It was no accident that they came as they did from confluent races, flowing together from India and Phœnicia, and settling in that sweet climate and romantic land, where the lovely Ægean, tossing its soft blue waters on the resounding shore, tempted them to navigation, and awakened their intellect by the sight of many lands. There they did their work. They made their calling and election sure. Greek architecture—one birth of beauty after another— was born. Athens was crowned with marvellous temples, whose exquisite proportions amaze and charm us to-day—inimitable creations of beauty. Homer came, and then epic poetry was born. Æschylus and tragedy came; Pindar and the lyric song; Theophrastus and pastoral music; Anacreon and the strain which bears his special name. And so Phidias and his companions created sculpture, Herodotus history, Demosthenes oratory, Plato and

Aristotle philosophy, Zeuxis painting, and Pericles statesmanship. This was their election, and they made it sure.

The Romans also had their chosen work. They were elected to develop the idea of law. A prosaic people, but filled with notions of justice, they developed jurisprudence. To show that a nation can be governed not by despotic will, nor by popular will, but by law,—this was the office of Rome. As long as it did this work it prospered; when it ceased to do it, it fell. All other races, no doubt, have their special calling too. Some make it sure; others seem to fail of making it sure, and so disappear. Thus the election of the Jews shows a principle of God's government, and is not an exceptional case.

That which is true of nations and races is also true of religions and of Christian denominations. All Christians are a chosen people. They are chosen for the work of teaching to the human race the great doctrines of the fatherhood of God and the brotherhood of man. Other religions were sent to men too. Mohammed had his mission—to convert the idolatrous Arabs to Monotheism. The religions of Asia were intended to prepare the way for Christianity by teaching the elementary ideas of religion and morality.

§ 7. How different Denominations are elected

Every great denomination, and small ones, too, are chosen to unfold some one Christian idea. The Catholic Church was chosen to carry forward the great central idea of unity—one Lord, one faith, one baptism. But the Catholic Church is not catholic enough: it has turned itself into a sect by excluding those who could not accept all its statements and methods, though they accepted Christ. The Jewish Church committed the same mistake. When it became narrow, bigoted, exclusive, it left its first love; it then ceased to enlarge itself, and was obliged to disappear. The Jewish religion, and all positive religions, are like vases in which a plant is growing. While the plants are young, they hold them easily; but as the plants grow, the vases, incapable of expansion, are shivered by the enlarging roots. So that, unless the Roman Catholic Church can be liberalized and enlarged, it must break to pieces.

Whatever is said of Jews as the chosen and elect people is intended to show us a principle which must be applied to others. It is a principle very visible in their case, but not confined to them. It is the law of divine Providence. By what we see of its working in their case, we are able to see it in other cases, where it is less distinct and less apparent.

§ 8. How Individuals are elected

And now let us apply the doctrine of election to individuals. When one is elected he is always elected to some special opportunity, which he can improve or not, and for which he is held accountable.

When God sends into the world a great and original genius, like Columbus, Sir Isaac Newton, Dante, Shakespeare, Mozart, Michael Angelo, Franklin, Washington, Byron, Napoleon, it is very plain that they are sent, provided with certain qualities, to do a certain work. It is evident that God meant Columbus to discover America, and Dante to write a poem. If Columbus had tried to write the "Inferno," and Dante had devoted himself to inventing a steam-engine, if Franklin had written sonnets and pastorals, and Isaac Newton had gone into trade, if Washington had composed symphonies, and Beethoven had travelled to discover the source of the Nile, they would not have made their calling and election sure. But such men (with an occasional exception, like that of Napoleon and Byron) were all faithful to their own inspiration, and each chose to abide in the calling in which he was called; and so each did the work God gave him to do in the world. Napoleon and Byron did their work only partially, for they allowed their egotism to blind them, so as to lose sight of their mission after a while. God sent Napoleon to bind together and organize the institutions of a new time—to organize liberty. He did it for a season, and then sought, egotistically, only to build up himself and his dynasty; then his work came to a sudden end. For it is vanity and egotism which make us fail. We wish for some calling finer or nobler than the calling God gives us; so we come to nothing.

In these great and shining examples we are taught how God elects men, how he elects all men, and how he elects all to work. These are not the exceptional cases, as we are apt to suppose, but they are the illustrations of a universal rule.

Every human being has his own gift and opportunity from God; some after this fashion, and others after that. If faithful, he can see what it is. If his eye is single, his whole body is full of light. If he is true to the light within his soul, it grows more and more clear to him what God wants him to do. Not every man's business is to do great works in the world; but every one is sent to do something and to be something—something which shall bring him nearer to God—something which shall make him more useful to man. At first he is confused; he cannot tell what his calling is. But each day, if he be faithful to each day's call, causes the whole calling of his life to become more luminous and clear. So we see that conscientious and faithful people, as they continue to live, grow more and more into specialty of work, and have more and more of a special place and duty. Thus we see that all God's callings are special, and none vague or general. "Every man has his proper gift from the Lord; one after this fashion, and another after that." Perhaps it is not a shining gift, it will not make him famous, but it is always a good one—always useful and noble. If we follow God's leadings, we shall always come out right. "Let every man," says the apostle, "abide in the calling in which he is called." Let him not be impatient of his own gift, nor covetous of another's; let him not be uneasy in his place, nor straining for something beyond his reach. But if faithful every day to his own gift, he may be sure that it will grow at last into something truly good, satisfactory, and sufficient.

§ 9. How Jesus was elected to be the Christ

Perhaps we can now better understand how Christ was "the chosen one of God." If Columbus was chosen and sent to discover a world, if Dante was sent to be a great poet, if Mozart, Rafaelle, had each his mission, can we doubt that Jesus also was specially selected and endowed for the work which he has actually done, to be the leader of the human race in religion and goodness—to lead it up to God? Yet those who will admit the mission in all other cases, question it in his case. But what was true in them was much more so in him. He was conscious from the first that he was selected. "Wist ye not that I must be about my Father's business?" "To this end I was born, that I might bear witness to the truth." "God sent not his Son into the world to condemn the world, but that the world, through him, might be saved." "For this cause came I to this hour." "I have finished the work given me to do."

Jesus, by his nature and organization, by his education, by the very time of his birth, by the inspiration and influence of the Holy Spirit, was elected and called. And he fulfilled his part perfectly; and so, the two conditions being met, he became Saviour of the world, and perpetual Ruler of the moral and spiritual nature of man.

§ 10. Other Illustrations of Individual Calling and Election

But it is not merely great men, and men of genius, who are thus providentially chosen and sent. *Every* man is chosen for something, and that something not vague and general, but special and distinct.

You go into some country village of New England. You find there some plain farmer, of no great education, perhaps, but endowed with admirable insight and sagacity, and of a kind and benevolent nature. He has come to be the counsellor and adviser of the whole community. He has no title; he is not even a "squire." He has no office; he is not even a justice of the peace. But he fulfils the mission of peace-maker and of sagacious counsellor. He is judge without a seat on the bench; he is spiritual guide without being called "reverend;" he is the stay, the centre, the most essential person in the place. He has had an evident calling from God, not from man, and he has made it sure by his diligence and fidelity in his work.

And perhaps in the same village is a woman, poor, old, and uneducated. But she, too, has a calling from God. She is always sent for in the hour of trial. If any accident happens, she is there. Her sagacity and experience help her to do what is needed. She has no medical diploma, but she is the good physician of the place. God gave to her native sagacity, gave to her benevolence, gave her acute observation and a good memory, and she has made her election sure by her own fidelity.

Some persons are called to love and teach little children: that is *their* work. They are happy with children, and children are happy with them. Some are called to sympathize; their natures overflow with sympathy; they enter readily into all trials and into the troubles of every soul, and they pour oil and wine into the wounds of the heart. God called them to be his good Samaritans, and they hear the call and obey.

"A place for everything, and everything in its place," says the prudent housekeeper. "A place for every man, and every man in his place," says the divine Housekeeper, who has so many mansions in his house, and whose Son said he went to prepare a place for us there in the other world—a working place, probably, and a sphere of labor there as here. But in this world, too, what a delight it is to see any one in his right place!

There are different ways in which God calls us, and different kinds of callings. But every calling of God is good and noble. He calls us to work; he calls us to Christian goodness; he calls us to heavenly joy, to glory, honor, and immortality. These are the three great callings of man—Christian work first, Christian goodness next, Christian glory last. Since God made every one of us, he made every one of us for something; he has appointed a destiny for each one, and he calls us to it. If we do not hear the gentle call, the whisper of his grace, he calls us by trial, by disaster, by disappointment. He chastens us for our profit. He prunes our too luxuriant branches that we may bring forth more fruit.

So this doctrine of election, in its other form, as usually taught by Orthodoxy, so harsh and terrible,—"*horrible decretum*,"—so dishonorable to God, so destructive to morality, so palsying to effort, grows lovely and encouraging when looked at aright.

As one grows old, and looks back over his past life, he sees the working of this divine decree—working where he concurred with it, working where he resisted it. He sees more and more clearly what his election was, and how he has fulfilled it, how far failed. He sees himself as a youth, fiery and ardent, striving for one thing, educated by God for another. He sees how he was partly led and partly driven into his true work; how he has been made an instrument by God for good he never dreamed of to God's other children. He says, "It is no doing of mine. It is the Lord's doing. He chose me for it before the foundation of the world. I builded better than I knew. I have failed in a thousand plans of my own, but I have ignorantly fulfilled God's plans. I am like Saul, the son of Kish, who went out to seek his father's asses, and found a kingdom. I am like Schiller's explorer, who went to sea with a thousand vessels, and came to shore saved in a single boat, yet having in that boat the best result of the whole voyage."

Chapter XII
Immortality And The Resurrection

§ 1. Orthodox Doctrine

The Orthodox doctrine of the future life is thus stated in the Assembly's Catechism, chapter 32:—

"I. The bodies of men, after death, return to dust, and see corruption; but their souls (which neither die nor sleep) having an immortal subsistence, immediately return to God who gave them. The souls of the righteous, being then made perfect in holiness, are received into the highest heavens, where they behold the face of God, in light and glory, waiting for the full redemption of their bodies. And the souls of the wicked are cast into hell, where they remain in torments and utter darkness, reserved to the judgment of the great day. Besides these two places for souls separated from their bodies, the Scripture acknowledged none.

"II. At the last day, such as are found alive shall not die, but be changed; and all the dead shall be raised up with the selfsame bodies, and none other, although with different qualities, which shall be united again with their souls forever.

"III. The bodies of the unjust shall, by the power of Christ, be raised to dishonor; the bodies of the just by his Spirit unto honor, and be made conformable to his own glorious body."

The views here given may be considered, on the whole, the Orthodox notions on this subject, although Orthodoxy is by no means rigorous on these points. Considerable diversity of opinion is here allowed. The nature of the life between death and the resurrection, and the nature of the resurrection body, are differently apprehended, without any discredit to the Orthodoxy of the belief. But, on the whole, we may say that the Orthodox views on these topics include the following heads:—

1. Man consists of soul and body.

2. The soul of man is naturally immortal.

3. The only satisfactory proof of this immortality is the resurrection of Christ.

4. Christ's resurrection consisted in his return to earth in the same body as that with which he died, though glorified.

5. Our resurrection will consist in our taking again the same bodies which we have now, glorified if we are Christians, but degraded if we are not.

On the other hand, those views which incline towards rationalism and spiritualism agree in part with these statements, and in part differ; thus:—

1. They usually agree with Orthodoxy in believing man to consist of soul and body.

2. They also agree in believing the soul of man naturally immortal.

3. They differ from Orthodoxy in thinking the proof of immortality to be found in human consciousness, not at all in the resurrection of Jesus.

We will therefore examine these two points of immortality and the resurrection, to see what the true doctrine of Scripture is concerning them.

§ 2. The Doctrine of Immortality as taught by Reason, the Instinctive Consciousness, and Scripture

The first class of proofs usually adduced for immortality are the rational proofs, which are such as these:—

The Metaphysical Proof.—This is based on the distinction of soul and body. The existence of the soul is proved exactly as we prove the existence of the body. If we can prove the one, we can equally prove the other. If any one asks, How do we know there is such a thing as body? we reply that we know it by the senses; we can touch, taste, smell, and see it. But to this the answer is, that the senses only give us sensations, and that these sensations are in the mind, not out of it. We have a sensation of resistance, of color, of perfume, and the like; but how do we know that there is anything outside of the mind corresponding to them? The answer to this is, that by a necessary law of the reason, when we have a sensation, we *infer* some external substance from which it proceeds. We look at a book, for example. We have a sensation of shape and color; we infer something outside of our mind from which it proceeds. In other words, we perceive qualities and infer substance. This inference is a spontaneous and inevitable act of the mind. Now, we are conscious of another group of feelings which are not sensations, which do not come from without, but from within. These are mental and moral. But they, too, are qualities; and, as in the other case, perceiving qualities, we infer a substance in which they inhere. This latter substance we name soul, and we know it exactly as we know body. It is known by us as a simple substance, having personal unity. The personality, the "I," is a fundamental idea. Now, as soon as we perceive the existence of soul, it becomes evident that soul *cannot* die. It may be annihilated, but it cannot die. For what is *death* when applied to the body? Dissolution or separation of the parts, but not destruction of the simple elements. Death is decomposition of these elements, and their resolution into new combinations. Now, the soul, being known by us as a simple substance, is incapable of dissolution.

This is the metaphysical proof of immortality. Then comes the teleologic proof, or that from final causes. Man's end is not reached in this life. We see everything in this world made for an end. The body is made for an end, and attains it, and then decays and is dissolved. The soul, with all its great powers, goes on and on, but the body dies before the soul is ever perfected. Every human life is like an unfinished tale in a magazine, with "to be continued" written at its close, to show that it is not yet ended.

And besides these proofs of immortality, there is the theological proof, founded on the attributes of God; and the moral proof, based on the conflict between conscience and self-love; and the analogical proof, based on the law of progress in nature; and the cosmic proof, founded on the relation of the soul to the universe; and the historic proof, resting on the universal belief in immortality; and lastly, the psychologic proof, or the instinct of life in man, which carries with it its own evidence of continuity.

But after all these proofs have been considered, the final result is probability. Only the last gives more, and this acts not as an argument, but as conviction. And the strength of this conviction depends on the strength in any individual of this instinct. Some have more of the instinct of life, others less.29 Those who have much are easily convinced by these various arguments. But those who have less, feel as Cicero did after reading the Phædo of Plato.30

This instinct of life appears not only to be different from the fear of death, but its exact opposite. When we have most of the one, we have the least of the other. Any great excitement lifts us temporarily above the fear of death by giving us more life. So a man will plunge into the sea, and risk his own life to save that of another. So whole armies go to die cheerfully in the great rage of battle. But this instinct receives a permanent strength by all that elevates the soul. All greatness of aim, all devotion to duty, all generous love, take away the fear of death by adding to the quantum of life in the soul.31

If it be asked what the Scriptures teach concerning immortality, it must be admitted that they have not much to say. They speak of life and of eternal life; but this, as we shall discover, is quite another thing from continued existence. It refers to the quality and quantity of being, and not merely to its duration.

§ 3. The Three Principal Views of Death— the Pagan, Jewish, and Christian

There are three principal views of death—the Pagan view, the Jewish view, and the Christian view.

Paganism, in all its various forms, is chiefly distinguished by its transferring to the other life the tastes, feelings, habits of this life. The other world is this one, shaded off and toned down. It is gray in its hue, wanting the color of this world; and is really inferior to it, and only its pale reflection. To the gods of Olympus the doings of men are matters of chief interest. Tartarus and the Elysian Fields are occupied by lymphatic ghosts, misty spectres, unsubstantial and unoccupied. When a living man enters, like Ulysses, Æneas, or Dante, they throng around him, delighted to have something in which they can take a real interest. "Better be a plough-boy on earth than a king among the ghosts." This expresses the Pagan idea of the other world. This world is more *real* than the other, to the Pagan.

Judaism, in its view of hereafter, is much more positive. It began with no idea of a hereafter. Nothing is taught concerning a future life by Moses, and little is to be found concerning it even in the prophets. The explanation is simple. Men hard at work in the present do not think much of the future; and the work of the Jews was to be servants of Jehovah and doers of his law here. However, all men must think a little of the region beyond death. When the Jews thought of it, they projected their law upon its blank spaces. It was a place where Jehovah would vindicate his law—where the just should be happy, the unjust miserable. The perplexity which tormented Job, David, and Elijah—namely, that bad men should succeed in this world and good men fail—was to find its solution there. Judgment was the Jewish idea of hereafter—a judgment to come. "I have a hope toward God, as they themselves also allow," said Paul, speaking of the Pharisees, "that there shall be a resurrection of the dead, of the just, and also of the unjust."

The Christian view of death is, that it is abolished—it has ceased to be anything. The New Testament distinctly says, "who has *abolished* death, and brought life and immortality to light."32 Death, to a Christian, is but a point on the line of advancing being; a door through which we pass; a momentary sleep between two days. In the same sense the Saviour says, "He that liveth and believeth on me shall never die."

So also he spoke of Lazarus as being only asleep, and said of the daughter of Jairus, "She is not dead, but sleepeth."

Certainly Jesus could not have spoken of death in this way if he regarded it as the awful and solemn thing which most believers consider it. If it is the moment that decides our eternal destiny, which shuts the gate of probation, which terminates for the sinner all opportunity of repentance and conversion, for the saint all danger of relapse and fall,—then death is surely something, and something of the most immense importance.

But Christ has really destroyed death both in the Pagan and in the Jewish feeling concerning it. He destroys the Pagan idea of death as a plunge downward from something into nothing, a descent into non-entity or half-entity, a diminution of our being, a passage from the substantial to the shadowy and unreal.

For, according to Christianity, we do not descend in death; we ascend into more of reality, into higher life. Death is a passage onward and upward.

The proof of this we find in the Christian doctrine of the Resurrection.

The meaning of the resurrection of Christ is not, as has been often supposed, that after death he came to life *again*, but that at death he rose; that his death was rising up, ascent. This we shall show in a future section of this chapter.

One power of Christ's resurrection was to abolish the *fear of death*. It brought life and immortality to *light*. It showed men their immortality.

The fear of death is natural to all men, but it is easily removed. The smallest and lowest power of the resurrection is shown in removing it.

The fear of death is natural. It consists in this—that we are, in a great part of our nature, immersed in the finite and perishing. "When we look at the things which are seen," which "are temporal," we have an inward feeling of instability—nothing substantial. Therefore it is said, "In Adam all die," for the Adam, the first man in all of us, is the animal soul. "The first man is of the earth, earthy." The law of our life is, that it comes from our love. When we love the finite, our life is finite. But besides the finite element in man, the animal soul, or Adam, is the spiritual element, or Christ, the life flowing from things unseen, but eternal.

Christ has abolished death. There is now to the Christian no such thing as death, in the common sense of the term. The only death is the sense of death, the fear of death, which insnares and enslaves. Jesus delivers us from this by inspiring us with faith. We rise with him when we look with him at the things unseen. Faith in eternal things brings into the soul a sense of eternity. Death is only a sleep: outward death is the sleep of the bodily life; inward death is the sleep of the higher life. We awake and rise from the dead when Christ gives us life; and when he, who is our life, shall appear, we shall also appear with him.

The philosopher Lessing says, "Thus was Christ the first *practical* teacher of the immortality of the soul. For it is one thing to conjecture, to wish, to hope for, to believe in immortality as a philosophical speculation—another thing to arrange all our plans and purposes, all our inward and our outward life, in accordance to it."

Jesus also destroys the Jewish idea of death, as a passage from a world where the good suffer and the bad triumph, to a world where this state of things is reversed. The kingdom of heaven, with him, begins here, in this world. Judgment is here as well as hereafter. The Jew lived, and all Judaizing Christians live, under a fearful looking for of judgment after death. The Christian sees that judgment is always taking place; that Christ is always judging the world; that God's moral laws and their retributions are not kept in a state of suspense till we die—that they operate now daily. The Christian knows that heaven and hell are both here, and he expects to find them hereafter, because he finds them here. He believes in law, but not in law only. He believes in something higher than law, namely, love—the love of a present, helpful Father, of a friend near at hand, of an inspiration from on high, of a God who forgives all sins when they are repented of, and saves all who trust in him. He is not under law, but under grace.

When he looks forward to the other world, it is not as to a place where he goes to be sentenced by a stern and absolute judge, but where judgment and mercy go hand in hand, where law remains, but is fulfilled by love.

This is what Paul means when he says, "The sting of death is sin, and the strength of sin is the law; but thanks be to God, who hath given us the victory through our Lord Jesus Christ."

The only real death is the fear of death—the Pagan fear of death, which is a dread of loss, change, degradation of being, to follow the dissolution of the body; and the Jewish fear of death, which is a fearful looking for of judgment, and the sting of which is sin. Christ abolishes both of these fears in every believing heart. He abolishes them in two ways—by the life and the resurrection. He is both resurrection and life: by inspiring us with spiritual or eternal life, he abolishes all fear of dissolution; and by showing us that he has ascended into a higher state by his resurrection, he gives us the belief that death is not going down, but going up. For, though "it doth not yet appear what we shall be, yet we know this, that when *he* shall appear, we shall be like him."

But, unfortunately, Christians are still subject to the fear of death. This fear has been aggravated by the current teaching in pulpits professedly Christian. The fear of that "something after death" has been made use of to palsy the will; and conscience, as instructed by Christian teachers, has made cowards of us all; so that few persons can really say, "Thanks be to God, who has given us the victory through our Lord Jesus Christ."

It is very certain that the Pagan view of death and the Jewish view of death still linger in the Church, and are encouraged by Christian teachers. Death is made terrible by false doctrine and false teaching in the Church. Christ has *not* abolished death to the majority of Christians. Christians are almost as much afraid of death as the heathen—sometimes more so.

Actual Christianity is a very different thing from ideal Christianity. Ideal Christianity is Christianity as seen and lived by Jesus; the gospel which he saw and spoke; the word of God made flesh in him. But actual Christianity is an amalgam; a portion of real Christianity mixed with a portion of the belief and habits of feeling existing in men's minds before they became Christians. The Jews took a large quantity of Judaism into Christianity; the Pagans a large quantity of Paganism. The Christian Church from the very beginning Judaized and Paganized. Paul contended against its Judaism on the one hand and its Paganism on the other. But Judaism and Paganism have always stuck to the Christian Church. She has never risen above them wholly to this day. They mingle with all her doctrines, ceremonies, and habits of life. The Romish Church has more of the Pagan element, the Protestant more of the Jewish. The mediatorial system of Rome is essentially Pagan. Its ascending series of deacons, sub-deacons, priests, bishops, archbishops, patriarchs, cardinals, and pope in the Church below; and beatified and sanctified spirits, angels, and archangels in the Church above; its processions, pilgrimages, dresses, its monastic institutions, its rosaries, relics, daily sacrifice, votive offerings—everything peculiar to the Roman Church, existed before, somewhere, in Paganism. So Protestantism has taken from the Jews its Sabbath, its idea of God as King and Judge, its exclusion from God's favor of all but the elect, its view of the divine sovereignty, its doctrine of predestination, day of judgment, resurrection of the body, material heaven and material hell.

I do not mean to say that there is no truth in these things. There is, because there is some truth in Paganism and in Judaism. We are all Pagans and Jews before we become Christians. The Jewish and Pagan element is in every human soul, and in all *constants* in man there is truth. But the Pagan and Jewish truths are but stepping-stones to the higher Christian truth. The law and Paganism are school-masters to bring us to Christ. The evil is, that Christianity has not been kept supreme; it has often been sunk and lost in the earlier elements. As the foolish Galatians were bewitched, and relapsed from the gospel to the law,—turning again to weak and beggarly elements, desiring to be in bondage to them again, going back to their minority under tutors and governors,—so the Church has been relapsing, going back to weak and beggarly elements, not keeping Christianity supreme in thought, heart, and life, but letting Paganism or Judaism get the upper hand.

So it has been in regard to this subject. We Paganize and Judaize in our view of death. We reëstablish again what Christ has abolished. We make death something where Christ made it nothing. It is made the great duty of life to "prepare for death." No such duty is pointed out in the New Testament. Our duty is to prepare every day *to live*; then, when we die, we shall be taken care of by God. We can safely leave the other world and its interests to Him who has shown himself so capable of taking care of us here.

The gloom of death has been heightened by artificial means. Mourning dresses, solemn faces, funeral addresses, the grave,—all have had an unnatural depth of awe added to the natural sense of bereavement. The Orthodox Church has deliberately and systematically Paganized and Judaized in what it has said and done about death. Its object has been always to make use of the great lever of fear of a hereafter in order to enforce Christian belief and action. Hence Death has been made the king of terrors, the close of probation, the beginning of judgment, the awful entrance to the final decision of an endless doom. All this is wholly unchristian, unknown to apostolic times, a relapse towards Paganism. It is utterly opposed to the great declaration that "Christ has abolished death, and brought life and immortality to light through the gospel."

What is called faith in immortality, therefore, is of two kinds: it is an instinct, and it is a belief. In the New Testament these are plainly distinguished. In the passage just quoted, it is said that Jesus "brought life and immortality to light." Jesus himself says, "I am the resurrection and the life." "He that believeth in me hath eternal life abiding in him, and I will raise him up at the last day."

Life is a matter of consciousness. It is a present possession, something abiding in us now.

Immortality, or the resurrection, is an object of intellectual belief. It is something future. We *feel* life; we believe in the resurrection.

We will pass on, in the next sections, to consider each of these.

§ 4. Eternal Life, as taught in the New Testament, not endless Future Existence, but present Spiritual Life

It is only necessary carefully to examine the passages in the New Testament where the phrase "eternal life" (ζωή αἰώνιος) occurs, to see that it does not refer to the duration, but to the quality, of existence. *Temporal life* is that life of the soul which through the body is subject to the vicissitudes of time. *Eternal* (or everlasting) *life* is that life of the spirit which is independent of change, and is apart from duration. God's being was regarded by the Semitic races as outside of time and space, as a perpetual Now, without before or after. ("I am the *I Am*." Exod. 3:14.) Man, made in the image of God, becomes a "partaker of the divine nature" (2 Peter 2:4) by the gift of eternal life.

That "eternal life" is not an endless temporal existence appears,—

(*a.*) From the passages in which it is spoken of as something to be obtained by one's own efforts, as (Matt. 19:16) when the young man asks of Jesus what good thing he shall do that he may have eternal life, and Jesus replies that he must keep the commandments, give his possessions to the poor, and come and follow him. Certainly that was not the method to obtain an endless existence, but it was the true preparation for receiving spiritual good. So Jesus tells Peter (Mark 10:30) that those who make sacrifices for the sake of truth shall receive temporal rewards "in this time;" and "in the coming age eternal life" ("ἐν τῷ αἰῶνι τῷ ἐρχομένῳ ζωὴν αἰώνιον"). The coming age is the age of the Messiah, when the gift of the Holy Ghost should be bestowed.

(*b.*) Passages in which eternal life is spoken of as a present possession, not a future expectation. (John 3:36.) "He that believeth on the Son *hath* (ἔχει) eternal life." So John 6:47, 54, &c.

(*c.*) Passages in which eternal life is defined expressly as a state of the soul. (John 17:3.) "This is life eternal, that they may know thee the only true God, and Jesus Christ whom thou hast sent," &c.

So (Gal. 6:8) it is represented as the natural result of "sowing to the Spirit;" (Rom. 2:7) of "patient continuance in well-doing;" as "the gift of God" (Rom. 6:23); as something which we "lay hold of" (1 Tim. 6:12, 19).

This view of "eternal life" is taken by all the best critics. Professor Hovey thus sums up their testimony:—33

> "On a certain occasion, Christ pronounced it necessary for the Son of Man to be lifted up, 'that whosoever believeth in him should not perish, but *have eternal life*' (John 3:15)—ἔχῃ

ζωήν αἰώνιον. Ζωὴν αἰώνιον, says Meyer, who is, perhaps, the best commentator on the New Testament, of modern times, 'signifies the eternal Messianic life, which, however, the believer already possesses—ἔχῃ—in this αἰών, that is, in the temporal development of that moral and blessed life which is independent of death, and which will culminate in perfection and glory at the coming of Christ.' And Lücke, whose commentary on the Gospel of John is one of the most thorough and attractive in the German language, says that the ζωὴ αἰώνιος, which is the exact opposite of ἀπώλεια (destruction), or θάνατος (death), is the sum of Messianic blessedness. It is plain, we think, that the life here spoken of as the present possession of every believer in Christ is more than endless existence; it is life in the fullest and highest sense of the word, the free, holy, and blessed action of the whole man, that is to say, the proper, normal living of a rational and moral being. The germ, the principle of this life, exists in the heart of every believer; it is a present possession. 'Whosoever,' says Christ, 'drinketh of the water that I shall give him shall never thirst; but the water that I shall give him shall be in him a fountain—πηγὴ—of water, springing up into everlasting life.' (John 4:14.) In another place our Saviour utters these words: 'He that heareth my word, and believeth on him that sent me, *hath eternal life, and shall not come into condemnation, but has passed from death into life*' (John 5:24)—μεταβέβηκεν ἐκ τοῦ θανάτου εἰς τὴν ζωήν. Here, again, the believer is said to *have* eternal life, even now; for he has passed from death into life. *Ingens saltus*, remarks Bengel, with his customary brevity and graphic power. We translate a part of Lücke's ample and instructive note on this important verse.

" 'The words, "Has passed from death into life" determine that ἔχει (*hath*) must be taken as a strict present. For the verb μεταβέβηκεν (*has passed*) affirms that the transition from death into life took place with the hearing and believing. Only if an impossible thought were thus expressed, could we consent, as in a case of extreme necessity, to understand the present ἔχει and the present perfect μεταβέβηκεν as futures. And then we should be compelled to say that John had expressed himself very strangely. But if a higher kind of life, a resurrection process prior to bodily death, is represented by "hath," and "hath passed," then ζωή and ζωὴ αἰώνιος are not to be understood of a life commencing after bodily death, but of the true and eternal Messianic life or salvation, beginning even here. This life does not, to be sure, exclude natural death, but neither does it first begin after this death. (Cf. 5:40.) Even so θάνατος cannot be understood of bodily, but only of spiritual death, of lying in the darkness of the world. This interpretation would be justified here, even if θάνατος elsewhere in the New Testament denoted uniformly nothing but bodily death. But the metaphorical idea of death stands out clearly in 1 John 3:14; 5:16, 17; John 8:51, 52; 2 Cor. 2:16; 7:10. Similar, also, is the use of the words θανατοῦν (Rom. 7:4; 8:13), and νεκρός, νεκροῦν, ἀποθνήσκειν (Matt. 8:22; Eph. 5:14; Heb. 6:1; Col. 3:5; Gal. 2:19).'

"With the passage now examined may be compared a statement of the apostle John to the same effect, namely: 'We know that we have passed from death into life, because we love the brethren; he that loveth not abideth in death.' (1 John 3:14.) This language, explained with a due regard to the preceding context, speaks, evidently, of spiritual death and life, of a passing from one moral condition into another and opposite one. To say that this new moral condition and blessed state is to endure and improve forever, may doubtless be to utter an important truth, but one which does not conflict in the slightest degree with its present existence. It begins in this life; it continues forever and ever.

"Again: we find our Saviour saying, 'He that believeth on me hath everlasting life;' 'Except ye eat the flesh of the Son of man, and drink his blood, ye have no life in you;' and, 'The words that I speak unto you are spirit, and are life.' (John 6:47, 53, 63.) By these verses we are taught once more, that the Greek terms which denote life and death, living and dying, were applied by Christ to opposite moral states of the soul. For, observe, (1.) he more than intimates that his words, his doctrines, are the source of present life to those who receive them, and that, by eating his flesh and drinking his blood, he signifies a reception of his words, and so of himself as the Lamb of God. And, (2.) he declares that one who believes *has* eternal life; that one who eats of the true bread shall not die, but shall live forever; and that one who does not eat the flesh and drink the blood of the Son of man *hath not life* in himself.

"Is it not plain that the words *life* and *death,* as well as the words *bread, flesh,* and *blood, eating* and *drinking,* are here used in a spiritual sense? Is it not plain that Jesus here speaks of something in the believer's soul which is nourished by Christian truth, and which is at the same time called *life?* But it is the function of truth to quicken thought and feeling, to determine the modes of conscious life, the character or moral condition of the human soul; and hence the rejection of it may involve the utter want of certain spiritual *qualities* and blessed *emotions,* but not the want of personal existence. In still another place we read, 'Jesus said unto her, I am the resurrection and the life: he that believeth in me, though he were dead, yet shall he live; and whosoever liveth and believeth in me shall never die.' (John 11:25, 26.) Christ here affirms that every believer is exempted from death. And it matters not for our present purpose whether the word ζῶν, translated in our version 'liveth,' refers in this passage to physical or to moral life. If it refers to physical life, then our Saviour pronounces the Christian to be already, in time, delivered from the power of death, and in possession of a true and immortal life. But if it refers to moral life, Christ declares that whoever possesses this life, whether in the body or out of the body, is delivered from the power of death; that is, his union with God and delight in him, which alone constitute the normal living of the soul, shall never be interrupted: οὐ μὴ ἀποθάνῃ εἰς τὸν αἰῶνα—*he shall never die....*

" 'And this is life eternal,' says the Great Teacher, 'that they should know thee, the only true God, and Jesus Christ, whom thou hast sent.' (John 17:3.) The best ancient and modern interpreters hold this verse to be a definition by Christ himself of the expression 'life eternal,' so often used by him, according to the record of John. De Wette says, '*And this is* (therein consists) *the life eternal*; not, this is the means of the eternal life; for the vital knowledge of God and Christ is itself the eternal life, which begins even here, and penetrates the whole life of the human spirit.' Meyer translates thus: 'Therein consists the eternal life,' and says, 'This knowledge, willed of God, is the "eternal life," inasmuch as it is the essential subjective principle of the latter, its enduring, eternally unfolding germ and fountain, both now, in the temporal development of the eternal life, and hereafter, when the kingdom is set up, in which faith, hope, and charity abide, whose essence is that knowledge.'34 The same view, substantially, is presented by Olshausen, Lücke, Bengel, Alford, and many others."

Eternal life is the gift of God to the soul through Jesus Christ. It is God's life communicated to man—the life of God in the soul of man. This is distinctly stated in the First Epistle of John (chap. 1:1), as the life which was from the beginning, the eternal life which was with the Father, but is manifested to us, giving us fellowship with the Father and with his Son.

The root of this eternal life is in every human being. It is what we call "the spirit" in man, as distinguished from the soul and body. It is the side of each person which touches the infinite and eternal.

Fichte, the most spiritual of German philosophers, says, "Love is life. Where I love, I live. What I love, I live from that."35 When we love earthly things, our life is earthly, that is, temporal; when we love the true, the right, the good, our life is spiritual and eternal. Then we have eternal life abiding in us. Then all fear of death departs. The great gift of God through Christ was to make the right and true also lovely, so that loving them, we could draw our life from them. When God becomes lovely to us, by being shown to us as Jesus shows him, then by loving God we live from God, and so have eternal life abiding in us.

The natural instinct of immortality is the spirit, or sense of the infinite and eternal. But it needs to be reënforced by the influence of Christian conviction, hope, and experience, in order completely to conquer the sense of death. It is not by logical arguments in proof of a future existence that immortality becomes clear to us, but by living an immortal life. Dr. Channing says truly, "Immortality must begin here." And so Hase (Dogmatic, § 92) says, "Any proof which should demonstrate, with mathematical certainty, to the understanding, or to the senses, the blessings or terrors of our future immortality, would destroy morality in its very roots. The belief in immortality is therefore at first only a wish, and a belief on the authority of others; but the more that any one assures to himself his spiritual life by his own free efforts and a pure love for goodness, the more certain also does eternity become, not merely as something future, but as something already begun."36

Whenever Jesus is said to give eternal life, or to be the life of the world; whenever the apostles declare Christ to be their life, or say that as in Adam all die, so in Christ shall all be made alive; when Paul says, "The law of the Spirit of life in Christ Jesus has made me free from the law of sin and death;" "to be spiritually minded is life and peace;" "the life of Jesus is manifested in our dying (mortal) flesh;" when John says, "He that hath the Son hath life;" when in Revelation we read of the book of life, and water of life, and tree of life,—the meaning is always the same. It refers to the spiritual vitality added to the soul by the influence of Jesus, who communicates God's love, and so enables us to LOVE God, instead of merely fearing him or obeying him. Love casts out all fear, the fear of death included. He who looks at the things unseen and eternal, partakes of their eternal nature, and though his outward human nature perishes, his inward spiritual nature is renewed day by day.

§ 5. Resurrection, and its real Meaning, as a Rising up, and not a Rising again

One part of the Christian doctrine of immortality is conveyed in the term "eternal life;" the other part in the other term, usually associated with it—"the resurrection." The common Orthodox doctrine of the resurrection, is that the dead shall rise with the same bodies as those laid in earth; and this identity is usually made to consist in identity of matter, though Paul expressly says, "Thou sowest *not* that body that shall be." On the other hand, many liberal thinkers of the Spiritual School deny any resurrection, and think the whole doctrine of the resurrection a Jewish error, believing in a purely spiritual existence hereafter. Others, like Swedenborg, teach that the soul hereafter dwells in a body, though of a more refined and sublimated character; and in this we think they approach more nearly the teaching of the New Testament.

It is a remarkable fact that the Greek words indicating the rising of men should have been translated, in our English Bible, by terms signifying something wholly different, and conveying another sense than that in the original. It is equally extraordinary that this change of meaning should seldom or never be alluded to by theological writers.

These words, translated "resurrection," "rise again," and the like, all have, in the Greek, the sense of rising up, not of rising again. They signify not return, but ascent; not coming back to this life, but going forward to a higher. The difference in meaning is apparent and very important. It is one thing to say, that at death we go down into Hades, or into dissolution, and at the resurrection we come back to conscious existence, or to the same life we had before, and quite a different thing to say that what we call death is *nothing*; but that we rise *up*, and go forward when we seem to die. This last is the doctrine of the New Testament, though the former is the one usually believed to be taught in it.

The immense stress laid, in the New Testament, on the resurrection of Jesus is by no means explained by supposing that after his death he came to life again, and so proved that there is a life after death. What he showed his disciples was, that death was not going down, but going up; not descent into the grave, or Hades, but ascent to a higher world. This is the evident sense of such passages as these. We have not room to go over all the passages which should be noticed in a critical examination, but select a few of the most prominent.

1. Ἀνάστασις, commonly translated "resurrection," or "rising again," but which literally means "rising up." (So Bretschneider, "Lexicon Man. in lib. Nov. Test." defines it as "resurrectio, *rectius* surrectio.")37

This word occurs forty-two times in the New Testament. In *none* of them (unless there be a single exception, which we shall presently consider) does it necessarily mean *a rising again*, or coming back to the same level of life as before. In a large number of instances the word *can only* mean a *rising up*, or ascent to a higher state. Of these cases we will cite a few examples.

Ten of the passages in which the word ἀνάστασις occurs, are in the account by the Synoptics of the discussion between Jesus and the Sadducees concerning the case of the woman married to seven brothers. After stating the case, they say, "Therefore, *in the resurrection*, whose wife of them is she?" It is plain that the word "resurrection" here is equivalent to "the future state," and cannot be limited to a return to life. This becomes more apparent in the answer of Jesus, as given, somewhat varied, by the three Synoptics: "In the resurrection they neither marry nor are given in marriage, but are as the angels of God in heaven." (Matt. 22:30.) Mark, instead of "the resurrection," has the corresponding verb, "when they shall rise from the dead." This certainly means, not rising again, but rising up, ascending to a higher state. And Luke adds another element, showing that the "resurrection" is a state to which all may not attain, but which is dependent on character; evidently therefore a higher state. "They which shall be accounted worthy to obtain that world (τοῦ αἰῶνος ἐχείνου), and the resurrection from the dead, neither marry nor are given in marriage; neither can they die any more, for they are equal unto the angels" (or rather "are like the angels") "and are children of God, being *children of the resurrection*." (Luke 20:35, 36.) This last phrase, "children of the resurrection," is very significant, and intends a character corresponding to this higher state. There seems, indeed, to be a contradiction between this passage, which makes the resurrection conditional, and those which declare it universal. (See John 5:29, and 1 Cor. ch. 15.) But perhaps the reconciliation can be found in the apostolic statement (1 Cor. 15:23) "every one in his order." All shall ascend into the higher state, called "the resurrection," but only as they become prepared for it. All are not now prepared to hear the voice of the Son of man (or of divine truth), which shall causes them to rise to the resurrection of life and of judgment; but, in due season, all shall come forth from their graves, and hear it.

Another passage in which this word occurs is in Luke 2:34, where Simon says, "This child is set for the fall and *rising again* (ἀνάστασιν) of many in Israel." A moral fall and rising are here evident; and only if the reduplication be dropped, and we read "for the fall and the rising up," do we get the true idea. It is not meant that Jesus comes to degrade us morally, and then lift us up again morally. Rather it means that he comes to test the state of the hearts of men: some cannot bear the test, and fall before it; others, better prepared, rise higher. Here, also, ἀνάστασις means rising up, and not rising again.

The most remarkable use of this word, however, is in that famous passage where the common meaning is wholly unintelligible, in the story of Lazarus. (John 11:24, 25.) Jesus says, "I am the resurrection and the life." If resurrection means coming back to life after death, in what sense can Jesus be "the resurrection and the life"? Then Jesus said that he was "the coming back to life," which is unintelligible. But if the resurrection means the ascent to a higher state, then Jesus declares that he is the way of *ascent to a higher state*, just as he says elsewhere, "I am the way;" "I am the door." It is the power of Christ within the soul, the power of his spirit of faith, hope, and love, which enables us to go forward and upward. Christ is not the principle of resuscitation to an earthly existence, or a merely human immortality. He does not bring us to life again, but he lifts us up. So he adds, "He who believeth in me, though he were dead, yet shall he live." Not, shall come to life again; no, but, shall rise out of death into life, ascend into a higher condition of being. Then he adds that to one who has faith in him, who has adopted his ideas, there is no longer any such thing as death. Death has disappeared—is abolished. "He who liveth and believeth in me shall never die."

But, it may be objected, if spiritual death and life are here spoken of,— if the passage means that he who believeth in Christ shall have inward religious spiritual life, a heavenly and celestial life,—then how could that comfort Martha, or apply to her case, who was mourning, not the spiritual, but the natural, death of her brother?

Christ is essentially a manifestation of the truth and love of God. To believe in him is therefore to believe in God's truth and love. But belief in this fills the soul with life. And the soul full of life cannot die. What seems death is only change, and a change from a lower to a higher state, therefore rising up, or resurrection. Christ, then, the love and truth of God in the soul, is the life and the resurrection. He fills the soul with that life which causes it to rise with every change, to go up and on evermore to a higher state. That which seems death is nothing; the only real death is the immersion of the soul in sense and evil, the turning away from truth and God.

Now, Martha believed, as most of us believe, in a *future* resurrection. She believed that, after lying a long time in the grave, one would come out of it at last, on a great day of judgment, and somehow the soul and body be reunited. She believed this, for it was the general belief of the Jews in her day. It is the general belief of Christians now. The majority of Christians have not got very far beyond that. They talk of the resurrection, as though it were merely the return of the soul into the old body; and when you comfort them over their dead by saying, "Your dead will rise," reply, "I know it—at the resurrection, at the last day." But Jesus tells Martha, and all the Martha Christians of the present time, that he *is* the resurrection and the life. Your brother is not to sleep in the dust till the last day, and then rise. He does not die at all. He rises with Christ here, and in whatever other world. His nature is to go *up*, not down, when he is Christianized. Now or then, to-day or at the last day, if he has the living faith of a son of God, he will be raised by that Christ within him, who is his life.

This, it seems to us, is the only adequate explanation of this passage, and shows conclusively that resurrection must mean, in this place, a rising up to a higher existence, and not a mere return to this life.

It appears, from 1 Cor. ch. 15, that there were some in the Christian church who said there was no resurrection of the dead (ἀνάστασις νεκρῶν,) or that it was past already. (2 Tim. 2:18.) These Christians did not deny the doctrine of immortality, or a future life. It is difficult to imagine the motive which could induce any one, in those days, to join the Christian church, if he denied a future life. Probably, therefore, they assumed that the only real resurrection takes place in the soul when we rise with Christ. They said, "If we are to rise into a higher life after this, *how* shall we rise, and with what bodies?" (1 Cor. 15:35.) They professed to believe in a simple immortality of the soul, but not an ascent of the personal being, soul and body together, to the presence of God. They did not question a future life, but a higher life to which soul and body should go up together.

To these doubting Christians, who could not gather strength to believe in such a great progress as this, Paul says that if man does not rise, if it is contrary to his nature to rise, then Jesus, being a man, has not risen, but gone down to Hades with other souls. Then he is not *above* us, with God, sending down strength and inspiration from our work. This faith of ours, which has been our great support, is an illusion. We have all been deceived—deceived in preaching forgiveness of sins through Christ from God; deceived in preaching a higher life above us, into which Christ has gone, and where he is waiting to receive us. But we have not been deceived—Christ *has* risen, and risen as the first fruits of humanity. He leads the way up, and in proportion as we share his life, we also have in ourselves the principle of ascent, and shall go up too. He goes first; then all who are like him follow and finally, in due order, all mankind. Death and Hades have been conquered by this new influx of life in Christ. Instead of remaining pale ghosts, naked souls, we shall rise into a fuller, richer, larger life, of soul and body.

There is one passage, however, where there seems a difficulty in considering ἀνάστασις, or resurrection, as implying an ascent of condition. It is in John 5:28, 29. Our common translation reads thus: "The hour is coming in which all that are in the graves shall hear his voice (that is, the voice of the Son of man), and shall come forth, they that have done good unto the resurrection of life, and they that have done evil unto the resurrection of damnation." At first sight it certainly seems that the "resurrection of damnation" (ἀνάστασιν χρίσεως) could hardly be considered a higher state. All depends, however, on the meaning of the word, here translated "damnation." The word, in the Greek, is the genitive of χρίσις. Now, by turning to the Concordance, we find that this word χρίσις occurs some forty-eight times in the New Testament. In these places,—

It is translated 3 times by "damnation."
It is translated 2 times by "condemnation."
It is translated 2 times by "accusation."
It is translated 41 times by "judgment."

It is evident, therefore, that our translators considered *judgment* to be the primary and usual meaning of the word. Why, then, did they not translate it here, "rising to judgment," or "resurrection of judgment"? It must have been because they believed either that (1.) "judgment" would make no sense here; (2.) that "damnation" would make better sense; or, (3.) that "damnation" was more in accordance with the analogy of faith. But we can decide these points for ourselves. "Judgment" is the better word here, for it accords with the doctrine of the New Testament, that in proportion as man goes wrong, he dulls his moral sense, and needs a revelation of truth to show him what he is. A true man, who has lived according to the truth here, has judged himself, and will not need to be judged hereafter. (1 Cor. 11:31.) He rises into the resurrection of life. But those who follow falsehood here, need to see the truth; and they rise into the resurrection of judgment. The truth judges and condemns them. But this is really an ascent to them also. It is going up higher, to see the truth, even when it condemns them. This passage, then, is no exception to the principle that wherever "resurrection" (ἀνάστασις) occurs in the New Testament, it implies going up into a higher state.

All the other places where the word occurs either evidently have this meaning, or can bear it as easily as the other. Thus (Luke 14:14), "Thou shalt be recompensed in the higher state of the just." (20:27), the Sadducees "deny a higher state." (Acts 1:21), "he is to be a witness with us of the ascended state of Jesus." (Acts 4:2), "preached, through Jesus, the higher state of the dead." (17:18), "preached to them Jesus and the higher state." (20:23), that Christ "should be the first to rise into the higher state." (Lazarus and others had returned to life again before Jesus, so that in this sense he was *not* the first fruits.) (Rom. 6:5), "planted in the likeness of his resurrection." This can only mean as Christ passed through the grave into a higher state, so we pass through baptism into a higher state.

The only text which presents any real difficulty is Heb. 11:35, translated, "women received their dead raised to life again," literally, "women received from the resurrection their dead" (ἐξ ἀναστάσεως), which may refer to a return to this life, as in the case of the child of the widow of Sarepta (1 Kings 17:17), and of the Shunamite (2 Kings 4:17).38 But in the same verse, the other and "better" resurrection is spoken of, for the sake of which these martyrs refused to return to this life. The case referred to is probably that of the record of the seven brothers put to death by Antiochus (2 Macc. 7:9), who refused life offered on condition of eating swine's flesh, and said, when dying, "The King of the world shall raise us up, who have died for his laws, unto everlasting life" (εἰς αἰώνιον ἀναβίωσιν ζωῆς ἀναστήσει ἡμᾶς), literally, "to an eternal renewal of our life."39 This verse shows, therefore, that though ἀνάστασις may mean a return to this life, yet that the other sense of a higher life is expressly contrasted with it, even here.

Our conclusion, therefore, with regard to this term ἀνάστασις, is, that its meaning, in New Testament usage, is not "rising again," but "rising up," or "ascent."

2. Ἀνίστημι. This word is the root of the former. It is used one hundred and twelve times in the New Testament. It is translated with *again* (as, "he must rise again from the dead") fifteen times. It is translated thirty-six times "rise up" or "raise up" (as, "I will raise him up at the last day"), and ninety-six times without the "again." It is rendered "he *arose*," "shall *rise*," "stood up," "raise up," "arise," and in similar ways.

3. Ἐγείρω. This word is also frequently used in relation to the resurrection, and is translated "to awaken," "arouse," "animate," "revive." The natural and usual meaning is ascent to a higher state, and not merely a "rising again."

From these considerations we see that the primitive and central meaning of the terms used to express the resurrection is that of ascent. It is going up. This is the essential Christian idea. But it soon became implicated with the Pagan idea of immortality, or continued existence of the soul, and the Jewish idea of a bodily resurrection at the last day. But though there is a truth in each of these beliefs, the Christian doctrine is neither one nor the other. The gospel *assumes*, but does not teach, a continued existence of the soul. Since the greater includes the less, in teaching that the man rises at death into a higher life, it necessarily implies that he continues to live. And in teaching that he is to exist as man, with soul and body, in a higher condition of development, it teaches necessarily the bodily resurrection of the Jews. Christ, who came "not to destroy, but to fulfil," fulfils both Pagan and Jewish ideas of the future state in this doctrine of an ascension at death.

The principal points of the teaching of Jesus concerning the life which follows the dissolution of the body are these: *First.* As against the Sadducees, he argues that the dead are living (Matt. 22:31, and the parallel passages), from the simple fact that God calls them *his.* If God thinks of them as *his*, that is enough. His thinking of them makes them alive. No one can perish while God is thinking of him with love. Such an argument, carrying no weight to the mere understanding, is convincing in proportion as one is filled with a spiritual conception of God. *Secondly.* Jesus abolishes death by teaching that there is no such thing to the soul which shares his ideas concerning God and the universe. This is implied in the phrases, "He that liveth and believeth in me shall never die." (John 11:26.) "He that believeth on me hath everlasting life." (John 6:47.) "I am the living bread, whereof if a man eat, he shall live forever." (John 6:51.) "Whoso eateth my flesh, and drinketh my blood, hath eternal life." (John 6:54.) "If a man keep my saying, he shall never see death." Here, "eating Christ's flesh, and drinking his blood," is plainly equivalent to "keeping his saying," and "believing on him." As "food which we eat and drink changes itself so as to become a part of our own body by assimilation," so Christ intends that his truth shall not be merely taken into the memory, and reproduced in words, but shall be taken into the life, and reproduced in character. *Thirdly.* He teaches that as feeding on his truth changes our natural life into spiritual life, and lifts temporal existence into eternal being, so it will also place us outwardly in a higher state and higher relations, to which state he applies the familiar term the "resurrection" or "ascent," the "going up." "I will raise him up at the last day." The "last day," in Jewish and New Testament usage, means the Messianic times, as appears from such passages as Acts 2:17, where the term is used of the day of Pentecost; Heb. 1:2, "hath in these last days spoken unto us by his Son;" 1 John 2:18, "Little children, it is the last time." Jesus tells his disciples that he is going to the Father (John 14:15), in whose house are many mansions, where he is to prepare a place for his disciples. (John 14:2.)

That "resurrection" was understood to mean a present higher state, and not a future return to life, appears also from its use by the apostles. Christians are spoken of as having already "risen with Christ" (Col. 3:1); "risen with him in baptism" (Col. 3:1); walking "in the likeness of his resurrection" (Rom. 6:5). And, no doubt, it was by making this idea of a present resurrection too exclusive, that some Christians maintained that it was wholly a present resurrection, and not at all future—that "it was past already."

This Christian faith in "resurrection" as ascent to a higher condition of being at death is practically borne witness to by such common expressions concerning departed friends as these: "He has gone to a better world;" "He is in a higher world than this;" "We ought not to grieve for him—he is better off than he was." The practical sense of Christendom has taken this faith from the Gospels, though the Creeds do not authorize it. The Creeds teach that the souls of the good either sleep till a future resurrection, or are absorbed into God until then, while the souls of the impenitent descend to a lower sphere. Christ teaches that at death *all* rise to a higher state—of life and love to the loving, or judgment by the sight of truth to the selfish; but *higher* to all. Paul declares that "as in Adam all die, even so in Christ shall all be made alive," making the rise equivalent in extent to the fall.

The great change in the faith of the apostles, in consequence of the resurrection or ascent of Christ, was this: They before believed that at death all went to Hades, to the gloomy underworld of shadows, there to remain till the final resurrection. But the belief that Christ, instead of going down, had gone up, and had assured them that all who had faith in him had the principle of ascent in their souls, and were already spiritually risen,—this took the victory from Hades and the sting from death.

To Christians, at least, Hades is no more anything; all who have a living faith rise with Christ; and sooner or later, each in his order, *all* shall rise. This was the "power of the resurrection" of Jesus to destroy the fear of death, to enable them "to attain" *now* "to the resurrection of the dead" (Phil. 3:10), teaching that "if the Spirit of Him who raised up Jesus from the dead dwell in you, he that raised up Jesus from the dead shall also quicken your mortal bodies by his Spirit that dwells in you." "For it is Christ that died, *yea, rather, that is risen,* who is even at the right hand of God, who also maketh intercession for us." It was, therefore, the duty of all Christians, since they were risen in Christ, "to seek the things which are above."

§ 6. Resurrection of the Body, as taught in the New Testament, not a Rising again of the same Body, but the Ascent into a higher Body

It is remarkable that those who profess to believe in the literal inspiration of the New Testament should nevertheless very generally teach that the future body is *materially* the same as this. We often hear labored arguments to show how the identical chemical particles which compose the body at death may be re-collected from all quarters at the resurrection. Yet the only place where any account is given of the future body, declares explicitly that it is different from the present, just as the stalk which comes out of the ground differs from the seed planted. "We sow *not* the body which shall be, but bare grain, and God giveth it a body as pleaseth him."

Many persons, however, take an opposite view, and have no belief in any future bodily existence. They speak much more frequently of the *immortality of the soul.* But the resurrection of the body is unquestionably a doctrine of the New Testament, while the immortality of the soul is not. The New Testament knows nothing of a purely spiritual existence hereafter, nothing of an abstract disembodied immortality. The reaction from materialism to idealism has caused us now to undervalue bodily existence. So it did among the Corinthians to whom Paul wrote, "How say some among you that there is no resurrection of the dead?" These Corinthians were not Sadducees, nor Epicureans. There is no evidence that these sects had any influence on the Christian Church. They did not deny a *future existence*, but they denied a rising up and a *future bodily existence.* They believed, like us, in an immortality of the soul, denying the possibility (probably on philosophical grounds) of the resurrection of the body. So Paul proceeds, in the fifteenth chapter of Corinthians, first to prove the fact, and then to explain the nature of a bodily resurrection.

Let us consider, first, what is meant by a resurrection of the body.

This word *resurrection* tends to mislead us by suggesting the rising from the grave of the material body there deposited; and accordingly we have the theory which makes the future body the mere revival of the same particles of matter composing the present body. But the Greek word, as we have fully shown, means not merely rising out of the grave, but rising to a higher state of existence. The *anastasis* of the body is its elevation and spiritualizalion. By the resurrection of the body, we mean that in the future life of man, he shall not exist in the same material and fleshly envelope as now, nor yet as a purely disembodied spirit. The true doctrine avoids both extremes — the extreme of pure idealism on the one hand, and of pure materialism on the other. It asserts three things: first, that we have a real body hereafter; second, that this will be identical with our *true* body now; third, that it will be this true body in a higher state of development than at present, a spiritual instead of a natural body.

First, it will be a real body. A real body is an organization with which the soul is connected, and by means of which it comes into connection with the material universe, and under the laws of space and time. This organization may be more or less refined and subtle; it may not come under the cognizance of our present senses; but if it is an organization by means of which we may commune with the physical universe, it is essentially a *body*.

Again, the future body is identical with the present true body of man. For what is our *true body*? Not the particles of flesh and blood, but the principle of its organization. The identity of our body does not consist in the identity of its material particles, for these come and go, are in constant flux, and are wholly changed, it is said, every seven years. But, notwithstanding this change, the body of the man is the same with that of the child. The same features, figure, temperament, morbid and passional tendencies, are reproduced year after year. These flying particles, gathered from earth and air, are manufactured into brain, bone, blood, according to an unvarying law, and then given back again to air and earth. There is, therefore, a hidden mysterious principle of organization working on during the whole seventy years of our earthly existence, which makes the body of the infant and the child identical with that of the man and the old man. This is the true body; and this, extricated at death from its present envelope, and clothed upon with a higher spiritual and immortal form, will constitute the future body.

But again, it will be a *higher development of the body*. Paul plainly teaches this. He uses the analogy of the seed, showing that the future body is related to this; and differenced from this, as the plant is related to the seed, and yet different from it. "Thou sowest *not* that body *that shall be*, but bare grain." You do not sow the stalk, but the kernel; you do not sow the oak, but the acorn. Yet the oak is contained potentially in the acorn, and so the future body is contained potentially in the present. The condition of the germination of the acorn is its dissolution; then the germ is able to separate itself from the rest of the seed, and start forward in a new career of development. In like manner the spiritual body cannot be developed until the present organization is dissolved.

Paul goes on to say that "there is a natural body and there is a spiritual." This body is the natural body; the future will be the spiritual. Two things may be implied in this distinction. As by the natural body we come into communion with the natural world, the world of phenomena, so by the spiritual we commune with the spiritual world, the world of essential being and cause. *Here* and *now* we see things through a glass, darkly, *then* face to face. *Here* we look at things on the outside only; but how often a longing seizes us to know the essences, to penetrate to their interior life! That longing is an instinctive prophecy of its own fulfilment hereafter. The spiritual body must also *manifest the spirit* hereafter, as the natural or soul body now manifests the soul. For while the present body expresses adequately enough present wishes and emotions, it fails of expressing the spiritual emotions, and fails of being a true servant of the higher life.

This, then, constitutes the future body. First, it is an organization connecting us with the outward universe of space and time. Second, it is identical with the present true body. Third, it is a development and advance of this into a higher organization. Let us now inquire what are the evidences and proofs of *this future body*. How do we know, or why do we think, that we shall have any such body?

The first proof of a future bodily existence is its reasonableness. There is a law of gradation in the universe by which the seed unfolds gradually into the stalk, the bud into the flower, the flower into the fruit. We see a gradual progress of vegetable life into animal, and a gradual transition from the lower forms of animal existence to the higher. The transition is so gradual that it is very difficult to say where vegetables end and where animals begin. Radiated animals ascend towards the mollusks, the mollusks towards the articulata, the articulata towards the vertebrata. And through this last class we see a steady ascent from one form of organization to another; from fishes to reptiles, from reptiles to birds, from birds to mammalia, until by steady rise we reach the human body, in delicacy, beauty, and faculty the crown of all. Why should we suppose this the end of bodily existence? Why not rather that this is to pass into a still more noble and beautiful type of organization? After this gradual development, why suppose the enormous change to a purely spiritual existence? Is it not more reasonable to suppose, instead, a higher order of bodily life?

If we may look at the question for a moment from a metaphysical point of view, we shall find it hard to comprehend the possibility of personal existence hereafter apart from bodily organization. Everything which is, must be either somewhere, or everywhere, or nowhere; that is, it must be present in some particular point of space, or omnipresent through all space, or wholly out of space. But to be wholly out of space is to lose that which distinguishes one thing from another, for all distinctions which we can conceive of are distinctions in space and time. To be everywhere is to be omnipresent, which is an attribute belonging to God and not to finite being, and would imply absorption into the divine nature. Therefore personal existence is existence somewhere in space, but locality in space is an attribute of body, not of spirit, and implies bodily existence.

Moreover, shall we suppose that after death we are to have no more communion with the material universe, no more knowledge of this vast order and beauty, which is a perpetual manifestation of God, the garment which he wears, one of his grand methods of revelation? These myriads of suns and worlds, these constellations of stars peopling space, this city of God full of wonder and infinite variety, are they to be nothing to us after the few years of mortal life are over? We cannot believe it. If, then, we are still to perceive the material universe, the faculties by which we perceive it will be more intense bodily faculties. If spiritual things are spiritually discerned, bodily things are discerned in a bodily manner.

Such considerations as these show that a future bodily existence is reasonable; but the proof of it must come, if at all, either from revelation or experience. Let us see, then, what bearing the resurrection of Jesus has upon this question.

According to the Gospels, Jesus rose from the dead in bodily form. This body resembled his former one, so as to be recognized by his disciples; it had the marks of the spear and nails; it could be touched, and was capable of eating food. In all these respects it seems exactly the same body he had before. This, too, is confirmed by the fact that he came from the tomb where his body had been placed, and that this had disappeared. But, on the other hand, many peculiarities indicate a difference; such as his not being recognized at once by Mary in the garden, nor by the disciples during the whole walk to Emmaus; his appearing and disappearing suddenly; his coming through the closed doors. Again, if the body of Jesus was exactly like that which he had before death, it is evident that he would have to lay it aside again before ascending into the spiritual world, for flesh and blood cannot inherit the kingdom of God. But if he was to lay it aside again, this would be equivalent to dying a second time, which would destroy the whole meaning and value of his resurrection, making it nothing but a mere revival, or coming to life again, like that of a person who has been apparently drowned. Such a revival would have produced no results, and the faith of the Church which has come from the resurrection of Jesus would never have taken place.

Accordingly, we must conclude that Jesus rose with a higher spiritual body. And this gives to the ascension its meaning. For otherwise, the ascension would be only a disappearance; whereas, in this view, the disciples saw him pass away in the shape and form he was to continue to wear in the other world. Then the gulf was bridged over, in their minds, and they had looked into heaven.

This was what the resurrection of Jesus did for the apostles. It changed doubt and despair into faith and hope; changed theoretical belief into practical assurance; imparted that commanding energy of conviction and utterance which only comes from life. Animated thus themselves, they were enabled to animate others. And so the resurrection of Christ was the resurrection of Christianity, the resurrection of a Christian faith and hope infinitely deeper and stronger than had before existed in the minds of the disciples.

We do not like the usual method of regarding the resurrection of Jesus as a great exceptional event, and an astounding violation of the laws of nature. Its power seems rather to have consisted in this, that it was a glorious confirmation of those everlasting laws announced by Jesus—laws boundless as the universe. The very essence of the gospel is the declaration that good is not only better than evil, which we all knew before, but stronger than evil, which we weakly doubt.

The gospel assures us that love is stronger than hatred, peace than war, holiness than evil, truth than error. It is the marriage of the goodness of motive and the goodness of attainment; goodness in the soul and goodness in outward life; heaven hereafter and heaven here. It asserts that the good man is always in reality successful; that he who humbles himself *is* exalted, he who forgives *is* forgiven, he who gives to others receives again himself, he who hungers after righteousness is filled. This was the faith which Christ expressed, in which and out of which he lived and acted; it was this faith which made him Christ the King, King of human minds and hearts. Was it then all false? Did his death prove it so? Was that the end, the earthly end, of his efforts for man? Were truth and love struck down then by the power of darkness? That was the question which his resurrection answered; it showed him passing through death to higher life, through an apparent overthrow to a real triumph; it gave one visible illustration to laws usually invisible in their operation, and set God's seal to their truth. Through that death which seemed the destruction of all hope, Jesus went up to be the Christ, the King.

In this point of view we see the value and importance of the resurrection of Jesus, and why Easter Sunday should be the chief festival of Christianity. It was the great triumph of life over death, of good over evil. It was the apt symbol and illustration of the whole gospel.

If, then, the resurrection of Christ means that Christ ascended through death to a higher state; if our resurrection means that we pass up through death, and not down; not into the grave, but into a condition of higher life; if the resurrection of the body does not mean the raising again out of the earth the material particles deposited there, but the soul clothing itself with a higher and more perfect organization; if it is, then, the raising of the body to a more perfect condition of development,—then is there not good reason why such stress should be laid upon this great fact?

All the proof rests on the historic fact of the resurrection. Was Christ seen in this higher spiritual and bodily state, or was he not? If he was, then we have a fact of history and experience to rely upon to show us that the future life involves an ascent both spiritual and bodily. And this is the reason why such stress has been laid on the resurrection.

This raising of man, through the power of Christ's life, to a higher state, is not a mere matter of speculation, then, not an opinion, not something pleasant to think of and hope for, but it is a fundamental fact of Christian faith. Because Christ has arisen and passed up, we must all arise and pass up, too, with him. He is the first fruits of those who sleep. In proportion as the Spirit of Christ is in us, in that proportion is the power in us which shall carry us upward towards him. He wishes that those who believe in him shall be where he is. We shall belong to him and to his higher world, not arbitrarily, but naturally; not by any positive decree of God, but by the nature of things.

The essential fact in the resurrection is, that Christ rose, through death, to a higher state. The essential doctrine of the resurrection is, that death is the transition from a lower to a higher condition in all who have the life which makes them capable of it.

Chapter XIII
Christ's Coming, Usually Called The "Second Coming," And Christ The Judge Of The World

§ 1. The Coming of Christ is not wholly future, not wholly outward, not local, nor material

It is a curious fact that, in direct contradiction to Christ's own explanations concerning his coming, this should frequently be considered by the Orthodox, (1.) as wholly future; (2.) as wholly outward; (3.) as local; (4.) as bodily and material.

It cannot be wholly future, for if it were, Jesus was mistaken in saying of the signs of his coming, "This generation shall not pass away until all these things be fulfilled." (Mark 13:30.)

Nor can it be wholly outward, for if it were, Jesus was mistaken when he declared of the signs of his coming, "The kingdom of God cometh not with observation" (Luke 17:20); "The kingdom of God is within you " (Luke 17:21); "My kingdom is not of this world" (John 18:36). See also Mark 4:26,27, and Matt. 13:33, where his kingdom is compared with seed sprouting and leaven working secretly.

Nor is Christ's coming local, that is, in a certain place, for if it were, Jesus was mistaken in telling his disciples not to believe those who said, "Lo, here!" or "Lo, there!" not to go into the desert when men say, "Behold, he is there," and not to believe those who declare that he is hidden somewhere in the city, for that the coming of the Son of man should be like that of the lightning, which shines all round the sky, and seems to be everywhere at once. (Matt. 24:26.)

And if not local, neither can it be a bodily coming; for all bodily coming must be in some one place. Since, therefore, Jesus distinctly denies that his coming is to be "here" or "there,"—that is, local,—it must be a spiritual coming, a coming in spirit and in power. All the material images connected with it—the clouds, the trumpet, &c.—are to be considered symbolical. The "clouds of heaven" may symbolize spiritual movements and influences; the "trumpet," the awakening power of new truth.40

§ 2. No Second Coming of Christ is mentioned in Scripture

It is also a remarkable fact that only one coming of Christ is mentioned in the New Testament. Orthodoxy speaks continually of Christ's *second* coming, but without any warrant. It assumes that the manifestation of Jesus in the flesh was his first coming as the Christ, and that consequently the predictions (in Matt. ch. 24, and the parallels) *must* refer to a second coming. Hence the phrase "second coming" has been introduced, and naturalized in theology. But, in truth, the life of Jesus on earth was not regarded as his coming as the Messiah.41 What the disciples expected was his manifestation or investiture as the Messiah, which evidently had not taken place at the time of their conversation. And this was to be, not "at the end of the world," but *at the end of the age.* They, like other Jews, divided time into two periods, "the present age," or times previous to the Messiah, and "the coming age," or times of the Messiah's reign. When, therefore, Jesus was with them, only teaching and healing, they did not at all consider him *to have come* as the Messiah. But when he spoke of the destruction of the Temple, as *that* indicated the end of the existing economy, they understood it to be synchronous with his coming as the Christ. So they said, "What shall be the sign of thy coming, and of the end of the age?" And so through the Epistles, when the "coming of Christ" is spoken of, is meant his manifestation in the world as the Messiah. This was a single event, to take place once, not to be repeated. Such a thing as "Christ's *second* coming" is unknown to the Scriptures.42

§ 3. Were the Apostles mistaken in expecting a speedy Coming of Christ?

It is often said that the apostles themselves were mistaken in expecting a speedy coming of Christ. No doubt they did expect his speedy coming, and with reason; for he himself had told them that the existing generation should not pass away till all those things were fulfilled. Therefore they were justified in looking for a near coming of Jesus as the Christ. We admit that they expected his speedy coming; but we think they were not mistaken, for he did come. He came, though not perhaps in the manner they anticipated. Possibly they interpreted too literally what he said concerning his coming.

For though Christ spoke so much in symbols and parables, literal people took him literally. And so they do still. When he said that except men ate his flesh and drank his blood they could not be his, the literalists said, "*How* can this man give us his flesh to eat?" And so many persons still think that somehow Christ's actual body is to be eaten in the Lord's supper. So, when he said that the Son of man should be seen "coming in the clouds of heaven with power and great glory, and send his angels with the sound of a trumpet, and gather his elect from the four winds," they took it literally. His apostles, even, may have supposed that he was to be seen up in the air in physical form,43 and that a material trumpet was to be blown. But all this was the flesh, the garb of his thought. The spirit of his thought only is of value; the flesh profits nothing. The apostles were wrong in supposing—if they did suppose it—that Christ was to come in their day in the air, in an outward physical fashion, with an outward noise, making a great demonstration to the senses of sight and hearing. Christ never came so, and he never will come so. The only coming of Christ possible is spiritual coming, for Christ is spirit. He did come, therefore, in the days of the apostles, in the great access of faith and power in their own souls, and in the souls of those whom they converted. He came in power and great glory, when his truth came to human minds, and his love to human hearts. He sent his angels then, and gathered his elect from the four quarters of the heavens. When Paul was converted, Christ came to him; when the negro chamberlain of the Queen of Ethiopia was converted, Christ came to him; when the people of Ephesus and Corinth, Philippi and Rome, were converted, Christ came to them. The trumpet sounded, but it was in their souls that it sounded; the angels summoned the elect, but these angels were the convictions sent into their reason, and the longings awakened in their hearts.

Materialists and Literalists are always the same. The apostles soon rose out of their literalism, and soon spoke of Christ as being revealed *within* them, not outside of them; dwelling, not in the air, but in their hearts. But literalists, down to this day, have always imagined the coming of Christ to be to the senses, rather than to the soul. They do not see that a great noise in the air is not so glorious a thing as a voice heard in the depths of the heart, and a great outward conflagration somehow seems to them more imposing than the burning up of falsehood and sin in the world. So we are always hearing people predict that Christ is to come in 1846, or 1856, or 1866, meaning thereby that they expect some great outward event then, visible to eyes and ears. "Fools, and slow of heart," not to see that the only possible coming of Him who is spirit and love is a coming in the soul, and that he has come, and is coming, and is to come more and more abundantly, from day to day. So they read about the heavens and earth being burned up, and of a new heavens and earth; and they imagine that the sky is somehow to be burned with material fire, and the surface of the earth to sink into the flaming abyss beneath us. But if this should happen, *that* would have nothing to do with the coming of Christ. The heavens and earth which he consumes with the breath of his mouth, and destroys with the brightness of his coming, are the religions and moralities, the institutions and works, of men. And the new heavens and new earth which take their place are the higher, nobler, purer religions and moralities which flow out of the Spirit of Christ.

§ 4. Examination of the Account of Christ's Coming given by Jesus in Matthew (chapters 24-26)

A great difficulty in regard to the coming of Christ is to combine in one view the different notions given in Scripture concerning it. Many of these ideas indicate that the coming of Christ took place at the destruction of Jerusalem, as, for example, the description of wars, destruction of the Temple, and especially the declaration that "this generation shall not pass away till all these things be fulfilled." On the other hand, the coming of Christ is expressly connected, in our translation, with "the end of the world," and with the general judgment. Hence a difficulty in interpreting these passages, some persons thinking that the coming of Christ took place at the destruction of Jerusalem; others thinking that it is yet to take place at the end of the world; others, again, maintaining two or more comings of Christ; and others spiritualizing the whole of it, and making it mean the spread of the spirit of Christianity.

Let us, therefore, examine the passage in which Christ's coming is spoken of, and endeavor to find its natural and obvious meaning, and so see how far the common Orthodox conception is correct.

The subject is not unimportant. Several chapters in the Gospel of Matthew (24-26) are devoted to the description of this event. All of the Epistles contain frequent allusions to it. The apostles unquestionably expected Christ's coming in their day, and they had a right to do so, inasmuch as Jesus himself had distinctly said that their generation would not pass away till all was fulfilled. And in the main fact they were not mistaken, however they may have been deceived, as we have before said, in taking too outward a view of the attending circumstances. For if Christ's coming did not take place in their day, not only were they themselves mistaken on a most important point, but Jesus was mistaken likewise.

Some of the other points in the description of this event are these: Christ's coming was to be like that of the thief in the night — that is, it was to be unexpected, and to take men unprepared. It was to be preceded by wars, commotions, and misery in every form; preceded also by the preaching of the truth in many lands. It was to be as difficult to locate Christ at his coming, as to fix the lightning, which comes out of the east and shines to the west. It was to be attended with great spiritual darkness, even in the minds of the wise and good. The sun, and moon, and stars of the moral world were to be darkened, and the powers of the heavens to be shaken; and of ten virgins, all going together to meet the bridegroom, half would be found spiritually asleep when he came. Christ's coming would be especially judgment and punishment. He would part the sheep from the goats. He would consume with the brightness of his coming the man of sin. Such are some of the traits with which the coming of Jesus is described by himself and by his apostles. How are these to be reconciled with the facts, and what was his coming?

The best way to get at the facts is to begin at the beginning, and ask *what the disciples meant* when they asked for the signs of Christ's coming. They were sitting with Jesus on the Mount of Olives, looking across the valley between, at the Temple. They saw and admired the gorgeous magnificence of this vast edifice towering before them, white with marble and yellow with gold, against the deep blue sky of that sunny land, and as they admired it, Jesus told them that every stone of that divine structure should be cast down. And then they asked, "*When* shall these things be? and what shall be the signs of thy coming, and of the end of the world?" What was the connection, in their minds, between the three events? Why should they have at once inferred that the destruction of the Temple was to take place at the coming of Christ, and that the coming of Christ was to take place at the end of the world? There was no connection at all, according to the common notions on this subject. If the coming of Christ was to be a great outward manifestation in the sky, to take place long after his death, after the lapse of thousands of years, and at the destruction of the visible universe, what had that to do with the Jewish Temple? or, indeed, what had that to do with any of their ideas concerning their Master? But the notion in their minds, when they asked the question, was something very different; not the present Christian idea, but the usual Jewish idea. They spoke as Jews, out of the notions of their day. Christ answered what was in their minds, not what is in ours. If we wish to know what he meant, we must place ourselves on their stand-point, look out of their eyes, and listen with their ears.

The coming of Christ had a very distinct meaning to the Jewish mind. It meant the manifestation of the Messiah, *as such*. It meant his coming to reign as king. It meant his manifestation in Judea, in Jerusalem, as the great Son of David, and the submission of the Jews, and Gentiles with them, to his authority. The disciples of Jesus, believing him to be the Christ, believed that he was to come as such. He had come as Prophet, as Teacher, as a worker of beneficent miracles, but he had not yet come as Christ, as King. They were not asking about any second coming after his death and resurrection, for they did not believe that he was to die. They were asking for his present triumphant manifestation and investiture as the Messiah.

Nor were they asking—as our translators make them ask—for "the end of the world." But they were asking for the *end of the age*—that is, of the first age. We have said that the Jews divided all time into two great periods; one the age preceding the Messiah, the other the age of the Messiah. The first was called this age, or the present age; the other the coming age. The end of the first period and beginning of the second were called the ends of the age; as where Paul says, "These are written for our admonition, upon whom the ends of the world are come;" and where he says that Christ has "now once appeared in the end of the world to put away sin." These were the ideas of the Jews, as we know from history. When, therefore, Christ spoke of the overthrow of the Temple, they inferred that he was speaking of the beginning of the Messianic age; since the Temple would not be overthrown while the Jewish theocratic and Levitical government continued. Now, as the Jewish age did come to an end at the destruction of Jerusalem, and Christianity, as the universal religion, took the place of Judaism in the education of the human race, this really was the coming of the Messiah and the end of the age.

We understand, therefore, Christ to have been really speaking of his coming, as an event soon to take place, and which did soon take place, when, at the destruction of Jerusalem, the Jewish Christians were scattered through the world, and Christianity took its place as a universal religion.44 If this exhausted the meaning of the idea, it would be of very little interest to us. But the contents of the passage are more rich and full; and, like most of Christ's sayings, besides its present and immediate application, it has more universal and far-reaching meanings. The principles of Christianity which were manifested then, continue to be manifested in other forms to-day. Jesus said on one occasion, "The hour is coming, and now is, when all that are in their graves shall hear the voice of the Son of man." And on another occasion, "The hour is coming, and now is, when the true worshippers shall worship the Father." The hour had come in its first manifestation, but was to come again in other and richer manifestations of the same principle. So Christ himself came as King at the taking of Jerusalem, but has come since, again and again, more plainly and fully, in other triumphs of his truth, in other manifestations of his power. We believe that the coming of Christ took place at the destruction of Jerusalem. We believe that it has taken place since, in other historical events. We believe that it is to take place more fully hereafter, in this life and in the other life.

Let us look and consider how this may be.

§ 5. Coming of Christ in Human History at different Times

As we look back through the eighteen centuries of Christian history, we can observe many events which may now be seen to have been each a coming of Christ. When, at the destruction of Jerusalem, the Mosaic theocracy went down before the iron power of Rome, amid those scenes of horror the firmest believers in Christ might have feared only evil. It seemed to be the overthrow of everything most sacred—the triumph of Paganism over the worship of Jehovah. Yet what was the result? Jesus then ceased to be the Jewish Messiah, and began to reign over all nations as the world-teacher, the Son of God, the prophet for mankind. Since then, more and more, the world has gone to him as to its great Master. This, therefore, was a coming of Christ.

Look again. The early centuries are disgraced with theological wars. Fierce conflicts are carried on about the Trinity, and the rank of Jesus in the universe. All regard for the pure, divine truth of Christianity seems forgotten in the fury of these controversies. Yet, nevertheless, amid all the absurdity and contradiction, one truth emerges, everywhere recognized— that in Jesus was something divine; that God was more fully manifest in him than elsewhere; that he is the moral image of the Infinite One. This is another coming of Christ. He comes now not merely as a prophet, but as the revealer of divine love and truth, in his own character. The theological doctrines, in which this truth has been wrapped, are the husks and shells which the world will throw away. But throughout Christendom the idea of God is derived from the character of Jesus, and in this way Jesus has come to rule the hearts of men as their divine King.

Other centuries passed by, and we find new and strange ideas taking possession of men's minds. A horror of life, a dread of the sins of the world, drive men into the desert, to live as hermits and anchorites. Thousands and tens of thousands of monks withdrew from the world into the wilderness. All Christianity appeared to be changing into a new form of heathenish, self-inflicted torture. Its blessed humanity, its genial influences on social life, seemed to be fast disappearing. Nevertheless, out of all this error one truth emerged, one Christian idea was developed—that of self-discipline and self-culture. And in the development of this idea Christ came to reign *over the individual soul* as its Master, Guide, and Redeemer from all sin.

After this arose the Papacy. The Church, as a powerful institution, became ambitious to rule the state and the world. A spiritual despotism appeared, surrounding itself with earthly splendor, grasping the sword of earthly power, and the farthest removed from the humble and gentle spirit of its Master. It would tolerate no opposition to its will, in high places or low. It hurled its thunders at the head of kings, and sent crusading armies to persecute and torture the peasants of the Piedmont valleys. Nothing could seem more full of the spirit of Antichrist than this spiritual despotism embodied in the Papacy. And yet, even through this evil there was developed a truth—that there was something in the world higher than kings, greater than the state. Papacy, with all its evils, was a standing proof, in an age of brute force, of the supremacy of mind over matter. So that, even here, the pride and selfishness of the priests and the popes have been overruled, in the providence of God, to give ascendency to a Christian idea, and to cause Christ to come as the King of the world.

Consider another important event in the history of Europe: the conversion of the barbarous tribes to Christianity. When the nations of the north poured from the forests of Germany and the deserts of Scandinavia over the Roman empire,—when Goths and Vandals, Franks, Lombards, and Normans, quenched the light of civilization and brought the dark ages over Europe,—how terrible seemed the gloom, and how hopeless the prospects, of the human race! But we now see the result in modern civilization. We see all these different nations subdued by the power of Christianity, and a new unity, a higher harmony, as the result. We see the great idea of the unity of the race, the harmony of nations, resulting from all this darkness and misery. So Christ has come again as the Prince of Peace, breaking down the partition walls, and proclaiming a brotherhood of man.

Let us look at one more event of history—the Lutheran Reformation. What evils attended it! What wars came out of it! How has the impulse to freedom given by Luther degenerated into licentiousness, run out in infidelity and unbelief! And yet, when we consider the ideas of personal responsibility and individual independence which have been born of it,— when we consider what an impulse it has given to thought, to free inquiry, to earnest investigation of truth, all the results of this fruitful principle,—we cannot doubt that this also was a coming of Jesus, the unfolding of a new and higher power in Christianity.

Thus has Christ come from age to age, and in the midst of apparent failure, increasing error, growing unbelief, and all forms of human wickedness, has acquired new power over the human mind. At the present day he is more the King of the world than ever. When he seems to go, then he comes. When iniquity most abounds, then he is nearest. When love grows cold in the hearts of his disciples, then a new impulse of faith is about to be given. When false prophets rise up and deceive many, then new champions of the truth are near at hand. Christ comes amid wars and persecutions. He comes unexpectedly, like the thief in the night; comes without observation; and while men say, "Lo, here!" and "Lo, there!" the kingdom of heaven is in the midst of them. He is not to be found in the desert, nor in the secret chambers; neither in public nor private; located neither in this nor that particular place; incarnate neither in this nor that particular person. But Christ comes like the lightning, seen over the whole heaven at once, in a new spirit pervading all parts of life, all parts of society.

§ 6. Relation of the Parable of the Virgins, and of the Talents, to Christ's Coming

We now see what is meant by the parable of the foolish and wise virgins, and of the talents, which follows it. We see their application to this description of Christ's coming. If the coming of Christ be thus unexpected, he will not be recognized by the sleeping servant, nor by those who beat their fellow-servants. Slothful Christians who make no effort to improve, persecuting Christians who spend their time in denouncing heretics, and saying, "My Lord delayeth his coming," never understand the signs of the times, nor recognize any new influx of divine light in the world. At each new coming of Christ those who have been faithful are rewarded by more light. To those who have, shall be given, and the faithless lose what they had before. From him who hath not, shall be taken away even what he seems to have. The capacity of seeing Christ when he comes, of recognizing him in any new manifestation of truth, depends on his previous fidelity.

§ 7. Relation of the Account of the Judgment by the Messiah, in Matt. ch. 25, to his Coming

But what is meant by the judgment described in the 25th chapter of Matthew, commencing, "When the Son of man shall come in his glory, and all the angels with him, then shall he sit upon the throne of his glory, and before him shall be gathered all nations, and he shall separate them one from another, as a shepherd divideth the sheep from the goats." This stands in such close connection with what goes before, that many refer this also to the destruction of Jerusalem. But the moral meaning is so prominent, that others apply it entirely to the final judgment in the future life. The difficulties on both sides disappear if we reflect that the principles which govern this life and the next are identical—that whether Christ came at Jerusalem, comes to-day, or comes in the future life, the laws of Christian retribution are the same. Wherever Christ judges men, the sheep go to the right, and the goats to the left. The generous, humane, and disinterested hear always the words, "Come, ye blessed of my Father; inherit the kingdom prepared for you from the foundation of the world." The judgment in this world, it may be, is only heard in the depths of the soul. It may be that no other mortal knows of it. Still it is the voice of Christ which speaks. Still it is the real kingdom which they inherit. The judgment in the future life, may be or may not be, before assembled multitudes whom no man can number, and the kingdom then inherited may be one shared with the angels, and extending over worlds. Still the sentence is the same in both cases. The judgment of Christ is one in all worlds. It was, and is, and shall be. Jesus Christ is the same yesterday, to-day, and forever.

It may be said, this is to make the coming of Christ merely figurative — the coming of ideas and principles only; only the coming of his religion; and this is but an invisible abstraction. We reply, that according to our view, Christianity cannot be conceived of as an abstraction, apart from the person of Jesus, nor can his religion come unless he comes with it. Jesus is with us always, in the world always, and none the less really, because invisibly. It is no figure of speech to say that Christ is with his Church, and with his truth; that where it goes, he goes; that when he comes, it comes. It may even be that his presence will not always be an invisible one. It may be that what we now believe, we shall one day see and know. But then those only will recognize their Master's presence who are awake and watching for him. To the others it will seem a mere illusion or enthusiasm.

§ 8. How Christ is, and how he is not, to judge the World

In some places Jesus says that he is made Judge of mankind, and in other places denies that he is to judge any one. Take, for example, the following passages, selected because they seem to contradict each other. They are all in the Gospel of John, and therefore the contradiction is not in the different limitations or special misconceptions of the different evangelists. The passages are, John 3:17; 9:39; 5:22; 8:15; 12:47. The first is as follows: "For God sent not his Son into the world to condemn the world, but that the world through him might be saved." The word here translated "*condemn*" is precisely the same as that which elsewhere is translated "*judge*." Consequently we should here read that God sent Christ into the world, not to judge the world, but to save it. But the next text referred to (John 9:39) is one in which Jesus says, "For judgment have I come into the world, that they which see not may see, and that they which see might be made blind." Again (in John 5:22) it is said, that "the Father judgeth no man, but hath committed all judgment unto the Son." But in the following passage (John 8:15) Jesus says, "Ye judge after the flesh. I judge no man." And in the last text he repeats the same idea. "And if any man hear my words and believe not, I judge him not; for I came not to judge the world, but to save the world." We have, therefore, in these passages, this apparent contradiction — that the

Saviour seems in some places to declare that he is to judge the world, and in others that he is not to judge the world. We therefore shall do well to inquire how these are to be understood, and in what way at all they are to be reconciled with each other, and with the common Orthodox doctrine concerning judgment.

And here we may remark, in passing, that there are many such seeming contradictions as these in the New Testament, and that to the student of the Gospels, who is a sincere seeker of truth, they are very precious and valuable. Such a one is always glad at finding statements in the New Testament which thus appear opposed to each other; for he knows, by experience, that they are the very passages from which he may learn the most, and where he will be likely to find some hitherto unnoticed truth concerning Christ or his gospel. Such truth, however, will not be found if he attempts to remove the contradiction by any artificial, hasty, or forced process. If his object is merely to find proof-texts in support of the doctrines he already believes, such paradoxes will afford him nothing but barren difficulties, and a sphere for the exercise of sophistry and misplaced ingenuity. But if he can bear to admit his ignorance, and is willing to examine these difficulties in order to correct his own errors, enlarge his own views, and learn something really new, he will often find here the clew to deeper insight and to a larger knowledge.

What, then, is the explanation of these passages? In what way is Christ to *judge*? How is it that he has come into this world for *judgment*? and how has the Father committed *all judgment* unto the Son? and how, nevertheless, can be say, "*I judge no man; for I came not to judge the world*"?

Christ's coming was simply to do good; to make men better; to save them from their sins; to reveal pardon; to offer salvation; to manifest God's love. "The law was given by Moses, but grace and truth came by Jesus Christ." It is the law, and not the gospel, which judges and condemns the evil-doer. The law given by Moses, or the law given in the conscience, in the reason, in the nature of things, written on the face of nature, written in the soul of man, — this law has not been made more strict by the coming of Christ. Men were bound before, by the law of nature and the law of Moses, to love God with all their heart, and their neighbor as themselves; and they are not bound to do more now. They were bound by nature and reason to obey their conscience, to do the best they could always, and they are not bound to do any more now. The whole influence of the gospel is a bountiful and gracious one, intended and adapted to make it easier to do right, to add new motives to virtue. Christ is no strict, severe judge, deciding by the letter of the law, bound by his office to show no favor or compassion, but the sinner's advocate and friend. And hence it may truly be said that he came not to judge the world, but to save the world.

Nevertheless, it is also true that the greatest blessings and the best gifts of God are also judgments. They test the character. They show what it is. According to the state of mind and heart in which a man is, so does he receive, or reject, or neglect the offered good. If he loves light, he comes to the light. If he loves darkness, he goes away. If his deeds are good, he gratefully receives any revelation which brings him nearer to God. If his deeds are evil, he rejects such revelation, avoids it, dislikes the thought of it. So it necessarily is that the best and kindest of men who wishes only to do good to all, nevertheless, by his very presence and his offers of good, judges and condemns the wicked. But what are the judgment and the sentence? Simply this—that light has come into the world, and that they have chosen darkness rather than light, because their deeds are evil. Therefore it was necessarily the case that the coming of Jesus into the world was a judgment, and that though he everywhere went with the purpose of saving and blessing men, yet that he necessarily was also a judge. The thoughts of many hearts were revealed by his presence. The pure in heart came to him in humility, penitence, and faith. The proud in heart, the self-willed, the self-righteous, turned away from him, and so judged themselves unworthy of receiving his truth. The Galilean peasants, the common people, heard him gladly. The Scribes and Pharisees murmured against him and rejected him. This was really a judgment on both: the sheep went to the right hand, and the goats to the left. Thus it is a law of human nature that all high truth by its coming judges men, and shows by its influence upon them what is their real state. And in this way, as Christ's truth was the highest of all, so he was, and is, a judge in the highest sense. But this is not quite all. The coming of such truth not only shows the good and evil which are in men, but it develops them, brings them out, increases the good, increases also the evil. It is necessarily so; it cannot be otherwise. When good comes to us, if it does not make us better, it makes us worse. Truth and goodness are like the magnet. They have two poles. They attract and they repel. Thus it was written that the coming of Jesus would be for the fall or the rising of many. Thus he said, "For judgment I have come into the world, that those which see not may see, and that those who see may be made blind." Peter was made better, Judas was made worse, by being in the company of Christ. His coming was not only judgment, but also reward and punishment. He came to the fishermen of Galilee: they were pure in heart, they were lovers of truth and goodness, and his coming transformed them into apostles, saints, and martyrs. He came to the Scribes and Pharisees: they were not pure in heart. They were proud of their position, their influence, their piety, and his coming transformed them into murderers.

We are now prepared to decide what is meant by Jesus in saying that he came to judge the world, and yet that he came not to judge, but to save. It was not the purpose of his mission to judge. The direct object of his coming was not to judge, but to save; but indirectly, and as a matter of necessity, one of the consequences of his coming was, that men were judged by the word which he spoke, by the truth which he manifested, by the holiness of his life, by the bliss which he offered, and which they rejected. And yet it was true that he did not judge them, and that he did not mean to judge them. They were already judged by their own choice and determination. Therefore he says, "He who believeth not on me is judged already, because he hath not believed on the name of the only begotten Son of God." It was not the will of Christ, but the truth itself, which pronounced the sentence upon him. "The word that I have spoken, the same shall judge him at the last day." And thus it is said, that God is the Judge of all, and yet again, that the Father judgeth no man, but hath committed all judgment unto the Son, and hath given him authority to execute judgment also, because he is the Son of man. The explanation is, that men are judged by the truth. But this truth is not abstract, but the truth embodied in the life and teaching of Jesus. God does not come into the world himself to show men their sins, but he embodies his truth and holiness in the life of his Son, and so judges the world.

In giving this explanation, we have looked steadily at the essential thing in judgment. We have regarded the substance, not the form. If we think of judgment as something outward, the judge seated on his throne, the criminal standing before him, and a formal sentence pronounced, of acquittal or condemnation, we confess that we should find it difficult to reconcile these different passages of Scripture, some of which declare that Christ is to be the judge, and others that he is not to be. But what is the essential thing in judgment? It is that justice shall be done, and that truth and right shall be vindicated; that the good shall be rewarded, and the wicked punished; that virtue and truth shall be seen and recognized in the consciences of men for what they are. This is the essential thing. *How* this is done, whether in an open tribunal, before the assembled universe, or in the secret places of every man's soul, belongs not to the essence, but to the form, and is comparatively unimportant.

§ 9. When Christ's Judgment takes Place

Nevertheless, there is a more important question to be answered in relation to the *time* of judgment. When is the judgment? For it may be thought, from what we have said, that we consider judgment as taking place only in this world. But such is not the fact. Christ's judgments take place at Christ's coming, whether here or hereafter. Whenever Christ comes, he comes to judge. His first coming, in Judea, was a judgment; and he said, "*Now* is the judgment of the world." His coming judged all those who were near him; revealed the state of their minds and hearts; showed them what they were. Wherever he went, men arranged themselves at once according to their real characters, and the thoughts of many hearts were revealed.

It is true that people at that day did not understand that they were thus condemning themselves. They did not know that the awful judgment of God was being pronounced upon them; that they were standing before his bar in the presence of angels. They did not know that the day of judgment had come, and that they were giving an account of every idle word even then. But so it was. When they scoffed at Jesus and said, "He is a gluttonous man and a wine-bibber," they may have forgotten their words almost before they left their mouths. But there they stand, recorded against them forever—an everlasting proof of their blindness of mind and their hardness of heart. When the penitent woman brought the ointment and anointed the feet of Jesus, and bathed them with her tears, little did she think that it was her day of judgment also, and that the approving sentence of her act would be read by angels in heaven and countless myriads on earth. None of them knew that it was a judgment then; but it was so.

But was that the only judgment? No; for whenever Jesus comes, he comes to judge; and since that, his first coming, he has come again and again to individuals and to the world, and every coming has been a new judgment on the state of the human mind and heart. It has therefore been well said, that the history of the world is the judgment of the world. And it is always true that this judgment is not understood when it is pronounced, but is seen and recognized afterwards. It is so with individuals; it is so with communities. Who is there who, in looking back over his past life, does not witness many an hour in which the truth has come to him, and he refused to admit it, and so sentenced himself to receive a lie? in which he has had opportunities of improvement, opportunities of doing good, and has refused to accept them, and so the talent has been taken from him and given to another. This is the judgment—that light has come into the world, and we have chosen darkness. At the time we did not know it: blinded by prejudice, heated by passion, we rushed recklessly on. But sooner or later comes the calm hour of recollection, and we see ourselves as we are.

But is this judgment which takes place in this world the only one? It is unreasonable to think so. There are, in fact, two extreme views on this subject. The views of those who say that all judgment is in this life, and the views of those who say that no judgment is in this life. The New Testament teaches that we are judged here, and that we are also judged hereafter. The coming of Christ is here, and also hereafter; and the judgment which commenced with his first coming will not be completed till all of us stand before the judgment seat to give an account of the deeds done in the body, whether they be good or evil. "It is appointed unto men once to die, but after this the judgment." There is a judgment in this life, and another to come. But those will be best prepared for that future judgment who understand the present judgment. Here is an example of the nature of the judgments which take place in this world.

In the year 1633, an old man was brought before the Court of the Inquisition, consisting of seven cardinals of the Roman Catholic Church, to hear a sentence and to pronounce a recantation. The crime he had committed was the publication of a book in the form of a dialogue, maintaining that the sun stood still, and that the earth moved; which proposition these holy cardinals pronounced to be absurd, false in philosophy, and formally heretical, seeing that it was expressly contrary to Holy Scripture. Whereupon they call upon him to abjure, execrate, and detest these errors and heresies; prohibiting his book and condemning him to confinement, with the penance of reciting once a week, for three years, the seven penitential psalms. And thereupon, this man, Galileo Galilei, of the age of seventy, on his knees, with his hands on the Gospels, abjures his opinion.

These seven cardinals thought that they were pronouncing sentence on Galileo and on the Copernican system. But, in reality, they pronounced sentence on themselves and their own church. They put it upon record forever, that the Roman Catholic Church, claiming to be infallible in matters of faith, had, by its highest judicature, declared the Copernican system a heresy, and thus declared its own claim to infallibility a lie. This was the condemnation—that light had come into the world, and they chose darkness rather than light.

So it is whenever a new truth comes into the world: it attracts the free-minded, the lovers of truth; it repels those bound by interest or passion. Those who believe, with Solomon, that a living dog is better than a dead lion, leave behind them the past, and with open eyes go forward, leaving the dead to bury the dead. Those who change the maxim, and love a dead dog more than a living lion, turn their backs to the east and to the rising sun, and hug their much-loved errors to their hearts. So the truth stands in their midst, awful in its beauty, and judges them—sending away its foes, drawing its friends to its embrace.

But it is not in abstract truth, whether of science or theology, that Christ comes to us now. It is in the truth in its concrete shape, embodied in the reforms which overthrow evil, in the great moral improvements which do away with the sin and woe of the world. Every new cause of this sort parts the sheep from the goats, and causes the thoughts of many hearts to be revealed. We do not mean to assert that all who sympathize with any particular reformatory measures, or any particular reformatory party, are on the side of Christ, and all who disapprove these measures, or this party, are against him. Such an assertion would be the sign of the narrowest bigotry or the most foolish ignorance of human nature. But we mean to say, that when any great human and moral movement comes to rouse men's minds to a great evil—such as the evil of *war, slavery, intemperance, licentiousness, popular ignorance, pauperism, infidelity,* it is impossible for good men not to take an interest in it, and in their own way to aid it. If men neglect and ridicule such movements, find fault with all that is done, and do nothing themselves, they show thereby that they do not care so much for their brother's happiness as for their own ease and comfort. In this way it becomes true that

> "Some great cause, God's new Messiah, offering each the bloom or blight, Parts the goats upon the left hand, parts the sheep upon the right, And the choice goes by forever 'twixt that darkness and the light."

We read in the book of Acts, that after Paul and Barnabas had preached the gospel to the Jews in Antioch, the Gentiles were interested also, and great multitudes came together to hear the word of God. But when the Jews saw the multitudes, they were filled with envy, and contradicted Paul and blasphemed. Then Paul and Barnabas waxed bold, and said, "It was necessary that the word of God should be first preached to you; but since you put it from you, and *judge yourselves unworthy of eternal life,* lo, we turn to the Gentiles." A hard judgment for a man to pronounce on himself—that he is not worthy of eternal life!

But do we not often all do the same? Christ comes to us in the form of a new truth, which will correct our errors and enlarge our hearts. But loving our own little creed better than the truth, we reject it without examination, and so judge ourselves unworthy of the light, strength, and peace it might bestow. Christ comes again in some opportunity of usefulness to our neighbor. But loving our own selfish ease, we excuse ourselves, and so judge ourselves unworthy of the happiness we should enjoy in doing the kind action. He comes in some deep conviction, calling us to a new life. We feel that we ought to leave our frivolity, and live for God and eternity— live for what is real and permanent. But we stifle these convictions, and go back to our old lives, and so judge that we are not worthy to become the friends and fellow-workers of Jesus, and companions of the pure and good.

The great feast is ready, and the invitation is sent to us, and we, with one consent, begin to make excuse. Do we think that in that moment we are standing before the judgment seat of God, and pronouncing sentence on ourselves? It is our own heart that condemns us, and God, and Christ, and the everlasting truth of things must confirm the sentence.

§ 10. Paul's View of the Judgment by Christ

What were the views of the apostle Paul concerning a future judgment? One of the passages is in Romans. (2:5-16.) In this passage Paul describes a day, or time, when God should judge and bring to light the secrets of the human heart. He refers probably to the coming of Christ, as described in the twenty-fifth chapter of Matthew. Christ's coming is represented as "that day" the "day of judgment," as, "it shall be more tolerable for Sodom and Gomorrah in the day of judgment." It was not, we have seen, as is commonly supposed, only a judgment in the other world after death, but also a judgment in this world. It was not when we should go to Christ in the other world, but when Christ should come to us in this world. It is spoken of as a particular day, or time, and, no doubt, it was thought at first by Paul, as by the other apostles, that the coming of Christ was to be sudden and outward—an imposing visible transaction. But, gradually, Paul's views on this subject changed, under the influence of a growing spiritual insight. At first he interprets literally what Jesus says of his coming. But afterwards, in his later Epistles to the Ephesians and Colossians, he ceases to dwell on the outward coming, and speaks of the inward revelation of Christ in the heart—speaks of our now sitting in heavenly places with Christ. We may, therefore, suppose that the apostle believed the essence of the judgment to be in this—that either in this world or the next, or both, there shall be a revelation of God's truth to the soul, so that every soul shall see itself as God sees it—see its own evil or good, and so be rewarded or punished by that sight. This idea is given by Jesus himself, in his description of the judgment which was to take place before that generation passed away—a judgment in which the Son of man should be seated on the throne of his glory, with all his angels, and all nations be collected before him. The judgment consists in showing to the good, that when they did anything good to man, they did it to Christ and God; and in showing to the bad, that when they refused anything to their poor brethren in want, they refused it to Christ and God. The judgment is therefore making known to each man his own real character. The consequence of that revelation is, that some men immediately go into spiritual happiness, and others into spiritual suffering.

This is the substance of the Christian doctrine of judgment, as taught in the New Testament. All else is accessory, and belongs to the rhetoric—is part of the *mise en scène*; but there are two points in the views of the apostle concerning judgment, which deserve further notice. The first is in 1 Cor. 6:2, where he says, "Know ye not that the saints shall judge the world?" and (verse 3), "Know ye not that we shall judge angels?" He speaks of this as of something which they already knew, or at any rate could know; something like an axiom, as when he says (verse 9), "Know ye not that the unrighteous shall not inherit the kingdom of God?" or (verse 19), "Know ye not that your body is the temple of the Holy Spirit?" This notion is based on the idea of the unity of Christ and his disciples. Christians are joint heirs with Christ. Whatever Christ inherits, they receive and share with him. If he judges the world, and judges angels, they do the same with him, because they share his spirit of insight. Paul thinks the essence of Christianity to be so profound, that even the angels, desiring to look into it, may not have seen it. Therefore Christians, to whose heart God has revealed it by his Spirit, may be able to set the angels right in some matters. But this does away with the notion of a literal day of judgment; for we can hardly imagine Christians to be assembled together and seated on a throne by the side of Christ, in order to judge the world. Some millions of Christians seated on a local throne as judges, with millions of men and angels standing before them, is an impossible picture.

The other point is the passage in 1 Cor. 11:31: "If we would judge ourselves, we should not be judged." Here a principle seems to be laid down—that just so far as we apply God's truth to our own hearts and consciences, we do not need to have it applied by God. And this corresponds with the account of the judgment to which we have before referred, in the twenty-fifth chapter of Matthew. Those who are there called up for judgment, and who stand before the throne, are not Jews or Christians, but Gentiles (τὰ ἔθνη). The holy angels are with Christ in his glory. The heathen appear before him; those who have been doing good without knowing it are received by him into his kingdom, as those who have been blessed by his Father. They are Christians, it appears, without knowing it. They inherit the kingdom, from which the original heirs who have been wicked and slothful servants, and who have buried their talent in the napkin, are excluded. Christians who have judged themselves, and applied Christianity by their own lives, are not to be judged at the coming of Christ, but only those who have been doing right or wrong ignorantly.45

§ 11. Final Result

The course of our investigations in the present chapter has brought us to this result. Orthodoxy is right in expecting the coming of Christ in this world, but wrong in supposing it wholly future and wholly outward. It is right in making it a *personal* coming, and not merely the coming of his truth apart from him, but wrong in conceiving of this personal coming, as material to the senses, instead of spiritual to the soul. It is right in expecting a judgment, but wrong in placing it only in the other world. It is right in supposing that all mankind, the converted, the unconverted, and the heathen, are to be judged by Christian truth, but wrong in supposing that this judgment must occur in one place or at one time. Finally, in this, as in regard to many other doctrines, Orthodoxy fails by neglecting the great saying of Jesus, "The spirit quickeneth, the flesh profiteth nothing," and the similar statement of Paul, "The letter killeth."

Chapter XIV
Eternal Punishment, Annihilation, Universal Restoration

§ 1. Different Views concerning the Condition of the Impenitent hereafter

The different views concerning the future state, held by the Christian Church, may be thus classified; arranging them, exhaustively, under eight divisions:—

I. The Roman Catholic Church makes three conditions hereafter; viz.,—

1. Everlasting joy.

2. Everlasting suffering.

3. Temporal sorrow in purgatory.

II. The Orthodox Protestant Church makes two conditions hereafter; viz.,—

1. Unmixed and everlasting joy.

2. Unmixed and everlasting suffering.

III. The Old School Universalists make one condition hereafter; viz.,—

1. Eternal joy.

IV. New School Universalists and Restorationists make two conditions hereafter; viz.,—

1. Eternal joy.

2. Temporal and finite suffering.

V. Unitarians make an indefinite number of conditions hereafter, according to the various characters and moral states of men.

VI. The Swedenborgians make an indefinite but limited number of heavens and hells, suited to the varieties of character, but having a supernatural origin.

VII. The Spiritualists make the other world like this world, with no essential differences, making it a continuation of the natural life.

VIII. The Annihilationists believe that the finally impenitent will perish wholly, and come to nothing.

This statement includes all, or nearly all, of the views held in the Christian Church concerning the condition of departed souls in the other world. We do not propose to examine them all at the present time; but we shall examine at some length three of them.

Eternal punishment, annihilation, and universal restoration are the three principal views taken in the Church of the condition hereafter of those who die impenitent, and in a state of hostility to God. The wicked may hereafter be reformed, may be annihilated, or may be kept in a state of permanent punishment. One of these views is held by the Universalists; another by Orthodoxy; the third is now adopted by those who are dissatisfied with the horrors of Orthodoxy, but not yet ready to accept the Optimism of the Universalist hope. We will consider these, beginning with the Orthodox doctrine of everlasting punishment. We wish we could say that this doctrine was not fully and decidedly Orthodox. But it is quite as much so as the Trinity, the deity of Christ, or the atonement. No one is allowed to have any doubts or questions concerning it. It seems to be believed that the whole system of Orthodoxy would be endangered, if this terror was not held to its bosom with an unfaltering grasp.

§ 2. The Doctrine of Everlasting Punishment, as held by the Orthodox at the Present Time

What is this doctrine, as it is taught at the present day in all Orthodox churches, and as it stands in all Orthodox creeds? It is, that the moment of death decides, and decides forever, the destiny of man; that those who die impenitent, unbelieving, and unconverted are forever lost, without the possibility of return; that those thus lost are to suffer forever and ever, without end, the most grievous torments in soul and body. These torments consist in banishment from the presence of God, and positive sufferings, in addition thereto, of an awful kind. Precisely what they are, it is not, perhaps, necessary for an Orthodox man to believe. There is no Orthodox definition which is authoritative on that point; and considerable range, therefore, is allowable. The suffering may be that of literal fire, or it may not. It may be physical suffering, or the pangs of conscience, the absence of love, and the sense of emptiness. On these points there is some liberty of opinion, doubtless. But we presume that it would not be Orthodox to admit a preponderance, in hell, of good over evil; or to admit, with Swedenborg, the existence of pleasure there, even though it be only a diabolical and sinful pleasure. The doctrine of Orthodoxy certainly is, that evil predominates over good, and pain over pleasure, in the condition of the damned; so that there existence is a curse, and not a blessing. Especially is hope shut out: there is no hope of return, no possibility of escape, no chance of repentance, even at the end of myriads of years. The man who is condemned to imprisonment for life, in solitary confinement, is in an unfortunate condition; but he has hope,— hope of escape, hope of pardon,—sure hope, at all events, of deliverance, one day, by death, from his condition, and a change to something better, or at least to something different. But, in the Orthodox opinion, there is no such alleviation as this to the sufferings of the future state.

It is usual, we know, for many Orthodox preachers to intensify in description the sufferings of the future state, and to task their imagination for multiplied pictures of horror; and we shall presently give some examples to show how far this is carried. We have no doubt that there are many Orthodox men who are as much shocked by these gross descriptions as those are who deny everlasting punishment. But are they not themselves really responsible for them? Those who admit the principle that God can torment his children forever, in the other life, for sins committed in this, have accepted the principle, from which *any* view of the Deity, however shocking, may very legitimately proceed.

But let us, for the present, only assume that Orthodoxy asserts a preponderance of evil over good in the other world, and that this preponderance is to be continued without end—forever. Let us see what this means.

It means that the suffering to be endured hereafter by each individual soul, as a punishment for sins committed in this world, will infinitely exceed in amount all the suffering borne on the surface of the earth, by its total population, from the creation of Adam to the destruction of the world. Each lost soul will suffer not only more, but infinitely more, than all the accumulated sufferings of the human race throughout all time. We shudder as we read the account of the sufferings from hydrophobia, or the burning alive of a slave at the South, or the tortures inflicted by the Holy Inquisition, or the horrors of a field of battle, or the cruelties inflicted by savages upon their victims; but all of these, added together, are finite, and the sufferings of a single soul hereafter are infinite. That is to say, all the pain and evil of this world, resulting from all human sin, through all time, is infinitely small and insignificant when compared with the punishment endured by a single soul hereafter for his share of that sin. And all this is inflicted by God; and he is a God of love.

There are some doctrines, the statement of which is their refutation. This, we think, is one of them.

But it must also be considered, that this doctrine, which throws such darkness over the future, also sends down a rayless night over the present. It refutes every theodicy; it nullifies every solution of evil. The consolation for the sufferings of this world is, that the fashion of this world passes away, and that there is a better world to come. The explanation of the evils of this life is, that they are finite, and that they are, therefore, to be swallowed up and to disappear in an infinite good. The Christian finds relief, in considering the sufferings of this world, by regarding them as the means of a greater ultimate joy; by looking forward to the time when all tears shall be wiped away; and by a firm faith that love is stronger than selfishness, good stronger than evil. But the doctrine of eternal punishment gives us, in the condition of a single lost soul, a greater amount of evil hereafter than all the evil, which is to be thus explained, here; and the myriads of lost souls, each of which is to suffer infinitely more than all the sufferings of the present world, present us with a problem, in the future, so appalling, that the problem of present evil, vast as it is, becomes insignificant by its side.

We are tormented with evil here. We seek a solution of the problem: we find it in the limited, finite, and ancillary nature of evil. But that solution is wholly taken away when we are told that evil is infinite and eternal.

It seems to us impossible to hold the common doctrine on this subject, without having the gospel view of the divine character essentially shaken; it is not possible to regard Him as a being in whom love is the essential attribute. If this is so, as we shall presently undertake to prove, it becomes a matter of vital importance that the doctrine should be disproved and rejected. It is not enough that it should be quietly laid aside: it is due to the truth that it should be distinctly and fully confuted. For this doctrine, if it be false, is deeply dishonorable to God: it takes away his highest glory; it substitutes fear of him, in the place of love, in the human heart; it neutralizes the peculiar power of the gospel; it degrades the quality of Christian piety, and poisons religion in its fountain.

The Orthodox doctrine of future punishment is, then, exceedingly simple. There is to be a judgment in the last day, universal and final. All mankind are to be collected before the judgment seat of Christ, and there to be divided into two classes, — one on the right hand, and the other on the left. These are to go upward, to heaven, to be eternally happy; those downward, to hell, to be eternally miserable. There are no degrees of suffering; for the torments of hell are infinite in degree, as well as everlasting in duration. Usually the suffering is made intensively as well as extensively infinite.

Sometimes degrees are allowed in suffering. No allowance is made for ignorance, or want of opportunity; for inherited evil, or evil resulting from force of circumstances. The purest and best of men, who does not believe the precise Orthodox theory concerning the Trinity, sits in hell side by side with Zingis Khan, who murdered in cold blood hundreds of thousands of men, women, and children, marking his bloody route by pyramids of skulls. The unbaptized child, who goes to hell because of the original sin derived from Adam, is exposed to God's wrath no less than Pope Alexander VI, who outraged every law of God and man, and who, says Machiavelli, "was followed to the tomb by the holy feet of his three dear companions— Luxury, Simony, and Cruelty."46

This is the doctrine which every denomination and sect in Christendom, except the Unitarians and Universalists, maintain as essential to Orthodoxy. It is but a year or two since twenty-one bishops of the Protestant Episcopal Church issued a declaration of their belief that this doctrine is maintained, without reserve or qualification, by the Church of England. Only recently an ecclesiastical council of Congregationalists refused the fellowship of the churches to a gentleman elected as its pastor by the Third Congregational Church in Portland, Maine. In the report of the result, the council says that it believes the candidate to be generally sound in his belief, and exemplary in his Christian spirit, and heartily extends to him its Christian sympathy. But it declines to install him as pastor, because it "understands him as saying, that he does not know but there may be another state of probation and offer of salvation, after death, for all to whom Christ is not personally preached; and that, whilst believing in a future retribution, he says that the everlasting punishment of the wicked may be an extinction of the wicked by annihilation." So that a mere doubt on this subject is considered a sufficient reason, by the most advanced and liberal of the whole Orthodox body at the present day, for refusing church fellowship.

The American Tract Society floods the land with loose leaves, all appealing to the fear of an eternal hell. We have one before us now, called "Are you insured?" which represents Christianity as a contrivance for escaping from everlasting torment, as a spiritual insurance office, where one must "take out a policy," and so escape everlasting fire.47

There is no theological journal, bearing the Orthodox name, which is more rational and liberal than the "New York Independent." But in its issue of January 5, 1860, it speaks of future endless misery thus, saying that there is a "vast amount and weight of evidence to the point—evidence enough to prove it, if provable; all nature, all law, all revelation uttering the doctrine, so that it is an amazing stretch and energy of unbelief not to believe it, implying a moral state and position that will not believe it on any testimony, however clearly and unqualifiedly, even to the exhaustion of the capabilities of language, God himself may declare and affirm it."

There is evidently an energetic attempt made in some quarters to revive the decaying belief in the doctrine of everlasting punishment in the future state, as a penalty for the sins of this. Dr. Thompson, of New York, has published a work to this end, called "Love and Penalty." Dr. J. P. Thompson, the author of this book, is considered the leader of New Haven theology — the Elisha on whose shoulders the mantle of Dr. Taylor, of New Haven, has fallen. Dr. Nehemiah Adams, of Boston, has labored in the same field, exerting himself to prove this doctrine in various tracts and other works. Professor Hovey, of the Baptist Seminary of Newton, has published a little book on the same subject.

It is probably thought dangerous by these gentlemen to relax at all the terrors of futurity. And, no doubt, if all those who have been restrained from evil by fear of eternal punishment were to lose that belief suddenly, the consequences, at first, would be sometimes bad. If you have exerted your whole force in producing fear of hell, instead of fear of sin, then, the terror of hell being taken away, men might rush at first into license. But the dread of a future hell is by no means so efficacious a motive as is often thought. We become hardened to everything, and neither the clergyman nor his parish eat any less heartily of their Sunday dinner, nor sleep any less soundly on Sunday night, in consequence of the terrible descriptions of eternal torments contained in the morning's sermon.48

§ 3. Apparent Contradictions, both in Scripture and Reason, in Regard to this Doctrine

Beside the practical motive for maintaining this doctrine, which we have intimated, there are also scriptural and philosophical reasons. Scripture and reason both do, in fact, seem to teach opposite doctrines on this subject. There are passages in the New Testament which appear to teach never-ending suffering, and others which appear to teach a final, universal restoration. It is written, "These shall go away into eternal punishment;" but it is also written, that Christ "shall reign till all things are subdued unto him;" when "the Son also himself shall be subject to Him who did put all things under him, that God may be all in all." As the same word is used to express the way in which all enemies are to be subject to Christ, and the way in which Christ himself is to be subject to God, it follows that the enemies, when subjected, shall be friends. It is said that the wicked shall be punished "with everlasting destruction from the presence of God;" but it is also said that "in the dispensation of the fulness of times, God will gather in one all things in Christ, both which are in heaven and on earth;" and "that at the name of Jesus every knee should bow, in heaven, in earth, and under the earth; and that every tongue should confess that Jesus Christ is Lord, to the glory of God the Father." It is said of the wicked, that "their worm never dies, and their fire is not quenched;" but it is also said that "it pleased the Father, having made peace through the blood of the cross, by Christ to reconcile all things unto himself, whether they be things in earth or things in heaven." So that Scripture, at first sight, seems to teach both eternal punishment and universal restoration.

There is a similar contradiction on this subject, if considered in the light of pure reason. When looked at from the divine attributes, the unavoidable conclusion seems to be, that all men must be finally saved. For God is infinitely benevolent, and therefore must wish to save all; is infinitely wise, and therefore must know how to save all; is infinitely powerful, and therefore must be able to overcome all difficulties in the way of saving all: hence all must be saved. But, on the other hand, when we consider the subject from the position of man's nature, an opposite conclusion seems to follow. For man, being free, is able to choose either evil or good at any moment; and, as long as he continues to be essentially man, he must retain this freedom; and therefore, at any period of his future existence, however remote, he may prefer evil to good—that is, may prefer hell to heaven. But God will not compel him to be good against his will (for unwilling goodness is not goodness); and therefore it follows that there is no point of time in the infinite future of which we can certainly say that then all men will be saved.

Of course these seeming contradictions of Scripture and antinomies of reason are not real contradictions. God does not contradict himself either in revelation or in reason. Whether we can reconcile such antagonisms *now*, or not, we know that they will be reconciled. Meantime, it is our duty to disbelieve whatever is dishonorable to God, or opposed to the character ascribed to him by Jesus Christ. Christ has taught us to regard God as our Father. It is our duty to refuse credence to any doctrine concerning him which is plainly opposed to this character. If I have formed my opinion of my friend's character from a large experience, I ought to refuse to believe, even on good evidence, anything opposed to it. What is faith in man, or in God, good for, that is unable to resist evil reports concerning them? If I am told that my friend has become a thief or a swindler, and he who tells me says, "I know that it is so—here is the evidence," I reply, "I do not care for your evidence. I know that it is impossible." So, if all the churches in the world, Catholic and Protestant, tell me that Jesus teaches everlasting punishment inflicted by God for the sins of this life, and produce chapter and verse in support of their statement, I reply, "If I have learned anything about God from the teachings of Jesus, it is that your assertion is impossible.

About the meaning of these passages you may be mistaken, for the letter killeth; but I cannot be mistaken in regard to the fatherly character of the Almighty."

These contradictions we shall consider in a paper printed in the Appendix (an examination of Dr. Neheimiah Adams's tract on the "Reasonableness of Everlasting Punishment"). At present we will only say that we should hold it less dishonorable to God to deny his existence than to believe this doctrine concerning him. We think that in the last day it will appear that the atheist has done less to dishonor the name of God than those who persistently teach this view. For what says Lord Bacon? (Essays, XVII. Of Superstition.) "It were better to have no opinion of God at all than such an opinion as is unworthy of him; for the one is unbelief, the other is contumely; and certainly superstition is the reproach of the Deity. Plutarch saith well to that purpose. 'Surely,' saith he, 'I had rather a great deal men should say there were no such man at all as Plutarch, than that they should say there was one Plutarch that would eat his children as soon as they were born,' as the poets speak of Saturn. And as the contumely is greater towards God, so is the danger greater towards men."

The doctrine of everlasting punishment, being essentially a heathen and not a Christian doctrine, cannot do any Christian good to any one. It is the want of faith in the Church which makes it afraid of giving it up. The Christian Church has not faith enough to believe in the power of truth and love. It still thinks that men must be frightened into goodness, or driven into it. Fear is a becoming and useful motive no less than hope; but fear of what? Not fear of God; but fear of sin, fear of ourselves, fear of temptation. To be afraid of God never did any one any good. These doctrines drive men away from God; or, if they drive them *to* God, drive them as slaves, as sycophants, as servants, not as sons. We are saved by becoming *the sons of God*; but you cannot drive a man into sonship by terror. You may make him profess religion, and go through ceremonies, and have an outward form of service; but you cannot make him love God by means of fear.

But good men teach these things, no doubt. Men far better than most of us believe them and teach them. It always has been so. The best men have always been the chief supporters of bad doctrines. A good man, humble and modest, is apt to shrink from doubting or opposing what the Church has taught. He accepts it, and teaches it too. When God wants a reformer, he does not take one of these good, modest, humble men. He does not take a saint. He takes a man who has ever so much will, a little obstinacy, and a great love of fighting; and he makes the wrath of such a man to serve him.

Neither St. Teresa nor Fénélon could have reformed the Catholic Church. It took rough old Martin Luther and hard-hearted John Calvin to do it. The first Universalists, the Abolitionists, all reformers, are necessarily men of that sort. They are rude debaters, not standing on ceremony or politeness. They are hard-headed logicians, going straight to their point, careless of elegances and proprieties. They are God's pioneers, rough backwoodsmen, hewing their way with the axe through the wilderness. After them shall come the peaceful farmer, with plough and spade, to turn the land into wheat fields, orchards, and gardens.

§ 4. Everlasting Punishment limits the Sovereignty of God

It is certain that the doctrine of eternal punishment, in the common form, can only be maintained by giving up some of the infinite attributes of the Almighty. If punishment is to exist without end; if hell is always to co-exist with heaven; if certain beings are to be continued forever in existence merely as sinful sufferers,—then, it is clear, God is not omnipotent. He shares his throne forever with Satan. Satan and God divide between them the universe. God reigns in heaven, Satan in hell. God desires that all shall be saved; but this desire is absolutely and forever defeated by a fate greater than Deity. Law divorced from love—that is, nature in its old Pagan aspect—is higher than God. God is not the Almighty to any one who really believes eternal punishment. God is not the Sovereign of the universe, but only of a part of it. The doctrine of eternal punishment, in its common form, does, therefore, virtually dethrone God.49

It is, in fact, impossible to conceive of an eternal hell co-existing with an eternal heaven, without also seeing that it limits eternally the divine Omnipotence; for the omnipotence of God is in carrying out his will to have all men saved by becoming holy. Unless God's laws are obeyed, God is not obeyed; and he is not sovereign if not obeyed. Hell is a condition of things hostile to God's will: it is a permanent and successful rebellion of a part of the universe. It is no answer to say, that it is shut up, and restrained, and made to suffer; for it is *not* conquered. God has conquered sin only when he has reduced it to obedience. Hell is no more subject to God than the Confederate States, during the rebellion, were subject to the United States government. They were shut up by a blockade; they were restrained by great armies and navies; they were made to suffer; but they were *not* reduced to submission and obedience.

Nor is it any answer to say, that the existence of sin and suffering hereafter no more limits God's omnipotence than their existence here and now limits his omnipotence. For the question is of eternal suffering. Temporal suffering hereafter, we grant, is no objection to the divine Omnipotence. Limited and finite evil, in this world or the other, is no philosophical difficulty; and for this reason—that finite evil, when compared with infinite good, becomes logically and mathematically *no* evil. The finite disappears in relation to the infinite. All the sufferings and sins of earth, through all ages, are strictly nothing when viewed in the light of the eternal joy and holiness which are to result from them. This is a postulate of pure reason. Make evil finite, and good infinite,—make evil temporal, and good eternal,—and evil ceases to be anything. But make evil eternal, as is done by this doctrine, and then we have Manicheism—an infinite dualism—on the throne of the universe.

§ 5. Everlasting Punishment contradicts the Fatherly Love of God

This doctrine is a relapse on Paganism, and derived from it. It has nothing to do with Christianity, except to corrupt it. No man was ever made better by believing it: multitudes have been made worse. It attributes to our heavenly Father conduct that, if done by the worst of men, would add a shade of increased wickedness to their character. It assumes that God has made intelligent creatures with the intention of tormenting some of them forever. It assumes that those who are thus created, exposed to this awful risk, are to be thus tormented, unless they happen to pass through what is called an Orthodox conversion in this short earthly life. God keeps them alive forever in order to torture them forever.

The barbarity of this opinion exceeds all power of language to express. We are accustomed to mourn over the anguish and misery that are in this world. The problem of earthly evil has been a burden and anxiety to good men in all times, a great question for thinkers in all ages. The only satisfactory solution is, that it is temporary and educational; that it is to pass away, and, in passing, to create a higher joy and goodness than could otherwise have come. But the doctrine of everlasting punishment not only annuls this explanation, and makes it impossible to explain earthly evil, but adds to it a tenfold greater mystery. The fatherly character of God disappears in Pagan darkness, in view of this horrid doctrine; for the everlasting suffering of one human being contains in itself more evil than the accumulated sufferings of all mankind from the creation of the world to the end of it. Add together all the sicknesses, bereavements, disappointments, of all mankind; all the wars, famines, pestilences, that have tormented humanity; add to these all the mental and moral pangs produced by selfishness and sin in all ages, and all that are to be to the end of time,—and these all combined are logically and mathematically *nothing*, compared with the sufferings of one human being destined to be everlastingly punished. For all temporal sufferings added together are finite; but this is infinite.

Now, the being who could inflict such torture as this is *not* the God and Father of our Lord Jesus Christ. There may be some deity of cruelty, some incarnation of wrath and despotism, in the Hindoo Pantheon, capable of such terrific wickedness. It is no answer to say that God inflicts suffering now in this world, and therefore he may inflict everlasting suffering in the other; for those are all finite; that is infinite. *Finite* suffering may result in greater good, may be an education to good; but *everlasting* suffering cannot. The finite and infinite cannot be compared together. There is no analogy between them.

The God of the New Testament is our Father. If he inflicts suffering, it is for our good; "not for his pleasure, but for our profit, that we may be partakers of his holiness." All earthly suffering finds this solution, and accords with the fatherly character of God in this point of view. Much, no doubt, cannot be now fully understood. We do not *see how* it tends to good; but all suffering *that ends* may end in good. Suffering that does not end cannot end in good.

If human beings are everlastingly punished, it must either be that they go on sinning forever, and cannot repent, lose all power of repentance, and so cease to be moral agents, or else that they retain the power of repenting, and therefore *may* repent. In the first case, God continues to punish forever those who have ceased to sin, because their freedom and moral power have ceased; or else he punishes forever those who have repented, and *so* ceased sinning. In either case, God must punish everlastingly those who have ceased to be sinners; which is incredible.

If God is a Father, he is at least *as good* as the best earthly father. Now, what father or mother would ever consent to place a child in a situation where there was even a chance of its running such an awful risk? God has *created* us with these liabilities to sin; he has (according to Orthodoxy) chosen and determined that we shall be born wholly prone to evil, and sure to fall into eternal and unending ruin, unless he saves us by a special act of grace. "What man among you, being a father," would do so? Custom dulls our sense to these horrors. Let us therefore imagine a case far less terrible. Suppose that a number of parents should establish a school, to which to send their children. Suppose they should arrange a code of laws for the school of such a stringent character that all the children are sure to break it. Under the school are vaults containing instruments of torture. For each offence against the laws of the school (offences which the children cannot fail to commit) they are to be punished by imprisonment for life in these cells, with daily torture, from racks, thumb-screws, and the like. A few of them are to be selected from the rest, not for any merit of their own, but by an arbitrary decree of the parents, and are to be rewarded (not for their superior good conduct, but according to the caprice of the parents) with every luxury and privilege. Among these privileges is included that of taking a daily walk through the cells, and witnessing the horrible sufferings of their brothers and companions, and hearing their shrieks of anguish, and praising the justice of their parents in thus punishing some and rewarding the rest.

But this, you may say, is not a parallel case. No, we grant it is not, for what are these torments to that of a never-ending futurity? They are all as nothing. Therefore every such comparison must utterly fail of doing justice to the diabolic cruelty ascribed to the Almighty by this Orthodox doctrine.

"But what right," says the Orthodox defender of this doctrine, "have we to reason in this way concerning the divine proceedings, by the analogy of earthly parents? What right have we to compare God's doings with those of a human father?" *No* right, perhaps, as philosophers; but as Christians we have not only the right to do it, but it is our duty to do so. Jesus has himself taught us to use this analogy, in order to acquire confidence in God's ways, and to assure ourselves that God cannot fail of acting as we should expect a good and wise earthly parent to act. "What man is there of *you*, whom, if his son ask bread, will he give him a stone? Or if he ask a fish, will he give him a serpent? If *ye* then, being evil, know how to give good gifts unto your children, how much more shall your Father, which is in heaven, give good things to them that ask him?" (Matt. 7:9-11.) Jesus authorizes and commands us to reason from the parental nature in man to that in God. Instead of simply assuring us of it, on the ground of his own authority to teach us; instead of saying, "Believe this, because I say it," he says, "Believe it, because it accords with your own convictions and with human nature."

§ 6. Attempts to modify and soften the Doctrine of Everlasting Punishment

The reasons for the late efforts to support this terrific doctrine are probably to be found in a widespread and increasing disbelief concerning it, pervading the churches nominally Orthodox. This has come from the growing intelligence and progressive movements of thought in the Christian Church. The evidences of this belief are numerous and increasing. Those who reject the Orthodox view are a numerous body, but divided into several parties. There are the old-fashioned Universalists, a valiant race,—men of war from their youth,—who, under the lead of such men as Hosea Ballou and Thomas Whittemore, have spent their lives in fighting the doctrine of everlasting punishment. Very naturally, perhaps, they went to the opposite extreme of opinion, and denied all future suffering. But this view has, we think, ceased to be the prevailing one among the Universalists. The doctrine of ultimate restoration has very generally taken its place. This doctrine also prevails widely in other denominations; not only among the liberal bodies, like the Unitarians, but also among Methodists, Presbyterians, and Congregationalists. It has widely spread, as is well known, in Germany. It was held by Schleiermacher, the father of modern German theology. It tinges the writings of such Orthodox men as Tholuck, Hahn, and Olshausen. Others profess to believe in everlasting punishment, but make it a merely negative consequence of lost time and opportunity: one will be always worse off hereafter in consequence of the neglect of duty. Others follow Swedenborg, and make the sufferings of hell rather agreeable than otherwise to those who bear them.

Various ineffectual attempts have indeed been made, in all ages of the Church, to soften the austerity of this doctrine. From the days of Origen, these merciful doctors50 have always been trying to soften this austere dogma, but ineffectually; for the dread of an eternal hell has been one of the chief motives which the Church has used in converting men from sin to holiness. Any suggestion of the possibility of future restoration would, it is feared, cut the sinews of effective preaching. For the baptized who are not fit for heaven the Roman Catholic Church has established, indeed, a temporary hell, with torments of an inferior sort; for bad Catholics there is purgatory, with the hope of ultimate escape from it; but for the unbaptized heathen, for heretics, and for excommunicated persons, there is nothing but eternal punishment.

Many, in all ages, have made the everlasting continuance of punishment not absolute, but *hypothetical*—depending on the question, "Will the sinner continue forever to sin?"51 Others have made future punishment *relatively* everlasting; that is, because even the repentant sinner will be always just so far behind the position he would have had if he had not sinned. This, however, is taking a material view of progress, as though it was limited, like the going of a horse, to so many miles a day.

Many of the early fathers, and some of the mediæval doctors, took milder views of the future sufferings of the impenitent or unconverted. Proceeding from the idea of freedom, as indestructible in the human soul, Origen declared that, no matter how low any moral being has fallen, a way to return is always open to him. Even the devil may, in time, regain the highest position in the angelic hierarchy.52 No doubt Origen admitted the need of external conditions for this restoration; but he said, God is able to heal the damage done to any part of his works.53 He will restore all things to their origin, uniting the end and the beginning, and so becoming indeed the Alpha and Omega. This may require long processes, through many ages.54 Since Jesus speaks of a sin which cannot be forgiven in this age (αἰών) nor the next, it follows, says Origen, that there is a series of ages, or worlds, through which we pass, and many of these ages of ages (sæcula sæculorum) must pass away before all bad men and angels shall have returned to their original state. Quoting the passage, "The last enemy that shall be destroyed," he says that he shall not be destroyed as to his substance, but as to his enmity. His being was made by God, and cannot perish; his hostile will proceeded from himself, and shall be destroyed.

Mr. Brownson (or rather a writer in Brownson's "Quarterly Review," July, 1863) takes another way of softening the terrors of hell. With him too, hell is an everlasting state; but he maintains that the Roman Church has not made it an article of faith to believe that there is any positive suffering therein. If you believe in an eternal hell, that is enough; you are not precluded from softening its horrors to any extent you can. Thus he maintains that the great Augustine allows hell to be only a negative state—only the absence of the exquisite beatitude of heaven. This writer (who is said by the editor to be a learned Catholic priest) asserts that there is a growing repugnance to the popular doctrine upon eternal punishment among the most intelligent of the Catholic laity, and this reluctance is the chief obstacle to the reception of the faith by a large class of non-Catholics. He attempts to meet this state of mind by showing that neither the doctrine of St. Augustine nor that of the Catholic Church supports this popular view, but allows a much milder one. He proceeds to make these points:—

1. St. Augustine nowhere teaches that human nature is intrinsically evil, but he invariably teaches that it is substantially good. ("Omnis natura in quantum natura est bona est." "Omnis substantia aut Deus est aut ex Deo." De Lib. Arbit.) Therefore it follows that the very notion of *total* depravity is impossible. St. Augustine distinctly says that "the very unclean spirit himself is good, inasmuch as he is a spirit, but evil inasmuch as he is unclean." Hence, not even the nature of the devil himself is evil. So St. Thomas ("Diabolus, in quantum habet esse, est bonus"), "the devil, so far as he *is*, is good."

2. St. Augustine teaches in explicit terms that existence is a good even to angels and men who are eternally bound by the consequences of evil.

3. Eternal death, according to St. Augustine, is a subsidence into a lower form of life, a privation of the highest vital influx from God in order to everlasting life, or supreme beatitude, but not of all vital influx in order to an endless existence, which is a partial and incomplete participation in good. These sinful souls, therefore, fulfil in a measure the end of their creation, and have a place and a function in harmony with the general order of the cosmos. There is no trace, in this view of Augustine, that God hates a portion of his creatures with an absolute, infinite, and eternal hatred, and

is hated by them in return. The original act of creative love is an enduring and eternal act, in which even Satan is included. "Their nature still remains essentially good, and far superior in excellence and beauty to material light, which is the highest corporeal substance."

4. Hell, therefore (Infernus), is simply a lower state of inchoate and imperfect being, "of saints nipped in the bud." Infant damnation is only a gentle sadness—"levis tristitia." All positive suffering in hell is probably temporal, and therefore must at last cease. The lost souls will enjoy there quite as much as they can do here, *minus* the temporal sufferings of this life. They continue *natural* beings, and therefore can enjoy all natural joy; and that which they lose, being the "beatific vision," of which they have no conception, is a loss of which they are wholly unconscious.

Swedenborg maintains, in the same way, the everlasting character of the punishment of those who have passed the final judgment, but admits many palliations to its sufferings. He teaches that delight is the universal substance of heaven, and also of hell, and that evil spirits are in the delight of evil, as good spirits in that of good. An evil spirit would be as unhappy in heaven as a good one would be in hell.

§ 7. The meaning of Eternal Punishment in Scripture

But what, then, is the vital truth in the doctrine of eternal punishment? Christ says, "These shall go away into eternal punishment."[55] What is this "eternal punishment"? It is commonly supposed to mean the same thing as punishment which shall never end, or punishment continued through all time. But this is to misunderstand both the philosophical and scriptural meaning of the word "eternal." Eternal punishments are the opposite of temporal punishments: they have nothing to do with time at all; they are punishments outside of time. To attempt to realize eternity by adding up any number of myriads of years of time, is necessarily a failure; for time and eternity are different things. You might as well attempt to produce thought or love, by adding up millions of miles of distance, as, by adding up millions of years of time, to get any idea of eternity. Eternal life, in the language of Scripture, has nothing to do with the future or the past. It is a present life in the soul, awakened within by the knowledge of God and Christ. "This *is* life eternal, to know thee, the only true God, and Jesus Christ, whom thou hast sent." "Eternal life and eternal death both come from the knowledge of God and of Christ." To one it is a savor of life, to another of death. Eternal punishment and eternal life are the punishments and the rewards of eternity, distinguished from those of time, and having their root in the knowledge of God which comes through Christ. Eternal life and eternal punishment both commence here, from the judgments which takes place now: but the last judgment, or the judgment of the last day, is that which will take place hereafter, when the soul shall have a full knowledge of itself and of God; see its whole life as it really is; have all self-deceptions taken away, all disguises removed, and know itself as it is known. God's love, when revealed, attracts and repels. Like all real force, it is a polar force. The one pole is its attractive power over those who are in a truth-loving state; the other pole is its repelling power to those who are in a truth-hating state. Love attracts the truthful, and repels the wilful. Eternal punishment, then, is the repugnance to God of the soul which is inwardly selfish in its will,—loving itself more than truth and right. It is the sense of indignation and wrath, alienation and poverty, which rests on it while in this condition. It is the outer darkness; it is the far country; it is the famine, which comes as a holy and blessed evil, sent to save, by bringing to repentance, the prodigal child, who has not yet "come to himself."

From this knowledge of God and of itself, therefore,—from this judgment of the last day,—will flow eternal life to the one class, and eternal punishment or suffering to the other. Those who have been conscientious and generous; who have endeavored faithfully to live for truth and right; who have made sacrifices, and not boasted of them; who have clothed the naked and fed the hungry, making the world better and happier by their presence,—will hear the Saviour say, "Come, ye blessed of my Father, inherit the kingdom prepared for you from the foundation of the world; for I was hungry, and ye gave me meat." Perhaps they have never even heard the name of Christ; perhaps they were the Buddhists of Burmah, of whom Mr. Malcom speaks, who brought food to him, though a stranger to them. "I was scarcely seated," says he, "when a woman brought a nice mat for me to lie on; another, cool water; and a man went and picked me a half dozen fine oranges. None sought or expected the least reward, but disappeared, and left me to my repose." Or perhaps they will be the poor black women in Africa, who took such kind care of Mungo Park, singing, "Let us pity the white man: he has no mother to bring him milk, no wife to grind him corn." The reward of their fidelity will be the gift of a greater power of goodness, coming from a knowledge of God and Christ. They were helping Christ, though they did not know him. They will say, "Lord, when saw we thee an hungered?" These Gentiles, without the law, who do by nature the things contained in the law, will come to know Christ, and receive a spiritual life— life flowing from that knowledge. On the other hand, those who have not endeavored to do what they knew to be right will receive from the same knowledge of God and Christ a spiritual or eternal punishment. Perhaps they have received some of it already in this world; but a deeper knowledge of the truth will bring a keener self-reproach. The worm that never dies is this gnawing[56] tooth of conscience. The fire which is not quenched is the heart still selfish, turned to evil, joined with a conscience which sees the good. For man, as long as he is man, cannot get away from himself. He may sophisticate himself with falsehoods, put his conscience to sleep, and imagine that he has escaped all the penalties of evil; but he cannot escape from himself. The longer and deeper the sleep of conscience, the more terrible its final awakening.

Eternal punishment, therefore, is the punishment which comes to man from his spiritual nature; from that side of man which connects him with eternity, in contradistinction from temporal punishment, which is that which comes from his temporal nature and the temporal world. Through the body he receives temporal pleasure or pain from the world of time and space; through the spirit he receives spiritual joy or sorrow from the world of eternity and infinity.

Thus intimately are judgment and retribution connected. There is nothing arbitrary about rewards or punishments. They follow naturally and necessarily from the revelation of divine and eternal truth. Sooner or later, the everlasting distinctions between right and wrong, good and evil, make themselves seen and known. The distinctions between right and wrong *are* eternal.

The idea of duration is not connected with eternal punishment or eternal life; for the idea of duration belongs to time, and not to eternity. Human law sentences men, for crime, to be punished by imprisonment for six months, three years, ten years, or for life; but in God's world there is not, and cannot be, any relation between a man's guilt and the precise time he is to suffer. He must suffer while he is guilty, be the time longer or shorter. When he ceases to be guilty, he must cease to suffer. He therefore fixes the *duration* of his suffering himself: that makes no part of the divine sentence. If he judges himself unworthy of eternal life during five, ten, one hundred, or ten thousand million years, that is for himself to say. God will never save him against his will; and God can wait. The sphere of time belongs to man's freedom; that of eternity, to the freedom of God.

And this reconciles the philosophic difficulty. Man, being *free*, can postpone his submission and obedience *indefinitely*; but, being finite, cannot postpone it *infinitely*. At any point of time, he may still resolve to resist the influx of eternal life, and continue in the sphere of death: but eternity surrounds time, and infolds it; and in eternity God's purposes will be realized, and every knee bow, of things in heaven, and in earth, and under the earth. Universal harmony must prevail at last.

"Eternal" and "everlasting" are two wholly different ideas. We fully believe in eternal punishment, but not in everlasting punishment. Eternal life is spiritual life: eternal suffering is spiritual suffering.

The whole of antiquity recognizes this distinction; and the Bible is saturated with it. When Jesus says, "He who believes in me has *eternal life* abiding in him," there is nothing about duration intended in that. When he says, "This is *life eternal*, to know thee the only true God," there is nothing about duration implied. It is the quality of the life which is conveyed—spiritual life, life flowing from the sight of God and Christ.

We believe in eternal punishment; but, because it is eternal, therefore it is not everlasting. Eternal suffering, flowing from the sight of the eternal truth and love of God, is real suffering, because it involves the sight of sin, the consciousness of failure, the deep conviction of what we ought to do and have not done; but all this leads to repentance and salvation. When the Lord turned and looked on Peter, Peter went into eternal suffering. He saw his own guilt and the infinite goodness of his Master at the same time. The one produced penitence; the other, hope. But, when Judas hanged himself, he did *not* go into eternal punishment, but into temporal. He saw his own baseness and his own folly; but he did not see God's love. If he had seen God's love and Christ's pardoning mercy, together with his sin, he would not have hanged himself; but, like Peter, he would have repented, and gone forth to preach the gospel.

When we see God's truth and love, we go into eternal life or into eternal suffering, according to the direction of our lives and hearts. If we are following Christ, and trying to do right,—if we are not selfish, but generous,—then the sight of God's love and truth in Christ leads us directly into spiritual joy; but if we are selfish, and seeking only our own good, if we are indifferent to the rights of our fellow-men, then we go into eternal or spiritual suffering.

The force of eternal punishment, therefore, is not in the statement that it is never to end; nor in any description, however vivid, of outward physical torments. Such descriptions produce excitement, agitation, terror. But this is not *conviction*. The doctrine, not being in harmony with the attributes of God or the nature of man, can never be sincerely or profoundly believed. It is inwardly opposed by every Christian conviction in the human soul; for it is not Christian, but Pagan. It is a relapse into Paganism, an importation of Pagan terrors into Christianity. It degrades every soul that teaches it, or that accepts it, in the same way that idolatry degrades it. It puts a veil between the soul and the true God.

But the true Christian doctrine of eternal punishment is, that the soul which sins shall eternally suffer; that there is an eternal distinction between truth and falsehood, good and evil; that spiritual distinctions are positive and real; and that evil is not a mere negative thing, implying a little less of good, but positive, being the state of a soul which is repelled, not attracted, by the divine goodness; which keeps away from God, as the shadow keeps on the side of the globe which is away from the sun.

Again: eternal suffering is the suffering of eternity, as distinguished from temporal suffering, which has its root in time. This is something which comes from within, while temporal suffering comes from without. Till man is reconciled to God by obedience and love, he has the sentence of death in himself. This suffering is not arbitrary, but fixed in the nature of things. As a sinner, man must be eternally separated inwardly from God, and therefore from bliss. His hell is within him, not without. And it is also here, as well as hereafter, since eternity is here, no less than time.

In this view of eternal punishment, there is an important truth—truth essential to the just spiritual growth of man. It is needed to resist the tendency to make light of sin. It is needed to oppose the view which makes evil, as well as good, a natural growth, and teaches that all men are on their way upward, and will ultimately fall into heaven by some specific levity. It is needed to remind us that we must choose whom we will serve, and that, consciously or unconsciously, we are at all moments tending either upward or downward—either towards God or away from him.

This is the great truth which is often lost sight of by Liberal Christianity, and by that easy optimism which declares that "whatever is, is right;" but darkly taught, because dimly seen, by Orthodoxy. Pagan in its form, there is often an essentially Christian idea communicated by the Orthodox pulpit. The Pagan form may be neglected and disbelieved: the Christian impression may remain. It tightens the nerves of the soul, as a cold bath invigorates the body made languid by too much warmth and ease. Yet, as long as the Pagan form remains, the interior truth is shorn of its full power. Let us pray that the truth, divested of its dark errors, may at last be recognized by the Christian Church. For very often the words of a great writer and thinker (who also was an earnest opponent of the Orthodox form of this doctrine) recur to us in these studies: "Few see the things themselves, but only the forms of things, in the mirror of reflection, as images. But we shall at last see the things themselves face to face, as it is said, and without a veil, if it please God, in part before the close of this present life, more fully in the life to come."57

§ 8. How Judgment by Christ is connected with Punishment

To what we have said of judgment by Christ, in the previous chapter, we add here some further thoughts in regard to its connection with punishment. Orthodoxy makes this connection arbitrary and outward. For such sins, it says, God has appointed such a punishment; and the object of judgment is to glorify God, by showing how exact he is in finding out every sinner, and fulfilling his every threat against evil. But, according to a better view, which alone can commend itself to minds of any large range—future judgment is simply the act by which God shows to a man the truth concerning himself, so that he can see it.

A deaf and dumb child being asked, "What is judgment?" replied, "Judgment is to see ourselves as we are, and to see God as he is." This is the essential thing in judgment; and in this sense Christ is declared "to be the judge of the quick and the dead;" that is, he judges us in this world, and will judge us in the other world. His judgments are not external, sentencing us to external punishments; but they are internal, causing us to judge ourselves. He shows us what we are. Whenever he comes, he comes to judgment, separating the good from the evil, testing the state of the heart, causing men to go to the right or the left. His coming always makes an issue which cannot be avoided; calls upon us to decide which course we shall take, what thing we shall do, what master we will serve. When Christ first came, he came for judgment, that the thoughts of many hearts might be revealed,—revealed to themselves and to others. Wherever he came, men immediately were divided into two classes,—becoming his disciples, or becoming his opponents. No longer was any compromise possible between truth and error, between right and wrong. They were obliged to choose which to serve; and they chose according to the inward tendency of their hearts. They whose hearts were right, chose the right: they whose hearts were wrong, chose the wrong.

Christ is thus the Judge of the living as well as the dead. Often in our lives he comes to us thus to be our Judge. Every time he calls upon us to do anything for him, he judges the state of our heart. Every time he offers an opportunity to the world of improvement or progress, he judges the world.

When he was on trial before Caiaphas and before Pilate, they were on trial, and not he. When they sentenced him, they condemned themselves. During the whole of those dark hours, when Christ was buffeted, spit upon, crowned with thorns, to the eyes of angels he was seen to be sitting on the throne of his glory. Caiaphas and the Jewish priests, Pontius Pilate and the Roman soldiers, Judas Iscariot, the Jewish people, each in turn received their sentence, and passed to the left hand. And so ever since, whenever any great opportunity has been given to the world to decide between right and wrong, the world has pronounced judgment on itself; has gone to the right hand with the sheep, or to the left hand with the goats. When Paul offered Christianity to the Jews, and they rejected it, he said "it was necessary that the word of God should first have been spoken to you; but seeing you put it from you, and judge yourselves unworthy of eternal life, lo, we turn to the Gentiles." So it always is. God does not judge us, nor Christ; but we judge ourselves. For this reason Jesus says, "If any man hear me, and believe not, I judge him not; for I came not to judge the world." And again he says, "The word which I have spoken, the same shall judge him at the last day." And yet again, "This is the judgment, that light has come into the world, and that men have chosen darkness rather than light, because their deeds are evil."

The account of judgment (in the 25th chapter of Matthew) at Christ's coming we considered in the last chapter. It will, however, bear a little further examination. There are *three* different judgments indicated in the three parables of the virgins, the talents, and the sheep and goats. The first is the judgment of opportunity, the second of work, the third of knowledge. In the first and second we judge ourselves, in the last we are judged. These two occur in time, the other in eternity. The first two are the judgments which take place at Christ's coming here; the third is the judgment of "the last day." The first takes place whenever we are "called" by a new opportunity; the second comes in all retribution; the third by the inward revelation of God's truth, showing men what they are, and what God is. The wise and foolish virgins represent those *who are invited to receive Christianity*; the servants with the talents, believers who have received it in different degrees; and the nations (heathen, τὰ ἔθνη)58 those (in Christendom or outside of it) to whom Christianity has never come.

§ 9. The Doctrine of Annihilation

This view of the final results of moral evil, as destroying personal existence, is hardly an Orthodox doctrine, though quasi-Orthodox. It is the refuge of that class of minds which are unable to accept universal restoration on the one side, or everlasting punishment on the other. To them a large number of human beings seem "too good for banning, and too bad for blessing," and in their opinion will be suffered quietly to drop out of conscious existence. The analogies of nature, in which out of many seeds and many eggs produced, only a few attain to the condition of plants and animals, tend to confirm this view. The state of human character here appears also to favor it, since multitudes pass out of this world in an undeveloped condition, seeming wholly to have failed of the end of their being. The chief scriptural argument in favor of the doctrine is found in the assumption that "life through Christ" is equivalent to continued conscious existence, and that "death" as the punishment of sin, is equivalent to annihilation. We have so fully discussed the meaning of these terms in the previous chapter, that it is not desirable to argue this point here. We agree with the Orthodox view, and differ from that of the annihilationists on this point. The God of the gospel is the Father of all his children—of the weakest, feeblest, and most sinful. If he is the God of *all*, then he is "the God, not of the dead, but of the living, for all live to him." Indian tribes and heathen nations may be willing that the sickly infants, and those worn with age, should perish; they may expose female infants, thinking them not worth bringing up; but Christian nations establish schools and hospitals for the deaf and dumb, the insane, the inebriates, the idiotic. If we, then, being evil, know how to care for the weak, undeveloped, and vegetative natures, how much more shall their Father in heaven care for them! The doctrine of annihilation rests fundamentally on a Pagan view of God.

§ 10. The Doctrine of Universal Restoration

This opinion has its roots, we think, in the gospel. It has prevailed in the church from the earliest times, having been held, as we have seen, by Origen, and a great number of eminent church fathers and doctors. What more Christian word has come to us from the earliest centuries than the cry out of the heart of the great Alexandrian teacher, "My Saviour, even now, mourns for my sins. My Saviour cannot be happy while I remain in my iniquity. He does not wish to drink the cup of joy alone in the kingdom of God; he is waiting till we shall come and join him there."59

Our object in this chapter is to consider the Orthodox view, and we shall not, therefore, enter into any extensive argument concerning universal salvation. We will only here indicate the general scriptural evidence in its support. The alternative to the Orthodox view of everlasting punishment is not, as we have shown, necessarily Universalism. It may be annihilation, or it may be, under the name of eternal punishment, a negative evil, being the privation of the highest kind of happiness. Still, it seems proper to suggest, if only very briefly, some reasons given by Universalists for their belief.

In the Epistles of Paul there are five or six passages, which appear to teach, or to imply, an ultimate restoration of salvation of all moral beings. Among them are these:—

1. Eph. 1:9, 10. "Having made known to us the mystery of his will, according to his good pleasure, which he hath purposed in himself, that in the dispensation of the fulness of times he might gather together in one all

things in Christ, both which are in heaven and which are on earth, even in him."

The apostle is speaking of the "riches of God's grace," wherein "he hath *abounded* toward us," and gives as the proof this revelation made in Christ of a great mystery—that "in the dispensation [economy] of the fulness of times" he might bring into one (under one head) "all things in heaven and on earth." The idea of the passage seems evidently to be that in the economy, or order, of the divine plan, which extends through indefinite periods of time, all things shall be united under one head in Christ. But if brought under one head (as the Greek word signifies), then all become Christians, all "in heaven and earth." This would seem to be a very plain statement of a universal restoration.

As such, Olshausen, one of the most Orthodox of commentators, regards it. He rejects all the explanations offered by the advocates of everlasting punishment as unsatisfactory. "It cannot be disputed," he says, "that in it the restoration of all things seems to be again favored—a view which Paul in general, as has already been remarked (on Rom. 11:32; 1 Cor. 15:24; Gal. 3:22) says more to support than the other writers of the New Testament." Olshausen declares the interpretations which suppose a merely external subjection of the world to Christ to be entirely inadequate, and have left unresolved the principal difficulty, which is, "how Paul could say that all have a share in redemption, if he held the common view that the numberless hosts of angels who fell, along with the far greatest part of mankind (Matt. 7:13, 14) are eternally damned, and thus shut out from the harmony of the universe." The defenders of universal restoration, says Olshausen, "understand the harmony of the universe seriously, in its literal meaning, and seem, according to that, to be here in the right."

2. Phil. 2:9, 10. "Wherefore God hath highly exalted him, and given him a name which is above every name, that at the name of Jesus every knee should bow, of things in heaven, and things on earth, and things under the earth, and that every tongue should confess that Jesus Christ is Lord, to the glory of God the Father." Here we have "*things under the earth*" (καταχθονίων) added to "things in heaven and on earth." This word only occurs here in the New Testament, but is by Bretschneider (Lex. Man.) translated "subterranean" or "infernal," and applied to the inhabitants of Hades, with a reference to Origen, who uses the word in relation to the demons. De Wette applies the language to angels, living men, and the dead. At all events, it appears to include all moral beings, and to declare that the whole human race shall bow to Christ, and accept him as Master. But this cannot mean a merely outward submission, for such a forced and reluctant homage would bring little honor to God, nor be worth such admiration on

the part of the apostle. It must therefore mean that all men, not only all who now live, but all who have lived, shall finally become Christians and enter into the glory of God.

3. Col. 1:20. "And, having made peace by the blood of the cross, by him to reconcile all things to himself; by him, I say, whether they be things in earth or things in heaven." Here a new feature is added to the statement by the word "reconcile," which evidently expresses the entire conversion of the heart, and therefore of human beings, to the law of Christ.

4. 1 Cor. 15:22. "As in Adam all die, even so in Christ shall all be made alive." The "all" must be as extensive on one side as the other. Now, whether the death in Adam be physical or moral, whether it mean the dissolution of the earthly body, or the loss of innocence by sin, it certainly includes *all* human beings, in the fullest sense. All men die, and all men sin. It would therefore seem that the other "all" must be quite as comprehensive. It must include all human beings. All men shall "be made alive in Christ." But this cannot mean a mere physical immortality, or an immortality in misery; for one cannot be said to be "alive in Christ" who is suffering endless torment. To be "alive in Christ" means to be spiritually alive, for "he that hath the Son hath life."

5. 1 Cor. 24:28. In this passage Paul declares that *all* enemies shall be subject to Christ. But this, again, cannot mean a forced submission, for that is in no sense being subject to Christ. *Christ's* subjects are willing subjects. It therefore must mean that, finally, all human beings shall become Christian in conviction and in heart.

These five texts from the apostle Paul seem to us very plain and conclusive as to his opinions. But perhaps the strongest evidence in proof of a universal restoration is to be found in Christ's own parable of the prodigal son. For in this the genuine spirit and purpose of the gospel is shown to be that God *never* loses his fatherly love for his rebellious and lost children. On the contrary, his heart yearns towards them with a more earnest affection than towards the holy and good. The prodigal son represents those who are "dead in sin." (Luke 15:24-32.) The parable teaches that God loves them all the while they are away, and that "there is more joy in heaven over one sinner that repenteth than over ninety and nine just persons who need no repentance." Now, if God loves the sinners thus whose bodies are yet alive, does he cease to love them when the bodily change takes place which we call death? Does his nature change then? And if not, does it ever change? After millions of years, if they have been lost and dead so long, has his love become weary of waiting, or does "his mercy endure forever"?

To us it seems clear, that if the parable of the prodigal son is to be taken as a true statement of the feeling of God towards every sinner, that every sinner must at last be brought back by the mighty power of this redeeming love. The power of the human will to resist God is indeed indefinite; but the power of love is infinite. Sooner or later, then, in the economy of the ages, all sinners must come back, in penitence and shame, to their Father's house, saying, "Make us as thy hired servants." If so, if universal restoration does not mean primarily restoration to outward happiness, but to inward obedience, it seems to us that the doctrine may be so stated as to be a new motive for *present* repentance and obedience. May we not say to the sinner, You may resist God to-day, to-morrow, for a million years; but, sooner or later, you *must* return, obey, repent, and submit? God will spare no means to bring you. His love to you requires him to use all methods, all terrors, all suffering. The "worm that never dies," the "fire that is never quenched," the "outer darkness,"—these are all blessed means, in the providence of the Almighty, to bring the sinner back to a sense of his evil state. In the other world, as in this world, God will "chasten us, not for his pleasure, but for our profit, that we may be partakers of his holiness."

Chapter XV
The Christian Church

§ 1. The Question stated

One of the most interesting questions of the present time, in practical theology, concerns the nature, authority, organization, functions, and future of the Christian Church. The interest in this subject has recently much revived, in consequence of a reaction towards the Roman Catholic or High Church view. This has appeared in the tendency among Protestants to join the Catholic Church as the only true and saving Church of Christ. The same tendency has taken into the Church of England, and into the Episcopal Church of the United States, those who were not ready to go as far as Rome. It is therefore important and useful to ask, What is the truth and what the error in the different views concerning the Church? These differ very widely. The Roman Catholics declare that theirs is the only true Church, and that out of it is no salvation. Many Protestants reply that the Roman Catholic Church is Antichrist, and the only true Churches are those which hold the Evangelical or Orthodox creed. The Swedenborgians say that the Old Church came to an end in 1758, and that since then the New Church has taken its place. Finally, a considerable number of persons maintain that all these churches are worse than useless, and that it is the duty of Christians to come out, and be separate from them all. They do not believe in the need of any church, but would substitute for it societies for special purposes,—lyceums and literary clubs for purposes of mental instruction; temperance societies, peace societies, and other associations for moral purposes; and Odd-Fellows associations, Masonic associations, and clubs for social purposes.

The question then is, Is a Christian Church needed for the permanent wants of man? Was such a Church established by Christ? If so, which Church is it? And what is to be its future character and mode of organization?

It is scarcely necessary to discuss here the abstract question—Is a church an essential want of man, so as to be needed by him forever? It is enough to show that a church is needed now, and will be, for a long time to come. Every religion has had its church. No sooner does a new idea arise, than it is incorporated in some outward union. The new wine is put into new bottles. Confucius has his church, Mohammed has his church; even Mormonism and Spiritualism have established their churches. The Christian Church arose immediately after the ascension of Jesus; it came as a matter of necessity, born not of flesh, nor of the will of man, but of God. It has continued ever since, in ever-varying forms, but one undying body. Other institutions have risen and passed away. The Roman empire has disappeared. The barbarous nations overflowed Europe, and then were civilized, Christianized, and absorbed into the Christian Church. Protestantism separated from Romanism, but *the Church* remained in both. Other sects, Presbyterian, Independent, Quaker, Methodist, Baptist, Swedenborgian, Unitarian, Universalist, separated from the main Protestant body, but each took with it the church; each has its own church. Even the Quakers, the most unchurched apparently of any, who renounced the visible ministry, and the visible sacraments, made themselves presently into the most compact church of all. So the word continues evermore to be made flesh. So all spirit presently becomes incarnate in body. The body is outward and visible; the spirit inward and invisible. Both are necessary to the life, growth, and active influence of the gospel. Without the spirit of Christianity, the body would be good for nothing; it would be only a corpse. Without the body of Christianity, the spirit would be comparatively inactive; it would be only a ghost. A body without spirit corrupts and is offensive; a spirit without body is inoperative and alarming. Through body alone the spirit can act; through spirit alone the body can live.

Without asking, therefore, for any other authority for the Church, than its adaptation to human wants, we may safely say, that it is a great mistake to suppose we can dispense with churches. You cannot overthrow the churches, not the weakest of them, by any agency you can use; for all came up to meet and supply a want of the human soul. They are built on that rock. What will you put in their place? A lyceum? A debating society? A reform club? What are you to say to the souls of men, hungering and thirsting for God? What to the sinner, borne down by the mighty weight of transgression? What to the dying man, who knows not how to prepare to meet his God? We need the Church of Christ—the Church whose great aim it is, and always has been, to renew and regenerate the soul from its foundation, to lay the axe at the root of the tree of evil, and the very sound of whose bell, rolling its waves of music over the sleeping hills on the Sabbath morning, is worth more to the soul than a thousand lyceums and debating societies.

No; the Church is not to be destroyed; it is to be renewed with a deeper and fuller life. We want a better Church, no doubt—one more free in its thought, more active in its charity, with more of brotherhood in it. We want an apostolic Church, fitted to the needs of the nineteenth century. The theological preaching which satisfied our parents is not what we wish now. We need Christianity applied to life—the life of the individual and of the state. A better Church, no doubt, is needed; but we want the churches *fulfilled*, not destroyed.

§ 2. Orthodox Doctrine of the Church— Roman Catholic and High Church

Admitting, then, the permanency of the Christian Church, we next ask, "What is its true form?" or, "Which is the true Church?" or, again, to state it in another way, "Is the form of the Church permanent, or only its substance? Is *any* union for Christian purposes, for worship and work, a Church, or must it be found in some particular organic form?" To this question Romanism and High Church Episcopacy reply, "It must." The rest of Protestantism answers, "No." Romanism says—Jesus established an essential form for his Church, as well as an essential substance. The true Church is an organization as well defined as any corporation for secular purposes. It has the monopoly of saving souls, a patent right of communicating spiritual life, which cannot lawfully be infringed by any other corporation. This right was originally bestowed on St. Peter, and has been transmitted by him to his successors, bishops of Rome. The proof is in the original deed of gift, "Thou art Peter," &c., and in the regularity of the succession of subsequent bishops.

"According to the Catholic dogma," says Guericke,60 "the Church is an outward community, by which all communion with Christ is conditioned and mediated. This outward community is the true Church, with the signs of unity, universality, apostolicity, and holiness, and is both the only infallible Church, and only one which can save the soul." This Church, according to Bellarmine, is a wholly visible and outward association; as much so as the kingdom of France or republic of Venice.61 According to Moehler,62 the Church "is the visible community of believers, founded by Christ, in which, by means of an enduring apostleship, &c., the works wrought by him during his earthly life are continued to the end of the world." The Roman Catholic idea is of a visible Church only, and not of a Church at once visible and invisible, which is the Protestant notion. It is composed of good and bad, while the Protestant notion makes the true Church consist only of the regenerate.63

The chief refutation of this claim of the Romish Church is to be found in the very vastness of its assumption. Assuming itself to be the only true Church, and the only one founded by Christ, we of course require full and exact evidence in proof of its assertion. It must prove, (1.) That Jesus founded an outward Church of this kind; (2.) That he made Peter its head; (3.) That he gave Peter power to continue his authority to his successors; (4.) That the bishops of Rome are the successors of Peter; (5.) That this succession has been perfect and uninterrupted; (6.) That the Roman Catholic Church *is* infallible, and has never committed any mistake; (7.) That it *is* Catholic, and includes all true Christians; (8.) That it *is* at one with itself, having never known divisions; (9.) That it *is* the only holy Church, bearing the fruits of Christian character in a quality and quantity which no other Church can rival. If any one of these nine propositions fail, the whole claim of Rome falls prostrate. But they *all* fail, not one being susceptible of proof. It cannot be made to appear that Jesus ever intended to found a Church having such a monopoly of salvation; nor that the apostle Peter was ever placed at its head, with supreme authority;64 nor, if he had this authority, that he ever was bishop of Rome; nor, if he were, that he transmitted his authority to his successors; nor, if he did, that the bishops of Rome are his successors; nor, if they are, that the succession has been unbroken; nor that the church has been actually infallible; nor that it includes all true Christians; nor that it has been free from schisms; nor that it has always been so pure and holy as to show that Romanism is eminently Christian, and Protestantism not so. The chain of proof, therefore, which, if one link parted, would be a broken chain, is broken at *every* link, and cannot carry conviction to any unbiassed mind.

In a little work lately published in France by the Protestant Pastor, Mr. Bost,65 the author gives as a reason for not being a Catholic, that while the Church calls on us to submit to its authority, it cannot tell where the authority resides.66 The Ultramontanes place it in the person of the pope; but the Gallicans have never admitted this idea, and place the supreme authority in a universal council.

Besides, what sort of infallibility is that which has tolerated the Inquisition, applauded the St. Bartholomew massacre, preached crusades against the heretics in France, massacred the Protestants in Holland, burned ten thousands at the stake in Spain? If it be said that Protestants also have persecuted, we reply, that they did it *against* their own principles, but that the Catholics persecuted in accordance with theirs; and that the Church which claims exclusive infallibility and holiness has no right to excuse itself *because it has done no worse* than those which it denounces as being in error and sin.

§ 3. The Protestant Orthodox Idea of the Church

Protestantism does not claim for its Church exclusive holiness or infallibility. It defines the Church to be "a congregation of faithful men, in which the pure word of God is preached, and the sacraments duly administered."67 Why, then, the reaction towards Romanism? It is partly owing to the passive element in man—the wish to be governed, the weariness of independent thought, which led Wordsworth to say,—

"Me this unchartered freedom tires,"—

and which, in "Van Artevelde," declares that,—

Thought is tired of wandering through the world,

And homeward fancy runs its bark ashore,—

and partly because the Protestant Churches are often less active and diligent in the practical part of Christian work than the Roman Catholic Churches. Instead of a manly Protestantism, they give us a diluted Catholicism. They insist on a creed which has neither antiquity nor authority to recommend it, on sacraments that are no real sacraments, but only symbols, and on a ritual which has neither the beauty nor variety of the Roman worship.

What does the Protestant Church propose to itself as its end? To produce an abstract piety, instead of a concrete piety—not a piety embodied in life and conduct, but taking only the form of an inward experience. If the churches should set themselves the work of feeding the hungry and clothing the naked, of removing the vices and crimes of men, of helping the outcasts and visiting the prisoners, they would have a more living piety growing out of this active charity. Their prayer meetings would be much more vigorous when they prayed in order to work, than when they pray in order to pray. Men should not be admitted into the Church because they are pious, but in order to become pious by doing Christian work. By loving, practically, the brother they have seen, they would come to love God, whom they have not seen.

Again: the Protestant Church feebly imitates the aristocracy of the Romish Church. In order to conquer Romanism, we must go on and leave it behind, seeking something better, and finding some more excellent way. Now, the sin of Romanism is its aristocracy; Protestantism ought, then, to give us, in its Church, a Christian democracy. But it keeps up the pernicious distinction between clergy and laity, making the clergy a separate class, and so justifying Milton's complaint that the "Presbyter is only the old priest written large." It makes a distinction between men and women in the Church, not encouraging the latter to speak or to vote. It makes a distinction between the rich and poor, selling its pews to those who can buy them, and leaving those who are unable to do so outside of the sanctuary. It makes a distinction between Orthodox and heretics, excluding the latter, instead of inviting them in where their errors might be corrected. And finally, it makes an unchristian distinction between good people and bad people; for while Jesus, its Master, made himself the friend of publicans and sinners, the Church too often turns to them the cold shoulder, and leaves them to be cured by the law, and not the gospel.

The following saying of a saint of the desert, Abbot Agatho, is reported by Dr. Newman, who tells it as something wise and good. It seems to us to illustrate, with much *naïveté*, the tendency of both Catholic and Protestant Orthodoxy, to put right opinion above right conduct.

"It was heard by some that Abbot Agatho possessed the gift of discrimination. Therefore, to make trial of his temper, they said to him, 'We are told that you are sensual and haughty.' He answered, 'That is just it.' They said again, 'Are you not that Agatho who has such a foul tongue?' He answered, 'I am he.' Then they said, 'Are not you Agatho *the heretic?*' He made answer, 'No.' Then they asked him why he had been patient of so much, but would not put up with this last. He answered, 'By those I was but casting on me evil; but by this I should be severing me from God.' "

According, therefore, to Agatho and Dr. Newman, the tongue "which is set on fire of hell," does not separate us from God, but an error of opinion does. Pride, "which comes before a fall," and sensuality, which makes of a man a beast, do not come between the soul and God so much as an honest error of opinion.

The Protestant Church fails to overcome the Catholic Church only by being too much like the latter. With Protestant ideas, we have semi-Catholic Churches. We claim as our fundamental principle the right of private judgment, and then denounce and exclude those who differ from us. We claim that the soul is not to be saved by monkish seclusion, by going away from the world; and yet we do not preach and carry out in our church-action the purpose of saving the bodies of men as well as their souls. When the Protestant Church work gets more into harmony with Protestant ideas, we shall then see fewer relapses into Romanism.

§ 4. Christ's Idea of a Church, or the Kingdom of Heaven

The Roman Catholics having made the visible Church, or outward Christian community, the central idea of Christianity, and having changed this into a close corporation of priests, it was natural, perhaps, that Protestants should go too far in another direction. Accordingly, the central idea in Protestantism is not the Church, but the salvation of the soul; not social, but personal religion; not the Christian community, but personal development; not the kingdom of heaven here, but heaven in a future life. Yet it is true, and has been shown lately with great power,[68] that the direct and immediate object of Jesus was to establish a community of believers. This was implied in his being the Christ,—for the Christ was to be the head of the kingdom of heaven,—and the kingdom of heaven was to be an earthly and human institution. Jesus took the idea of the kingdom of God, as it was announced by the prophets; purified, developed, deepened, and widened it; and it resulted in his varied descriptions of the "kingdom of heaven," This phrase, in the mouth of Jesus, expresses essentially what we mean by "the Church." This will appear more plainly if we sum up the principal meanings of the phrase "kingdom of God" in the New Testament. It is,—

1. *Something near at hand.*

Mark 1:15. "The kingdom of God is at hand." Luke 9:27. "There are some standing here who shall not taste of death till they see the kingdom of God." Mark 9:1. "There be some of them which stand here which shall not taste of death till they have seen the kingdom of God come with power."

2. *It was already beginning.*

Luke 17:20. "And when he was demanded of the Pharisees when the kingdom of God should come, he answered them and said, The kingdom of God cometh not with observation, neither shall they say, Lo, here! or, Lo, there! for behold, the kingdom of God is within (or 'among') you."

3. *It was not of this world.*

John 18:36. Jesus said, "My kingdom is not of this world."

4. *But was to be in this world.*

Matt. 6:10. "Thy kingdom come, thy will be done on earth, as it is in heaven."

5. *In some respects it was to be an outward and visible kingdom, or an outward institution.*

Parable of the grain of mustard-seed. Matt. 13:31, 32.

6. *It would contain good and bad.*

Parable of the net. Matt. 13:47.

7. *It would belong to Christ.*

Col. 1:13. "Hath translated us into the kingdom of his Son." Luke 22:30. "Ye shall eat and drink in my kingdom." John 18:36. "My kingdom is not of this world." Matt. 16:28. "Shall see the Son of man coming in his kingdom."

8. *It would be finally given up to God.*

1 Cor. 15:24. "Then the end; when he shall have delivered up the kingdom to God, even the Father," &c.

9. It is a spiritual kingdom.

Rom. 14:17. "For the kingdom of God is not meat and drink, but righteousness, peace, and joy in the Holy Ghost."

10. Flesh and blood cannot inherit it.

1 Cor. 15:50. "Flesh and blood cannot inherit the kingdom of God; neither doth corruption inherit incorruption."

11. The conditions of admission are spiritual.

John 3:3. "Except a man be born again," &c. Matt. 5:3. "Blessed are the poor in spirit," &c. 1 Cor. 6:9. "The unrighteous shall not inherit the kingdom of God." See Gal. 5:21. Eph. 5:5.

12. The kingdom was to be established by the Son of man at his coming.

Matt. 24:30; 25:1. "They shall see the Son of man coming in the clouds of heaven," &c. "Then shall the kingdom of heaven be likened."69

Christ, therefore, had in his mind, as the direct object of his coming, to cause God's kingdom to come, and his will to be done on earth as in heaven. It was not his direct purpose to teach the truth in abstract forms, like the philosophers; nor to make atonement by his death for human sins; nor to set an example of a holy life; nor to make a revelation of God and immortality; nor to communicate new life to the world. These he did; but they came as a part of the kingdom of heaven. They were included in this great idea. His kingdom was a kingdom of *truth*, in which his *word* was to be the judge. He was to reconcile the world to God by his death. He was to show what man was made to be and could become. He was to reveal God as a Father to his human children. He was to set in motion a tide of new spiritual life. But the method by which all this was to be done was the method of a community of disciples and brethren, who should be his apostles and missionaries. They were to be an outward, visible association with the symbols of baptism and the supper. They were also to be an influence in the world, a current of religious life. We find that such was the result. We see the disciples embodied and united in a visible community, which spread through all the Roman empire, which soon had its teachers, officers, its meetings, its worship, its sacred books, its sacred days. But we find also the larger and deeper current of life, which constitutes the invisible Church, flowing, like a great river, down through the centuries. All Christians in all Christian lands drink from this stream, and all their ideas of God, man, duty, immortality, are colored and tinged by it. We read the Bible by the light of the convictions we absorbed at our mother's knee in our infancy. We carry on our churches in the power of the holy traditions which have become a part of our nature. There is a Christian consciousness which grows up in every child who is born in Christendom, and is the best part of his nature. This makes him a member of the invisible Church before he outwardly becomes a member of the visible Christian community.

§ 5. Church of the Leaven, or the Invisible Church

There are two parables of Christ which apply to the Church visible and invisible. The Church Visible is the Church of the Mustard-seed; the Church Invisible is the Church of the Leaven. The former is an organization, the latter an *influence*; the one is body, and the other spirit. The Visible Church is limited by certain boundaries; defined by its worship, creeds, officers, assemblies, forms. It has its holy days, holy places, holy men, holy books. But the Invisible Church is not limited by any such boundaries; it exists wherever goodness exists. The Church of the Leaven is to be found inside and outside of Orthodoxy; inside and outside of professing Christianity; among Jews, Mohammedans, Heathen; among Deists and unbelievers of all sorts, who build better than they know. For says Jesus, "The wind bloweth where it listeth, and we hear the sound thereof.... So is every one who is born of the Spirit." A locomotive must run on a track, a wagon on a road. But there is no track laid through the sky for the south wind; there is no time-table to determine the starting and arriving of the soft breeze which comes from the far prairies, laden with the sweet fragrance of ten thousand flowers.

"So is every one who is born of the Spirit." Get out your Catechism, my Orthodox friend; establish, dear Methodist brother, your experience to determine whether one is converted or no. Settle for yourself, excellent formalist, the signs of the true Church, out of which there is no salvation; and when you have got all your fences arranged, and your gates built to your satisfaction, you are obliged to throw them all down with your own hands, to let the Church of the Leaven pass through. "Nobody can be saved," says Dogmatic Christianity, "who does not believe in the Trinity and the Atonement." "Nobody can be saved," says Sentimental Christianity, "who has not had a conscious change of heart." " Nobody can be saved," says Formal Christianity, "who is out of the true Church and its sacraments." Here are the three fences of the Church of the Mustard-seed. But see! here comes an innumerable multitude of little children, who have never believed in Trinity or Atonement; have never been baptized at all; have never been converted. Yet neither Dogmatist, Sentimentalist, nor Formalist dares to exclude them from heaven. Logic steps aside; good feeling opens the three gates; and the little ones all walk quietly to the good Shepherd, who says, "Let them come to me, and forbid them not;" gathering the lambs in his arms, carrying them in his bosom, and tenderly leading them in the green pastures beside the still waters.

The little children must be allowed to go through; consistency requires them to be damned; but consistency must take care of itself; so much the worse for consistency. But who comes next? Here are all the heathen, who have not heard of Christ. Must they be damned? According to the creeds, yes; but modern Orthodoxy has its doubts; its heart has grown tender. Somehow or other we think that we shall have to let them pass, before a great while. Then here are all the people whom we have known and loved. They did not believe as they should. They were never converted, so far as we know; they were not members of any Church, true or false. But we loved them. Cannot the three fences be put aside again, just to let these friends of ours pass by. What kind-hearted Orthodox man or woman was ever wanting in an excuse for letting his heretical friends into heaven. "He changed his views very essentially before he died. He used very Orthodox language, to my certain knowledge. He said he relied on the merits of Christ; or, at least, he said he believed in Christ." And so all the good and kind dead people must follow all the little children, and pass the triple fence. They do not belong to the Church of the Mustard-seed; but they belong to the Church of the Leaven. These fences are like the flaming wall in Tasso; they seem impassable, but as soon as one comes up to them they are found to be nothing. Blessed be God that common sense is stronger than logic; that humanity is stronger than forms; and that large, kind Christian hearts are more than a match for the somewhat narrow Christian head.

§ 6. The Church of the Mustard-seed

This is not the spirit, but the body; not the life, but the organization of that life. There is no doubt that we need a Church visible as well as a Church invisible; need a body as well as a soul; and it is a very important question what sort of a body we shall have. Soul, no doubt, is infinitely more important than body; still we do not wish our body to be lame, blind, or dyspeptic. Because soul is better than body, we do not like rheumatism or neuralgia. Our visible Church, the body of Christ, is sometimes a little dyspeptic, and goes about looking very gloomy and miserable, when it ought to be as gay as a lark. Sometimes also it seems to be rheumatic; at any rate, it cannot go and attend to its work. It is very subject to fever and ague; plenty of meetings to-day, all alive with zeal and heat, but to-morrow it is cold and shivering. It has its pulmonary disease too; its lungs are not strong enough to speak when it ought; to cry out for truth and right in the day of trial. And as we find that hygienics are better than therapeutics for physical diseases, so, perhaps, it will be better for us to prevent the diseases of the Church by wise arrangements, which shall give it air, exercise, and a wholesome diet, than to cure it, when sick, by the usual medicine of rebuke, reproof, and ascetic mortification.

The visible Church may be looked at in four points of view. We may consider it as, —

1. The Primitive Church, or Church as it was.
2. The Church Actual, or Church as it is.
3. The Ideal Church, or Church as it ought to be.
4. The Possible Church, or Church as it can be.

§ 7. Primitive and Apostolic Church, or Church as it was

If we study the nature, organization, and character of the primitive Christian Church, as it appears in the book of Acts and in the Epistles, we recognize easily the warm, loving life which was in its spring time, when all buds were swelling, and all flowers opening. It was far from being a perfect Church. It had many errors, and included many vices. Some persons in the Church did not believe in the resurrection of the dead. (1 Cor. 15:12.) Some disciples had not heard there was a Holy Ghost. (Acts 19:2.) Some even became intoxicated at the Lord's Supper. (1 Cor. 11:21, ὅς δὲ μεθύει). Some Christians had to be told not to steal (Eph. 4:28); nor to lie, (Col. 3:9); nor to commit other immoralities. Peter (supposed to be the infallible head of the Church) was rebuked by Paul for dissimulation. Paul and Barnabas could not get along together, but quarrelled, and had to separate. Part of the Church Judaized, and denounced Paul as a false apostle. Another part Paganized, and carried Pauline liberty into license. And yet, though there was so little of completed Christian character, there was a great amount of spiritual life in the apostolic Church. They are styled saints, but never was anything less saintly than the state of things in the beginning. But they were looking the right way, and going in the right direction. They were full of faith, zeal, enthusiasm, and inspiration; so they had in themselves the promise and expectation of saintship, if not its reality.

Directly after the ascension of Christ, and the wonderful experiences of the day of Pentecost, we find the Christian community in active operation. Its organization was as yet very indefinite; that was to come by degrees.

It was a Church without a creed; its only creed was a declaration of faith in Jesus as the Christ, the Son of God. It was a Church without a bishop, or a single head of any kind; for Peter, James, and John seem all three to have possessed an equal influence in it, and that influence was derived from their character. Paul tells us expressly, in the Epistle to the Galatians, that when he went up to Jerusalem, long after his conversion, Peter, James, and John "seemed to be pillars" there. No mention is made anywhere in the book of Acts of a single bishop presiding over the Church at Jerusalem, or over any other Church. And as to the Romish Church, which claims to be the oldest Church, and the mother of all the rest, it was not yet founded at all, when the Church at Jerusalem was established. Nor was the Church at Rome as old as the Churches at Antioch, at Lystra, at Iconium, and elsewhere, for Paul and Barnabas ordained elders in all these churches, as we are expressly told in Acts 14th; and in Acts 15:7 we find Peter still at Jerusalem. If there was any church at Rome, Peter was not its bishop; then either it was a church without a bishop, or Peter was not its first bishop.

We find also that as the apostolic Church had no creed and no bishop, neither had it any fixed or settled forms. Its forms and usages grew up naturally, according as convenience required. Thus (Acts 6:1-5) we find that the apostles recommended the disciples to choose seven persons to attend to the distribution of charity. "A murmuring arose" because the Greek widows were neglected—neglected, probably, because not so well known as the others. This shows that there were no fixed, established forms; even the order of deacons was originated to meet an occasion.

That they had no form of service, no fixed Liturgy, in the apostolic Church, appears from 1 Cor. 14:26. "How is it, brethren, when ye come together, every one of you hath a psalm, a doctrine, a tongue, a revelation, an interpretation? Let the prophets speak, two or three, and the others judge, and if anything be revealed to another that sitteth by, let the first hold his peace. You may all prophesy one by one, that all may learn, and all be comforted." Now, it is very evident no fixed or formal service could have been established in the churches when he recommended this.

But though the apostolic Church had neither bishop, nor creed, nor fixed forms, nor a fixed body of officers, it had something better—it had faith in God, and mutual love. "The multitude of them that believed were of one heart and one soul; neither said any man that aught that he possessed was his own, but they had all things common." We do not find an absolute community of property established by a law of the Church, as in the monastic orders, or as in the school of Pythagoras, and some modern communities, as that of St. Simon; for Peter says to Ananias, of his property, "While it remained, was it not thine own? and after it was sold, was it not in thine own power?" But though their property was in their own power, they did not call it their own, or consider it so; it belonged to God: they were only stewards, and they readily brought it, and gave it to the use of the Church.

The apostolic Church was a home of peace and joy. Whatever tribulations they might have in the world, when they met together they met Christ, and ate their meat with gladness and singleness of heart. They were in an atmosphere of love and freedom. We hear of no rules, no laws, no constraining forms; but all were led by the Spirit of God. Even in their public service, as we have seen, though Paul recommended a greater order, it was not based on authority, but on the sense of propriety of each individual, because God was not the God of confusion, but of peace.

Such was the original Church, as described in the Acts and Epistles. It sprang up because it was wanted, and Christ foresaw that it would be. It was founded not on an arbitrary command, but on the needs of human nature. Man is not a solitary, but a social being. He needs society in his labors and in his joys; society in study, society in relaxation. Even in the highest act of his life, —in the act of prayer, in communion with God; in that act, called by an ancient Platonist "the flight of one alone to the only One," —even then he cannot be alone. In the union of man with man in any natural and true relation, his thought becomes more clear, his will more firm, his devotion more profound, his affections more enlarged. The broader and deeper the basis of the union, the more it blesses and helps him. A friendship based upon the knowledge and love of the same God, what can be better for us than this?

Thus we see that the apostolic Church was a home for Christ's family (Matt. 12:49); a school for his disciples; a fraternity of brethren. For discipline, it had officers, but no clergy, nor priesthood, for all were priests, and all took part in the services. (1 Peter 2:5; Rom. 1:6; 1 Cor. 14:26.) Its only creed was a belief in Jesus as the Christ, the Son of God. (Acts 8:37; 16:31. 1 John 4:15; 5:5, 10. Rom. 10:9.) The unity of the Church was not the unity of opinion, nor the unity of ceremonies, but the bond of the Spirit (Eph. 4:3), and the central unities of faith, not of doctrine (Eph. 4:5.) The object of the Church service was not merely to partake the Lord's Supper together, nor to maintain public worship, nor to defend and propagate a creed, nor to call men into an outward organization, nor to gather pious people together, and keep them safe as in an ark, but to *do good* and *get good*—to grow up in all things into Him who is the Head. And the condition of membership was to wish to be saved from sin, and to have faith in Christ that he could save them; it was to hunger and thirst after righteousness.

§ 8. The Actual Church, or the Church as it is

Now, if we turn from the Church as it was to the Church as it is, —from the apostolic Church to those around us, —we see a difference. Instead of the freedom and union which were in the early Church, we find in the Roman

Catholic communion union, but no freedom; in the Protestant Churches freedom, but no union. In both we find the Church built on the ministry, instead of the ministry on the Church; the priests everything, the people nothing; fixed forms, instead of a free movement; dead creeds, instead of a living faith. The spirit of worldliness has entered the churches, and they try to serve God and Mammon; God on Sunday, and Mammon on the week days. The members of the churches are more devout and more religious, but not more moral or more humane, than many who are out of their body. And because they do not love man whom they have seen, they find it hard to love God, whom they have not seen. Their want of humanity destroys their piety.

A vast amount of good is done by the churches, even in their present state; but when we think of what they might do, it seems nothing. Yet it is *not* nothing. Could we know the good done by the mere sound of the church bells on Sunday, by the quiet assembling of peaceful multitudes in their different churches; could we measure the amount of awe and reverence which falls over every mind, restraining the reckless, checking many a half-formed purpose of evil, rousing purer associations and memories, calling up reminiscences of innocent childhood in the depraved heart of man; could we know how many souls are roused to a better life, made to realize their immortal nature, reminded of a judgment to come; could we see how many souls, on every Sabbath, in our thousands of churches, are turned from sin to God, how many sorrowing hearts are consoled by the sweet promises of the gospel; could we see, as God sees and the angels see, all this,—we should feel that the churches, in their greatest feebleness, are yet the instruments of an incalculable good. But when we look at what *is* to be done, what *ought* to be done, what *could* be done by them, their present state seems most forlorn.

It is one of the most difficult of our duties not to despise an imperfect good, and yet not to be satisfied with it.

One of the greatest evils of our churches is, that they are churches of the clergy, not of the people. Our clergy are generally pure-minded, well-intentioned men, less selfish and worldly than most men; but they are not equal to the demands of their position. We take a young man, send him to college, then to a theological school, where he studies his Greek very faithfully, and learns to write sermons. He comes out, twenty-two years old, a pleasing speaker, and is immediately settled and ordained over a large long-established church. As he rises in the pulpit and looks down on his congregation, one would think he would despair. What can he say to them? He knows nothing of human nature, of its struggles and sins, its temptations in the shop and the street. Men do not curse at him, nor try to cheat him, nor entice him into bar-rooms, oyster-cellars, billiard-rooms, and theatres. He cannot speak to men of their vices, their stony and hard hearts, their utter unbelief, their crying selfishness, for he knows nothing of it. He must speak of sin in the abstract, not of sin in the concrete. If he did, what could he say? What weapons has he? The sword of the Spirit is in his hands, but he has not tried it; he has no confidence in it. The awful truths of the Bible, which smite the stoutest sinner to the earth, these he might utter, if he dared; but he knows not how. And yet he is the teacher of these gray-headed men, and their only teacher. Had he gone out as Jesus sent his disciples, without purse or shoes or two coats, and preached the gospel for ten years by the way-side, in cottages, in school-houses, living hard, sleeping on the floor, seeing men and women everywhere without disguise, and taking no thought beforehand what to say, but leaning on God for his inspiration,— then might he have learned how to say something weighty even to a great congregation. Or if this poor boy were surrounded by a living active church, helping him by advice, going with him into the house of sorrow, the haunt of sin, kneeling with him by the sick couch and death-bed, and adding to his small experience the whole variety and richness of theirs,—then might he be a man of God, thoroughly furnished for every work.

If there were Judaism and Paganism in the early Church, they still, no doubt, linger in our churches to-day. The Church Judaizes in this—that it still puts forms above life. For example, the Roman Catholic Church teaches that if you take a child, and put water upon him, repeating the baptismal formula, and with the *intention* of baptizing him, the child becomes in that moment regenerate. If he had died the moment before, he would have been damned forever in eternal torments; if he dies the moment after, he will go to eternal bliss in heaven. Now, if an earthly parent should cover his child's body with camphene, and then set it on fire, because somebody had not baptized it, we should say he was a very cruel parent. But this conduct is attributed to the good God by the Roman Catholic doctrine. Moreover, when an outward form is made thus essential, when everlasting salvation or damnation depends on it, it behooves us to know what it is. Baptism consists of three parts—the water, the formula, and the intention of the baptizer. But as to the water, we may ask, *How much* is essential? Is it essential that there be enough to entirely immerse the body? The Catholic Church replies, "No." Is the aqueous vapor always present in the air enough? It answers, "No, *that* is *not* enough." At what precise point, then, between these two, does *enough* begin, does baptism take place, and the child cease to be a child of perdition, and become an heir of salvation? The Roman Catholic Church, being obliged to answer this question, has answered it thus: There is no baptism until water enough to *run* is put on the child. A drop which will not *run*, does not baptize him; a drop which will run, baptizes him. The difference, then, between these two drops, is the difference to the child between eternal damnation and eternal salvation.70

How does this sound by the side of the declaration of the apostle Paul— "He is not a Jew who is one outwardly, neither is circumcision outward in the flesh; but he is a Jew who is one inwardly, and circumcision is of the heart"? Judaism, if anything, was an outward institution; Christianity, if anything, is an inward life. And yet that which the apostle Paul said of Judaism we hardly to-day would venture to say of Christianity. "He is not a Christian who is one outwardly, neither is Christianity in outward belief, profession, or aspect; but he is a Christian who is one inwardly." "O, no!" we say, "there must be a distinction. A man who does not believe in the miracles, for example, may be a good man, but you must not call him a Christian." But he who follows Christ, we think, is a Christian. And as Christ walks before mankind on the divine road of goodness, truth, love, purity, he who walks on that road *cannot help being a follower* of Christ, whatever he may call himself.

How the Church Judaizes about the Sabbath—pretending, first, that there *is a Sabbath* in Christianity, and teaching people that there is a sort of piety in calling Sunday *the Sabbath*, and next putting this ritual observance, this abstinence from labor and amusement, on a level with moral duties! When men tithe mint, they are apt to forget justice and mercy. If Jesus were to return, after all these centuries, and were only to do and say just what he did and said about the Sabbath when he was here before, there are many pious Protestants who would think him rather lax in his religious principles. How long he has been with us, and yet we have not known him!

An American Protestant bishop once forbade a clergyman of his church to officiate again, because this clergyman had invited a Methodist minister to assist him in the administration of the sacrament. This is backsliding a good way from the position of Him who said, "Forbid him not: he that is not against us is with us." And again: "Whosoever wishes to do the will of God, the same is my mother, my sister, and my brother." Dear Master! is *thy* Church so broad as to include all who desire to do the will of God, and are *our* churches so narrow that they cannot hold any but those who agree with us in our little notions about ceremony and form? Hast thou been so long time with us, and yet have we not known thee?

The Church Actual is a timid Church. It is afraid of truth, and afraid of love. Its creed is full of mysteries too solemn and sacred to be examined. They are the sealed book of the prophet, which is given to the learned clergy, and to the unlearned laity; and the answer of the unlearned laity is, "We are not learned." And the answer of the learned clergy is, "It is sealed.

It is a mystery. We must not even try to understand it." The Actual Church is not fond of a free examination of its tenets, but rather represses it by the flaming terrors of perdition impending over honest error.

The Church Actual sticks in the letter. How it idolizes the Bible! But when you ask, *What?* you find it is rather the letter of the Bible than its manly, generous, humane, and holy spirit. It babbles of verbal inspiration and literal inspiration, which are phrases as absurd as it would be to say "bodily spirit." Question the inspiration of the letter, and a thousand voices cry, "You are cutting away the very foundations of our faith. If we cannot believe every letter of the Bible to be from God, we have nothing to hold by." But the apostle Paul thought somewhat differently, when he said, "Who hath also made us able ministers of the New Testament, *not of the letter, but of the spirit; for the letter killeth, but the spirit giveth life.*"

The American Bible Society appointed a committee of learned persons to revise the present translation of the Bible—not to make a new translation by any means, but merely to correct palpable blunders of the press, palpable errors in the headings of chapters, or universally admitted mistakes of the translators. The learned men did their work. It was examined, printed—about to be published. But an outcry was made, that the Bible Society, in taking away these few errors of the press, was taking away *our* Bible. The Christian public, in the middle of the nineteenth century, has been so instructed, that when a few errors in the letter of the outward word are corrected, it cries out, "They have taken away my Lord, and I know not where they have laid him."

The Church Actual is sectarian. Every church is trying to swell its numbers at the expense of its neighbors. We do not think that a Christian Church should be constructed on the principle of a mouse-trap, which it is easy enough to get into, but hard to get out of. We do not think it right that young persons, in the glow of their piety, should be drawn into a church, without being told that if they should change their views on any important point, they cannot leave it except by being excommunicated publicly. But there are churches in New England which have many very easy and agreeable entrances, but only two exits—very difficult and disagreeable. If one wishes to leave, he is dismissed with a letter directed to some other church of the same creed, and not till he has joined some such church, and a certificate is sent back to that effect, is he released from his obligations. The Church is therefore like a city on a hill, with a palisade fence all round, with openings by which one can get in, but not out; and having only two outlets—one by a gate kept carefully locked, and the other over a steep wall, fifty feet high. You have your choice of three things: 1. Stay where you are;

2. Go through the gate into another palisaded enclosure; 3. Be pitched down the Tarpeian rock of excommunication.71

Thus we see that the Church Actual differs much, and often for the worse, from the Church Primitive. It is not now a home or a fraternity, for its members often do not know each other by sight. It is not a school of disciples, for it is thought necessary to take your whole creed at once, ready made, and not learn it by degrees. The worship is too often by the minister and choir, the people being only spectators. Instead of the simple original faith in Jesus as the Christ, the people are taught long and complicated creeds. Instead of a unity of conviction, seeing the same things, there is only a unity of expression, *saying* the same things. Instead of seeking to save the outcasts, infidels, vicious; churches are built and occupied by Christians themselves, as though Christ came to call only the righteous to repentance. There may be, in our great cities, a church to every two thousand persons; but every seat in every church is bought and occupied by the respectable and comfortable classes. The gospel is preached, but no longer to the poor. There is something wrong in all this.

§ 9. The Church Ideal, or Church as it ought to be

The Church Ideal is full of life, power, love, freedom. It is a teaching Church; calling men out of darkness into marvellous light, throwing light on all the mysteries of human existence. It takes the little child and teaches it concerning its duty and destiny. It organizes schools through every Christian nation, so that all Christian children shall be taught of God, and that great shall be their peace. It teaches systematically and thoroughly all classes of society; so that all, from least to the greatest, know the Lord. It organizes missions to all heathen lands, and its missionaries are so true, noble, kind, so reflect the life of Jesus in their own, that the heathen come flying like clouds, and like flocks of doves, to the windows of the holy home. The dusky, and swarming races of Hindostan, the mild and studious Chinamen, come flowing to Christ, as the long undulating clouds of pigeons darken along the October sky in our western forests. The ideal Church is a loving Church. It loves men out of their sins. It seeks the poor and forlorn, the hard-hearted and impenitent, and by unwearied patience soothes their harsh spirit. Enter its gates, and you find yourself in an atmosphere of affection. The strong bear the infirmities of the weak. Each seeks the lowest place for himself. They love to wash the disciples' feet.

The Ideal Church is an active Church. All the members work together for the building up of the body; some after this fashion, others after that. "So the whole body, fitly joined together, and compacted by that which every joint supplieth," is built up in love. Is there any ruinous vice, any corroding sin, any festering moral disease in the land? The Ideal Church searches for its root, and finds its cure. It takes the intemperate man by the hand, and will not let him go till he abstains. It penetrates into every haunt of sin and pollution, and brings forth the half-ruined child, triumphantly leads out the corrupt woman, and places them in new homes. The Ideal Church does not dispute about doctrines or dogmas. It says to each, "To your Master you shall stand or fall, not to me."

Therefore the Ideal Church is an earthly heaven. There is in it a warm, serene, sunny atmosphere; a sky without clouds; the society of love, the solitude of meditation, the inaccessible mountain tops of prayer; the low-lying, quiet valleys, where the wicked cease from troubling, and the weary are at rest.

But where is the Ideal Church? We have seen that it is not in the past, where many look for it. The golden age of the Church, the Paradisiacal state of Christianity, is not behind us. Was the Ideal Church that which persecuted Paul for renouncing Judaism? Was it any of the Churches described by John in the book of Revelation? that of Ephesus, which had "left its first love"? that of Pergamos, which contained heretical teachers? that of Thyatira, which communed with Jezebel and the depths of Satan? that of Sardis, which had "a name to live, and was dead"? or that of Laodicea, which was lukewarm?

Was that an Ideal Church where Paul was obliged to write to Titus that a bishop must not be a striker, nor given to wine, nor to filthy lucre? and to advise Timothy to avoid "profane and vain babbling"?

There was more life in it than in the Church now; a great struggling, but undeveloped power of life, heaving and tossing the Church, as with subterranean fire—smoke and flame bursting forth together; a great power of life, but little chance of doctrine as yet; little harmony of action; little in accordance with our ideas of decency and order. It was the spring time, and as in the spring there is a great power of life in nature, swelling all buds, pushing all shoots, unfolding leaves,—but all things still bare; few flowers, no fruit,—so it was in the Primitive Church. It was not Ideal. The Ideal Church is before us, not behind us; it is to come.

§ 10. The Church Possible, or Church as it can be

Is any Church possible but the Actual? We think there is. We think that a Church may be something more and better than any we have now. Without reaching the ideal standard we can yet do something.

We think it possible for a Church to be united on a basis of study and action rather than on that of attainment. Instead of having it consist of those who have formed opinions, let it consist of those who wish to form them. Instead of having it consist of those who have been converted, and who believe themselves pious, let it consist of those who wish to be converted, and who desire to be pious. Instead of having it consist of good people, let us invite in the bad people who desire to be good. Do you send your children to school because they are learned, and not rather because they are ignorant? Why should we not become disciples of Christ because of our ignorance, rather than our knowledge.

We think it possible to have a Church, and even a denomination, organized, not on a creed, but on a purpose of working together. Suppose that the condition of membership was the desire and intention of getting good and doing good. The members of a church are not those who unite in order to partake the Lord's Supper, but to do the Lord's work. The Lord's Supper is their refreshment after working. They come together sometimes to remember his love, and to get strength from him. Let them sit together, express their desires, confess their faults, say what they have been trying to do, where they have failed, where succeeded, and so encourage each other to run with diligence the race set before them.

We therefore think it possible for a Church to be built on Christ himself, and not on a minister. The Church might even do without a sermon; the members might pray together and sing together, when they had no minister, and be a true family of Christian men and women, brothers and sisters in the Lord. The lowest view of a Christian Church is that which makes it a body of pew-holders; the next lowest, that which makes them an audience met to hear a sermon; the next lowest, a mere congregation or assembly of worshippers; a little higher is that of a body of communicants, bound together by the desire of knowing Christ; but highest of all is that which regards a Church as the body of Christ. Such a Church is to learn of him, and to do his will; it is his eyes, to look on all things with a Christian vision; his hands, by which he shall still touch and heal the wretched; his feet, to go through the world, to search out its evils and sins; his mouth, through which he shall speak words of divinest help and encouragement. "The body of Christ, and members one of another." The body of Christ; always active, always progressing, always advancing; advancing into a deeper and better knowledge of his will, into a purer love of his kingdom, into a further and divine life of union with him; the body fitly joined together, and compacted by that which every joint supplieth, making increase of the body to the building of itself up in love.

It is possible to have a Church which shall be ready to teach and preach the gospel, not to a few pew-holders only, but to the whole community. Every child born in New England is taught the elements of secular knowledge without money and without price. Are the waters of earthly knowledge, then, so much more essential to the safety of the state than the waters of life, that we cannot risk the chance of leaving any child uninstructed in reading and writing, but may leave him untaught in the gospel? It would seem to be possible, since we have free schools, to have also free Churches, and so really to have, what we profess to maintain, *Public Worship!* There is no such thing now as public worship. The churches are not public places—each belongs to a private corporation of pew-holders.

It is possible to have a Church which shall consider it its duty to obey its Master's first command, and "preach the gospel to every creature." Its mission shall be to go out into the highways and the hedges, to seek and save the lost. It will regard the world as its field, and the whole community as its sphere of labor—the whole community, according to its needs, to be taught, helped, comforted, and cured by the gospel.

It is possible to have a Church which shall be united, not on ceremonies, nor on a creed, but on study and labor, on loving and doing. The condition of admission should be the purpose to get good and do good. They should enter this school to learn, and not because they were already learned; to become good, and not because they were already so.

It is possible to have a Church which shall make it its purpose to educate the whole man—spirit, soul, and body; and not merely the spirit; to present the human being to God perfect and entire, wanting nothing.

It is possible to have a Church which shall combine union and freedom. The Roman Church, aiming at union, and neglecting freedom, has a union which is no real union; which is an outward shell of conformity, without inward unity of heart and thought. The Protestant Church, desiring freedom and neglecting union, has a freedom which is not really freedom, being only the outward liberty of tolerated opinions, but one in which free thought is discouraged, and honest difference of opinion disallowed. Only by combining in a living whole such antagonist needs, can either of these be fully secured. Union without freedom is not union; freedom without union, not freedom. There is no harmony in the juxtaposition of similar notes, but in the concord of dissimilar ones. Difference without discord, variety in harmony, the unity of the spirit with diversity of the letter, difference of operation, but the same Lord, many members, but one body,—this is very desirable, and wholly possible.

The day is coming in which our dogmatic Churches, formal Churches, sentimentally pious Churches, and professedly liberal Churches, shall be all taken up into something higher and better. The very discontent which prevails everywhere announces it. It is the working of the leaven—mind agitating the mass. In Protestant countries there is a tendency to Rome; but in Roman Catholic countries an equal or greater tendency to Protestantism. Orthodoxy tends to Liberal Christianity. Liberal Christianity tends to Orthodoxy. Each longs for its opposite, its supplement, its counterpart. It is a movement towards a larger liberty and a deeper life.

Chapter XVI
The Trinity

§ 1. Definition of the Church Doctrine

"The fundamental formula for the doctrine of the Trinity, as defined by the Church," says Twesten,72 "is, that in one divine essence or nature there are three persons, distinguished from each other by certain characteristics, and indivisibly participating in that one nature." The "Augsburg Confession," says, in like manner, "three persons in one essence."73 So the "Gallic Confession," and other Church Confessions, which say almost the same thing in the same words.74

The explanations given to these phrases vary indefinitely. Nitzsch (System d. Christ. Lehre, § 80) says, "We stand related in such a way, with all our Christian experience (Gewerdensein und Werden), to the one, eternal, divine essence, who is love, that in the Son we adore love as mediating and speaking, in the spirit as fellowship and life, in the Father as source and origin." Schleiermacher considers this doctrine as not any immediate expression of the Christian consciousness, and declares that "our communion with Christ might be just the same if we knew nothing at all of this transcendent mystery." Hase says,75 "This Church dogma always has floated between Unitarianism, Tritheism, and Sabellianism, asserting the premises of all three, and denying their conclusions only by maintaining the opposite."

All sorts of illustrations have been used from the earliest times—such as fountain, brook, river; root, stalk, branch; memory, understanding, will;76 soul, reason, sense;77 three persons in grammar, the teacher, the person spoken to, and that spoken of.78 Some mystics argued the necessity of three persons in the Deity for the sake of a divine society and mutual love.79 Lessing argues that "God from eternity must have contemplated that which is most perfect, but that is himself; but to contemplate with God, is to create; God's thought of himself, therefore, must be a being, but a divine being, that is, God, the Son God; but these two, God the thinker and God the thought, are in perfect divine harmony, and this harmony is the Spirit."80 Leibnitz also considers the Trinity as illustrated best by the process of reflection in the human mind. Strauss objects to this class of definitions, that they are two elements united in a third, while the Church doctrine requires three united in a fourth.

The Church doctrine concerning the Trinity appears most fully developed in its Orthodox form in what is called the Creed of St. Athanasius. It was not written by him, but by some one in the fifth or sixth century.

1. Whosoever will be saved, before all things must take care to keep the Catholic faith:

2. Which except one keeps it entire and inviolate, he shall without doubt perish everlastingly.

3. But the Catholic faith is this: that we adore one God in Trinity, and the Trinity in Unity;

4. Neither confounding the persons, nor dividing the substance.

5. For there is one person of the Father, another of the Son, and another of the Holy Spirit.

6. But the divinity of the Father, Son, and Spirit, is one, the glory equal, the majesty equal.

7. As is the Father, so is the Son, and so is the Holy Spirit.

8. The Father is uncreated, the Son is uncreated, and the Holy Spirit uncreated.

9. The Father immeasurable,81 the Son immeasurable, and the Holy Spirit immeasurable.

10. The Father eternal, the Son eternal, and the Holy Spirit eternal.

11. And yet there are not three Eternals, but one Eternal.

12. And so there are not *three* uncreated, nor *three* immeasurable, but *one* uncreated, and *one* immeasurable.

13. So the Father is omnipotent, the Son is omnipotent, and the Holy Spirit is omnipotent.

14. And yet there are not *three* omnipotents, but one omnipotent.

15. So the Father is God, the Son is God, and the Holy Spirit is God.

16. And yet there are not *three* Gods, but *one* God.

17. So the Father is Lord, the Son is Lord, and the Holy Spirit is Lord.

18. And yet there are not *three* Lords, but *one* Lord.

19. For as we are compelled by Christian truth to confess of each one, that each person82 is God and Lord; so we are forbidden by the Catholic religion from saying three Gods or three Lords.

20. The Father is not made, nor created, nor begotten.

21. The Son is from the Father alone; not made, nor created, *but begotten.*

22. The Holy Spirit is from the Son and the Father; not created, nor begotten, but *proceeding.*

23. Therefore there is one Father, and not three; one Son, and not three; one Holy Spirit, and not three.

24. And in this Trinity there is none before or after, none greater or less, but all three Persons are coeternal and coequal.

25. So that everywhere we must adore the Unity in Trinity, and the Trinity in Unity.

26. Whoever, therefore, would be saved, must think thus of the Trinity.

§ 2. History of the Doctrine

In the Christian Church, the history of this doctrine is interesting and important. Some sort of Triad, or Trinity, existed in very early times, although the Orthodox form was not established until later.

At first, the prevailing doctrine is that of subordination; that is, that the Son and the Spirit are inferior to the Father. But, as the Son and the Spirit were also called divine, those who thought thus were accused of believing in three Gods.83 Some then said, that the Father was alone divine; and these were called Monarchians. Others, wishing to retain the divinity of the Son and Spirit, and yet to believe in one God, said that the *divinity* in the Father, in the Son, and in the Spirit, was essentially the same, but that the divinity of the Father was the fountain from which that of the Son and Spirit was derived. This was fixed as Orthodox at the Council of Nice, A.D. 325, and was the beginning of Orthodoxy in the Church. It was a middle course between Scylla and Charybdis, which were represented on the one side by Arius, who maintained that the Son was created out of nothing; and by Sabellius on the other hand, who maintained that the Son was only a mode, manifestation, or name of God; God being called the Father, as Creator of the world; called Son, as Redeemer of the world; and Spirit, as Sanctifier of the world. The Council of Nice declared that the Son was not a manifestation of God, as Sabellius said, nor a creation by God, as Arius said, but a derivation from God.84 Just as the essence of the fountain flows into the stream derived from it, so the essence of the Father flows into the Son, who is derived from him. Here, then, we have the three formulas of the early Church—that of Arius, who says, "The Son was created by the Father, and is inferior to him;" that of Sabellius, who says, "The Father, Son, and Spirit, are manifestations of God, and the same essence;" and Orthodoxy, as the Council of Nice, trying to stand between them, and saying, "The Son is derived from the Father, and is of the same essence with him."

The Church, ever since, has been like a ship beating against head winds between opposing shores. It has stood on one tack to avoid Arianism or Tritheism, till it finds itself running into Sabellianism; then it goes about, and stands away till it comes near Arianism or Tritheism again. Unitarianism is on both sides: on one side in the form of one God, with a threefold manifestation of himself; on the other side in the form of a Supreme God, with the Son and Spirit subordinate. It has always been very hard to be Orthodox; for, to do so, one must distinguish the Persons, and yet not divide the substance, of the Deity. In keeping the three Persons distinctly separate, there was great danger of making three distinct Gods. On the other hand, if one tried to make the Unity distinct, there was danger that the Persons would grow shadowy, and disappear.

The heaviest charge against the Church doctrine of the Trinity is, that, driven to despair by these difficulties, it has at last made Orthodoxy consist, not in any sound belief, but only in sound phrases. It is not believing anything, but saying something, which now makes a man Orthodox. If you will only use the *word* "Trinity" in any sense, if you will only call Christ God in any sense, you are Orthodox.

§ 3. Errors in the Church Doctrine of the Trinity

The errors in the popular view concerning the Trinity, as it is at present held, appear to be these:—

1. *The Trinity is held as a mere dogma*, or form of words, not as a reality. It is held in the letter, not in the spirit. There is no power in it, nor life in it; and it is in no sense an object of faith to those who accept it. They do not believe it, but rather believe that they ought to believe it. There are certain texts in Scripture which seem to assert it, certain elaborate arguments which appear convincing and irrefutable. On the strength of these texts and these arguments, they believe that they ought to believe it. But it is a matter of conscience, not of heart; of logic, not of life; of law, not of love. It is not held as a Christian doctrine ought to be held, with the heart; but only philosophically, with the head. If it should cease to be preached for a few years in Orthodox pulpits, it would cease to be believed; it would drop out of the faith, or rather out of the creed, of the community. Unitarianism has extended itself, without being preached, from the simple reading of the Bible.

But Trinitarianism cannot be trusted to its own power. It has no hold on the heart. Here, in Massachusetts, the ministers left off preaching the Trinity, and the consequence was, that the people became Unitarian. Unitarianism in New England was not diffused by preaching: it came of itself, as soon as the clergy left off preaching the Trinity. This shows how worthless, empty, and soulless the doctrine was and is. Instead of this formal doctrine, we want something vital.

2. *Another objection to the present form of the Trinity is, that it is not only scholastic, or purely intellectual, but that it is also negative.* It is not even a positive doctrine. It is often charged against Unitarianism, that it is a mere negation; and, in one sense, the charge is well founded. Unitarianism is a negation, so far as it is a mere piece of reasoning against Orthodoxy; but, as asserting the divine Unity, it is very positive, But the doctrine of the Trinity *is* a mere negation, as it is usually held; because it is an empty form of denial. It only can be defined or expressed negatively. The three Persons are not substances, on the one hand; nor qualities, on the other hand. It is not Sabellianism, nor is it Arianism. Every term connected with the Trinity has been selected, not to express a truth, but to avoid an error. The term "one essence" was chosen in order to exclude Arianism; the term "three Persons," or subsistences, was chosen in order to avoid Sabellianism.

Because the doctrine is thus a negation, it has failed of its chief use. It has become exclusive; whereas, when stated truly, as a positive truth, it would become inclusive. Rightly stated, it would bind together all true religion in one harmonious whole, comprehending in its universal sweep everything true in natural religion, everything true in reason, and uniting them in vital union, without discord and without confusion. Every manifestation which God has made of himself in nature, in Christ, and in the human soul, would be accepted and vitally recognized by Christianity, which comes, not to destroy, but to fulfil. The doctrine of the Trinity would be the highest form of reconciliation or atonement,—reconciling all varieties in one great harmony; reconciling the natural and supernatural, law and grace, time and eternity, fate and freedom.

But, before illustrating this, we must consider further some of the objections to the common form of the doctrine.

3. *It is also charged against the doctrine of the Trinity, "that it is a contradiction in terms, and therefore essentially incredible."* To this it is replied, that it would be a contradiction if God were called Three *in the same sense* in which he is called One; but not otherwise. The answer is perfectly satisfactory; and we therefore proceed to ask, In what sense is he called Three, and in what sense is he called One? The answer is, The Unity is of essence, or substance:

the Trinity is of persons. This answer, again, is satisfactory, provided we know what is meant by these two terms. But the difficulty is to know what is meant by the word "person." We are expressly informed, that this term is not used in its usual sense; for, if it were, it would divide the essence, and three Persons would be the same as three Gods. On the other hand, we are told that it means more than the three characters or manifestations. Here lies the difficulty, and the whole of the rational difficulty, in the doctrine of the Trinity. It is all on the side of the Triad. When we ask, What do you mean by "the three"? there can be given but three answers,—two of them distinct, and one indistinct. These answers are, (1.) We mean three somethings, which we cannot define; (2.) We mean three Persons, like Peter, James, and John; (3.) We mean three manifestations, characters, or modes of being. Let us consider these three answers.

(*a.*) "The three Persons are three somethings, which cannot be defined. It is a mystery. It is above reason. There is mystery in everything, and there must be mystery in the Deity." So Augustine said, long ago, "We say three Persons, not because we have anything to say, but because we want to say something."85 But if one uses the phrase "three Persons," and refuses to define it positively, merely defining it negatively, saying, "It does not mean this, and it does not mean that, and I don't know what it does mean," he avoids, it is true, the difficulties, and escapes the objections; but he does it by giving up the article of faith. No one can deny that there *may be* three unknown distinctions in the divine nature; but no one can be asked to believe in them, till he is told what they are. To say, therefore, that the Trinity is a mystery, is to abandon it as an article of faith, and make of it only a subject of speculation. We avoid the contradiction; but we do it by relinquishing the doctrine.

This fact is not sufficiently considered by Trinitarians. They first demand of us to believe the doctrine of the Trinity, and, when pressed to state distinctly the doctrine, retire into the protection of mystery, and decline giving any distinct account of it. Now, no human being ever denied the existence of mysteries connected with God, and nature, and all life. To assure us, therefore, that such mysteries exist, is slightly superfluous. But, on the other hand, no human being ever *believed*, or could *believe*, a mystery, any more than he could see anything invisible or hear anything inaudible. To believe a doctrine, the first condition is, that all its terms shall be distinct and intelligible.

(*b.*) The second answer to the question is, "We mean, by Persons, three Persons, like Peter, James, and John." According to this answer, the *Trinity* remains, but the *Unity* disappears. This answer leaves the Persons distinct, but the Unity indistinct. The Persons are not confounded; but the essence is divided. The Tri-personality is maintained, but at the expense of the Unity. In fact, this answer gives us Tritheism, or three Gods, whose unity is only an entire *agreement* of feeling and action. But this answer we may set aside as unorthodox, no less than unscriptural.

(c.) Having thus disposed of each other possible answer, there remains only that which makes of the three Persons three revelations or manifestations of God, or representations of God. This answer avoids all the difficulties. It avoids that of *contradiction*; as we do not say that God is one in the same sense in which he is three, but in a different sense. It avoids the objection of *obscurity*; for it is a distinct statement. It avoids the objection of Tritheism; for it leaves the Unity untouched. Moreover, it is a real Trinity, and not merely nominal. The Father, the Son, and the Holy Ghost are not merely three different names for the same thing, but they indicate three different revelations, three different views which God has given of his character, which, taken together, constitute the total divine representation. It remains, therefore, simply to ask, Is this view *a true one*? Is there any foundation for it in Scripture, in reason, and in Christian consciousness, the three sources of our knowledge of the truth?

§ 4. The Trinity of Manifestations founded in the Truth of Things

We repeat, that this view is an Orthodox view of the Trinity, according to the teaching of the greatest fathers of the Church. If we suppose that the Deity has made, and is evermore making, three distinct and independent revelations of himself, — each revelation giving a different view of the divine Being, each revelation showing God to man under a different aspect, — then each of these is a personal manifestation. Each reveals God as a Person. If we see God, for example, in nature, we see him not merely as a power, a supreme cause, but also a living Person, who creates evermore out of a fulness of divine wisdom and love. God in nature is, then, a Person. Again: if God reveals himself in Christ, it is not as abstract truth or as doctrinal statement. But we see God himself, the personal God, the Father and Friend, the redeeming grace, the God who loved us before the foundation of the world, approaching us in Christ to reconcile us and save us. It is a God who "so loved the world" that we see in Christ, therefore, a Person. And so the Spirit, which speaks in the human conscience and human heart, is not a mere influence, or rapture, or movement, but is one who communes with us; one who talks with us; one who comforts us; one who hears and answers us; therefore a Person.

If, then, there is no antecedent objection to this form of the Trinity as a threefold manifestation of the divine Being, we have only to ask, Is it *true* as a matter of fact? Has such a threefold manifestation of God actually taken place? We reply, that it is so. According to Scripture, observation, and experience, we find such to be the fact. Scripture shows us God, the Father, as the source of all being, the fountain and end of all things; from whom all things have come, and to whom all things tend. As the Creator, he reveals himself in nature and providence (as the apostle Paul declares), "being understood by the things that are made," and "not leaving himself without a witness."

Supreme power, wisdom, and goodness are manifested in nature as unchanging law, as perfect order. But God is seen in Christ again as Redeemer, as meeting the exigencies arising from the freedom of the creature by what we call miracle; not contrary to nature, but different from nature, showing himself as the Friend and Helper of the soul. As the essence of the first revelation of God is the sight of his goodness, and wisdom, and power, displayed in law, so the essence of the second revelation is of the same essential Being displaying himself as love. In the first revelation, he is the universal Parent; in the second, he is the personal Friend. But there is a third revelation which God makes of himself,—within the soul as life. The same power, wisdom, and goodness which we see displayed externally in outward nature, we find manifested internally in the soul itself, as its natural and its spiritual life. That which is displayed outwardly as power is manifested within the soul as cause; that which is manifested outwardly as wisdom is revealed inwardly as reason; and that which is manifested outwardly as goodness is manifested inwardly as conscience, or the law of right.

§ 5. It is in Harmony with Scripture

The Scriptures also speak of the Father, the Son, and the Holy Ghost. When they speak of the Father, they usually mean God as the Supreme Being. Matt. 11:25: "Jesus said, I thank thee, *O Father*, Lord of heaven and earth." As omniscient: "Of that day knoweth no man, nor the angels, nor the Son, but *the Father* only." As omnipotent: "Abba, *Father*, all things are possible to thee." As having life in himself, and as spirit: "They shall worship *the Father* in spirit and in truth." As the source of all power, life, and authority of the Son: "I came forth *of the Father;*" "*the Father*, which hath sent me;" "the works which *the Father* hath given me to do." The apostle Paul says, "To us there is but *one God, the Father;*" and calls him "the God of our Lord Jesus;" also "the one God *and Father* of all, who is above all, and through all, and in us all." The great order of the universe depends on him: "He has put the times and the seasons in his own power." Christ will at last "deliver up the kingdom to God, *the Father*." By Christ, "we have access in one spirit *to the Father*." "All things were delivered" to Christ "of *his Father*," whose will Christ always sought. Thus is *the Father* spoken of in the New Testament as the Source from which all things have proceeded, and the End to whom all things tend.

The Son (or Son of God) is spoken of in the New Testament as distinct from the Father, but intimately united with him. The Father gives power; the Son receives it. The Father gives light; the Son receives it. The Son does nothing but what he seeth the Father do. "The Father hath sent me," he says, "and I live by the Father." "I am not alone; but I, and the Father who sent me." "The Son is in the Father, and the Father in him." "No man cometh to the Father but by" him. He shows the Father to the world. The Father is glorified in the Son. He is in the bosom of the Father. The Father sent him to be the Saviour of the world. "He that hath the Son hath life;" "And in him is everlasting life."

The Holy Spirit, which came after Jesus left the world (also called the Holy Ghost and the Spirit of God), is an inward revelation of God and of Christ. It teaches all things, comforts, convinces. It is a spirit of life, lifts one above the flesh, makes one feel that he is a Son of God, communicates a variety of gifts, produces unity in the Church, sanctifies, sheds the love of God into the heart, and renews the soul. The New Testament speaks of joy in the Holy Ghost, power of the Holy Ghost, and communion of the Holy Ghost.

According to the New Testament, the Father would seem to be the Source of all things, the Creator, the Fountain of being and of life. The Son is spoken of as the manifestation of that Being in Jesus Christ; and the Holy Ghost is spoken of as a spiritual influence, proceeding from the Father and the Son, dwelling in the hearts of believers, as the source of their life,—the idea of God seen in causation, in reason, and in conscience, as making the very life of the soul itself.

There are these three revelations of God, and we know of no others. They are distinct from each other in form, but the same in essence. They are not merely three names for the same thing; but they are real personal manifestations of God, real subsistences, since he is personally present in all of them. This view avoids all heresies, since it neither "divides the substance" nor "confounds the persons." And these are really the two heresies, which are the most common and the most to be avoided. We think it can be easily shown that these are the great practical dangers to be avoided. To "divide the substance" is so to separate the revelations of God as to make them contradict or oppose each other: to "confound the persons" is not to recognize each as an independent source of truth to the soul.

§ 6. Practical value of the Trinity, when rightly understood

There is, therefore, an essential truth hidden in the idea of the Trinity. While the Church doctrine, in every form which it has hitherto taken, has failed to satisfy the human intellect, the Christian heart has clung to the substance contained in them all. Let us endeavor to see what is the practical value of this doctrine, for the sake of which its errors of statement have been pardoned. What does it say to the Christian consciousness?

The Trinity, truly apprehended, teaches, by its doctrine of Tripersonality, that God is *immanent* in nature, in Christ, and in the soul. It teaches that God is not *outside* of the world, making it as an artisan makes a machine; nor *outside* of Christ, sending him, and giving to him miraculous powers; nor outside of the soul, touching it *ab extra* from time to time with unnatural influences, revolutionizing and overturning it; but that he is personally present in each and all. So that, when we study the mysteries and laws of nature, we are drawing near to God himself, and looking into his face. When we see Christ, we see God, who is in Christ; and when we look into the solemn intuitions of our soul, the monitions of conscience, and the influences which draw our heart to goodness, we are meeting and communing with God.

Moreover, the Trinity, truly apprehended, teaches, by its doctrine of *One Substance* (the Homoousion), that these three revelations, though distinct, are essentially at one; that nature cannot contradict revelation; that revelation cannot contradict nature; and that the intuitions of the soul cannot be in conflict with either. Hence it teaches that the Naturalist need not fear revelation; nor the Christian believer, natural Theism. Since it is one and the same God who dwells in nature, in Christ, and in the soul, all his revelations must be in harmony with each other. To suppose otherwise is to "divide the substance" of the Trinity.

And again: the Trinity, rightly understood, asserts the distinctness of these three personal revelations. It is the same God who speaks in each; but he says something new each time. He reveals a new form of his being. He shows us, not the same order and aspect of truth in each manifestation, but wholly different aspects.

And yet again: as the doctrine teaches that the Son is begotten of the Father, and the Spirit proceeds from the Father and Son, it thereby shows how the revelation in nature prepares for the revelation in Christ, and both for the revelation in the soul.

The error of "dividing the substance" is perhaps the most common. The man who sees God in nature, sees him only there: therefore God loses to him that personal character which seems especially to be seen through Christ; for God, as a person, comes to us most in Christ, and then is recognized also in nature and the soul as a personal being. So, without Christ, natural religion is cold: it wants love; it wants life. But, on the other hand, the Christian believer who avoids seeing God in nature, and who finds him only in his Bible, loses the sense of law or order, of harmonious growth, and becomes literal, dogmatic, and narrow. And so, too, the mystic, believing only in God's revelation through the soul, and not going to nature or to Christ, becomes withdrawn from life, and has a morbid and ghastly religion, and, having no test by which to judge his inward revelations, may become the prey of all fantasies and all evil spirits, lying spirits, foul spirits, and cruel spirits.

Such errors come from "dividing the substance;" and they are only too common. So that, when the true doctrine of Trinity in Unity is apprehended, the most beneficial results may be expected to flow into the life of the Church. No longer believed as a dead formula, no longer held in the letter which killeth, no longer accepted outwardly as a dogma or authority, but seen, felt, and realized in the daily activity of the intellect and heart, the whole Church will recover its lost union, sects will disappear, and the old feud between science and religion forever cease. Science will become religious, and religion scientific. Science, no longer cold and dead, but filled through and through with the life of God, will reach its hand to Christianity. Piety, no longer an outlaw from nature, no longer exiled from life into churches and monasteries, will inform and animate all parts of human daily action. Christianity, no longer narrow, Jewish, bigoted, formal, but animated by the great liberty of a common life, will march onward to conquer all forms of error and evil in the omnipotence of universal and harmonious truth.

Natural religion, Christianity, and spiritual piety, being thus harmonized, nature will be more warm, Christ more human, and the divine influences in the soul more uniform and constant. Nature will be full of God, with a sense of his presence penetrating it everywhere. Christianity will become more natural, and all its great facts assume the proportion of laws, universal as the universe itself. Divine influences will cease to be spasmodic and irregular, and become calm, serene, and pure, an indwelling life of God in the soul.

A simple Unity, as held by the Jews and Mohammedans, and by some Christian Unitarians, may be a bald Unity and an empty Unity. Then it shows us one God, but God withdrawn from nature, from Christ, from the soul; not immanent in any, but outside of them. It leaves nature godless;

leaves Christ *merely* human; leaves the soul a machine to be moved by an external impulse, not an inward inspiration.86

We conclude, finally, that no doctrine of Orthodoxy is so false in its form, and so true in its substance, as this. There is none so untenable as dogma, but none so indispensable as experience and life. The Trinity, truly received, would harmonize science, faith, and vital piety. The Trinity, as it now stands in the belief of Christendom, at once confuses the mind, and leaves it empty. It feeds us with chaff, with empty phrases and forms, with no real inflowing convictions. It seems to lie like a vessel on the shore, of no use where it is, yet difficult to remove and get afloat; but when the tide rises, and the vessel floats, it will be able to bear to and fro the knowledge of mankind, and unite various convictions in living harmony. It is there for something. It is providentially allowed to remain in the creeds of the Church for something. It has in itself the seed of a grand future; and, though utterly false and empty as it is taught and defended, it is kept by the deeper instinct of the Christian consciousness, like the Christ in his tomb, waiting for the resurrection.

Appendix
Critical Notices

In this Appendix we shall add a brief critical examination of certain recent works on points connected with our previous subjects. These criticisms will complete the discussion in these various directions, so far as space will allow here. The largest part of what follows has been printed already, either in the "Christian Examiner," or in the "Monthly Journal of the American Unitarian Association."

§ 1. On the Defence of Nescience in Theology, by Herbert Spencer and Henry L. Mansel

Mr. Herbert Spencer, in his book called "First Principles," lays down the doctrine of theological nescience, as the final result of religious inquiry. In his chapter on "Ultimate Religious Ideas" he argues thus: The religious problem is, Whence comes the universe? In answer to this question only three statements are possible. It is self-existent. It was self-created. It was created by external agency. Now, none of these, says Spencer, is tenable. For, (1.) Self-existence means simply an existence without a beginning, and it is not possible to conceive of this. The conception of infinite past time is an impossibility. (2.) Self-creation is Pantheism. We can conceive, somewhat, of self-evolution, but not of a potential universe passing into an actual one. (3.) The theistic hypothesis is equally inconceivable. For this is to suppose the world made as a workman makes a piece of furniture. We can conceive of this last, because the workman has the material given; he only adds form to the substance. To produce matter out of nothing is the real difficulty. No simile enables us to conceive of this production of matter out of nothing. Again, says Spencer, space is something, the non-existence of which is inconceivable; hence the creation of space is inconceivable. And lastly, says Spencer, if God created the universe, the question returns, Whence came God? The same three answers recur. God was self-existent, or he was self-created, or he was created *ab extra*. The last theory is useless. For it leads to an endless series of potential existences. So the theist returns to self-existence; which, however, says Spencer, is as inconceivable as a self-existent universe, involving the inconceivable idea of unlimited duration.

Nevertheless, continues Spencer, we are compelled to regard phenomena as effects of some cause. We must believe in a cause of that cause, till we reach a *first cause*. The First Cause must be infinite and absolute. He then follows Mansel in showing the contradiction between the two ideas.

But total negation is not the result,—only nescience. Atheism, Pantheism, and Theism agree in one belief, namely, that of a problem to be solved. An unknown God is the highest result of theology and of philosophy. "If religion and science are to be reconciled, the basis of the reconciliation must be their deepest, widest, and most certain of all facts—that the power which the universe manifests is utterly inscrutable."

Thus Mr. Spencer proposes to take back human thought eighteen centuries, and ignoring the conquests of Christian faith in civilization, theology, and morals, carries us to Athens, in the time of Paul, to worship at the altar of an unknown God. He makes a solitude in the soul, and calls it peace. He makes peace between religion and science, by commanding the first to surrender at discretion to the other. Science knows nothing of God; therefore theology must know nothing of God. But not so. Let each impart to the other that which it possesses, and which the other lacks. Let science enlarge theology with the idea of law, and theology inform science with the idea of a living God.

It is not difficult to detect the fallacies in this argument of Spencer for religious nescience. His notion of conception is that of a purely sensible image. He assumes that we have no knowledge but sensible knowledge, and then easily infers that we do not know God. We can conceive, he says, of a rock on which we are standing, but not of the whole earth. No great magnitudes, he declares, can be conceived. The conception of infinite time is, therefore, an impossibility.

But it is clear to any one, not bound hand and foot by the assumptions of sensationalism, that it is just as easy to conceive of the whole globe of earth, as of the piece of it which we see. We cannot have *a visual image* of the whole earth, indeed, but the mental conception of the globe is as distinct as that of the stone we throw from our hand. And so far from the conception of infinite duration being an impossibility, not to conceive of time and space as infinite is the impossibility. It is impossible to imagine or conceive of the beginning of time, or the commencement of space.

Looking at his trilemma concerning the universe, namely, that it was either, (1.) Self-existent, (2.) Self-created, or, (3.) Created by an external power, we say,—

1. The real objection to a self-existent universe, is not that we cannot conceive of existence without beginning. Nothing is easier than to conceive of an everlasting, unchanging universe, without beginning or end. It is not existence, but change, that suggests cause. Phenomena, events, require us

to believe in some power which produces them. Now, the events which take place in the universe suggest an intelligent, absolute, and central cause, that is, a cause combining supreme wisdom, power, and goodness. A self-existent universe is not inconceivable, but it is incredible.

2. Self-creation, he objects, is Pantheism. But this is no reason for denying it, since Pantheism may, for all we see at this stage of the argument, be the true explanation of the universe. The real objection to the hypothesis of a self-created universe (or of a self-created God), is that it involves the contradiction of something which exists and which does not exist at the same moment; at the moment of self-creation, the universe must exist in order to create, but must be non-existent in order to be created. A self-created universe, then, is not incredible because it involves Pantheism, but because it involves a contradiction.

3. He objects to the Theistic hypothesis, that we cannot conceive of the production of matter (more strictly, of substance) out of nothing. He adds that no simile can enable us to imagine it.

But I can produce, out of nothing, something visible, tangible, and audible. There is no motion and no sound. I move my arm by the power of will, and I produce both sound and motion. The motion of a body in space is a material phenomenon; for whatever is perceived by the senses is material. We do then constantly perceive material phenomena created out of nothing, by human will.

His argument against the Theist, that space could not have been created by God, since its non-existence is inconceivable, is much more plausible. But suppose we grant that space, supposed to be a real existence, was not created in time. Does it follow from that, that it does not proceed from God? Not being an event in time, it does not require a cause; but being conceived of as a reality, it may have eternally proceeded from the divine will, and so not be independent of the Creator.

And as regards his trilemma concerning Deity, that also fails in the failure of his thesis that eternal duration is inconceivable. His argument against the self-existent Deity, only rests on that assumption which we have shown to be untenable.

But Mr. Spencer, who is not a theologian, is at this point reënforced by Mr. Mansel, on whose former work, "The Limits of Religious Thought," we proceed to offer some criticism. This also is an argument for nescience in theology, in the presumed interests of revelation. Mr. Martineau has ably shown the weakness and the dangerous tendency of this whole argument of Mansel, in an article to which we earnestly refer our readers.

The work of Mr. Mansel is a desperate attempt to save Orthodox doctrines from the objections of reason, not by replying to those objections and pointing out their fallacy, but by showing that similar objections can be brought against all religious belief. For example, when reason objects to the Trinity, that it is a contradiction, Mr. Mansel does not attempt to show that it is *not* a contradiction, but argues that our belief in God is another contradiction of the same kind. His inference therefore is, that as we believe in God, notwithstanding the contradiction, we ought to believe in the Trinity also, notwithstanding the contradiction. If we believe one, we may believe both.

But this is a dangerous argument; since it is evident that one might reply, that there remains another alternative; which is, to believe *neither*. If Mr. Mansel succeeds in convincing his readers, the result may be a belief in the Trinity, or it may be a disbelief in God altogether; one of two things— either a return to Orthodoxy, or a departure from all religion. Either they will renounce reason in order to retain religion, or they will renounce religion in order to retain reason.

At the very best, also, the help which this argument offers us is to be paid for somewhat dearly. It proposes to save Orthodoxy by giving up the use of reason in religion. Mr. Mansel would say, "by giving up the unlimited use of reason;" but, as we shall presently see, this comes very much to the same thing at last.

What, then, is the nature of Mr. Mansel's argument? It is an argument founded upon Sir William Hamilton's philosophy of the Unconditioned. Now, this has been generally considered the weak side of Hamilton's system. According to him, the unconditioned is inconceivable: in other words, of the Absolute and Infinite we have no conception at all. But this denies to man the power of conceiving of God, and so leads directly to Atheism. This charge has already been brought against Hamilton's philosophy, in various quarters; for example, in the "North British Review " for May, 1835. But we will not here attempt any examination of Hamilton's theory, but confine ourselves to Mr. Mansel.

The argument of Mansel is this : "To conceive the Deity as he is, we must conceive him as First Cause, as Absolute, and as Infinite. By the First Cause is meant that which produces all things, and is itself produced of none; by the Absolute is meant that which exists in and by itself, having no necessary relation to any other being; by the Infinite is meant that which is free from all possible limitation."

Having thus defined the Deity as the First Cause, the Absolute, and the Infinite, Mansel goes on to show that these ideas are mutually contradictory and destructive. A First Cause necessarily supposes effects, and therefore cannot be absolute: nor can the Infinite be a person; for personality is a limitation. By a course of such arguments as these, Mansel endeavors to show that the reason is as incapable of conceiving God as it is of conceiving the Trinity, the Atonement, or any other Orthodox doctrine; and since we do not renounce our belief in God because of these contradictions, neither ought we, because of similar contradictions, to renounce our belief in the Trinity.

Such is the substance of Mansel's statement, though the arguments by which it is proved are varied with great ingenuity and to great extent. This course of thought is by no means original, either with Mr. Mansel or Sir William Hamilton. A far greater thinker than either of them (Immanuel Kant) had long before shown the logical contradictions of the understanding in what he called the Antinomies of the pure reason. But the important question is, If the reason contradicts itself thus in its conception of Deity, how are we to obtain a ground for our belief in God? Mansel answers, "Through revelation; that is, through the direct declarations of Scripture." This he calls faith. We are to believe in a personal God on the ground of a Bible confirmed by miracles.

This result is so strange, that it may well seem incredible. Yet we cannot think that we have misrepresented the tendency of the argument; though, of course, we have given no ideas of the acuteness and flexibility of the reasoning, the extent of the knowledge, and mastery of logic, in this work. That such a position should be taken by a religious man, in the supposed interest of Christianity, is sufficiently strange; for it seems to us equally untenable in its grounds, unfounded in its statements, empty of insight, destructive in its results. We will add, very briefly, a few of the criticisms which occur to us.

The first thing which strikes us in the argument is, that everywhere it deals with words rather than with things. The whole object of the discussion concerns the meaning of terms, and it deals throughout with the relation of words to other words. It is an acute philological argument. We feel ourselves to be arguing about forms, and not about substances. Now, such arguments may confuse, but they cannot convince. We do not know, perhaps, what to say in reply; but we remain unsatisfied. One not used to logic may listen to an argument which shall conclusively prove that white is black; that nothing is greater than something; that a man who jumps from the top of the house can never reach the ground; but, though the thing is proved, he is not convinced. So, when Mr. Mansel proves to us that we cannot conceive of a Being who is at the same time Infinite and Personal, we are unable, perhaps, to reply to the argument; but we know it to be false, since we actually have the two conceptions in our mind.

We *do* conceive of the Deity as an infinite personality. Of what use to tell us that we *cannot* have an idea, when we know that we *do* have it?

Mansel tells us that we cannot think the idea of the Infinite and Absolute. He says , "The Absolute and the Infinite are thus, like the Inconceivable and Imperceptible, names indicating, not an object of thought or of consciousness at all, but the mere absence of the conditions under which consciousness is possible."

But, then, they are only words, with no meaning attached; and, if so, how can we argue about them at all? All argument must cease when we come to an unmeaning phrase; therefore the existence of Mr. Mansel's argument proves the falsehood of his assertion. Since he argues about the Infinite, it is evident that he has the idea of the Infinite in his mind.

Mr. Mansel agrees in principle wholly with the Atheists; for the Atheists do not say that God does not exist, or that God cannot exist, but that we cannot know that he exists. So says Mr. Holyoake, a leading modern Atheist. This is what Mansel also asserts, only he goes farther than they, contending that the very idea of God is impossible to the human reason. It is true that he believes in God on grounds of revelation, which the Atheists do not; but he agrees with them in setting aside all natural and reasonable knowledge of Deity.

But how is it possible to obtain an idea of God from revelation, if we are before destitute of such an idea? When Paul preached to the Athenians, he addressed them as having already a true, though an imperfect, idea of God. "Whom, therefore, ye ignorantly worship, him declare I unto you." But, if they had not already an idea of God, how could he have given them such an idea? Suppose that he works a miracle, and says, "This miracle proves that God has sent me to teach you." But, by the supposition, they know nothing about God; consequently, they have nothing by which to test the truth of a revelation professing to come from him. Neither miracles, nor the nature of the truth taught, nor the character of the teacher, avail anything as evidence of a revelation from a Being of whom we know nothing. Without a previous knowledge of God, only immediate revelation is possible.

Mr. Mansel, therefore, is one who, without a foundation, builds a house on the sand. He attempts to erect faith in God after taking away the foundation of reason. The apostles built revealed religion upon natural religion, revealed theology upon natural theology, according to the rule, "That is not first which is spiritual, but that which is natural; afterward that which is spiritual." Christ said, "Ye believe in God: believe also in me." Mr.

Mansel reverses all this, and makes Christ say, "Ye believe in me: believe also in God."

But, even if it were possible to ascend to belief in God through belief in Christ, we must ask, Is not belief thought? If the mind cannot *think* the Infinite, how can it believe the Infinite? Must we not apprehend a proposition before we can believe it? Does not the conception of a thing logically precede the belief of it? If it is impossible to apprehend the Absolute, if this is only an empty name, how is it possible to believe in the Absolute on grounds of revelation, or on any other grounds? A miracle cannot communicate to the mind an idea which is beyond its power of conception.

Mr. Mansel declares that our religious knowledge is *regulative*, but not *speculative*.

He lays great stress on this distinction: by which he means that we have ideas of the Deity sufficient to guide our practice, but not to satisfy our intellect; which tell us, not what God is in himself, but how he *wills* that we should think of him. According to this view, all revelation is overturned, just as all natural religion has been previously overturned. Revelation does not reveal God on this theory. We have no knowledge of God in the gospel, any more than we had in nature. Instead of knowledge, we have only law. But this seems to despoil Christianity of its vital force. Christ says, "This is life eternal, to *know* thee, the only true God." But Mr. Mansel tells us that such knowledge of God is impossible. Therefore, instead of the gospel, he gives us the law; for it is certain that his *regulative* truths are simply moral precepts, addressed to the will, not to the intellect; capable of being obeyed, but not of being understood.

The radical error of Mansel seems to be this,—that his mind works only in the logical region belonging to the understanding, and is ignorant of those higher truths which are beheld by the reason. He has tried to find God by logical processes, and, of course, has failed. He therefore concludes that God cannot be known by the intellect. He has fully demonstrated that God cannot be comprehended by the logical understanding; and in this he has done a good work. But he has not shown that God cannot be known by the intuitive reason. The understanding comprehends: the reason apprehends. The understanding perceives the form: reason takes holds of the substance. The understanding sees how things are related to each other: the reason sees how things are in themselves. The understanding cannot, therefore, see the infinite and absolute; cannot apprehend substance or cause; knows nothing of the eternal. But the reason is as certain of cause as of effect; knows eternity as really as it knows time; it is as sure of the existence of spirit as it is of matter; and sees the infinite to be as real as the finite. Therefore, though we cannot comprehend God by logic, we can apprehend him by reason. We can be as sure of his being as we are of our own, and we are not obliged to explain away all those profound scriptures which teach us that the object and end of our being is to know God.

Since, therefore, Mr. Mansel's argument, with all its acuteness, learning, and honesty, tends directly to Atheism; since, by overturning the foundation of Christianity, it overturns Christianity itself; since it substitutes mere moral laws in place of the vital forces of the gospel,—it is no wonder that its positions have been rejected with much unanimity by the most eminent Orthodox scholars. Its defence of Orthodoxy costs too much. Leading thinkers of very different schools—for example, Mr. Brownson, the Roman Catholic, in his "Quarterly Review;" Professor Hickok, the Presbyterian, in the "Bibliotheca Sacra;" and Mr. Maurice, of the Church of England, in an able pamphlet—have opposed with great force the arguments and conclusions of this volume. It is true that some Orthodox divines consider that Mr. Mansel has *demonstrated* that the human consciousness is unequal to the speculative conception of a Being at once absolute, infinite, and personal, and seem gladly to have the aid of this book in defending the Trinity. But the more distinguished and experienced thinkers mentioned above are cautious of accepting the help of so dangerous an ally.

§ 2. On the Defence of Verbal Inspiration by Gaussen

Following the declaration of the apostle Paul, that "the letter killeth," we have, in the text of this volume, set aside all the theories of the Bible which assume its absolute and literal infallibility. But within a few years, a work in defence of this doctrine has been published abroad, by an excellent man, M. Gaussen, of Geneva, and translated and republished in America by Rev. Dr. Kirk, of Boston. Such a work, coming from such sources, deserves some examination. We shall, therefore, show the course of argument followed in this book, and the reasons which lead us to consider its conclusions unsound, and its reasoning inadequate.

Inspiration, as defined by Gaussen, is "that inexplicable power which the divine Spirit formerly exercised over the authors of the Holy Scriptures, to guide them even in the employment of the words they were to use, and to preserve them from all error, as well as from every omission.

"We aim," says he, "to establish, by the word of God, that the Scriptures are from God—that all the Scriptures are from God—and that every part of the Scripture is from God."

Let us consider the arguments in support of this kind of inspiration, and the objections to them.

Argument I. Plenary Inspiration is necessary, that we may know with certainty what we ought to believe.

Great stress is laid upon this supposed *necessity*, both by Gaussen and Kirk.

"The book so written," say they, "is the Word of God, and binds the conscience of the world; and nothing else does so bind it, even though it were the writings of Paul and Peter.

"With the Infidel, whether he be Christian in name or otherwise, the sharp sword of a perfect inspiration will be found, at last, indispensable. If the ground is conceded to him that there is a single passage in the Bible that is not divine, then we are disarmed; for he will be sure to apply this privilege to the very passages which most fully oppose his pride, passion, and error. How is the conscience of a wicked race to be bound down by a chain, one link of which is weak?"

Reply to Argument I.—It is no way to prove a theory *true* to assume its *necessity*. The only legitimate proof of a theory is by an induction of facts. This method of beginning by a supposed necessity, this looking first at consequences, has always been fruitful of false and empty theories. The great advance in modern science has come from substituting the inductive for the ideological method. Find what the facts say, and the consequences will take care of themselves. An argument from consequences is usually only an appeal to prejudices.

Again: This argument is fatal to the arguments drawn from the Scriptures themselves. In arguing from the Scripture to prove that every passage is divine, we have, of course, no right to assume that every passage is divine, for that is the very thing to be proved. Then the texts which we quote to prove our position may themselves not be divine, and if we grant that, "we are disarmed." For, according to this argument, nothing can be proved conclusively from Scripture except we believe in plenary inspiration—then plenary inspiration itself cannot be proved from Scripture. But Gaussen admits that this doctrine can be proved "only by the Scriptures;" therefore (according to this argument) it cannot be proved at all.

If, therefore, the doctrine of plenary inspiration is necessary "to bind the conscience of the world," it is a doctrine incapable of proof. If, on the other hand, it can be proved, it is then clearly not necessary "to bind the conscience of the world."

But again. This theory of plenary inspiration does *not* bind the consciences of men. If men are naturally disposed (as Messrs. Gaussen and Kirk maintain) to deny and disbelieve the doctrines and statements of the Bible, they have ample opportunity of doing so, notwithstanding their belief in this theory. For, after admitting that the words of Scripture, just as they stand, are perfectly true and given by God, the question comes, What do they mean? For instance, I wish, we will suppose, to deny the doctrine of the Deity of Christ. Now, you quote to me the text Rom. 9:5. "Of whom, as concerning the flesh, Christ came, who is over all, God, blessed forever," — which is the strongest text in the Bible in support of that doctrine. Now, though I believe in the doctrine of plenary inspiration, I am not obliged to accept this passage as proof of the Deity of Christ. For I can, 1. Assert that the verse is an interpolation; 2. Assert that it is wrongly pointed; 3. Assert that it is mistranslated; 4. Assert that Christ is called God in an inferior sense, as God over the Church. And, as a matter of fact, these are the arguments always used, even by those who deny the doctrine of a plenary inspiration. They seldom or never accuse the writer of a mistake, but always rely on a supposed mistranslation, or misinterpretation, in order to avoid the force of a passage. Hence, also, we find believers in this doctrine of plenary inspiration, differing in opinion on a thousand matters, and with no probability of ever coming to an agreement.

Argument II. Several Passages of the New Testament plainly teach the Doctrine of the Plenary Inspiration of the Bible.

The passages quoted by Gaussen, and mainly relied upon, are 2 Tim. 3:16. "All Scripture is given by inspiration," &c.; 2 Peter 1:27, "Holy men of God spake as they were moved," &c. Besides these, he refers to many passages in the Old and New Testaments, but his chief stress is laid on these.

Reply to Argument II.—It is well known that both these passages refer only to the Old Testament Scriptures. It is well known that the first may be translated so as to read, "All Scripture, given by inspiration, is profitable," &c. But it is reply enough to both these passages, to say, that neither of them indicates what kind of inspiration is intended. They assert an inspiration, which we also maintain. But they do *not* assert a verbal inspiration, nor one which makes the Scriptures *infallible*, but simply one which makes them *profitable*.

The stress laid on the passage 2 Tim. 3:16, "All Scripture," &c., is itself an argument against the theory of plenary inspiration. The most which can be made of this text, by *any* punctuation or translation, is, that all the Scripture is written by inspired men. What was the degree or kind of their inspiration, is not in the least indicated. It might have been verbal, it might have been the inspiration of suggestion, or of superintendence, or the general inspiration of all Christians.

Gaussen's only argument on this point is, "that it is the *writing* which is said to be inspired, and writing must be in words; hence the inspiration must be verbal." To this we must reply, that inspired writing can only mean what is written by inspired men. The writing itself cannot be inspired. This argument is too flimsy to be dwelt upon.

But further still. There is another argument which lies against every attempt to prove plenary inspiration out of the Scripture. *Every such attempt is necessarily reasoning in a circle.* Gaussen and Kirk have labored earnestly to reply to this argument, but in vain. The answer they make is, "We are not reasoning with Infidels, but with Christians. We address men who respect the Scriptures, and who admit their truth. The Scriptures are inspired, we affirm, because, being authentic and true, they declare themselves inspired; and the Scriptures are plenarily inspired, because, being inspired, they say that they are so totally, and without any exception."

But we answer Messrs. Gaussen and Kirk thus: "You are indeed reasoning with Christians, not with Deists; but you are reasoning with Christians who do not believe that *every passage* of Scripture is infallibly inspired. To prove your doctrine from any particular passages or verbal expressions, you must prove that those particular passages and expressions are not themselves errors. You yourselves assert that this cannot be done, except we believe these passages to be infallibly inspired. Therefore you must assume infallible inspiration in order to prove infallible inspiration. In other words, you beg the question instead of arguing it."

In this vicious circle the advocates of a verbal inspiration of infallibility are necessarily imprisoned whenever they attempt to argue from the words of Scripture. They contend that one must believe their theory in order to be sure that any passage is absolutely true, and then they quote passages to prove their theory, as if they were absolutely true.

Argument III. The theory of plenary inspiration is simple, precise, intelligible, and easy to be applied.

We admit this to be true. It has this merit in common with the opposite theory of no inspiration. Both are simple, precise, and very easy of application. But simplicity is not always a sign of truth. The facts of nature and life are more apt to be complex than simple. Theories distinguished by their simplicity most commonly ignore or omit a part of the facts. Simplistic theories are generally one-sided and partial. Materialism, Atheism, Idealism, Fatalism, are all very simple theories, and explain all difficulties with a marvellous rapidity. This makes them, at first, attractive to the intellect, which always loves clear and distinct views; but afterwards, when it is seen that they obtain clearness by means of shallowness they are found unsatisfactory.

Argument IV. The quotations from the Old Testament, by Jesus and his apostles, show that they regarded its language as infallibly inspired.

This argument, upon which great stress is laid, both by Prof. Gaussen and Dr. Kirk, though plausible at first sight, becomes wholly untenable on examination.

Thus, in the temptation of Jesus, in his reply to the tempter, he says, "Thou shalt not live by bread alone;" the whole force of the argument depending on the single word *alone.*

Replying to the Sadducees, who denied the resurrection, he says, "Have ye not read that God says, I *am* the God of Abraham, and of Isaac, and of Jacob? God is not the God of the dead, but of the living." Then the whole stress of the argument rests on the use of the verb in the present tense, *"I am."*

Arguing with the Pharisees, "How did David, by the Spirit, call him *Lord,* saying, The Lord said to my Lord," &c.? Here the argument depends on the use of the single word *Lord.*

Many more instances could be produced of the same kind; and Gaussen contends, that when Jesus and his apostles thus rest their argument on the force of a single word of the Old Testament, they must have believed that the very words were given by inspiration. For otherwise the writers might not have chosen the right word to express their thought in each particular case. And unless the Jews had also believed in the verbal inspiration of their Scriptures, they would have replied that these particular words might have been errors.

Reply to this Argument.—Plausible as this argument may seem, it turns out to be wholly empty and worthless. Whenever any writer is admitted to be an authority, then his words become authoritative, and arguments are necessarily based on single words and expressions. In all such cases, we assume that he chose the best words by which to convey his thought, and yet we do not ascribe to him any inspiration or infallibility.

Thus, go into our courts of law, and you will hear the language of the United States constitution, of the acts of legislature, of previous decisions of the courts, argued from, word by word. Counsel argue by the hour upon the force and weight of single words in the authorities. Judges in their charges instruct the jury to determine the life and death of the criminal according to the letter of the law. And this they do necessarily, according to the rule, "*Cum recedit a litera, judex transit in legislatorem.*" But will any one maintain that the counsel and court believe that the legislature was infallibly inspired to choose the very language which would convey their meaning?

In this very argument for plenary inspiration, Gaussen and his associates rest their argument on the single word "all," in the text, "All Scripture is given by inspiration," &c. Yet, say they, we are not assuming that this text is plenarily inspired, for that, we admit, would be begging the question. If, then, Mr. Gaussen can argue from the force of the single word *all*, without assuming the doctrine of plenary inspiration, why could not Jesus and his apostles argue from single words, without assuming the doctrine of plenary inspiration?

There is, however, a passage in Paul (Gal. 3:16), in which the apostle quotes a text from the Old Testament, and lays the whole stress of his argument on two letters. "He says not, 'And to seeds' σπέρμασιν, as of many, but as of one, 'And to thy seed' σπερματι." According to Gaussen's argument, Paul must have believed in the inspiration of the letters. But Gaussen is careful not to adduce this instance, which seems at first so much in his favor. For, in fact, both in Hebrew and Greek, as in English, "seed" is a collective noun, and does mean *many* in the singular. The argument of Paul, therefore, falls through; and it is evident that he is no example to be imitated here, in laying stress on one or two letters. Most modern interpreters admit that he made a mistake; and so, among the ancients, did Jerome, who nevertheless, said the argument "was good enough for the foolish Galatians."

Having thus replied, very briefly, but we believe sufficiently, to the main arguments in support of this theory, we say, in conclusion, that it cannot be true, for the following reasons, which we simply state, and do not now attempt to unfold.

1. The New Testament writers nowhere claim to be infallibly inspired to write. If they had been infallibly inspired to write the Gospels and Epistles, they certainly ought to have announced this important fact. Instead of which Luke gives as his reason for writing, not that God inspired him to write, but that "inasmuch as others have taken in hand" to write, it seemed good to him also to do the same, and that for the benefit of Theophilus. John and Paul assert the truth of what they say, but not on account of their being inspired to write, but because they are disciples and apostles.

2. The differences in the accounts of the same transactions show that their inspiration was not verbal.

These differences appear on every page of any Harmony of the New Testament. They are numerous but unimportant; they go to prove the truth of the narrative, and give probability to the main Gospel statements. But they utterly disprove the theory of plenary inspiration.

3. Paul declares that some things which he says are "of the Lord," other things "of himself;" that in regard to some things he was inspired, in regard to others, not.

4. Every writer in the New Testament has a style of his own, and there is no appearance of his being merely an amanuensis.

5. While the New Testament writers lay no claim to any such inspiration as this theory assumes, they do claim for themselves and for all other Christians another kind of inspiration, which is sufficient for all the facts, and which gives them ample authority over our faith and life, and makes them independent sources of Christian truth.

This view we have already sufficiently considered in our chapter on inspiration.

§ 3. Defence of the Doctrine that Sin is a Nature, by Professor Shedd

In the "Christian Review" for 1852 appeared an article of great power, written by a gentleman who has since become eminent as a thinker and writer—Professor W. G. T. Shedd. The title of the article was calculated to attract attention, as a bold attempt to defend an extreme position of Calvinism—"Sin a Nature, and that Nature Guilt." The article was so rational and clear that we consider it as being even now the best statement extant of this thorough-going Calvinism, and therefore devote a few pages here to its examination.87

After some introductory remarks, which it is not necessary to notice, the writer lays down his first position, that sin is a nature. His statement is, that we all sin necessarily and continually in consequence of *our nature*, i.e., the character born with us, original and innate.

The proofs of this position are, 1. The language of St. Paul (Eph. 2:3), "We were by nature the children of wrath, even as others." 2. That we are compelled by the laws of our mind to refer volitions to a nature, as qualities to a substance. We cannot stop in the outward act of sin, but by a mental instinct look inward to the particular volition from which the sin came. Nor can the mind stop with this particular volition. There is a steady and uniform state of character, which particular volitions cannot explain. The instinct of reason causes us to look back for one common principle and source, which shall give unity to the subject; and, having attained a view both central and simple, it is satisfied. As our mind compels us to refer all properties to a substance in which they inhere, so it compels us to refer all similar volitions to a simple nature. When we see exercises of the soul, we as instinctively refer them to a nature in that soul, as we refer the properties of a body to the substance of that body. 3. Christian experience proves that sin is a nature. The Christian, especially as his experience deepens, is troubled, not so much by his separate sinful actions and volitions, as by the sinful nature which they indicate, and out of which they spring. We are compelled to believe, as we look inward, that there is a principle of evil within us, below those separate transgressions of which we are conscious. There is a diseased condition of the soul, which these transgressions, indicate. There are secret faults from which we pray to be cleansed. 4. The history of Christian doctrine shows that the Church has in all ages believed in a sinful nature, as distinguished from conscious transgressions.

These are the proofs of the first position, that sin is a nature. We have stated them concisely, but with sufficient distinctness and completeness. Let us now examine their validity.

The first argument is the text in Ephesians, "We were by nature children of wrath," ἦμεν τέκνα φύσει ὀργῆς. The word φύσις, the writer contends, "always denotes something original and innate, in contradistinction to something acquired by practice or habit." This text, we know, is the proof-text of original sin, and is considered by many commentators as teaching that man's nature is wholly corrupt. But plainly this is going too far. Granting the full meaning claimed for the word φύσις, the text only asserts that there is something in man's nature which exposes him to the divine displeasure by being the source of sin. It does not assert the corruption of the whole nature, nor preclude the supposition that we are born with tendencies to good, no less than to evil. That we are so, the writer is bound by his own statement to admit; for if this Greek word "always denotes something original and innate," it denotes this in Rom. 2:14,88 which declares that the Gentiles "do by nature the things contained in the law." According to this passage in Romans, if there be such a thing as natural depravity, it is not total; and if there be such a thing as total depravity, it is not natural. Those who wish to maintain both doctrines can only do it by admitting two different kinds of sinfulness in man, one of which is natural, but not total; the other total, but not natural—a distinction which we esteem a sound one. According to this passage in Rom 2:14, we must understand φύσις as referring to the good side of man's nature, and the same word in Eph. 2:3 as referring to the corrupt side of man's moral nature. The first refers to the "law of the mind;" the second, to the other "law in the members" (Rom. 7:23). But there is another passage (Gal. 2:15), which asserts that the Jews by nature are not sinners, like the heathen. Now, as we can hardly suppose that the original instincts and innate tendencies of the Jewish child were radically good from birth, and essentially different from those of the heathen, and as such a supposition would contradict the whole argument of Paul in Rom. ch. 2, it is evident that φύσις in Gal. 2:15 does not denote something original and innate. The meaning of this verse probably is, that the Jew from birth up, and by the mere fact of being born a Jew, came under the influences of a religious education, which preserved him from many forms of heathen depravity. The word, therefore, means in that passage, not a Jew by nature, but a Jew by birth; and, if so, we are at liberty, if we choose, to ascribe the same meaning to the word in Ephesians, and to understand the text to teach that we were by birth placed under circumstances which tended necessarily to deprave the character.

This passage, therefore, quoted by the writer, does not teach entire depravity by nature, but a partial depravity, either found in the hereditary tendencies and instincts, or acquired by means of the evil circumstances surrounding the child from his birth.

The second argument of the writer is, that the laws of mind compel us to refer sinful volitions to a sinful nature, as they compel us to refer qualities to a substance.

We admit that, where we see uniform and constant habits of action, we are compelled to refer these to a permanent character or state of being. If a man once in his life becomes intoxicated, we do not infer any habit of intemperance, or any vicious tendency; but if he is habitually intemperate, we are compelled, as the writer justly asserts, to look beneath the separate single actions for one common principle and source. But in assuming that this source is a nature brought with us into the world, the writer seems to us to jump to a conclusion. It may be an acquired character, not an original nature. It may be an induced state of disease either of body or mind, a depravity which has commenced this side of childhood. We know that there are acquired habits both of mind and of body; otherwise, not only would it be impossible for a man to grow worse, but it would also be impossible for him to grow better, and there would be an end to all improvement and progress. Such an acquired character introduces unity into the subject of investigation, as completely as does an original nature, and therefore satisfies all the wants of the mind.

A precisely similar answer may be made to the writer's third argument, drawn from Christian experience. He is perfectly right, we think, in saying that the Christian is troubled, not merely, nor chiefly, by the recollection of single acts and volitions of evil, but in the evidence which they seem to give of a sinful state of mind and heart. He is right in considering any theory of moral evil shallow and inadequate which only takes into account sinful actions and sinful volitions. What earnest man, who has seriously set about correcting a fault, or improving his character, but has been obliged to say, "To will is present with me; but how to perform that which I will, I find not"? Every earnest effort shows us more plainly how deep the roots of evil run below the surface. We find a *law* in the members warring against the law of the mind, and bringing us into captivity to the law of sin. This is the description which Paul gives of it. It is a *law*; that is, something regular, constant, permanent—a steady stress, a bias towards evil. The apostle, however, differs from the writer in placing this law, not in the will, but in the members; and also in stating that there is another law,—that of the mind,—which has a tendency towards good. In the unregenerate we understand him to teach that the law of evil is the stronger, and holds the man, the personal will, captive. In the regenerate, the reverse is the case. Nor does Paul teach that this sinful tendency is guilt. It is not "O *guilty* man that I am!" but "O *wretched* man that I am!"

Now, while we agree with the writer in rejecting as superficial and inadequate any theory of evil, whether emanating from our own denomination or from any other, which does not recognize this evil state or tendency lying below the volitions, we differ from him in that we think it not always a nature, but a character. He has not proved, nor begun to prove, that this dark ground of evil in man is always innate or original. It may or may not be; but the argument from Christian experience shows nothing of the sort.

The writer's fourth and remaining argument is, that the Church has, in all ages, believed in a sinful nature, as distinguished from conscious transgressions. If this were so, we admit that it should have weight in the inquiry; but we deny the fact so far, at least, as the sinful nature is concerned.89

The writer proceeds thus: "Assuming, then, that the fact of a sinful nature has been established, we pass to the second statement of St. Paul, that man is by nature a child of wrath. We pass from his statement that sin, in its ultimate form, is a nature, to his statement that this nature is guilt." If we have done justice to the writer's arguments,—and it has been our object to state them fairly, though briefly,—we submit that the fact of a sinful nature has not been established by them. He has shown that in man there is a tendency to evil running below the conscious, distinct volitions—that there is a permanent character, good or evil, which manifests itself, and becomes first apparent to ourselves, or to others, in these separate, spiritual exercises or actions. But that this stress either to good or evil, this law either of the mind or members, is original and inborn, is yet to be proved. Let us then consider the second point, namely, whether this character or nature, whichever it may be, is also guilt.

As the writer's first argument to prove a sinful nature was drawn from the Greek word φύσις, so his first argument to prove that nature guilt is derived from the Greek word ὀργή in the same passage. "The apostle teaches," he says, "that sinful man is a child of wrath. Now, none but a guilty being can be the object of the righteous and holy displeasure of God." But this word, translated *wrath*, is confessedly used in other senses besides that of the divine anger or displeasure. It may mean the sufferings or punishments which come as the result of sin, in which sense it is used in Matt. 3:7, "Who hath warned you to flee from the wrath to come?" and other places. This word is used in the passage just quoted for some future evil; in John 3:36, for a present evil—"The wrath of God abides on him;" and in 1 Thess. 2:16, for a past evil—"For the wrath is come [lit. *has* come] on them to the uttermost." It may mean the subjective feeling of guilt; the sense that we deserve the divine displeasure, which is removed by the assurance of forgiveness. It may mean the state of alienation from God, which results by a law of the conscience from this sense of guilt—an alienation removed by the divine act by which God reconciles the sinner to himself. And the radical meaning, from which these secondary meanings flow, may be the essential antagonism existing between the holy nature of God and all evil. But whatever it means, it cannot intend anything like human anger. In the divine wrath there is neither selfishness nor passion; and it must consist with an infinite love towards its object. The word, therefore, as used in Eph. 2:3, does not convey the idea of guilt, *a vi terminis*. It may mean as well, that this sinful tendency in man, manifesting itself in sinful actions, produces a state of estrangement or alienation between man and God. How far this is a guilty alienation, and how far it is evil and sorrowful, is not to be learned from the term itself.

But the main proof of the writer in support of his second position is found in the assertion, that this sinful tendency in man, out of which evil acts continually flow, is not a tendency of the physical nature, but of the will itself. He distinguishes the will proper from the mere faculty of single choices, and considers it to be a deeper power lying at the very centre of the soul, which determines the whole man with reference to some great and unlimited end of living. It is, in fact, the man himself—the person. For man, he asserts, is not essentially intellect or feeling; but is essentially and at bottom a will, a self-determining creature. "His other faculties of knowing and feeling are grafted into this stock and root; and hence he is responsible from centre to circumference." He then affirms the will, thus defined, to be the responsible and guilty author of the sinful nature; being nothing more nor less than its constant and total determination to self as the ultimate end of living. This voluntary power, which is the man himself, has turned away from God and directed itself to self as an ultimate end; and this state of the will is the sinful nature of man.

We have no disposition to quarrel with the psychology of this statement. We admit man to be essentially will, in the sense here described. He is essentially activity; an activity limited externally, by special organization and circumstances, — limited internally, by quantity of force, and knowledge.

Nor, again, do we deny that in the unregenerate state the will of man is directed to self rather than to God as its ultimate end; and that this is guilt, and in a certain sense total guilt. No man can serve two masters. If he is obedient to one, he is necessarily disobedient to the other. This disobedience may, or may not, appear in act; but it is there in state. He whose ultimate end is self-gratification is always ready to sacrifice the will of God to his own. He whose ultimate end is God is always ready to sacrifice his own will. In this sense, the unregenerate man may be said to be wholly sinful; and he who is born of God, not to commit sin.

Thus much we grant; and the admission is a large one. But we must now object to the writer, that this is but one side of the question; and that he has omitted to see the other side. The sources of evil are not so simple as he seems to suppose; for man is a very complex being, and the world in which he lives is a very complex world. We therefore would inquire, —

What proof have we that this guilty direction of the will is a *nature*, in the sense claimed, i.e., something innate or original? Why may not the will have been turned gradually in this direction as we grow up, by enticements of pleasure; and why might not the will, in like manner, by means of wise culture, have been gradually directed to God?

Again: what proof have we that we are so wholly *unconscious* of this direction of the will, as our author contends? That a great many of the acts of the will are unconscious acts, like the separate movements of the finger in a skilful pianist, or lifting of the feet in walking, we admit; and we are not responsible for these separate acts, but for the *preceding choice*, by means of which we determine to play the tune, or walk the mile. In like manner, the direction of the soul to self rather than to God may be moral evil; but is not moral guilt, until we become conscious of it, in a greater or less degree. Then, when partially or wholly awakened to the evil direction of the soul, if we allow ourselves to neglect this discovery, to turn away from the fact and forget it, on that conscious act presses the whole burden of guilt, and not on the unconscious volitions which may result from it. We say, therefore, in opposition to the writer, that though there may be depravity without consciousness of the depraved state, there cannot be guilt without consciousness of the evil choice, or, as the apostle says, "Sin is not imputed where there is no law."

Again: we totally dissent from the statement that this deep-lying will in man is unable to obey the commands, "Turn ye, turn ye from your evil way, for why will ye die?" — "Repent and be converted, that your sins may be blotted out," — "Make you a new heart and a new spirit," — "Choose you this day whom you will serve," — "Believe in the Lord Jesus Christ and be saved." The writer says, that "such a power as this, including so much, and running so deep, which is a determination of the whole soul, cannot, from the very nature of the case, be such a facile and easily managed power as that by which we resolve to do some particular thing in every-day life." True: not *so* easily managed; but can it not be managed at all? It may require *more* self-examination to understand what the direction of the will is, and more concentration of thought and will, and more leaning on God's help; but *with* all these are we able or not able to turn to God? He says, the great main tendency of the will to self and sin as an ultimate end, though having a free and criminal origin, "is not to be reversed so easily." True, again; but why not *less* easily? The writer speaks of the sinful will as a "total determination of itself to self;" and asks "how the power that is to reverse all this process can possibly come out of the will thus shut up, and entirely swallowed in the process. How is the process to destroy itself?" But what! Has man become *a process*? He is essentially will, but is this will blind mechanism? Has it not, according to our author's own theory, intelligence, conscience, affection, rooted into it? The moment that the writer begins to speak of the will, as unable to change its direction, he is compelled to conceive of it materially and mechanically, and not as the moral, responsible soul. He says, "The human will becomes a current that becomes unmanageable simply because of its own momentum." And therefore, again, he is obliged to conceive of the whole voluntary power as lost, and lost before man was born; and he reduces all our real freedom to the original act of the will previous to birth, which took place when we were present in Adam's soul, and committed the first transgression with him.

This is plainly the denial of all human freedom since the fall of Adam. We bring into the world, according to the writer, a will wholly and inevitably bent to evil. We have no consciousness of this tendency, and if we were conscious of it we have no power to change it; but we yet are responsible for it, and guilty because of it, inasmuch as we began this state ourselves when all our souls were mystically present in the soul of Adam. Of this theory, we merely say now, that, if it be true, man is not *now* guilty of any sin which he commits in his mortal life; for he is not now a free being. He is only responsible for the sin which he freely committed in Adam. He is no more responsible when we suppose his sin to proceed from his will, than when we suppose it to proceed from a depraved sensuous nature, or from involuntary ignorance, for he is no more free in the one case than in the other. He may be an infinitely depraved and infinitely miserable being, but he can in no true sense be called a *guilty* being. Again we say, if this theory be true, it is an awful theory, and one which we cannot possibly reconcile with the justice or goodness, and still less with the fatherly character, of God. That God should so have constituted human nature that all the millions of the human race should have had this fatal opportunity of destroying themselves utterly, by one simultaneous act, in Adam, is, to say the least, an *awful* theory to propound concerning our heavenly Father. We might put Christ's argument to any man not hardened by theological study, as it seems to us, with irresistible force. "What man is there among *you*, being a father," who could do anything of this sort? But we know too well that all such appeals fall harmless from the sevenfold shield of a systematized theology.

Therefore we will only say further, concerning this theory, that, as being *apparently* in direct conflict with the divine attributes as taught in the New Testament; as making man a mere process deprived of real freedom; as proving man not guilty for any sin committed in this life; and as thereby deadening the sense of responsibility, and showing that we cannot possibly obey the command, "Repent and turn to God,"—this theory of a sin committed in Adam *ought to have the amplest proof* before we believe it. We admit that it may be true, though opposed to all our ideas of God, man, and duty. But being thus opposed, it ought to be sustained by the most unanswerable arguments. If Jesus and his apostles have told us so plainly, we will believe it if we can. How is it, then? Not a word on the subject in the four Gospels. Not a text from the lips of Jesus which can be pretended to lay down any such theory. He does not even mention the name of Adam once in the Gospels, nor allude to him, except when speaking of marriage. This theory rests, not on anything contained in the Gospels, book of Acts, or Epistles of Peter, James, or John, but on two texts in two Epistles of Paul (Rom. 5:14; 1 Cor. 15:22). In the latter passage Paul says not a word of Adam's sin, but only of his death,—the whole chapter treating, not of sin, but of death and the resurrection. This passage, therefore, can hardly be considered a plain statement of the theory. The other, in Romans, is confessedly so far from plain, that it is difficult to make it agree with any theory; but the most evident meaning, to one who has no theory to support, is, that sin began with Adam, and the consequences of sin, which are moral and physical evil, began also with him; and as he thus set in motion a series of evil tendencies which we find in our organization, and which Paul elsewhere calls the law of the members, and a series of evil circumstances which we find around us in the world, both of which are the occasion of sin, we may trace back to him the commencement of human disobedience. If the passage teaches anything more than this, it certainly does not teach it plainly or explicitly.

§ 4. Defence of Everlasting Punishment, by Dr. Nehemiah Adams and Dr. J. P. Thompson

Two defences of this dreadful doctrine have appeared within a few years—one by Rev. Nehemiah Adams, D. D. (chiefly known by his many and determined pleas for slavery), and the other by Dr. Thompson of New York.

We will first examine Dr. Adams's tract on "The Reasonableness of Eternal Future Punishment."

We have these three objections to it:—

I. It, throughout, denies the sovereignty of God.

II. It is, throughout, a system of naturalism.

III. It, throughout, ignores the central truth of the gospel.

It is our business to substantiate these assertions by sufficient proof.

1. The view taken in his tract, of God, cannot be true, because it conflicts with his supreme and sovereign deity.

Of course, this is to dethrone God. God, if not sovereign, is not God. Any view which disturbs, however remotely, the supremacy of the Deity, must be a relapse towards Pagan idolatry. We charge this tendency on the whole tenor of this tract. We affirm that it seriously impairs that confidence and strength which can only come from reliance on Omnipotence, and remands us to the terrors and narrowness of Polytheism: not consciously, of course, or intentionally, but by the logic of its ideas and the tendency of its argument.

According to Dr. Adams's view of the world, it is a scene of conflict between God and the Devil. The prize contended for is the souls of men. God wishes to save them: the Devil wishes to damn them. By immense efforts,— by the unparalleled sacrifice of himself on the cross,—God succeeds in saving a portion of this race, whom the Devil had plunged into fearful and desperate sin. As for the rest, He can do nothing with them, but must go away and leave them; escaping with the saved to some other region, where the sin and misery of the rest may be lost sight of.

The only divine supremacy which Dr. Adams admits is that of force. God is, on the whole, *stronger* than the Devil; so that He can prevent him from carrying his ravages beyond certain limits. God can "hem in and overrule" the power of sin; but he cannot conquer it. He has no complete power over the heart and will of men to become supreme there; but he has power over their conduct, and can restrain that within certain limits.

God's sovereignty, according to Dr. Adams, is only like that of a human government, and that, again, a weak one. A human government is strong when it is able to dispense with standing armies, with an omnipresent police, with prisons and dungeons: it is weak when its authority is only maintained by these. In the first case, it rests on the love of the people; in the other case, only on force.

Now, according to Dr. Adam's tract, God's sovereignty is essentially one of force. He is not sovereign by overcoming sin through his own holiness, but only by restraining its outbreaks by externally applied force. So far from conquering sin, he is represented as giving up all hope of conquering it. He has tried everything in his power, and has failed. He can do nothing more. Dr. Adams speaks of God's "having expended upon us all which the gospel of his grace includes," and of "the failure of that which is the brightness of his glory." Now, Dr. Adams says, "What God will probably do is, to go away and leave us," God says, according to the idea of this tract, "I will place all of you, who sin, in a world by yourselves, from which I and my friends will forever withdraw." In substance, He gives up, and acknowledges himself defeated. He is beaten by sin, which is more powerful than his gospel. Sin compels the Deity to compromise; to take some souls, and to leave others; to divide the universe, — love reigning in one part of it, hatred and wickedness in another.

2. The second objection to the doctrine of everlasting punishment, as taught in these works, is, that it is a system of pure materialism. It is naturalism, as opposed to supernaturalism. All its arguments from Scripture interpret Scripture according to its letter, and not according to its spirit. While much stress is laid on the word "eternal," no real eternity is believed in, or even conceived of. The fundamental law of religious knowledge — namely, that a man must be born of the Spirit in order to see the kingdom of God, and that spiritual things must be spiritually discerned — is wholly lost sight of. The spiritual world, with its bliss and its woe, is supposed to be a continuation of the natural world, instead of being its exact opposite. The same conditions of space and time are supposed to prevail there as here. Hell is regarded by Dr. Adams as a large place, located in some remote part of the universe, where the sufferings and blasphemies of damned souls and devils will not disturb the sentimental happiness of himself and his pious

companions. Eternity he regards as an enormous and quite inconceivable accumulation of time, instead of being the very negation of time. An unlimited quantity of days, months, and years, is his notion of eternity.

In like manner, all the arguments by which the school to which he belongs maintains this doctrine, are drawn from relations which exist in this world. Great use is made of the analogies of human government. It is said that it would not be safe for the Deity to forgive sins on the simple condition of repentance, without an atonement, because it would not be safe for human governments to do so. The government of God is made wholly similar to the imperfect and ignorant governments of men. When we say that God, as described in the New Testament, is not a Being to inflict everlasting suffering hereafter, we are told that he inflicts suffering here; as though there were no essential distinction between the finite and the infinite, the temporal and the eternal. When we argue that God would not suspend the eternal destiny of a soul upon the conduct and the determination of a brief earthly life, we have instances given us of great risks to which we are exposed, and great evils which we may incur, in this world; as though there were no difference between a partial loss and total destruction. When we say that the justice of God will not permit him to punish everlastingly those who, like the heathen, have never known Christ, we have instances given of those who have ignorantly burned themselves or have fallen down precipices. In all such examples, these reasoners overlook the essential distinction between the finite and the infinite. They forget that all finite evil can be made the means of a greater ultimate good, but that infinite evil cannot.

It is a curious fact, that those who are most Orthodox fall most easily into a very hard and dry naturalism. God is to them a king sitting on a throne in some far heaven outside of the world, not a spirit pervading it and sustaining it. He governs men from without by offering them rewards and threatening them with punishments, not by inward inspirations and influence. He teaches them from without by an outward Christ, an outward Bible, outward preachers, pulpits, creeds, Sabbaths, and churches; not by Christ formed within us, not by epistles and gospels written on the fleshly tables of the heart. The day of judgment is a particular time, when God shall sit on his throne, and all appear before him; not the perpetual spiritual sentence pronounced in each human soul by the divine law. And so heaven is a place where there is to be some singing of psalms, and such amusements as are here considered proper in Orthodox families; hell, another place, where souls are shut up, to suffer from physical fire, or at least from some external infliction. The doctrine taught by the Saviour in the first twelve verses of his first sermon, that the humble, the generous, the merciful, are already blessed, and have heaven now, does not appear to be at all comprehended. That heaven and hell are in this world already; that truth, love, and use are its essence, whilst falsehood and selfishness are the essence of hell,—these, though rudimental facts of Christianity, are commonly considered mere mysticism. But those who do not see all this have not seen the kingdom of heaven, and must be born again, into a new world of spiritual ideas, in order to see it.

3. The third and principal argument against the doctrine of everlasting punishment is, that it is *inconsistent with the divine love to his creatures.* It is impossible for God to manifest love to a human being by inflicting everlasting torment upon him. It cannot do him good, because, according to this theory, the period of probation is past, and he has no power now to repent. As far, therefore, as the man himself is concerned, it is gratuitous suffering—torment inflicted without any purpose. It cannot be said that God has any love for the soul which he is treating in this way. He has cast it off. To that soul, nevermore, throughout the ages of an everlasting existence, shall God appear as a friend, but always as an enemy.

We sometimes hear of a father who disinherits a child in consequence of some act of disobedience. In one of the most touching tragedies in the English language, a father refuses to forgive his daughter who had married contrary to his wishes. He leaves her to starve, and refuses to forgive her or to see her. No one approves of this conduct in the parent. But every Orthodox man, who believes in everlasting punishment, attributes an infinitely greater cruelty to God; infinitely greater, because the obstinacy of the human parent endures only during a short life, but the severity of God endures forever.

The force of this objection is such, that Dr. Adams has felt obliged to add to his tract on "Everlasting Punishment" another tract upon the text, "God is love," endeavoring to show a consistency between the two. But he does this by substituting something else in the place of the last. It is curious enough, that a master in Israel should have written a tract upon the "love" of God, and should have substituted "benevolence" instead of it. In other words, instead of that fatherly love to every individual which is the essential fact revealed in the gospel, he gives us a general good-will towards the human race. Such a general benevolence he finds not inconsistent with the doctrine of everlasting punishment; for, if love be only general good-will, then, the greatest good of the greatest number being the object, there is nothing to complain of if a few are sacrificed for the sake of the rest. It is not, to be sure, easy to see how those who have safely reached glory, and are in no danger of relapse, can be benefited by the knowledge that their old neighbors and friends are in hell; but there may be some benefit which is not apparent. By quietly substituting, therefore, the idea of benevolence in the place of love, the difficulty may be evaded, which otherwise is unanswerable.

But what an entire confusion of ideas is this, which substitutes a general benevolence for a personal affection, good-will towards the race for love to the individual! It is, in fact, abolishing the idea of Father, and substituting that of Ruler. The kind ruler, actuated by benevolence, desires the good of all his subjects; but he does not love them as individuals. But the father loves the child with a wholly different feeling. The tie is personal, not general. It is one of mutual knowledge and mutual dependence. We cannot love one whom we do not know; but we can exercise benevolence towards him very easily. Benevolence depends wholly on the character of the benevolent person; but love is drawn out by the object loved. I do not love my child because I am benevolent, but because it is my child. The infant draws forth a host of feelings, before unknown, in the mother's heart. She does not love her infant because she is a benevolent woman, but because the infant excites her love. A man is benevolent towards the sufferers in Kansas, whom he has never seen; but he does not love them. He loves his wife, but is not benevolent towards her. Benevolence and love, therefore, are not only essentially different in their nature, origin, and manifestations, but so different as often to exclude each other.

Now, it has always been seen that God is benevolent. This is taught by natural religion. We see it in all the arrangements of divine Providence. The infinitely varied provisions for the good of his creatures, the myriad adaptations by which their wants are met, are ample evidence of this. But Christianity comes to teach us something else, —to teach us that God is our Father, and so to see in him benevolence swallowed up in love. God does not love his children because he is benevolent, but because they are his children. He does not love them for the sake of others, but for their own sake. His love does not depend upon their being good, pious, or Christian; it depends only upon the fact that they are his children. This is the doctrine of the prodigal son; in which wonderful parable it is more distinctly stated than in any other part of the New Testament. The doctrine there taught, that there is more joy in heaven over one sinner who repents than over ninety and nine just persons who need no repentance, is somewhat different from that other doctrine, that the redeemed in heaven look down with joy upon the sufferings of the damned below. This parable teaches that God has a personal, fatherly love towards the impenitent sinner who has gone away from him into a far country. The father's joy when his child returned is the evidence of the love which had continued in his heart while his child was absent from him.

This being the character ascribed by Christ to the Deity, we assert that it is wholly inconsistent with the doctrine of everlasting punishment as taught in the pamphlet before us. There are, it is true, many widely different doctrines to which the term "eternal punishment" is applied. Some of these may not be inconsistent with the love of God. Let us give some instances.

Some, by eternal punishment, intend the punishments of eternity, as distinguished from those of time. They mean spiritual punishment, as distinguished from temporal punishment. They mean the sufferings which have their root in the sight of eternal things, as distinguished from those which originate in the sense of earthly things—sufferings which come to us from within, and not from without. "Eternal," in this sense, describes the quality, and not the quantity, of the suffering; and in this sense eternal punishment is not inconsistent with the divine love. But this is not the sense which Dr. Adams intends.

Some mean by endless punishment, that, as long as men continue to sin, they will continue to suffer; that sin is eternally suffering. But this is not the sense which Dr. Adams intends.

And some say that they believe in eternal punishment; meaning thereby, that the consequences of sin are everlasting,—either positively, by leaving forever some remorseful sorrow in the mind, or negatively, by leaving men forever lower down in the scale of excellence and happiness than they would otherwise be. But this is not what Dr. Adams means by it.

And some men believe in eternal punishment in the sense of a dark background to the universe, which will always continue, a shadow as permanent as light,—necessary for the full perfection and beauty of an infinite divine creation. Into this shadow man may forever plunge; out of it he may forever emerge: and it will always continue so to be. But this is not the view taken by Dr. Adams.

The view which Dr. Adams takes is of endless punishment inflicted as a consequence of temporal sin committed in this life. There will be no opportunity to repent hereafter, no pardon offered. There is nothing done by God, after this life, to save men. The heathen who have never heard of Christ, unconverted infants, those who have been brought up in the midst of evil, and heretics who do not accept the theory of Calvin concerning Christianity, are to be tormented forever in the other world. This view he thinks not only scriptural, but reasonable. It corresponds nearly to the human penalty of imprisonment for life; except that, instead of a few years of earthly life, it is a never-ending existence; and, instead of simple imprisonment, it is imprisonment with torture added.

We are accustomed to complain of the "horrors of the Inquisition;" but wherein do they differ in principle from the doctrine of Dr. Adams? The inquisitors tortured men for heresy; Dr. Adams thinks that God will do the same. The power of the Inquisition, however, was limited, on the principle, *Dolor, si dura, brevis; si longa, levis.* But not so with everlasting punishment.

That this view is absolutely inconsistent with the fatherly love of God to every soul, is apparent. It would be impossible for a father to torment his child forever in consequence of temporal sin. No earthly parent could be found cruel enough to inflict a million years of torture upon his child for each sin committed by him; but a million years for every sinful action would be but a trifling penalty compared with everlasting punishment.

As it is absolutely impossible to defend this doctrine on the ground of the fatherly love of God, it is defended by Dr. Adams and his companions on other grounds, namely, of the divine benevolence, and the duty of God as a governor. The argument is this: If God was dethroned, all sorts of evil would ensue. But sin is always endeavoring to dethrone God; therefore it is his duty to use the most strenuous measures to prevent this result. These strenuous measures consist in the highest rewards offered to obedience, and the severest punishments threatened to disobedience. But no punishment is so severe as everlasting punishment; therefore the benevolence of God requires him to threaten it; and, if threatened, his truth requires him to inflict it. This is the sort of argument by which the doctrine is defended. Its fallacies are manifest. It is based on a sort of Manicheism, making evil a hostile power in the universe, which threatens the supremacy of God. It makes God in danger of outward overthrow in consequence of the external assaults of sin. But we have always supposed that the essence of sin was the state of the heart, and the evil of sin to consist in the estrangement of the heart from God, and not in any danger that Omnipotence would be dethroned by it. Besides, though the fear of future punishment may restrain the outward act, it cannot change the heart, and cannot, therefore, remove the real evil of sin. Here is the fallacy of this whole argument.

Another weak point in the argument for everlasting punishment regards its proof, that all opportunity for repentance is confined to this life. Only two or three texts are quoted in proof of this very important position. One is taken from the book of Ecclesiastes, and declares, that, "in the place where the tree falleth, there it shall be;" of which there is no evidence that it has any relation to the subject; or, if it has, that it carries the least authority with it. Another passage asserts that "there is no work, nor device, nor knowledge, nor wisdom, in the grave whither thou goest." But this would prove too much; for it would prove that there was no knowledge in the other life. Another passage, quoted by Dr. Adams from the book of Revelation, says,

"Let him that is unjust be unjust still;" from which it is inferred that men have no opportunity hereafter for repentance. But, as this is said to those who are in *this* world waiting for the coming of Christ, it also proves too much, if taken literally; since it would declare that men cannot repent even in this world. Such is the extremely slight foundation on which this essential part of the doctrine is made to rest. Never was there so weak a support for so important a position.

The arguments from reason, by which our writer supports this part of his doctrine, are all taken from the plane of the lowest naturalism. He thinks it reasonable that the Almighty should suspend the everlasting destiny of his creatures upon what they do or omit doing in this life, because men, in earthly transactions, adopt a similar principle. A railroad train is advertised to start at a certain hour. If we are there a minute too late, we lose our opportunity of going on an important journey. We think this reasonable; why, then, argues Dr. Adams, should we think it unreasonable for God to make us lose our chance throughout eternity if we do not take the opportunity during life? God has given us full notice, he says, of his intention; we have been duly notified; and, after due notice, it is thought reasonable, in earthly business transactions, for people to run their chance. A man may commit a crime in a minute, for which he is sentenced to imprisonment for life or to capital punishment. We think this reasonable; why should we think it unreasonable that God should send men to an everlasting hell in consequence of sin committed in a short lifetime?

All these arguments are fallacious, because they apply to the infinite, conditions belonging wholly to the finite; because they transfer to Him, whose ways are not as our ways, and whose thoughts are not as our thoughts, the poor necessities of human ignorance and weakness. To those who reason thus, the Almighty may say, "Thou thoughtest me altogether such a one as thou thyself." It is because man is weak and ignorant that he is obliged to live under these limitations. If we were able to do differently, we should not make such severe consequences flow from human ignorance and weakness. We do such things, not because we think them absolutely just and good, but because we cannot help it. To argue that, because it is reasonable for human weakness to do something which it cannot help, it is reasonable for divine Omnipotence to do an infinitely more injurious thing of the same kind, is to fly in the face of all logic and reason.

Men make a rule, that, if I am not at the station when the train starts, I shall lose my trip for that day. Yes; but suppose the rule should be, that, if I arrived a moment too late, I should be crucified. Suppose a father should give full notice to his children, that, whenever any of them mispronounced a word, he should be burned alive. But it is easier, according to Dr. Adams's theory, for a child never to make a mistake, than not to commit the sins for which it is to be punished with everlasting torment. "What man among you is there, being a father," who would cause his children to come into the world exposed to such fearful risks; who would allow them to be born with constitutions tending inevitably to sin, the inevitable consequence of which, after a few short years of life, is never-ending torment, the only possible escape from which is salvation through a Being of whom the majority never heard, according to a system which the majority cannot believe, and by a process, which, except by a special help, none of them are able to accomplish? We should say, that we would not have children under these conditions. It were better that such children had never been born. If we then, being evil, would not subject our children to such risk, how much less would our Father in heaven do anything of the kind!

The reply to such arguments, by those whom Thomas Burnet calls the "unmerciful doctors" and "ferocious theologians," is always the same. Because finite evil exists, and is not inconsistent with the divine plan, therefore infinite evil may also exist, and not be inconsistent with the divine plan. Because one may suffer for a time in this world, therefore he may be compelled to suffer forever in the other world. It is assumed that there is no essential distinction between time and eternity, between finite and infinite evil. Here is the immense fallacy of the argument. The difference is simply this: All finite *suffering*, however great, is as nothing when compared with everlasting happiness afterwards; but all finite *happiness*, however great, is as nothing when compared with everlasting suffering afterwards. If we deny, therefore, the doctrine of everlasting suffering, evil virtually disappears from the universe; if we accept it, good virtually disappears, as far as the sufferers are concerned. If all evil is finite, the goodness of God can be fully justified; but, if to any one it is infinite, no such theodicy is possible.

This is the fatal objection to the doctrine of everlasting punishment. It clouds the face of the heavenly Father with impenetrable gloom. It takes away the best consolations of the gospel. When Jesus tells us to forgive our enemies, that we may be like our heavenly Father, who sends his blessings upon the evil and the good, this doctrine adds, that God's character is thus forgiving only in this world; but that, in the other world, he will torment his enemies forever in hopeless suffering. When we seek consolation amid the griefs and separations of this world by looking to a better world, where all tears will be wiped away, we have presented to us instead this awful vision of unmitigated horror. Instead of finite evil being swallowed up into infinite good, it darkens down into infinite woe.

Dr. Adams quotes Thomas Burnet, Master of the Charter-house, as a striking instance of one, who, though he denied or doubted this doctrine, admitted, nevertheless, that the Scriptures were probably against him. He quotes him correctly as saying, "Human nature shrinks from the very name of eternal punishment; yet the Scriptures seem to hold the other side." Though Dr. Adams gives the Latin, and refers to the page of the book, let us hope, for his own sake, that he quotes it at second-hand; which, as he twice misspells the name, is not unlikely; for Dr. Burnet, so far from admitting that the Scriptures are "probably against him," concludes, after an examination of the leading passages, that they prove nothing certainly as to the eternal duration of future punishment. He quotes the passage in which the Jewish servant is said to become a slave *forever*,—meaning till the year of jubilee; in which circumcision is called an *everlasting covenant*,—meaning that it shall be abolished by the same divine authority; in which the land of Canaan was given for an *everlasting possession* to Abraham and his seed, from which they have long since been expelled; &c. Dr. Burnet does, indeed, say that the Scriptures *seem* to favor the doctrine he opposes; but he then goes on to show that such is not the case. He also "awakens antiquity," and calls to his aid the merciful doctors of the early church (Justin Martyr, Jerome, the Gregories, &c.) to support his hope in a merely limited future suffering.

We will now consider the meaning of some of the texts usually adduced in support of this doctrine. Of these texts, there are some six or seven only upon which much stress is laid; and of these the principal ones are as follows:—

1. Matt. 18:8, "Having two eyes, two hands," &c., "to be cast into hell fire," or "into everlasting fire" (τὸ πῦρ τὸ αἰώνιον)—(τὴν γέενναν τοῦ πυρός).

2. Matt. 25:46, "These shall go away into everlasting (eternal) punishment, but the righteous into life eternal "(κόλασιν αἰώνιον and ζωὴν αἰώνιον). The same adjective is used in both places here, in the Greek; but our translators have seen fit to render it "everlasting" in the first place, and "eternal" in the second. There is no authority for such a different translation. The word κόλασις, translated "punishment," occurs in one other place in the New Testament: this is (1 John 4:18), "Perfect love casteth out fear, because fear hath torment." In this last instance, it is evident that the idea of punishment is not found, but only that of suffering. In the LXX. (Ezek. 14:3, 4, 7) it is translated "stumbling-block," and means, says Schleusner (Lexicon in LXX.), "all that is the source of misfortune or suffering." Donnegan gives as its meaning, "the act of clipping or pruning; *generally*, restriction, restraint, reproof, check, chastisement; *lit. and met.*, punishment."

The true translation of the passage, then, is,—

"These shall go away into the sufferings or punishments of eternity; and the righteous, into the life of eternity."

The simple, direct, and natural meaning, therefore, of this passage is, that, besides temporal joy and suffering, there are eternal joy and suffering: besides the joys and sufferings which have their root in time and in temporal things, there are joys and sufferings which have their root in eternity and in eternal things. In the twenty-fifth chapter of Matthew, the sufferings of eternity are described as following directly upon judgment, and as being its natural consequence. The judgment on each soul consists, according to this passage, in showing it its real character. Both the good and the bad are represented as needing such a judgment as this. Until the judgment takes place, men are described as being ignorant of the true nature of their own past conduct. They do not know their own good or their own evil: they do not understand themselves as they really are. They have done good and bad actions, but have not understood the value of those actions. They have not seen, that in every deed of charity, in every act of humble benevolence, they were helping Christ and his cause. They have not understood, that, by every selfish and cruel deed, they were injuring their Master. But the judgment reveals all this to them, and lifts them immediately out of temporal joy or pain into eternal joy or pain. They rise out of temporal things into eternal things, and the new insight is to them a source of spiritual joy or spiritual suffering.

In some instances, if αἰώνιος were translated "everlasting" or "never-ending," it would make such palpable nonsense, that our translators have been obliged to give it an entirely different rendering. Thus (2 Tim. 1:9; Tit. 1:2) we have the phrase πρὸ κρόνων αἰώνιον; which would be, literally, "before eternity," or "before everlasting time began," according to the common rendering. They have, therefore, translated it "before the world began." In the same way (Matt. 24:3; 1 Cor. 10:11), they are obliged to change their usual rendering, or they would have to say, "So shall it be at the end of forever;" or, "The ends of eternity have arrived."

Mark 9:43-50, it is said that the "worm does not die" in Gehenna, and "the fire is not quenched." This, therefore, is thought to teach the doctrine of never-ending punishment hereafter; but this was a proverbial expression, taken from the book of Isaiah.

Chap. 66:24, the prophet says, that, in the times of the Messiah, all men shall come, and worship in the presence of Jehovah; and shall then go out, and look upon the dead bodies of the men who had transgressed against the Lord; "for their worm shall not die, neither shall their fire be quenched; and they shall be an abhorring unto all flesh." Our Saviour, therefore, is not making an original doctrinal statement, but he is quoting from Isaiah. Now, the passage in Isaiah refers, not to punishment of the soul hereafter, but to the destruction of the bodies of transgressors in the valley of Hinnom. The fire and the worms in that valley were not everlasting in any strict sense. When Isaiah says, "Their worm shall not die, nor their fire be quenched," he expresses merely the utter destruction which would fall upon them. The fire and the worms of the valley of Hinnom have long since disappeared; but, while the fire lasted, it was the emblem, to the Jews, of the destruction which was to fall upon those who resisted the will of Jehovah. But it is not to be supposed that the idea of eternity, which is not in the original image, should be added in the figure. The fire and the worms were to last in the valley of Hinnom as long as there were idolaters to be punished for their idolatry; and so the spiritual suffering consequent upon sin lasts as long as sin lasts. Sin is perpetual misery; conscience is a worm which never dies; bad passions are a fire which is never extinguished. This is the simple and natural meaning of this passage.

3. Matt. 26:24. In this passage, as it stands in our translation, Jesus says concerning Judas, "Woe to that man by whom the Son of man is betrayed! It were good for that man if he had never been born." (Mark 14:21.) The argument is, that, if it were good for Judas not to have been born, it must be impossible that he should ever repent and be saved; because, if he should ever be saved, and his punishment should cease (though at ever so remote a period), it would be better for him to have been born than not to have been born; since there would remain an eternity of happiness to be enjoyed afterwards. And if this be true of Judas, it may be also true of others.

But, in reply to this argument, we say, —

1. The translation is doubtful. The literal translation is, "Woe to that man by whom the Son of man is betrayed! It had been good for him if that man had never been born." This is the literal rendering of the Greek; and the apparent meaning seems to be, "that it had been good for the Son of man if Judas had not been born." Jesus seems to say that it is a great woe to him, a great sorrow, to be betrayed by one of his own friends, by a member of his own household. It would have been good for Jesus, if this traitor, who was to wound his heart so deeply, had never existed.

2. But, retaining our present translation, the natural application of it is to this life. It means simply this: The earthly life of this man is an entire failure. His life is wholly thrown away. He had better never have been in the world, than to stand, as he will to all time, a monument of the basest treachery. The idea of the future life does not come it at all here.

On the whole, one must feel, in reading these books and tracts, that such writers are more to be pitied than to be blamed. Confined in the strait-jacket of an austere theology; steeped to the lips in Calvinism; working painfully all his life in sectarian harness; with an angry heaven over his head, and a ruined earth about his feet; his friends and neighbors dropping into hell by thousands every year; never having had any real sight of the blessed face of Jesus; having for them no hope full of immortality, but, instead thereof, a tenor full of damnation,—even a kindly nature and an affectionate heart must suffer, be dwarfed and crippled.

It is not an agreeable task to refute such errors; but believing them equally destructive, in their tendency, to piety and morality,—corrupting the Christian life at its centre, and weakening its chief source of power,— we feel it a duty not to be avoided. Advancing age does not make us conservative in regard to such doctrines. The longer we live, the more we see of their evil tendency. When young, we shrank from attacking them, fearing lest they might contain some truth beyond the range of our limited experience. But, having come to see wherein the essence of Christian truth lies in all varieties of pious experience, we know that this doctrine is an excrescence, weakening always the vital power of the gospel. It rests on custom, on cowardice, on the fear of change, not on any positive insight or substantial knowledge. But, as Tertullian declared of another doctrine defended by precedent, "Christ did not say, 'I am the Custom,' but, 'I am the Truth.' "

The time will come in which the Christian Church will look back upon its past belief in this doctrine as it looks back now on its former universal belief in the duty of persecution, the primacy of the pope, or the atonement made by Christ to Satan. It will regard it with the horror with which it now regards its former universal conviction, that God was pleased when his children burned each other alive for difference of opinion. We now shudder when we hear of "An Act of Faith," consisting in burning at the stake ten or twenty Jews and Protestants. Our children will shudder with a still more inward grief that we could make it *an act of faith* to believe that God burns millions of his own children in unquenchable fire forever because they deny Calvin's view of the atonement, or the Church definition of the Trinity, or because of any possible amount of sin committed in this world.

We now proceed to add some remarks upon a recent work by Dr. Thompson of New York, a zealous and favorite disciple of the late Dr. Taylor of New Haven. This book, the title of which is, "Love and Penalty," consists of nine lectures delivered in the Broadway Tabernacle.

With the contents of some of the chapters we have nothing to do. All the arguments for retribution, derived from the nature of God, the nature of man, the course of Providence, the demerit of sin, have for their object to prove what all Christians fully believe. Unitarians and Universalists, Theodore Parker and R. W. Emerson, teach retribution, present and future, with a force which leaves little need of additional arguments from Orthodoxy. They teach a perfect and inevitable retribution, proceeding both from the truth and goodness of God, by means of which every man reaps as he sows. Orthodoxy, they complain, teaches no such full and perfect retribution. All that part of this volume, therefore, which is intended to show the probability of retribution, is wasted, so far as any opposers are concerned. In this part of his book, Dr. Thompson fights as one who beats the air. He is very zealous to disprove that which no one asserts, to prove that which no one denies, and to show the folly of a position which no one assumes.

The confusion referred to runs through the whole book; and perhaps there is no better illustration than this volume presents of that logical fallacy which is called "the irrelevant conclusion." This fallacy consists in proving one thing, and making men think you have proved another. Dr. Thompson's hearers saw that he proved future retribution, and thought that he proved eternal punishment. We do not suppose that he intended to sophisticate them: the difficulty seems rather to be, that he has sophisticated himself. The *ignoratio elenchi* is in his own mind. He thinks, because he sees penalty, that he has seen vengeance; that, because he has established retribution, he has demonstrated everlasting punishment.

A reasoner has, no doubt, a perfect right to try to prove two distinct and independent propositions; but he must keep them distinct and independent, and not pretend to be proving one when he is proving the other. He has also a perfect right, if he desires to establish one proposition, to prove another, as the first step towards it; but he has no right to assume or imply that he has made out one of his points, when he has only shown the probability of the other.

Now, our author declares that he has one object; viz., to show the truth of the doctrine of everlasting punishment. He says, "It will be the aim of this series of lectures to show that *the doctrine of the eternal punishment of the wicked is in entire harmony with the paternal character of God.*" He then proceeds to give the substance of his argument, under eight heads. Six of these only prove future retribution, and only two of them have any direct bearing upon the main question. Yet, through all of them, there runs a quiet assumption, that they are bearing directly on the main question. This is the radical sophism of the whole volume. We may see this more plainly by analyzing some of his chapters.

His first position is this, in Lecture I.: "Our own nature, which is appealed to as refusing to recognize the attribute of punitive justice in a God of love, in fact demands this attribute, as essential to the moral perfection of the Deity—an attribute without which he could not command the confidence and homage of his intelligent creatures."

Before attempting to demonstrate any theorem, it is important to define its terms. An accurate definition at first of what we wish to prove would often make a long discussion unnecessary. What is meant by the *"attribute of punitive justice"*? Does it mean that God's nature is such that he causes happiness to flow from goodness, and suffering from wickedness, in the constitution of the universe? If this is meant, Dr. Thompson will find no one to oppose him; for all this can take place in perfect accordance with divine love to the sinner himself. What he *needs* is suffering: this is the way by which he is to be cured of that sin which is a greater evil than suffering. Or does the author mean, by "punitive justice," some attribute of the divine nature which finds pleasure in punishing the sinner, without regard to any good which is to come from it, either to him or to any one else? Apparently, this last is what he means; for he goes on to quote from Pagan authorities and Pagan religions, to show that conscience in man requires that the wicked should be punished, without any regard to any good to result from it. But these authorities only show, that, in the one-sided action of man's nature, the sense of justice acts independently of love. What Dr. Thompson has undertaken to show is, that it can act in God in harmony with love. In man, conscience produces hatred of sin, without regard to the good of the sinner; but the divine conscience acts in no such one-sided way. "Mercy and truth meet together; righteousness and peace kiss each other." The law is vindicated and the sinner benefited at the same moment.

The atonement of Christ, objectively considered, consisted exactly in this, that he showed a perfect reconciliation, in his own life, of God's hatred to sin, and love to the sinner. No one was ever so averse from sin, no one was ever so in sympathy with the sinner, as Jesus. The power of his life, death, and higher life, lay in this union of holiness and love. This was the objective atonement in Christ, and in this he was God manifest in the flesh. He who has seen him has seen the Father. The Christianized conscience, following Christ, pities the sinner, while it abhors the sin. Christian legislation lays aside the vindictive tendencies of natural law, and seeks at the same time to destroy evil, to protect society, and to reform the criminal. From this gospel view our author remands us to Paganism, and to the dicta of the natural conscience in unregenerate man. These testimonies only show, that conscience, in its unregenerate state, demands that the sinner be punished, and does not care whether that punishment does him good or harm, makes him better or worse. But conscience, when Christianized, does care: it wishes to save the sinner, while it punishes the sin. As far as the natural conscience goes, it speaks truly in saying that evil should follow sin. But why it should follow it, and what shall be the result, it does not say. That was left to Christ to reveal.

Dr. Thompson himself bears witness, unconsciously, to the truth of this distinction. Along with his testimonies from the Heathen conscience, he gives us two testimonies from the Christian conscience. The one is his own feelings on seeing a woman carried to the Tombs. He says he felt sympathy for her, and would fain have saved her from that shame, while he wished her crime to be punished. The other is the testimony of Dr. Bushnell, that the "necessary reason" why wicked people, remaining wicked, should not be in heaven, is, that it would destroy the happiness of heaven. These two Christians, therefore, have consciences which do not testify to punishment proceeding from naked, arbitrary, and vindictive law, such as the Pagan conscience accepts, but punishment having a reasonable end, a benevolent purpose, and accompanied with sympathy for the sinner.

Another position of Dr. Thompson is, however, so extraordinary, that it needs more consideration. His fifth proposition is this: "*The high and sacred Fatherhood which the gospel reveals is a Fatherhood in Christ towards those who love him, and not a general Fatherhood of indiscriminate love and blessing for the race.*"

A certain want of logical clearness in our author's mind appears in the very statement of this proposition. He joins together a positive and a negative, which have no antithetical relation. We entirely agree with him, that the Fatherhood of God is *not* one of *indiscriminate* love and blessing for the race; but we utterly reject the proposition, that the Fatherhood which Christ reveals is only one towards those who love him. The apostle John tells us that "we love him because he first loved us." And again: "Herein is love; not that we loved God, but that he loved us, and sent his Son to be the propitiation for our sins." The doctrine of the apostle is exactly opposite to that of Dr. Thompson. The modern divine teaches that God only loves those who first love him; but the ancient divine teaches that only by God's loving us first do we come to love him. Nor is this doctrine peculiar to John. It is a fundamental truth of the New Testament, that God's fatherly love, manifested to the soul, creates an answering love, and that nothing else can create it. Jesus said of the woman, "She loved much; but to whom little is forgiven, the same loveth little." God's forgiving love comes first, and creates a grateful love in return. And again we read (John 3:16), "God so loved the world, that he gave his only-begotten Son." He therefore loved the world while it was still alienated from him. And again we are told by the Saviour (Matt. 5:44) to "love our enemies, that we may be the children of our Father in heaven," who loves his enemies.

Possibly our friend may say, "Yes, God loves the sinner; but he does not love him with a *fatherly* love, but only with a general love." Perhaps a copy of the New Testament may be used in the Tabernacle Church, New York, which does not contain the Parable of the Prodigal Son. Only on some such supposition can we account for this assertion of Dr. Thompson, that "the high and sacred Fatherhood which the gospel reveals is a Fatherhood in Christ towards those who love him." Is that "*high and sacred Fatherhood of God*" revealed anywhere more fully and plainly than in this parable? and does it not teach expressly that the father loved the son, while he was absent, as a son? Is not his joy at the return of his son the evidence of that love which clung to him while he was away? Even after the son returned, he had not begun to love his father as a son: he did not think he had any right to do so. He did not expect that his father would love him again: he only expected to be as a servant. It is evidently, then, utterly false to say that God's Fatherhood, revealed in the gospel, is only a Fatherhood towards those who love him: it is a Fatherhood to those who hate him and to those who fear him. His love creates theirs, and is not created by it. Such a doctrine as this of Dr. Thompson, if generally believed, would sap the foundations of Christian life, and turn the gospel of reconciling grace into a cold system of retribution.

As a proof of this melancholy opinion,—an opinion which takes the life out of the gospel,—the author relies chiefly on that passage in which Jesus says to the Jews that they were of their father the devil. (John 8:44.) From this he argues that they had no right to regard God as Father, and that no one has that right except pious believers in Christ. But was not God at that very moment their Father, in the same way that the father of the prodigal son was his father while he was yet in the far country? The prodigal son could not see his father's love: while absent from him, he could not tell how much his father loved him. Only when he returned, and came back to his father's house, could he behold that blessed countenance and feel that pardoning love. But none the less did his father love him during all that absence; none the less did he desire his return.

When Jesus said to the unbelieving Jews, "Ye are of your father the devil," was he describing God's state of mind, or their state of mind? Did he mean that God was alienated from them, or that they were alienated from God? He evidently meant to say that they were in a *devilish* state of mind; that in their character and feelings they partook of the spirit of the devil, and not of the spirit of God. He was describing their position in relation to God, not God's position in relation to them. The text, therefore, appears to have no direct bearing on the subject. It teaches, indeed, that they could have no truly filial feeling towards God; but it does not show that he might not have a truly parental feeling towards them. If they could not truly say, "Abba, Father," he could say, "My son, give me thy heart."

We dwell on this because our author seems to us to have assumed a position injurious, if not fatal, to the most vital force of the gospel. That which subdues and converts the heart, and makes all things new in the soul, is not to be told, that God will be our Father when we love him, but that he is our Father now. "Herein is love; not that we loved God, but that he loved us." "God commends his love toward us, that, *while we were sinners*, Christ died for us." But why multiply quotations to prove that which is written on the face of the gospel, and to which all Christian experience bears testimony? It is God's love to us, descending in Christ, while we are estranged and far off, which draws up our affection to him: it is not our love which takes the initiative, and draws his down.

The sixth position argues future retribution from the demerit of sin, and asserts that "no punishment equal to the demerit of sin is, or can be, inflicted in the present life."

The boldness of this proposition is only equalled by the poverty of the reasoning by which it is supported. To assert that it is not in the power of God adequately to punish sin in this world, is to profess a knowledge of the resources of Omnipotence, and an acquaintance with the deserts of man, which it seems to us presumptuous to claim. On this point it is not necessary to enlarge. An *a priori* argument to prove that God cannot punish sin in this life as much as it deserves to be punished, can carry conviction to no mind which possesses any intellectual humility.

The seventh position declares that "there is no conceivable mode and no revealed promise by which the Fatherhood of God can make one, dying in impenitence and unbelief, holy and blessed in the future world."

This is, of course, the very key-stone of the argument in support of the doctrine of everlasting punishment. The burden of proof rests upon those who assert that doctrine. It is not enough that Scripture does not expressly declare that there is an opportunity in the other life for repentance and pardon; for Scripture is dealing with us in this life, and has no occasion to say much of the opportunities of the other. Those who wish to prove that there is no opportunity hereafter must show some text which expressly declares it. No such text is produced, and there is no such text in the Bible. If Jesus had said, "You must repent in this life, for after death there will be no opportunity;" or, "At death, man's spiritual condition is finally determined;" or, "After this life, man cannot turn from evil to good,"—we should have some distinct proof of the doctrine. But now we have none.

The Parable of Dives and Lazarus is referred to more than once by our author in support of his position. It is sufficient to say in regard to this, that the most Orthodox commentators, provided they are scholars, expressly deny that this refers to the doctrine of everlasting punishment. Olshausen, for instance, says, "Rightly to understand the whole delineation, we must, above all, keep clearly in view, that it is not everlasting salvation or condemnation which is here described, but the middle state of departed souls, between death and the resurrection." "In our parable, there is no possible reference to the everlasting condemnation of the rich man, inasmuch as the germ of love, and of faith in love, is clearly expressed in his words." The word translated "hell" in this parable is not Gehenna, but Hades.

Our author says, and says justly, that we can form no opinion as to another probation hereafter from *a priori* reasoning, but that the question must be answered only from Scripture. Having said this, he immediately proceeds to argue it, *a priori*, stating that there are only three conceivable modes by which those dying impenitent can be saved; and then tries to show that neither is possible. After this, he quotes a few passages bearing only indirectly, and by inference, upon the question. The Parable of the Ten Virgins is one of these, because in it it is said, "The door is shut;" and, "Depart! I know you not." With regard to this parable, also, Olshausen says that "the words 'I know you not' cannot denote eternal condemnation;" that the foolish virgins were "saved, but not sanctified;" and that the parable does not distinguish between the penitent and the impenitent, but between the penitent believers who watch and those who do not watch.

Of course, we have not been able to notice all the arguments of this book, or all the texts referred to; but we have perhaps said enough to show that its positions are not all tenable, and that its arguments are not absolutely unanswerable. This book of Dr. Thompson, though able, cannot be called conclusive.

§ 5. Defence of the Trinity, by Frederick D. Huntington, D. D

The last section of this Appendix shall be devoted to an examination and criticism of Dr. Huntington's sermon, printed some time since, in defence of the Trinity. The course of our argument will be as follows. We shall give the reasons which have induced Unitarians to reject the Church doctrine of the Trinity; also examining Dr. Huntington's positions and arguments in its support.

The principal reasons, then, for rejecting the Church doctrine of the Trinity, as assigned by Unitarians, are these:—

1. That it is nowhere taught in the New Testament.

2. That every statement of the Trinity, which has ever been made, has been either, (1.) Self-contradictory; (2.) Unintelligible; (3.) Tritheistic; or, (4.) Unitarian, in the form of Sabellianism, or of Arianism.

3. That the arguments for it are inadequate.

4. That the arguments against it are overwhelming.

5. That the good ascribed to it does not belong to it, but to the truths which underlie it.

6. That great evils to the Church come from it.

7. That it is a doctrine of philosophy, and not of faith.

8. That we can trace its gradual historic formation in the Christian Church.

9. That it is opposed to a belief in the real divinity of Christ, and to a belief in his real humanity; thus undermining continually the faith of the Church in the divine humanity of Christ Jesus the Lord.

Proceeding, then, to an examination of these reasons, we say,—

I. The Church doctrine of the Trinity is nowhere stated in the New Testament.

To prove this, as it is a negative proposition, would require us to go through the whole New Testament. But we are saved this necessity by the fact that we have a statement on this point from one of Dr. Huntington's own witnesses, and one on whom he mainly relies. He brings forward Neander, the great Church historian, as a believer in the Trinity , and again , by an error which he has since candidly admitted, quotes him as saying, "It is the fundamental article of the Christian faith," —which is just what he denies in the following passage. We call Neander to the stand, however, *now*, to have his unimpeachable testimony as a Trinitarian (and a Trinitarian claimed by Dr. Huntington with pride) to the fact, that the doctrine of the Trinity is nowhere stated in the New Testament. This is what Neander says of the Trinity, in the first volume of his great work on Church History (p. 572, Torrey's translation):—

> "We now proceed to the doctrine in which Theism, taken
> in its connection with the proper and fundamental essence
> of Christianity, or with the doctrine of redemption, finds
> its ultimate completion—*the doctrine of the Trinity.* This

doctrine does not strictly belong to the fundamental articles of the Christian faith, as appears sufficiently evident from the fact, that it *is expressly held forth in no one particular passage of the New Testament*; for the only one in which it is done, the passage relating to the three that, bear record (1 John 5:7), is undoubtedly spurious, and in its ungenuine shape, testifies to the fact, how foreign such a collocation is from the style of the New Testament Scriptures. We find in the New Testament no other fundamental article than that of which the apostle Paul says, that other foundation can no man lay than that is laid—the annunciation of Jesus as the Messiah."

With this authority we might be content. But Dr. Huntington differs from Neander in thinking that Jesus has himself stated the doctrine of the Trinity, and stated it clearly and fully, in the baptismal formula. (Matt. 28:19.) He says that this is "a clear and full declaration of the fundamental article of Christian belief." He says, "Now, if ever, Christ will distinctly proclaim the doctrine of Christendom;" and he then declares that Christ, in this passage, told his Church to baptize "in the Triune name."90

Not in the Tri*une* name, certainly. This is an assumption of our friend. He may think that this is implied; that this is to be inferred; that this is what Christ meant; but certainly it is not what Christ said. Christ gives us here *three* objects of baptism, no doubt; but he does not say that they are one. How far this baptismal formula is "a clear and full declaration" of the doctrine of the Trinity will appear thus. The doctrine of the Trinity declares,—

1. That the Father is God.

2. That the Son is God.

3. That the Holy Ghost is God.

4. That the Holy Ghost is a person, like the Father and the Son.

5. That these three persons constitute one God.

Of these five propositions, all of which are essential to the doctrine of the Trinity, *not one is stated in the baptismal formula*. Christ here says *nothing* about the deity of the Father, the Son, or the Holy Ghost; *nothing* about the personality of either of them; and *nothing* about their unity: It is difficult to conceive, therefore, how Dr. Huntington can bring himself to call this a command to baptize in the Triune name.

Dr. Huntington adds, "Our faith is summoned to the three persons, of the one God." But nothing is said of three *persons*; nothing is said of their being one God.

He says, "No hint is given that there is any difference of nature, dignity, duration, power, or glory, between them."

We admit it, but also say, that no hint is given of any *equality* of nature, dignity, duration, power, or glory, between them. Which way, then, is the argument? Christ does not state, on the one hand, that the three are unequal or different: he does not state, on the other hand, that they are equal and the same. The inference of proof from this fact seems to us to be this: If the apostles, when Christ spoke to them, were already full believers in the church doctrine of the Trinity, the fact that Christ did not deny it would be an argument in its favor; but if the apostles were, at that time, wholly ignorant of the Trinity, then the fact, that he did not assert it distinctly, at least shows that he did not mean to teach it at that time. That inference appears to us a very modest one. But Dr. Huntington will admit that they did not know the doctrine; for he tells us that it was the purpose of Christ to teach it to them at that time. To which we can only reply, If he meant to teach the doctrine, why did he not teach it?

That the *word* Trinity is not to be found in the New Testament, and that it was invented by Tertullian, is a matter of little consequence; but that the doctrine itself should be nowhere stated in the New Testament we conceive to be a matter of very great consequence. We have seen that Dr. Huntington's attempt to show that it *is* stated in the baptismal formula is a failure. If not stated there, we presume that he will not maintain that it is stated anywhere. We therefore agree with Neander in saying, that, whether the doctrine be true or not, it is not taught distinctly in the New Testament. If taught at all, it is only taught inferentially; that is, it is a matter of reasoning, not a matter of faith. It is metaphysics: it is not religion.

II. The second reason why Unitarians reject the Church doctrine of the Trinity is this:—

That every statement of the Trinity has proved, on examination, to be either, (1.) A contradiction in terms; or, (2.) Unintelligible; or, (3.) Tritheistic; or, (4.) Unitarianism under a Trinitarian form.

Let us examine this objection. What is the general statement of the Trinity, as made by the Orthodox Church, Catholic and Protestant? Fortunately, this question is easily answered.

Orthodoxy has been consistent since the middle ages in its general statement, however much it may have varied in its explanations of what it meant by that statement.

The doctrine of the Trinity, as it stands in the creeds of the churches, is this:—

There is in the nature of God three persons,—the Father, the Son, and the Holy Ghost,—and these three are one being. They are the same in substance, equal in power and glory. Each of these three persons is very God, infinite in all attributes; and yet there are not three Gods, but one God.

According to the general doctrine of Orthodoxy, the unity of God is in being, essence, and substance; that is, God is one being, God is one essence, God is one substance. The threefold division stops short of the being of God: it does not penetrate to his essential nature: it does not divide his substance.

What, then, is the Trinity? It is a Trinity of persons.

But what is meant by "person," as used in this doctrine? According to the common and familiar use of the word at the present time, three persons are three beings. Personality expresses the most individual existence imaginable. If, therefore, the word "person" is to be taken according to the common use of the phrase, the doctrine of the Trinity would be evidently a contradiction in terms. It would be equivalent to saying, God is one being, but God is three beings; which again would be equivalent to saying that one is three.

Now, Trinitarians generally are too acute and clear-sighted to fall into such a palpable contradiction as this. It is a common accusation against them, that they believe one to be three, and three one; but this charge is, in most cases, unjust. This would be only true in case they affirmed that God is three in the same way in which he is one; but they do not usually say this. They declare that he is one being,—not three beings. They declare that the threefold distinction relates to personality, not to being, and that they use the word "person," not in the common sense, but in a peculiar sense, to express, as well as they can, a distinction, which, from the poverty of language, no word can be found to express exactly. Thus St. Augustine confessed, long ago, "We say that there are three persons, not in order to say anything, but in order not to be wholly silent." *Non ut aliquid diceretur, sed ut ne taceretur.* And so Archbishop Whately, in the notes to his Logic, regrets that the word "person" should ever have been used by our divines; and says, "If *hypostasis*, or any other completely foreign word, had been used instead, no idea at all would have been conveyed, except that of the explanation given; and thus the danger, at least, of being misled by a word, would have been avoided."

(1.) *The Unintelligible Statement.*

The Trinitarian thus avoids asking us to believe a contradiction; but, in avoiding this, he runs upon another rock—that, namely, of not asking us to believe anything at all; for if "person" here does *not* mean what it commonly means, and if it be impossible, from the poverty of language, to define precisely the idea which is intended by it, we are then asked to believe a proposition which Trinitarians themselves are unable to express. But a proposition which is not expressed is no proposition. A proposition, any important term of which is unintelligible, is wholly unintelligible.

To make this matter clear, let us put it into a conversational form. We will suppose that two persons meet together,—one a Unitarian, the other a Trinitarian.

Trinitarian. You do not believe the Trinity? Then you cannot be saved. No one can be saved who denies the Trinity. It is a vital and fundamental doctrine.

Unitarian. Tell me what it is, and I will see if I can believe it. What is the Trinity?

Trin. God exists as one being, but three persons.

Unit. What do you mean by "person"? Do you mean a person like Peter, James, or John?

Trin. No; we use "person" from the poverty of language. We do not mean that.

Unit. What, then, do you mean by it?

Trin. It is a mystery. We cannot understand it precisely.

Unit. I have no objection to the doctrine being mysterious; I believe a great many things which are mysterious; but I don't want the *language* to be mysterious. You might as well use a Greek, or a Hebrew, or a Chinese word, and ask me to believe that there are three *hypostases* or three *prosopa* in Deity, if you do not tell me what you mean by the word "person."

Trin. It is a great mystery. It is a matter of *faith*, not of *reasoning*. You must believe it, and not speculate about it.

Unit. Believe *it*? Believe *what*? I am waiting for you to tell me what I am to believe. I am ready to exercise my faith; but you are tasking, not my faith, but my knowledge of language. I suppose that you do not wish me to believe *words*, but thoughts. I wish to look through the word, and see what thought lies behind it.

Now, it seems to us that this is a very fair demand of the Unitarian. To ask us to believe a proposition, any important term of which is unintelligible, is precisely equivalent to asking us to believe no proposition at all. Let us listen to Paul: "Even things without life, giving sound, whether pipe or harp, except they give a distinction in the sounds, how shall it be known what is piped or harped? For, if the trumpet give an uncertain sound, who shall prepare himself for battle? So likewise ye, except ye utter by the tongue words easy to be understood, how shall it be known what is spoken? *for ye shall speak into the air*.... For, if I know not the meaning of the voice, I shall be unto him that speaketh a barbarian; and he that speaketh, a barbarian unto me."

It is of no use to talk about mystery in order to excuse ourselves for not using intelligible language. That which is *mysterious* is one thing; that which is *unintelligible* is quite another thing. We may understand what a mystery is, though we cannot comprehend *how* it is; but that which is unintelligible we neither comprehend nor understand at all. We neither know *how* it is, nor *what* it is. Thus, for example, the fact of God's foreknowledge and man's freedom is a mystery. I cannot comprehend how God can foreknow what I am to do to-morrow, and yet I be free to do it or not to do it. I cannot comprehend how Jesus should be delivered to death by the determined counsel and foreknowledge of God, and yet the Jews have been free agents in crucifying him and accountable for it. These things are mysteries; but they are not unintelligible as doctrines. I see what is meant by them. There is no obscurity in the assertion that God foreknows everything, nor in the other assertion that man is a free agent. I can see clearly what is implied *in both statements*, although my mind cannot grasp both, and bring them together, and show the way in which they may be reconciled. So, too, infinity is a mystery. We cannot comprehend it. Our mind cannot go round it, grasp it, sustain it. Our thought sinks baffled before the attempt to penetrate to the depth of such a wonderful idea. But we understand well enough what is meant by infinity. There is nothing obscure in *the statement* of the fact, that the universe is unbounded. So the way in which a flower grows from its seed is mysterious. We cannot comprehend how the wonderful principle of life can be wrapped up in those little folds, and how it can cause the root to strike downward, and the airy stalk to spring lightly upward, and the leaves to unfold, and, last of all, the bright, consummate flower to open its many-colored eye. But certainly we can understand very well *the statement* that a flower grows, though we do not comprehend how it grows.

Do not, then, tell us, when you have announced a doctrine, the language of which is unintelligible, that you have told us a mystery. You have done no such thing. Your proposition is not mysterious: it is unintelligible. It is not a mystery: it is only a mystification.

(2.) *The Tritheistic Statement.*

Leaving, then, this ground of mystery, and attempting to define move clearly what he means by three persons and one substance, the Trinitarian often sinks the Unity in the Triplicity, and so runs ashore upon Tritheism. This happens when he explains the term "person" as implying independent existence; in which case the Unity is changed into Union. Then we have really three Gods: the Father, who devises the plan of redemption; the Son, who goes forth to execute it; and the Holy Spirit, who sanctifies believers. If there are these three distinct beings, they can be called one God only as they are one in will, in aim, in purpose,—only as they agree perfectly on all points. The Unity of God, then, becomes only a unity of agreement, not a unity of being. This is evidently not the Unity which is taught in the Bible, where Jesus declares that the *first of all the commandments is,* "Hear, O Israel! the Lord our God is one Lord."

Moreover, against such a Trinity as this there are insuperable objections, from grounds of reason as well as of Scripture. For God is the Supreme Being, the Most High; and how can there be *three* Supreme Beings, three Most High Gods? Again: God is the First Cause; but if the Father, the Son, and the Holy Ghost are each God, and all equal in power and majesty, and have each an independent existence, then there are three first causes; which is evidently impossible. Again: one of the attributes of God is his independent or absolute existence. A being who depends on another cannot be the Supreme God. The Father, Son, and Spirit, therefore, cannot depend on each other; for each, by depending on another, would cease to be the independent God. But, if they do not depend on each other, then each ceases to be God, who is the First Cause; for that being is not the First Cause who has two other beings independent of him. Other arguments of the same kind might be adduced to show that there cannot be three necessary beings. In fact, all the arguments from reason, which go to prove the Unity of God, prove a unity of nature, not of agreement.

"But why argue against Tritheism?" you may say. "Are any Tritheists?" Yes: many Trinitarians are in reality Tritheists, by their own account of themselves. There are many who make the *Unity* of God a mere unity of agreement, and talk about the society in the Godhead, and the *intercourse* between the Father, Son, and Spirit.91

Opposed to this kind of Trinity is another view, in which the Unity is preserved, but the Trinity lost. According to this view, God is one Being, who reveals himself in three ways,—as Father, as Son, as Spirit,—or sustains three relations, or manifests himself in three modes of operation. The Trinity here becomes a nominal thing, and is, in reality, only Unitarianism with an Orthodox name. This kind of Trinity also is very prevalent, and is the one really maintained by men of high standing in the Orthodox Church, both in Europe and America. According to this view, the word "person" in the doctrine of the Trinity means the same as the corresponding word in Greek and Latin formerly meant; namely, the outward character, not the inward individuality. Thus Cicero says, "I, being one, sustain three persons or characters; my own, that of my client, and that of the judge" — *Ego unus, sustineo tres personas.*

This view of the Trinity is commonly called Modalism, or Sabellianism, and is also widely held by those who call themselves Trinitarians. It is, in fact, only Unitarianism under a Trinitarian name.92

(3.) *The Subordination View.*

Avoiding these two extremes, and yet wishing to retain a distinct idea of Unity and Tri-personality, the Trinitarian is necessarily driven upon a third view, in which the Father is the only really Supreme and Independent Being, the Son and the Holy Spirit subordinate and dependent.

This view, which is called the subordination scheme, or Arianism, is Unitarianism again in another form; and this view also is entertained by many who still retain the name of "Trinitarians." According to this view, the Son and the Holy Ghost are really God, but are so by a derived divinity. God the Father communicates his divinity to the Son and the Holy Ghost. This is the view really taken in the Nicene Creed, though adopted in opposition to the Arians, and was the doctrine of the earliest Church Fathers before the Arian controversy began. In the Nicene Creed, we read that the Son is "God of (ἐκ) God, Light of (ἐκ) Light, true God of true God;" the "*of*" here being the same as "from," and denoting origin and derivation.

This doctrine seems, in reality, to have less in its favor than either of the others. By calling the Son and Holy Spirit God, it contrives to make three distinct Gods, and so is Tritheism; and yet, by making them dependent on the Father, it becomes Unitarianism again. Thus, singularly enough, this attempt at making a compromise between Unity and Trinity loses both Unity and Trinity; for it makes three Gods, and so loses the Unity; and yet it makes Christ not "God over all," not the Supreme Being, and so loses the Trinity.

Between these different views, between Tritheism, Sabellianism, and Arianism, the Orthodox Trinity has always swung to and fro,—inclining more to one or to the other according to the state of controversy in any particular age. When the Arian or Tritheistic views were proclaimed and defended, the Orthodoxy of the Church swung over towards Sabellianism, making the Unity strong and solid; and the Trinity became a thin mode or an airy abstraction. When Sabellianism, thus encouraged, came openly forward, and defended its system and won adherents, then Church Orthodoxy would hasten to set up barriers on that side, and would fall back upon Tritheistic ground, making the Threefold Personality a profound and real distinction, penetrating the very nature of Deity, and changing the Unity of Being into a mere Unity of Will or agreement. We will venture to say, that there has never yet been a definition of the Trinity which has not been either Tritheistic or Modalistic; and Church Orthodoxy has always stood either on Tritheistic or on Sabellian ground. In other words, the Orthodox Trinity of any age, when searched to the bottom, has proved to be Unitarianism, after all—Unitarianism in the Tritheistic or in the Sabellian disguise; for the Tritheism of three coequal, independent, and absolute Gods, is too much opposed both to reason and Scripture to be able ever to maintain itself openly as a theology for any length of time.

The analogies which are used to explain the Trinity are all either Sabellian or Tritheistic. Nature has been searched in all ages for these analogies, by which to make the Trinity plain; but none have ever been found which did not make the Trinity either Sabellianism or Tritheism. They are either three parts of the substance, or else three qualities or modes of the substance.

Thus we have instances in which the three are made the three parts of one being, or substance; as in *man*,—spirit, soul, body; thought, affection, will; head, heart, hand.

One Being with three distinct faculties is Tritheism: one Being acting in three directions is Sabellianism.

Time is past, present, and future. Syllogism has its major, minor, and conclusion. There are other like analogies.

St. Patrick took for his illustration the three leaves of trefoil, or clover. Others have imagined the Trinity like a triangle; or they have referred to the three qualities of space,—height, breadth, width; or of fire,—form, light, and heat; or of a noun, which has its masculine, feminine, and neuter; or of a government, consisting of king, lords, and commons; or of executive, legislative, and judiciary.

This survey of Church Trinity shows that it is either one in which,—

1. The persons are not defined; or an unintelligible Trinity.

2. Or which defines person and Unity in the usual sense; or a contradictory Trinity.

3. Or which defines person as usual, and the Unity as only Union; or Tritheism.

4. Or which defines person as only manifestation; or Sabellianism.

These four are all the views ever hitherto given, and are all untenable. We might stop here, and say that the Trinity is utterly unsupported. There is no need of going to the Scripture to see if it is taught there; for we have, as yet, nothing to look for in Scripture.

The Trinitarian's difficulty appears to be in defining person. But possibly he may say, "I cannot, indeed, give a positive idea of person; but I can give a *negative* one. I cannot say what it *is*; but I can say what it is *not*. It is *not* a mere *mode* on the one hand; and not *being*, on the other. We must neither confound the persons nor divide the substance."

We will, then, go further, and say, as Trinitarians have never yet defined person, without making it either a mode or a being, so they never can define it otherwise. There is no third between being and mode. They *must* either confound the persons or divide the substance.

Again: that which differences one person in the Deity from another must be either a perfection or an imperfection. There is nothing between these. But it cannot be an imperfection; for no imperfection exists in God: and it cannot be a perfection; for then the other two persons would want a divine perfection, and would be imperfect.

III. The arguments in support of the Trinity are wholly inadequate. Since, according to Neander, the Trinity is not stated in the New Testament, it follows that it is a doctrine of *inference* only; that is, a piece of human reasoning. Now, we have, no doubt, a perfect right to infer doctrines from Scripture which are not stated there; but, as Protestants, we have no right to make these inferences fundamental, or essential to the religious life. They may, indeed, be metaphysically essential; that is, essential to a well-arranged system; but they are not morally essential; that is, not essential to the moral and spiritual life of the soul.

But this is just what Dr. Huntington attempts to do. He tries to show that there is a doctrine essential to the life, peace, and progress of man, which the New Testament has omitted to state; which is neither distinctly stated by our Saviour nor by any of his apostles; which has been left to be inferred, and inferred by the mere processes of unaided human reason.

What arguments does he allege for this?

His first and principal argument is the *universal belief of the Christian Church in the doctrine of the Trinity.*

On this Dr. Huntington lays great stress. He says,—

"Truth is not determined by majorities; and yet it would be contrary to the laws of our constitution not to be affected by a testimony so vast, uniform, and sacred as that which is rendered by the common belief of Christian history and the Christian countries to the truth of the Trinity. There is something extremely painful, not to say irreverent, towards the Providence which has watched and led the true Christian Israel, in presuming that a tenet so emphatically and gladly received in all the ages and regions of Christendom, as almost literally to meet the terms of the test of Vincentius,—believed always, everywhere, and by all,—is unfounded in revelation and truth. Such a conclusion puts an aspect of uncertainty over the mind of the Church, scarcely consistent with any tolerable confidence in that great promise of the Master, that he would be with his own all days."

To which we answer,—

(1.) That, according to Dr. Bushnell (Dr. Huntington's own witness), there never has been, nor is now, any such belief in the doctrine of the Trinity as he asserts. The largest part of the Church have always "divided the substance" of the deity, and another large portion have "confounded the persons;" and so the majority of the Church, while holding the word "Trinity," have never believed in the Triunity at all.

Dr. Huntington summons Dr. Bushnell as a witness to the practical value of the Trinity; and we may suppose something such an examination as this to take place:—

Dr. Huntington. Tell us, Dr. Bushnell, what instances you know of persons who have been converted or deeply blessed by the holy doctrine of the Trinity.

Dr. Bushnell. I have known of "a great cloud of witnesses," "living myriads," "who have been raised to a participation of God in the faith of this adorable mystery," (Huntington, p. 413.)

Dr. H. Mention some of them.

Dr. B. "Francis Junius," "two centuries and a half ago,"—a professor "at Heidelberg (Leyden?), testified that he was, in fact, converted from atheism by the Christian Trinity;" also "the mild and sober Howe;" "Jeremy Taylor;" also "the Marquis de Rentz;" "Edwards," and "Lady Maxwell." (Huntington, p. 414.)

Unitarian. Say, Dr. Bushnell, whether, in your opinion, the majority of Christians really believe in the Church doctrine of the Trinity.

Dr. B. "A very large portion of the Christian teachers, together with the general mass of disciples, undoubtedly hold three living persons in the interior nature of God." (Bushnell: "God in Christ," p. 130.)

Unit. Is that scriptural or Orthodox?

Dr. B. No. It is only "a social Unity." It is "a celestial Tritheocracy." It "boldly renounces Orthodoxy at the point opposite to Unitarianism." (Bushnell: "God in Christ," p. 131.)

Unit. Do I understand you to be now speaking of the properly Orthodox ministers and churches generally?

Dr. B. "Our properly Orthodox teachers and churches, while professing three persons, also retain the verbal profession of one person. They suppose themselves really to hold that God is one person; and yet they most certainly do not: they only confuse their understanding, and call their confusion faith. This I affirm on the ground of sufficient evidence; partly because it cannot be otherwise, and partly because it visibly is not." (*Ibid.* p. 131.)

Unit. Do you believe, Dr. Bushnell, that spiritual good can come from such a belief in the Trinity as you describe to be "undoubtedly" that of "the general mass of disciples"?

Dr. B. "Mournful evidence will be found that a confused and painfully bewildered state is often produced by it. They are practically at work in their thoughts to choose between the three, sometimes actually and decidedly preferring one to another; doubting how to adjust their mind in worship; uncertain, after, which of the three to obey; turning away, possibly, from one with a feeling of dread that might well be called aversion; devoting themselves to another, as the Romanist to his patron saint. This, in fact, is Polytheism, and not the clear, simple love of God. There is true love in it, doubtless; but the comfort of love is not here. The mind is involved in a dismal confusion, which we cannot think of without the sincerest pity. No soul can truly rest in God, when God is in two or three, and these in such a sense that a choice between them must be continually suggested." (*Ibid.* p. 134.)

Unit. This state of mind is undoubtedly that of the general mass of the disciples?

Dr. B. It is. (*Ibid.* p. 130.)

Unit. Are there others, calling themselves Trinitarians, who hold essentially the Unitarian doctrine?

Dr. B. Yes. "It is a somewhat curious fact in theology that the class of teachers who protest over the word 'person,' declaring that they mean only a *threefold distinction*, cannot show that there is really a hair's breadth of difference between their doctrine and the doctrine asserted by many of the later Unitarians. They may teach or preach in a very different manner; they probably do: but the theoretic contents of their opinion cannot be distinguished. Thus they say that there is a certain divine person in the man Jesus Christ; but that, when they use the term 'person,' they mean, not a person, but a certain indefinite and indefinable distinction. The later Unitarians, meantime, are found asserting that God is present in Christ in a mysterious and peculiar communication of his being; so that he is the living embodiment and express image of God. If, now, the question be raised, 'Wherein does the indefinable *distinction* of one differ from the mysterious and peculiar *communication* of the other?' or 'How does it appear that there is any difference?' there is no living man, I am quite sure, who can invent an answer." (*Ibid.* p. 135.)

Unit. Is it not true that both of these views are sometimes held alternately by Trinitarians?

Dr. B. "Probably there is a degree of alternation, or inclining from one side to the other, in this view of Trinity, as the mind struggles, now to embrace one, and now the other, of two incompatible notions. Some persons are more habitually inclined to hold the three; a very much smaller number, to hold the one." (*Ibid.* p. 134.)

Unit. But can they not hold the Unity with this Trinity?

Dr. B. "No man can assert three persons, meaning three consciousnesses, wills, and understandings, and still have any intelligent meaning in his mind, when he asserts that they are yet one person. For, as he now uses the term, the very idea of a person is that of an essential, incommunicable monad, bounded by consciousness, and vitalized by self-active will; which being true, he might as well profess to hold that three units are yet one unit. When he does it, his words will, of necessity, be only substitutes for sense." (*Ibid.* p. 131.)

(2.) But suppose that the belief of the Church in the Trinity was as universal as Dr. Huntington asserts and Dr. Bushnell denies, what would be its value? His argument proves too much. If it proves the Trinity to be true, it proves, *a fortiori*, the Roman Catholic Church to be the true Church, and Protestantism to be an error; for Martin Luther, at one time, was the only Protestant in the world. Suppose that a Roman priest had come to him then. He might have addressed him thus:—

"It is certainly an impressive testimony to the truth of the Church of Rome, that the Christian world have been so generally agreed in it. Truth is not determined by majorities; and yet it would be contrary to the laws of our constitution not to be affected by a testimony so vast, uniform, and sacred as that which is rendered by the common belief of Christian history and the Christian centuries to the doctrines and practices of the Roman Catholic Church. We travel abroad, through these converted lands, over the round world. We enter, at the call of the Sabbath morning light, the place of assembled worshippers; let it be the newly planted conventicle on the edge of the Western forest, or the missionary station at the extremity of the Eastern continent; let it be the collection of Northern mountaineers, or of the dwellers in Southern valleys; let it be in the plain village meeting-house, or in the magnificent cathedrals of the old cities; let it be the crowded congregation of the metropolis, or the 'two or three' that meet in faith in upper chambers, in log-huts or under palm-trees; let it be regenerate bands gathered to pray in the islands of the ocean, or thankful circles of believers confessing their dependence and beseeching pardon on ships' decks, in the midst of the ocean. So we pass over the outstretched countries of both hemispheres; and it is well nigh certain—so certain that the rare and scattered exceptions drop out of the broad and general conclusion—that the lowly petitions, the fervent supplications, the hearty confessions, the eager thanksgivings, or the grand peals of choral adoration, which our ears will hear, will be uttered according to the grand ritual of the Church of Rome. This is the voice of the unhesitating praise that embraces and hallows the globe."

What would Luther have replied to that? He would have said, "Truth must have a beginning. It is always, at first, in a minority. The gate of it is strait, the path to it narrow, and few find it. All reforms are, at the beginning, in the hands of a small number. If God and truth are on our side, what do we care for your multitudes?" We can make the same answer now.

Dr. Huntington proceeds to give his own creed in regard to the Trinity,— to state his own belief.

God, in himself, he declares, we cannot know at all. We know him only, in his revelation. "Out of that ineffable and veiled Godhead—the groundwork, if we may say so, of all divine manifestation; a theocracy— there emerge to us, in revelation, the three whom we rightly call persons— Father, Son, and Holy Ghost."

We can only conceive of God, he says, in action; and in action we behold him as three. But action and revelation take place in time. The Trinity, therefore, according to Dr. Huntington, is only known to us in temporal manifestation: whether it exists in eternity or not, we cannot tell. And yet, in the next sentence, he goes on to say that "the Son is eternally begotten of the Father," and "the Holy Ghost proceeds out of the Father, *not in time;*" which is the very thing he had a moment before professed to know nothing about. It is very difficult, therefore, to tell precisely what his view is. With regard to the incarnation of the Son, he is still more obscure. He says that "Christ comes forth out of the Godhead as the Son;" that he "leaves the glory he had with the Father;" that, while he is on earth, the Father alone represents the unseen personality of the Godhead, and that therefore the Son appears to be dependent on him, and submissive; that temporarily, while the Son is in the world, he remains ignorant of what the Father knows, and says that his Father is greater than he. "He lessens himself to dependency for the sake of mediation." "All this we might expect." This he calls an "instrumental inequality between Son and Father:" it "is wrought into the biblical language, remains in all our devotional habit, and ought to remain there."

In other words, Dr. Huntington believes that the Infinite God became less than infinite in the incarnation. The common explanation of those passages, where Christ says, for example, "My Father is greater than I," does not satisfy him. He is not satisfied that Jesus said it "in his human nature." No. It was the divine nature which said it; and it was really God the Son, who did not know the day nor the hour of his own coming. He lost a part of his omniscience. He ceased to be perfect in all his attributes. We should say, then, that he ceased to be God; but Dr. Huntington maintains that he was God, nevertheless; but God less than omnipotent,—God less than omniscient; God the Son, so distinct from the Father as to be ignorant of what the Father knew, and unable to perform what the Father could do.

Dr. Huntington ascribes it to "condescension" in Christ, to say that "of that day and hour knoweth not the Son." "*It is condescension indeed!*" says he. But this word "condescension" does not well apply here. One does not condescend to be ignorant of what he knows: still less does a truthful person condescend *to say* he is ignorant of what he knows. We may wisely condescend to help the feeble, and sympathize with the lowly, but hardly to be ignorant with them, or to pretend to be ignorant. It is a badly chosen word, and seems to show the vacillation of the writer's thought.

IV. The arguments against the doctrine of the Trinity are unanswerable.

We infer that they are unanswerable from the fact that they are not answered. It is to be presumed that Dr. Huntington, having been for so many years a preacher of Unitarian doctrine, is acquainted with our arguments. It is a remarkable fact that, in this sermon, he has nowhere attempted to reply to them. He has passed them wholly by. You would not know, from reading the discourse, that he had ever been a Unitarian, or had ever heard of the Unitarian objections to the Trinity; still less that he had himself preached against it. Unitarians, for instance, have said, that *if the Trinity be true, and if it be so important to the welfare of the soul as is contended, it would be somewhere plainly taught in the New Testament.* Does Dr. Huntington answer this argument? No; he answers the argument from the *word* "Trinity" not being in the Bible, and his answer is sufficient; but he does not answer the argument from the fact, that the doctrine itself is not anywhere distinctly taught, and that none of the terms which have been found essential to any Orthodox statement of the doctrine are to be met with in the New Testament.93

Nor does Dr. Huntington anywhere fairly meet the Unitarian argument from the impossibility of stating the doctrine in intelligible language. He tells us, with his usual eloquence, what we have often enough been taught before, that there are many things which we do not understand, and that we must believe many facts the *mode* of which is unintelligible. But when we say, "Can we believe *a doctrine* or proposition which cannot be distinctly stated?" He has no answer. The Trinity is *a doctrine*, and must therefore be distinctly stated in order to be believed. It has not been distinctly stated,94 and therefore cannot be believed. To this objection Dr. Huntington has no reply; and we may conclude that it is an unanswerable objection.

Dr. Huntington uses an unnecessary phrase about those who object to mystery. He calls the objection "shallow self-illusion," and proceeds with the usual declaration, that all of life is mysterious. Can he have been a Unitarian preacher for twenty years, and not have known that Unitarians object to mystery only when it is used by Trinitarians as a cover for obscurity and vagueness of statement?

You ask us to believe a precise statement, viz., that "there are three *persons* in the Godhead." We say, "What do you mean by 'person'?" The Trinitarian answers, "It is a mystery." We say, "We cannot believe it, then." The Trinitarian replies, "Why, all is a mystery. How the grass grows is a mystery; yet you believe it." "No," we say, "we do not believe it. When the mystery begins, our belief ends; we believe up to that point, and no farther." The statement, "the grass grows," is *not* a mystery; the fact, "the grass grows," is *not* a mystery. We believe the fact and the statement. The *way* in which it grows *is* mysterious; and we do not believe anything about it. "You cannot understand *how* the grass grows." No; and, accordingly, we do not believe anything about *how* the grass grows. But the whole purpose of the Trinity is to show *how* the Father, the Son, and the Holy Spirit exist. You are not satisfied that we receive *what* the Scripture teaches; you try to show us the *how*, and then leave it in obscurity at last.

Nor does Dr. Huntington reply to the Unitarian explanation of the Trinitarian proof-texts. Trinitarians have often quoted the texts—"*I and my*

Father are one;" "He who has seen me has seen the Father" —in proof of the Deity of Christ. Unitarians have often replied to both of them: to the first passage, that since Jesus has also said that his *disciples were to be one with him, as he is one with God*, it either proves that the disciples are also to be God, or does *not* prove that Christ is God. To the second passage, Unitarians have replied by reading the next clause, in which Christ says, "Believest thou not that I am *in* the Father?" showing how it is that he reveals the Father. He is *in* the Father, and his disciples are *in* him. Those who see him, see the Father; those who see his true disciples, see the face and image of Christ. These answers are so obvious, and Dr. Huntington must have heard them so often, that he should, as a controversialist, have taken some notice of them. He has not done so.

He quotes the passage from Eph. 1:20, 21, and says, *"Can this be a creature?"* We reply, "Can he be anything *but* a creature?—he who was *set* by God in this place of honor." Does God set God, as a reward, above principalities and powers? Does God make God "head over all things in the Church"? Again: Dr. Huntington quotes, "that, at the name of Jesus, every knee should bow, and every tongue confess that he is Lord;" but he omits the conclusion, "to the glory of God the Father."

He even quotes the passage, "Him *hath God exalted* to give repentance and forgiveness of sin."

And he quotes the passage, which has staggered the strongest believers in the Trinity, where Paul declares (1 Cor. ch. 15), that, *at the end*, Christ will give up his kingdom to the Father, that "God may be all in all," and explains it as meaning that "he will resume his place in the coequal Three, the indivisible One." Has he *left* his place, then? Is that Orthodox? Dr. Huntington evidently thinks so; for he says, "The Son, in his character of Sonship, is retaken, so to speak, into the everlasting undivided One." *So to speak.* We may *speak* so: "But what do we mean by it?" is the question. Did God the Son leave his place in the Godhead? Did he become less than God? Did he become ignorant? Did he suffer and die? Did he arise, and at last reascend, and take his place, "so to speak," in the Godhead? If this is meant as real statement, what better is it than the Avatars of Vishnu? What sort of Unity is left to us? We have a Trinity of council; but where is the Unity, except of agreement? One divine Being descending, and leaving the other divine Being alone, temporarily, on the throne of the universe, until the divine Being who had descended should reascend to take his seat again "in the coequal Three and indivisible One"!

One Unitarian argument, which appears to us unanswerable, is in the fact, that the very passages in which the highest attributes are ascribed to

Christ are always those in which his dependence and subordination are most strongly asserted. We could throw aside all the passages in which Jesus asserts directly his inferiority,—as, "My Father is greater than I;" "Of mine own self I can do nothing,"—and take the strongest proof-texts of the Trinitarians, and ask for no better proof for the Unitarian doctrine: "All power is given to me in heaven and earth;" "The image of the invisible God, the first-born of every creature;" "In him dwelt all the fulness of the Godhead bodily." Are these passages written of Christ in his divine or human nature? Not his divine nature; for to God the Son all power cannot be "given." God the Son cannot be "the image of God," or the "first-born of every *creature*." The "fulness of the Godhead" cannot dwell in God the Son. They must, then, be said of him in his human nature; and, if so, they show that the loftiest titles and attributes do not prove him to be God.

V. The good ascribed to the doctrine of the Trinity does not belong to it, but to the truths which underlie it.

Dr. Huntington asserts, for example, that "the Triunity of God appears to be the necessary means of manifesting and supporting in the mind of our race, a faith in the true personality of God."

If so, it is remarkable that the two forms of religion in which the personality of God, as absolute will, is most distinctly recognized (i.e., the *Jewish* religion and the *Mohammedan* religion), should both be ignorant of the Trinity. It is equally remarkable that the most Pantheistic religion in the world, in which the personality of God most entirely disappears (i.e., Braminism), should have a Trinity of its own. It is also remarkable, on this hypothesis, that idolatry in the Christian Church (as worship of Mary, worship of saints and relics, &c.) should come up with the Trinity, and flourish simultaneously with it.

No; it is not the Trinity which brings out most distinctly the personality of God, but the faith in a divine revelation through inspired men. If God can dwell in the souls of men, teaching and guiding them, he must be a person like the soul with which he communes. Especially does the religious consciousness of Jesus, his simple and child-like communion with the heavenly Father, bring God near to the soul as a personal being. It is not the Trinity, but the Christian faith which underlies it, which teaches the divine personality.

Nor is it the doctrine of the Trinity which is necessary for a living faith in God through Christ, reconciling the world unto himself. All that Dr. Huntington says of the evil of sin is well said, but has no bearing on the point before us. According to Dr. Huntington's own witnesses, as we have seen above, the Trinity was unknown in the earlier ages of the Church. Was reconciliation unknown? Was the forgiving love of Christ unknown? If he cannot assert this, the doctrine of the Trinity is not necessary to a living faith in a reconciling God.

Dr. Huntington argues, that only the sufferings, and actual sufferings, of God himself, can touch the sinful heart; and, therefore, the Trinity is true. The conclusion is a long way from the premise, even supposing that to be sound. But as regards the premise, he has read and quoted Mansel. Has he not verged towards the dogmatism which that writer condemns? Would it not be more modest, and better accord with Christian humility, to be satisfied with believing the scriptural assertions, that "God so loved the world, that he gave his only-begotten Son;" that "He who spared not his own Son, but gave him up for us all,—shall he not, with him, freely give us all things?" Is not this enough, without an argument to prove that the *only* way by which man can be saved is the method of a suffering God?

We will not dwell further on this head, nor examine our friend's argument to show that we cannot consistently, as Unitarians, have any piety. We will try, then, to have it inconsistently.

VI. Great evils to the Church have come from the doctrine of the Trinity.

It has tended to the belief in three Gods. It has tended to a confusion of belief between three Gods of equal power and majesty, united only in counsel; one supreme and two inferior Deities; one Deity with a threefold manner of manifestation; and a vague, undetermined use of words, with no meaning attached to them—unhappy confusion, which none have been more ready to recognize and to point out than Trinitarians themselves.

And what shall we say of the continual struggles, conflicts, and bitter controversies, which this doctrine has caused from the time of its entrance into the Church? What is there more disgraceful in the history of the Church, than the mutual persecutions of Arians and Athanasians, and of all the minor sects and parties, engendered by this disputed doctrine?

This is what Dr. Bushnell says of one of these matters; and his testimony is, perhaps, sufficient on this point,—

"No man can assert three persons,—meaning three consciousnesses, wills, and understandings,—and still have any intelligent meaning in his mind, when he asserts that they are yet one person; for, as he now uses the term, the very idea of a person is that of an essential, incommunicable monad, bounded by consciousness, and vitalized by self-active will; which being true, he might as well profess to hold that three units are yet one unit. When he does it, his words will, of necessity, be only substitutes for sense.

"At the same time, there are too many signs of the mental confusion I speak of not to believe that it exists. Thus, if the class I speak of were to hear a discourse insisting on the proper personal Unity of God, it would awaken suspicion in their minds, while a discourse insisting on the existence of three persons would be only a certain proof of Orthodoxy; showing that they profess three persons, meaning what they profess, and one person, really not meaning it.

"Such is the confusion produced by attempting to assert a real and metaphysical Trinity of persons in the divine nature. Whether the word is taken at its full import, or diminished away to a mere something called a *distinction*, there is produced only contrariety, confusion, practical negation, not light."

So far Dr. Bushnell. On another point thus testifies Twesten:—

"There are many to whom the biblical and religious basis of the doctrine is exceeding sure and precious, who are dissatisfied with the Church form of the doctrine, and even feel themselves repelled or fettered by it. It is to them more negative than positive, more opposed to errors than giving any insight into truth. It solves no difficulty, it unseals no new revelation."

Twesten goes on to admit that the Trinity has really hemmed in the free movement of the mind, substituting a dead uniformity for a manifold and various life; and yet Twesten is a very strong and able Trinitarian.

VII. The doctrine of the Trinity is a doctrine of philosophy, and not of faith.

As philosophy, it might be ever so true and important; but, when brought forward as religion (as Dr. Huntington has done), it would become at once pernicious. To offer theology for religion, belief for faith, philosophy born of speculative reflection in place of spiritual insight and pious experience, have always been most deleterious both to religion and to philosophy.

The objects of faith are the Father, the Son, and the Holy Spirit. Through Christ we have access to the Father in the Spirit. We see the Father revealed to us in the Son; we feel the power of the Spirit in our hearts. This is religion; but this has nothing to do with the doctrine of the Trinity.

VIII. We can trace the gradual formation of the doctrine in the Christian Church.

The following facts we suppose to be incontrovertible:—

1. Down to the time of the synod of Nice (A.D. 325), the Son was considered to be subordinate, or inferior to the Father, by the great majority

of writers and teachers in the Christian Church, and by the multitude of believers; and no doctrine of Trinity existed in the Church.

2. The *Nicene symbol*, which declared Christ to be "God from God, Light from Light, true God from true God, of the same substance with the Father,"95 was directed against the two Arian positions,—that Christ was created, and that there was a time when he did not exist; but it did not declare his equality with God the Father, nor teach the personality of the Holy Spirit, nor say anything of the Trinity.

3. The councils vacillated to and fro during three hundred years, gradually tending towards the present Church doctrine of the Trinity; thus,—

1. *Synod of Nice* (A.D. 325) opposed the Arian doctrine of the creation of Christ out of nothing, and maintained that his substance was derived from that of God.

2. *Synod of Tyre* (A.D. 335) favored the Arians, and deposed Athanasius.

3. *Council of Antioch* (A.D. 343) opposed the views of the Arians, and also the views of their opponents.

4. *Council of Sardica* (A.D. 344) resulted in a division between the Eastern and Western Churches—the East being semi-Arian, and the West, Athanasian—in their view of the nature of Christ.

5. The Western Church tending to Sabellianism (taught by Marcellus and his pupil Photinus), this view was condemned by two councils in the East and West, viz.:—

Second council of Antioch (A.D. 343).

Council of Milan (A.D. 346).

6. Constantius, an Arian emperor, endeavored to make the Western Churches accept the Arian doctrine, and, at two synods (A.D. 353 and 355, at Arelate and Mediolanum), compelled the bishops to sign the condemnation of Athanasius, deposing those who refused so to do.

7. The Arians, being thus dominant, immediately divided into Arians and Semi-Arians,—the distinction being the famous distinction between *o* and *oi*. Both parties denied the *Homoousios*; but the Semi-Arians admitted the *Homoiousios*.

8. At the synod of Ancyra (A.D. 358), the Semi-Arian doctrine was adopted, and the Arian rejected. The third synod of Sirmium (A.D. 358) did the same thing.

9. Down to this time (A.D. 360), nothing was said about the Holy Spirit in its relation to the Trinity. The Emperor Valens, an Arian, persecuted the Athanasians from A.D. 364 to 378. Then Theodosius, an Athanasian emperor, persecuted the Arians. Semi-Arianism, however, continued Orthodox in the East.

10. The Nestorian controversy broke out A.D. 430. Council of Ephesus (A.D. 431) condemned Nestor. The Nestorians (who were Unitarians) separated entirely from the Church, and became the Church of the Persian empire.

11. The Monophysite controversy broke out. The council of Chalcedon (A.D. 451) decided that there were two natures in Christ; and the Monophysites separated, and formed the Coptic Church. Their formula was, that "God was crucified in Christ." The Nestorians were too Unitarian, and the Monophysites too Athanasian. The Church decided (against the Nestorians) that Mary was God's mother, but decided (against the Monophysites) that God was not crucified.

12. *First Lateran Council* was called (in A.D. 640) to settle a new point. It having been decided that there were *two* natures in Christ, it was now thought best by many to yield to the Monophysites—that there was only one will in Christ. Hence the Monotheletic controversy, finally settled at the,—

13. Sixth General Council (A.D. 680), when *two* wills in Christ were accepted as the doctrine of the Church.

Thus it appears that it took the Church from A.D. 325 to A.D. 680 to settle the questions concerning the relation of Christ to God. During all this time, opinion vacillated between Arianism on the one hand and Sabellianism on the other. At the end of this period, the Church had become consolidated, and strong enough to compel submission to its opinions: but the relation of the Holy Spirit to the Trinity remained unsettled for several centuries more; and finally the Eastern Church separated altogether from the Western Church on this point. The whole Greek Church remains, to this day, separated from the Latin Church on a question belonging to this very doctrine of the Trinity. So much, then, for Dr. Huntington's assertion, that the Trinity is a doctrine which can almost literally be said to have been believed "always, everywhere, and by all."

IX. The doctrine of the Trinity is opposed to the real divinity of Christ and to his real humanity; thus undermining continually the faith of the Church in the divine humanity of Jesus Christ the Lord.

Our final and chief objection to the Trinity is, not that it makes Christ divine, but that it does *not* make him so. It substitutes for the divinity of the Father, the Supreme God, which Unitarians believe to dwell in Christ, a subordinate divinity of God the Son. This is subordinate, because derived; and, because derived, dependent. The Son may be said to be "eternally generated;" but this is only an eternal derivation, and does not alter the dependence, but makes it also to be eternal. The tendency of the Church doctrine of the Trinity is always to a belief, not in the supreme divinity dwelling in Christ, but in a derived and secondary divinity.

How is it, for example, with the Nicene doctrine concerning Christ? Dr. Huntington claims Nice as Trinitarian.

But what says Prof. Stuart concerning the Nicene doctrine? Listen.

"The Nicene symbol presents the Father as the Monas, or proper Godhead, in and of himself exclusively; it represents him as the *Fons et Principium* of the Son, and therefore gives him superior power and glory. It does not even assert the claims of the blessed Spirit to Godhead, and therefore leaves room to doubt whether it means to recognize a Trinity, or only a Duality." (Moses Stuart, Bib. Repos., 1835, quoted by Wilson, Trin. Test., p. 264.)

And how is it with the ante-Nicene fathers, whom Dr. Huntington also considers to be Trinitarian? else certainly his rule of "always, everywhere, and by all," does not hold. If, for the first three hundred years after Christ, there were no Trinitarians, it cannot be said that the Trinity has "always" been held in the Church. Listen, again, to Prof. Stuart, whose learning no one can question.

"We find that all the Fathers before, at, and after the Council of Nice, who harmonize with the sentiments there avowed, declare the Father only to be the self-existent God." (See the whole paragraph in Wilson, Trin. Test.)

"To be the author of the proper substance of the Son and Spirit, according to the Patristical creed; or to be the author of the *modus existendi* of the Son and Spirit, according to the modern creed,—both seem to involve *the idea of power and glory in the Father, immeasurably above that of the Son and Spirit.*" (Moses Stuart, Bib. Repos., 1835.)

So Coleridge asserts that "both Scripture and the Nicene Creed teach a subordination of the Son to the Father, independent of the incarnation of the Son.... Christ, speaking of himself as the coeternal Son, says, 'My Father is greater than I.' " (Wilson, Trin. Test., p. 270.)

According to the Trinitarian doctrine, then, we do not find God—the Supreme God, our heavenly Father—in Christ; but a derived, subordinate, and inferior Deity. Not the one universal Parent do we approach, but some mysterious, derived, inscrutable Deity, less than the Father, and distinct from him. Do we not, then, lose the benefit and blessing of the divinity of Jesus? Can we believe him when be says, "He who has seen me has seen the Father?" No; we do not believe that, if we are Trinitarians; but rather, that, having seen him, we have seen "the Son;" whom Coleridge declares to be an inferior Deity; over whom Bishop Pearson, in his "Exposition of the Creed," says, the Father holds "preeminence,"—the Father being "the Origin, the Cause, the Author, the Root, the Fountain, the Head, of the Son." The doctrine of the Trinity is therefore opposed, as Swedenborg ably contends, to the real divinity of Christ.96

But it is equally opposed to his real humanity. It constantly drives out of the Church the human element in Christ. Dr. Huntington is astonished at Unitarians not perceiving that the humanity of Christ is as dear to Trinitarians as his Deity; yet it cannot be denied, that the mysterious dogma of deity has quite overshadowed the simple human life of our dear Lord, so that the Church has failed to see the Son of man. All his highest human traits become unreal in the light of this doctrine of his deity. He is tempted; but that is unreal, for God cannot be tempted. He prays, "Our Father;" but this also is no real prayer, for he is omnipotent, and can need nothing. He encounters opposition, hatred, contumely, and bears it with sweetest composure; but what of that? since, as God, he looked down from an infinite height upon the puny opposition. He agonizes in the garden; but it is imaginary suffering: how can God feel any real agony, like man? Jesus ceases to be example, ceases to be our best beloved companion and brother, and becomes a mysterious personage, inscrutable to our thought, and far removed from our sympathy.

Footnotes

1. The following passage, from an article in the "Independent," by Henry Ward Beecher, is valuable, perhaps, as the testimony of one who has "summered it and wintered it" with Orthodoxy:—

"Does anybody inquire why, if so thinking, we occasionally give such sharp articles upon the great religious newspapers, 'The Observer,' 'The Intelligencer,' and the like? O, pray do not think it from any ill will. It is all kindness! We only do it to keep our voice in practice. We have made Orthodoxy a study. And by an attentive examination of 'The Presbyterian,' 'The Observer,' 'The Puritan Recorder,' and such like unblemished confessors, we have perceived that no man is truly sound who does not pitch into somebody that is not sound; and that a real modern orthodox man, like a nervous watch dog, must sit on the door-stone of his system, and bark incessantly at everything that comes in sight along the highway. And when there is nothing to bark at, either he must growl and gnaw his reserved bones, or bark at the moon to keep up the sonorousness of his voice. And so, for fear that the sweetness of our temper may lead men to think that we have no theologic zeal, we lift up in objurgation now and then—as much as to say, 'Here we are, fierce and orthodox; ready to growl when we cannot bite.' "

2. Thus Theodore Parker ("Experience as a Minister") speaks of a review of his "Discourse on Religion" in a Trinitarian work, which did it no injustice.

3. According to the "Chart of Religious Belief" in Johnston's Physical Atlas, there are in the world 140,000,000 of Catholics, 70,000,000 of Protestants, 68,000,000 of the Greek Church, and 14,000,000 of minor creeds. *About*, in his "Question Romaine," gives the Roman Church 139,000,000. He says, "The Roman Catholic Church, which I sincerely respect, is composed of 139,000,000 of individuals, not including the little Mortara."

4. Mr. Taylor shows that the Church, A.D. 300, was essentially corrupt in doctrine and practice; that the Romish Church was rather an improvement on it; that Jerome, Ambrose, Gregory, and Athanasius are full of false doctrine; and that a Gnostic theology, a Pagan asceticism, and a corrupt morality prevailed in the Church in those early centuries.

5. Of course we do not mean to charge our Orthodox friends with believing in persecution. We only show that *if Orthodoxy is in the letter*, they *ought*, consequentially, to believe in persecution. No doubt Protestantism has put an end to persecution. When Luther came, all believed in persecution; now, no one does. This is because the Reformation contained a double principle: first, that we are saved by faith, not by sacraments, and that faith is the belief of doctrines; second, that to see them aright, we must use our own minds, and consequently seek for truth as the paramount duty of life. But in order to seek effectually, we must seek freely—hence the right of private judgment as against authority in Church and State. The last principle is that of toleration; the first is the principle of intolerance. The last has proved the stronger, because it rests on the logic of things, the other only on the logic of words.

6. Heb. 11:1.

7. Jacobi—whose words have been said to let the thoughts shine through, as wet clothes around the limbs allow the form to be seen—says that all knowledge begins with faith. Faith is, according to Jacobi, (1) a knowledge proceeding from immediate revelation; (2) knowledge which does not need, and cannot have, proofs; (3) much more certain knowledge than any derived from demonstration; (4) a perception of the super-sensual world; (5) A well-grounded and reliable prepossession in favor of certain truths; (6) a faith which sees, and a sight which believes; (7) a vision, an impenetrable mystery, a perception of the thing in itself.

8. See "Broken Lights," p. 207, note.

9. A story is told of a clock, on one of the high cathedral towers of the older world, so constructed that at the close of a century it strikes the years as it ordinarily strikes the hours. As a hundred years come to a close, suddenly, in the immense mass of complicated mechanism, a little wheel turns, a pin slides into the appointed place, and in the shadows of the night the bell tolls a *requiem* over the generations which during a century have lived, and labored, and been buried around it. One of these generations might live and die, and witness nothing peculiar. The clock would have what we call an established order of its own; but what should we say when, at the midnight which brought the century to a close, it sounded over the sleeping city, rousing all to listen to the world's age? Would it be a violation of law? No; only a variation of the accustomed order, produced by the intervention of a force always existing, but never appearing in this way till the appointed moment had arrived. The tolling of the century would be a variation from the observed order of the clock; but to an artist, in constructing it, it would have formed a part of that order. So a miracle is a variation of the order of

nature as it has appeared to us; but to the Author of nature it was a part of that predestined order—a part of that order of which he is at all times the immediate Author and Sustainer; miraculous to us, seen from our human point of view, but no miracle to God; to our circumscribed vision a violation of law, but to God only a part in the great plan and progress of the law of the universe.—*Ephraim Peabody.*

10. Trench, "Notes on the Miracles of our Lord."

11. We use the term "plenary inspiration" rather than "literal inspiration," or "verbal inspiration," for "*literal inspiration*" is a contradiction in terms, like "*bodily spirit.*"

12. Tholuck, in his Essay on the Doctrine of Inspiration, ascribes the origin of the belief in the infallibility of Scripture to this supposed need of an authoritative outward rule of faith among Protestants. He says, "In proportion as controversy, sharpened by Jesuitism, made the Protestant party sensible of the necessity of an externally fortified ground of combat, in that same proportion did Protestantism seek, by the exaltation of the outward authoritative character of the Sacred Writings, to recover that infallible authority which it had lost through its rejection of inspired councils and the infallible authority of the pope. In this manner arose, not earlier than the seventeenth century, those sentiments which regarded the Holy Scripture as the infallible production of the Divine Spirit,—in its entire contents and its very form,—so that not only the sense, but also the words, the letters, the Hebrew vowel points, and the very punctuation were regarded as proceeding from the Spirit of God."—*Tholuck's Essay—Noyes's "Collection."*

13. The doctrine of the Roman Catholics, as stated by Moehler, a distinguished Roman Catholic, is as follows:—

"The doctrine of the Catholic Church on original sin is extremely simple, and may be reduced to the following propositions: Adam, by sin, lost his original justice and holiness, drew down on himself, by his disobedience, the displeasure and judgments of the Almighty, incurred the penalty of death, and thus, in all his parts,—in his body as well as soul,—became strangely deteriorated. Thus his sinful condition is transmitted to all his posterity as descended from him, entailing the consequence that man is, of himself, incapable—even with the aid of the most perfect ethical law offered to him from without (not excepting even the one in the Old Covenant)—to act in a manner agreeable to God, or in any other way to be justified before him, save only by the merits of Jesus Christ."

The doctrine of the Church of England concerning original sin and free will is in its ninth and tenth articles, and declares that,—

"Original sin is ... the fault and corruption of the nature of every man, that naturally is engendered of the offspring of Adam; whereby man is very far gone from original righteousness, and is, of his own nature, inclined to evil, ... and therefore in every person born into the world it deserveth God's wrath and damnation....

"The condition of man after the fall of Adam is such that he cannot turn and prepare himself by his own natural strength and good works to faith and calling upon God. Wherefore we have no power to do good works, pleasant and acceptable to God, without the grace of God by Christ preventing us, that we may have a good will, and working with us when we have that good will."

The early Fathers took different views of the origin of sin. Tertullian ascribed it to human *impatience*. "Nunc ut compendio dictum sit, omne peccatum impatientiæ adscribendum." (Tertul. *De Patien*. 5.) Origen thinks *laziness* the cause of sin; sin is a negation—*not* doing right. Justin Martyr ascribes the origin of sin to *sensuality*. Origen (after Philo) considered the story of the fall as an allegory, and a type of what takes place in all men.

14. See, in the Appendix, an examination of Professor Shedd's article.

15. Ovid. Metam. 7:18.

"Si possem, sanior essem. Sed trahit invitam nova vis; aliudque cupido, Mens aliud suadet, video meliora, proboque, Deteriora sequor."

See, also, the story, in the Cyropædia, of Araspes and his two souls.

16. See Dr. Cox's Sermon on Regeneration, reviewed by Dr. Hodge, in "Essays and Reviews."

17. Luther, in his "Table-talk," says of his preaching against the pope, and the enormous labors it entailed, "If I had known then what I now know of the difficulty of the task, ten horses should not have drawn me to it." "At that time Dr. Jerome withstood me, and said, 'What will you do? They will not endure it.' But said I, 'What if they *must* endure it?' "

18. See Raumer, "Geschichte Europas," zweiter Band.

19. God in Christ, by Horace Bushnell, p. 193, &c.

20. Heb. 2:9, 17, 18. 4:15. 5:8, 9.

21. No sooner was Socrates dead than he rose to be the chief figure in Greek history. What are Miltiades, Pericles, or Alcibiades to him? Twenty years after Joan of Arc was burned by a decree of the Roman Catholic Church, the same Church called a council to reconsider and reverse her sentence. Twenty years after the death of Savonarola, Rafaelle painted

his portrait among the great doctors, fathers, and saints in the halls of the Vatican. Within a few years after John Brown was hanged, half a million of soldiers marched through the South chanting his name in their songs. Abraham Lincoln was killed, and he is now the most influential figure in our history.

22. "Doctrinal Attitude of Old School Presbyterians." By Lyman B. Atwater, Professor of Mental and Moral Philosophy in Princeton College. Bibliotheca Sacra, January, 1864.

23. "The Old School in New England Theology." By Professor Lawrence, of East Windsor. Bibliotheca Sacra, April, 1863.

24. "Doctrines of the New School Presbyterians." By Rev. George Duffield, D. D., of Detroit. Bibliotheca Sacra, July, 1863.

25. "Hopkinsianism." By Rev. Enoch Pond, D. D., Professor in Bangor Theological Seminary. Bibliotheca Sacra, July, 1862.

26. "Doctrines of Methodism." By Rev. Dr. Whedon. Bibliotheca Sacra, April, 1862.

27. "Theologische Zeitscrift." Herausgegeben von Dr. Friedr. Schleiermacher, Dr. W. M. L. DeWette, und Dr. Friedr. Lücke. Erstes Heft, Berlin, 1819. *Ueber die Lehre von der Erwählung.*

28. Rom. 11:29. "The gifts and callings of God are without repentance." By this we understand the apostle to mean the same thing as is implied in Ecclesiastes (3:14): "I know that what God doeth, it is forever." God, having chosen the Jews for a work, will continue to them the gifts, and will see that somehow or other, some time or other, the work is done.

29. A person who never had an intellectual doubt concerning a future life may be so poorly provided with an inward sense of immortality that he may never feel quite willing to die, or confident in view of death. Such a man was Dr. Johnson, who had not the least scepticism; who was a dogmatic believer, and hated a heretic; who, yet, never attained to any sort of comfort in view of death, and was always afraid to die. So there may be another person who may have no intellectual belief in a future life, but who will have the instinct of immortality so strong as to be quite easy and happy in looking forward to death. Such a person is Miss Martineau, who, in consequence of a poor philosophy of *materialism* which she was taught in her childhood, and has always held, has been brought very logically at last to disbelieve immortality, and even the existence of God, and yet is very contented about it, and quite happy.

30. "Nescio, quomodo, dum lego, assentior; cum posui librum, et mecum ipse de immortalitate animorum cœpi cogitare, assensio omnis illa illabitur."

31. Thus it is said, "In Christ shall all be made alive." The meaning is, that when we live in reference to God, to immortal truth, to the infinite law of right,—when we really love anything out of ourselves,—we lose all fear of death. "Perfect love casts out fear;" that is, pure love. The love of a mother for a child casts out fear. She is not afraid of death; she will run the risk of death twenty times over to save her child. The immortal element is aroused in her. The soldier is roused by the general's fiery speech to a thrill of patriotism, and thinks it sweet and beautiful to die for his country. Love of his country has cast out his fear. This is something more than any mere insensibility. Men can harden themselves against danger and death; they can think of something else. But that insensibility is merely a thick shell put round it—a sevenfold shield perhaps; but the mortal fear lies hidden all the same within. True life is very different.

32. The word here rendered abolished is elsewhere translated "destroyed," "made void," "made of none effect," "brought to nothing," "vanished away," "done away," "put down." The meaning is, that all its force, importance, value, is taken out of it.

33. "The State of the Impenitent Dead. By Alvah Hovey, D. D." Boston, 1859.

34. For ἵνα before a defining clause, see John 6:29; 4:34; 1 John 3:11, 23; 4:21; 2 John 6.

35. Die Bestimmung des Menschen. Berlin, 1800.

36. In addition to the extracts from Professor Hovey, Meyer, Lücke, and De Wette, the following passages from F. D. Maurice ("Theological Essays") are interesting, as showing a concurrence of testimony from yet another quarter to the thesis of this section:—

"When any one ventures to say to an English audience, that eternity is not a mere negation of time, that it denotes something real, substantial, before all time, he is told at once that he is departing from the simple, intelligible meaning of words; that he is introducing novelties; that he is talking abstractions. This language is perfectly honest in the mouths of those who use it. But they do not know where they learned it. They did not get it from peasants, or women, or children. They did not get it from the Bible. They got it from Locke. And if I find that I cannot interpret the language and thoughts of peasants, and women, and children, and that I cannot interpret the plainest passages of the Bible, or the whole context of it, while I look through the Locke spectacles, I must cast them aside....

"Suppose, instead of taking this method of asserting the truth of all God's words, the most blessed and the most tremendous, we reject the wisdom of our forefathers, and enact an article declaring that all are heretics, and deniers of the truth, who do not hold that eternal means endless, and that there cannot be a deliverance from eternal punishment. What is the consequence? Simply this, I believe: the whole gospel of God is set aside. The state of eternal life and eternal death is not one we can refer only to the future, or that we can in any wise identify with the future. Every man who knows what it is to have been in a state of sin, knows what it is to have been in a state of death. He cannot connect that death with time; he must say that Christ has brought him out of the bonds of *eternal* death. Throw that idea into the future and you deprive it of all its reality, of all its power. I know what it means all too well while you let me connect it with my present and personal being, with the pangs of conscience which I suffer now. It becomes a mere vague dream and shadow to me when you project it into a distant world. And if you take from me the belief that God is always righteous, always maintaining a fight with evil, always seeking to bring his creatures out of it, you take everything from me—all hope now, all hope in the world to come. Atonement, redemption, satisfaction, regeneration, become mere words, to which there is no counterpart in reality."

37. In the German Bible we have the true word—"Auferstehung."

38. So De Wette, Kurzgefasstes exegetisches Handbuch zum N. T., ad locum.

39. So Schleusner, Lexicon in LXX.

40. So Usteri (Paulinischen Lehrbegriff) says that σάλπιγξ appears to denote partly the startling power of the truth, and partly its power of calling men together from all the regions of the earth.

41. Christ only comes when he comes to reign. His first coming was as Jesus, not as Christ. The human life is "the life of Jesus." Christian history is "the life of Christ." In his earthly life he was Prophet; in his death he was Priest; in his resurrection, or risen state, he was King.

42. The book of the Revelation of John is the account of Christ's coming; and the true interpretation of that book depends on the proper understanding of his coming. If Christ's coming began at the destruction of Jerusalem, and has continued in all the developments of human history, then the key to "the Revelation" is to be found in the progress of Christian principles and ideas in the world. Bertholdt (Christologia Judæorum Jesu

Apostolorumque ætate), note to § 11, quotes from the Sepher Ikkarim this passage—"The future age will come *gradually* to men after the day of the great judgment, which will take place after the resurrection." Resurrection and judgment both come with Jesus, and his were "the last days."

43. 1 Thess. 4:17. "We, who are alive, and remain, shall be caught up together with them, in the clouds, to meet the Lord in the air." Usteri (Paul. Lehrbeg.) says that "this εἰς ἀέρα has no analogy in any other passage of the Epistles, or indeed of the New Testament." But Paul outgrew this literalism, and in his later Epistles speaks of sitting already with Christ in "heavenly places."

44. Olshausen, an Orthodox commentator, speaks thus in regard to Christ's predictions concerning his coming, in Matt. ch. 24, 25: —

"One of the most striking examples of the binding of the present and future in one narrative, and one which presents many difficulties, is to be found in these passages. Plain descriptions of the impending destruction of Jerusalem and of the Jewish state blend with no less apparent descriptions of the coming of Christ in his kingdom. It cannot be denied that the Orthodox interpreters are far less natural and unforced than the others, in their treatment of this passage. Their dogmatic views lead them to put apart from each other elements which are blended together by Matthew and by the other evangelists. For example, Schott says, that the description of Christ's coming begins (Matt. 24:29) immediately after 'the tribulation,' &c., and that all before that belongs to the destruction of Jerusalem. But apart from the impossibility of regarding the 29th verse as the beginning of something entirely new, there are also in the passages which follow distinct references to the present generation (verse 34), and in the first part as distinct references to 'the last time.' We do not, therefore scruple (says Olshausen) to accept the simple explanation which alone suits the text, that Christ speaks of his coming as coincident with the destruction of Jerusalem, and with the downfall of the Jewish state."

The most interesting question, perhaps, is as to the opinions of Jesus *himself* about his coming. That he forsaw the overthrow of Jerusalem and the Temple is certain. Everything indicates that he possessed a marvellous power of reading the future in the present, and saw in the condition of the Jewish mind the inevitable overthrow of their state. He also saw that through his death all men should be brought to him, and that he should become King in the way in which he described to Pilate his royalty, i.e., King of the truth. All who love the truth shall, sooner or later, obey his voice. In what way, then, did he expect to come? In the way he himself indicates the coming of his kingdom—like leaven, working secretly in the dough; like seed, sprouting mysteriously in the ground; like lightning, seen everywhere at once. By these images alone could he convey to his disciples his ideas. He longed to tell them many things more, but they were not able; to bear them.

45. The difficulties (of which Olshausen and other candid Orthodox interpreters speak) in harmonizing the different parts of Matthew's two chapters (24 and 25) about Christ's coming and judgment, may perhaps be relieved in some such way as this. (1.) The end of the Mosaic age and the beginning of the Messianic age are fixed at the destruction of Jerusalem. (2.) Christ's coming begins there, and continues through Christian history, till all mankind are Christians. His coming, therefore, verifies what Schiller says of truth, that it *"nimmer ist, immer wird."* (3.) Whenever he comes, he judges men according to the state of mind in which they are. (4.) The three parables (virgins, talents, king on his throne) represent the judgment of three different classes. The first class (of wise and foolish virgins) are those who *are not yet converted*, and have not become disciples of Christ. When he comes, those of them who have oil in their lamps—or who receive truth into an honest heart (Luke 8:15)—are ready to receive him, and to become Christians; those who have no oil reject him. The second class (in the talents) are Christians, who receive more or less of power and of good, according to past fidelity. The third class (the "nations ") are the heathen, and others, who have never known of Christ at all, but are Christians outside of Christianity.

46. The latest illustration of Orthodox ideas on this subject we have met with is contained in a little tract which has fallen in our way, containing "extracts from a sermon addressed to the students in the United Presbyterian Theological Seminary of Xenia, Ohio, by Rev. William Davidson." It begins in this somewhat enigmatical way:—

"It is an unspeakably terrible thing for any one—for even a youth or a heathen—to be *lost*."

Why this limiting particle "even" is introduced is not explained. It seems to be implied either that a youth and a heathen have not as much to lose as others, or else that we are not bound to feel so much for their loss as for that of others. After a little poetry (which we omit, as it is altogether too stern a matter for any sentimental ornament), Mr. Davidson proceeds:—

"Nor is this all to those who suffer *least*. It is not only the loss of all, and a horrible lake of ever-burning fire, but there are *horrible objects*, filling every sense and every faculty; and there are *horrible engines and instruments of torture*. There are the 'chains of darkness,' thick, heavy, hard, and smothering as the gloom of blank and black despair—chains strong as the cords of omnipotence, hot as the crisping flames of vengeance, indestructible and eternal as justice. With chains like these, every iron link burning into the throbbing heart, is bound each doomed, damned soul, on a bed of burning marl, under an iron roof, riven with tempests, and dripping with torrents of unquenchable fire."

The object of the preacher being to make as terrific a picture as possible, he accumulates these material images of bodily torment in order to excite the imagination to the utmost. We can conceive of his writing these sentences carefully in his comfortable study, in an easy chair, by the side of a cheerful fire, with a smile of self-complacency, as he selects each striking expression. Then he proceeds:—

"Nor is this all. Unmortified appetites, hungry as death, insatiable as the grave, torture it. Every passion burning, an unsealed volcano in the heart. Every base lust a tiger unchained—a worm undying, let loose to prey on soul and body. Pride, vanity, envy, shame, treachery, deceit, falsehood, fell revenge, and black despair, malice, and every unholy emotion, are so many springs of excruciating and ever-increasing agonies, are so many hot and stifling winds, tossing the swooning, sweltering soul on waves of fire. And there will be deadly hunger, but no food; parching thirst, but no water; eternal fatigue, but no rest; eternal lust of sensuous and intellectual pleasures, but no gratification. And there will be *terrible companions*, or rather *foes*, there. Eternal longings after society, but no companion, no love, and no sympathy there. Every one utterly selfish, hateful, and hating. Every one cunning, false, malignant, fierce, fell, and devilish. All commingle in the confusion and the carnage of one wide-spread, pitiless, truceless, desperate strife. And there will be terrible sights and sounds there. Fathers and sons, pastors and people, husbands and wives, brothers and sisters, with swollen veins and bloodshot eyes, straining towards each other's throats and hearts, reprobate men, and devils in form and features, hideous to as great a degree as are the beauties of the blest in heaven beautiful. And there are groans and curses, and everlasting wailings, as harsh and horrible as heaven's songs, shouts, and anthems are sweet, joyous, and enrapturing. And there will be terrible displays of the divine power and skill, and infinitely awful displays of merciless and omnipotent justice, in the punishment of that rebel crew, that generation of moral vipers full grown, that congregation of moral monsters."

All this, however, is not enough. It is necessary to go further, and represent God in the character of the devil, in order to complete the picture.

"Upon such an assembly, God, who is of purer eyes than to behold iniquity, cannot look but with utter detestation. His wrath shall come up in his face. His face shall be red in his anger. He will whet his glittering sword, and his hand shall take hold on vengeance; and he shall recompense.

He shall launch forth his lightnings, and shoot abroad his arrows. He shall unseal all his fountains, and pour out his tumbling cataracts of vengeance. He shall build his batteries aloft, and thunder upon them from the heavens. His eye shall not pity them, nor shall his soul spare for their crying. The day of vengeance is in his heart, and it is what he has his heart set on. He will delight in it. He will show his wrath, and *make his power known.* That infinite power has never been fully made known yet; but it will be then. It is but a little that we see of it in creation and providence; but we shall see it, fully revealed, in the destruction of that rebel crew. He will tread them in his anger, and trample them in his fury, and will stain his raiment with their blood. The cup of the wine of his fierce wrath shall contain no mixture of mercy at all. And they will not be able to resist that wrath, nor will they be able to endure it; but they shall, in soul and body, sink wholly down into the *second death.* The iron heel of omnipotent and triumphing justice, pitiless and rejoicing, shall tread them down, and crush them lower still, and lower ever, in that burning pit which knows no bottom. All this, and more and worse, do the Scriptures declare; and that preacher who hesitates to proclaim it has forsworn his soul, and is a traitor to his trust."

Now, it is simple truth to say that the blasphemer and profane swearer who spends fifty years in cursing God and Christ is not so blasphemous as the man who writes such sentences as these about the Almighty, and utters them to young men as a preparation for their work in the ministry. The people of Sodom and Gomorrah shall rise up in the day of judgment against those who speak thus of God, and shall condemn them. The Pagans, who represent their gods as horrid idols, pleased with blood and slaughter, have an excuse, which Mr. Davidson has not, for they do not have the gospel of the Lord Jesus in their hands. Thus he continues:—

"And *all this shall be forever.* It shall never, never end. (Matt. ch. 25.) The wicked go away into everlasting torments. This is a bitter ingredient in their cup of wormwood, a more terrible thing in their terrible doom. If after enduring it all for twice ten thousand times ten thousand years, they might have a deliverance, or at least some abatement, it were less terrible. But this may never, never be. Their estate is remediless. There is a great gulf fixed, and they cannot pass from thence. Or, if after suffering all this as many years as there are aqueous particles in air and ocean, they might then be delivered, or if, after repeating that amazing period as many times as there are sand-grains in the globe, they might then be delivered, there would be *some* hope. Or, if you multiply this latter sum—too infinite to be expressed by figures, and too limitless to be comprehended by angels—by the number of atoms that compose the universe, and there might be deliverance when they had passed those amazing, abysmal gulfs of duration, then there would be *some* hope. But no! when all is suffered and all is past, still all beyond is eternity."

47. To show how some *Roman Catholics* write in the middle of the nineteenth century, we quote the following from a Roman Catholic book, published in England, by Rev. J. Furniss, being especially "a book for children." Wishing to spare our readers such horrors, we put it here, advising no one of weak nerves to read its atrocious descriptions.

"The fourth dungeon is 'the boiling kettle.' Listen: there is a sound like that of a kettle boiling. Is it really a kettle which is boiling? No. Then what is it? Hear what it is. The blood is boiling in the scalded veins of that boy; the brain is boiling and bubbling in his head; the marrow is boiling in his bones. The fifth dungeon is the 'red-hot oven,' in which is a *little child.* Hear how it screams to come out; see how it turns and twists itself about in the fire; it beats its head against the roof of the oven. It stamps its little feet on the floor of the oven. To this child God was very good. Very likely God saw that this child would get worse and worse, and would never repent, and so it would have to be punished *much more* in hell. *So God in his mercy called it out of the world in its early childhood.*"

48. We take the following from the "Monthly Religious Magazine:" —

"The 'Country Parson,' in his late work, the 'Autumn Holidays,' contends that the fear of future punishment in another world has little influence in deterring from crime. He ought to have added, that the reason may be, that there is so little belief in any spiritual world whatever, among men of grosser sensuality; and that future punishment, as it is preached in the old theology, is so arbitrary as to seem unreal, and is losing its power over all thinking minds. The following case is cited from the experience of a Scotch minister. No ministers, let it be remembered, preach the literal flames of a local hell in tones more awful than they.

"His parishioners were sadly addicted to drinking to excess. Men and women were given alike to this degrading vice. He did all he could to repress it, but in vain. For many years he warned the drunkards, in the most solemn manner, of the doom they might expect in another world; but, so far as he knew, not a pot of ale or glass of spirits the less was drunk in the parish in consequence of his denunciations. Future woe melted into mist in the presence of a replenished jug or a market-day. A happy thought struck the clergyman. In the neighboring town, there was a clever medical man, a vehement teetotaler; him he summoned to his aid. The doctor came, and delivered a lecture on the *physical* consequences of drunkenness, illustrating his lecture with large diagrams, which gave shocking representations of the stomach, lungs, heart, and other vital organs as affected by alcohol. These things came home to the drunkards, who had not cared a rush for final perdition. The effect produced was tremendous. Almost all the men and women of the parish took the total abstinence pledge; and since that day drunkenness has nearly ceased in that parish. Nor was the improvement evanescent; it has lasted two or three years."

49. So Erigena (quoted by Strauss), *De Divis Nat.* "Vera ratio docet, nullum contrarium divinæ bonitati vitæque ac beatitudini posse esse coeternum; divina siquidem bonitas consumet malitiam, æterna vita absorbet mortem, beatitudo miseriam."

50. The name given to them by Augustine ("Civ. Dei," lib. 21, c. 17): "Denique hujus sententiæ Patronos S. Augustinus appellat titulo non incongruo, 'Doctores Misericordes' tractatque non inhumaniter." Thomas Burnet, "De Statu Mortuum et Resurgentium." Chap. XI.

51. See Bretschneider, "Dogmatik," and Strauss, "Christliche Glaubenslehre."

52. "Nos et angelos futuros dæmones si egerimus negligenter; et rursum dæmones, si voluerint capere virtutes, pervenire ad angelicam dignitatem." Origen, quoted by Jerome.

53. "Nihil enim omnipotenti impossibile est, nec insanabile aliquid est factori suo."

54. "Quod tamen non ad subitum fieri, sed paulatim et per partes intelligen dum est, infinitis et immensis labentibus sæculis, cum sensim per singulos emendatio fuerit et correctio prosecuta, præcurrentibus aliis, aliis insequentibus." See these quotations in Strauss, Hase, &c.

55. Matt. 25:46. The Greek word translated in the English as "everlasting" punishment in the beginning of the verse, and as life "eternal" at the end, is the same word (αἰώνιος) in both places, and should be translated "eternal" in both.

56. *Remorse*—from *mordeo*, to gnaw. So St. Thomas (Summa, Pars III. 2, 97): "Vermis non debet esse intelligi corporalis sed spiritualis, qui est con scientiæ remorsus."

57. "Pauci res ipsas, sed rerum imagines, tanquam in speculo, intuentur: at res ipsas, facie ad faciem, ut dicitur, et ablato velo, visuri sumus tandem si Deo placuerit, partim sub occasu hujusee mundi, plenius autem in futuro." — *Thomas Burnet*, De Statu Mortuorum et Resurgentium Tractatus. Londini. Typis et impensis J. Hooke, in vico vulgò dicto *Fleet Street*, 1737. — No one has spoken more powerfully and eloquently than he against everlasting

punishment, particularly in the passage beginning "Nobis difficile est omnem exuere humanitatem." p. 309.

58. Is it not remarkable (as showing how little the New Testament has as yet been really studied) that there should be so many discussions as to the future doom of *the heathen*, when Jesus himself here distinctly tells us what it will be. The word ἔθνη is the only word in the New Testament which is ever translated *heathen*: wherever the word *heathen* occurs in our Bible, it is always this. Jesus teaches that the heathen (inside and outside of Christendom) will be judged *according to their humanity*, their obedience to the law written in their hearts; and he shows that this is coincident with the law of Christianity. So, when the Church of England says (in its 18th article) that "they also are to be had accursed that presume to say that every man shall be saved by the law or sect he professeth, so that he be diligent to frame his life according to that law and the light of nature;" it denounces this curse on Christ himself, and thus proves conclusively that it is not speaking by the Spirit of God, since "no man, speaking by the Spirit of God, calleth Jesus accursed." (1 Cor. 12:3) This comes of the habit (happily less common now than formerly) of throwing about curses at random, against those who differ from our opinions. Some of them may thus, accidentally, hit the Master himself. It is, perhaps, of less consequence that this anathema also touches the apostle Paul, who declares that the heathen who have not the law are a law to themselves when they do right, and are absolved by their conscience. (Rom. 2:14.)

59. Origen, Homil. in Levit. 7:2. "Salvator meus luget etiam nunc peccata mea; Salvator meus lætari non potest, donec ego in iniquitate permaneo. Non vult solus in regno Dei bibere vinum lætitiæ—nos expectat."

60. Guericke, Christ. Symbolik, § 70.

61. "Ecclesia enim est cœtus hominum ita visibilis et palpabilis ut est cœtus populi Romani, vel regnum Galliæ, aut respublica Venetorum." Bellarmin. Eccles. Milit. c. 2.

62. Moehler, Symbolism, § 36.

63. "Bonos et malos ad ecclesiam pertinere Catholica fides vere et constante affirmat." Cat. Rom.

64. The chief passage in proof of this, as is well known, is Matt. 16:18, 19 "Thou art Peter," &c. But even Augustine, the great light of the Latin Church, says that "Peter was not the Rock, but Christ was the Rock." (Neander, vol. ii. p. 168.) The same power was given to the other apostles. Matt. 18:18. John 20:23. Rev. 21:14.

65. Le Protestantisme Libéral par le Pasteur Bost. Paris, Baillière, 1865.

66. "Il est de fait que le Catholicisme, qui est essentiellement un principe d'authorité, ne sait pas dire où reside cette authorité."

67. "Thirty-nine Articles, art. xix." So Augs. Conf. art. 7: "Congregatio sanctorum, in qua evangelium recte docetur, et recte administrantur sacramenta." But it may be asked, Who is to decide on the "*recte*"?

68. In the remarkable work "Ecce Homo".

69. Tholuck, in his charming work on the Sermon on the Mount, speaks thus ("*Bergpredigt Christ. von A. Tholuck.*") "Two principal defects are found in the usual treatment of this doctrine: first, the different aspects and relations of the kingdom of God are by many considered as different *meanings* of the word, and are left standing side by side, without any attempt to ground their unity in some fundamental idea. Or, secondly, and still worse, a single aspect of the term is taken up, and the rest are wholly neglected. Examples of the first defect are to be found in Zwingle, in his note to John 3:3. (Here the kingdom of God is considered as divine doctrine and preaching of the gospel, as in Luke 18; sometimes it is taken for eternal life, Matt. 25; Luke 14; sometimes for the church and congregation of the faithful, as Matt. 13:24.) The later lexicographers, as Schleusner and Bretschneider, have not avoided these vague statements; and the last of them is particularly defective in his article on this phrase. Trahl more correctly sums up all these significations of the word thus: 'Happiness, present and future, obtained through Christ.' But in this definition the notion of 'a kingdom' is omitted. The opposite defect of taking only one of the meanings of the matter, to the neglect of the rest, is to be found, for example, in Koppe and Keil, according to whom the expression relates merely to the future reign of the Messiah one day to be established.

"Our own explanation of this expression starts from the phrase 'kingdom of God,' which explains the others, 'kingdom of heaven' and 'kingdom of Christ.' We think that the fundamental idea has been grasped by none more correctly than by Origen among the ancients, and by Calvin among the reformers. The phase of the idea principally dwelt upon by the Church Fathers may be seen in their explanation of the third petition of the Lord's Prayer, which Augustine especially examines profoundly. Most of them understand by it the realm of glory, the future revelation of Christ. Origen alone, in his book on Prayer, taken a more exact view of the subject. In like manner Calvin, in his Commentary on the Harmony. So Luther, in his fine Sermon on the Kingdom of God. Our own fundamental view we express thus: 'A community in which God reigns, not by force, but by being obeyed freely from love, and which is therefore necessarily united in itself by mutual love.' The Saviour came upon the earth to found such a community, and since it can only be completely established after he has conquered all his enemies, this kingdom of Christ belongs in its perfection to the other world."

70. An eminent and learned gentleman told me of this conversation which he had with a Roman priest: "When the wine of the Eucharist is consecrated, it becomes the real blood of Christ—does it not?" Priest, "It does." "What, then, do you do with that which remains in the cup, after communion?" Priest, "We drink it." "Does not some adhere to the glass?" Priest, "Yes; but we wash the glass." "What do you do with the water?" Priest, "We drink it." "But must there not yet remain, on the napkin, with which you wipe the glass, some portion of the blood of Christ, even though it be an infinitesimal portion?" Priest, "Yes." "Then, might it not happen that when the napkin is washed, this portion of Christ's blood may go into the water, and be poured on the ground, and be taken up by the root of a plant—say a cabbage. Would, then, the flesh of that cabbage contain, or would it not a portion of the blood of Christ?"

71. See, in the New York "Independent," June 9, 1866, the account of the "Recognition of Congregational Churches in Philadelphia," where the existence of this principle is admitted and defended by some eminent Congregational ministers; admitted and deplored by others.

72. Twesten, "Vorlesungen," &c., vol ii., p. 216. He adds to this definition its Latin form, in which the words "certain characteristics" stand "certis characteribus hypostaticis."

73. Quoted by Schleiermacher, "Glaubenslehre," § 170.

74. See the full discussions of these terms in Twesten (as above), Hase, "Christl. Glaubenslehre," § 56. Strauss, "Christl. Glaubenslehre," vol. i. Hase, "Dogmatik," &c.

75. Dogmatik, § 239.

76. Augustine (de Trinit.), says, "One life in man, but three faculties—memory, intelligence, will." But how if this is bad psychology?

77. Erigena, "The Father in the soul, the Son in the reason, the Spirit in the sense—this makes the most luminous illustration."

78. Abelard (quoted by Strauss).

79. Richard St. Victor (quoted by Hase), "There can be no possible communion of affection between a less number than three persons." So Augustine, "Cum aliquid amo, tria sunt—*ego*, et *quod* amo, et ipse *amor*." Such illustrations are hardly satisfactory at the present day. Poiret says the Father is *"Deus a se,"* the Son is *"Deus ex se,"* the Holy Spirit *"Deus ad*

se refluens." Angelus Silecius makes the Trinity a divine kiss. "God kisses himself—the Father kisses, the Son is kissed, the Spirit is the kiss."

80. Translated from the Latin in Hagenbach (Compend of the History of Doctrines, vol. i. p. 289). We agree with Strauss, who says, "Fürwahr, wer das *Symbolum Quidcunque* beschworen hatte, der hatte die Gesetze des menschlichen Denkens abgeschworen." So the Pastor Bost (Le Protestantisme Liberal), after giving the Creed, in a somewhat different form, adds, "ubi insana faciunt, mysterium appellant."

81. "Incomprehensible," Church of England Liturgy.

82. Or "each person by himself." The word in the Latin is "sigillatim," a word not in most of the dictionaries, but in some of them made equivalent to "singulatim."

83. Tertullian said, we can call Christ "God" when we speak of him alone; but if we mention him with the Father, then we must call the Father "God," and call Christ only "Lord." "For a ray of light shining into a room, we may call the sun shining there; but if we speak of the sun at the same time, then we must distinguish the ray, and call it not sun, but sunbeam."

84. The decrees of the Council of Nice inclined to Sabellianism. The term ὁμοούσιος (*of the same essence*) was a Sabellian term. Sabellianism could, in fact, stand most of the tests of modern Orthodoxy, since it maintains *three persons and one essence*, μίαν ὑπόστασιν and τρία πρόσωπα; and Schleiermacher, in one of his most elaborate treatises (Ueber den Gegensatz zwischen der Sabellianischen und der Athanasianischen Vorstellung von der Trinitat. Theolog. Zeitschrift. Berlin, 1822), has sought to rehabilitate Sabellianism. Moses Stuart translated this treatise, and plainly advocated a similar view. Hase (Kirchengeschichte, § 91) defines the view of Sabellius as making "Father, Son, and Spirit the different forms of revelation of the Supreme Unity unfolding itself in the world history as the Triad." Perhaps (see Baur) the chief peculiarity of Sabellius is in making the Triad begin and end with the process of revelation. The Monad is God in himself: the Triad is God in the process of self-revelation (Baur, "Christliche Lehre von der Dreieinigkeit," and "Lehrbuch der Christlichen Dogmengeschichte").

85. "Dictum est tamen tres personæ, non ut illud diceretur, sed ut ne taceretur." Aug. de. Trin., quoted by Hase, Dog. § 238.

86. John of Damascus (quoted by Twesten) made his boast of Christianity, that it united what was true in Polytheism with what was true in Judaism. "From the Jews," he says, "we have the oneness of nature, from the Greeks the distinction in hypostases."

87. The substance of what follows in this section, appeared in the "Christian Examiner."

88. The *nature* by which the heathen "do the things contained in the law," i.e., obey God, which is here (Rom. 2:15) called "the law written in the heart," is in Rom. 7:23 called the "law of the mind." Olshausen (a sufficiently Orthodox commentator), says, "It is wholly false to understand ὅταν ποιῇ of a mere ideal *possibility*; the apostle speaks evidently of a real and actual obedience. Paul infers that, because there are actually pious heathen, they must have a law which they obey." *Ad locum.*

89. We have no room to enter into an examination of this question at this time, and can only give a general statement on this subject from one of the authorities which happens to be at hand:—

"*All* the Fathers" (before Augustine, fourth and fifth century) "differed from Augustine in attributing freedom of will to man in his present state. Thus Justin: 'Every created being is so constituted as to be capable of vice or virtue.' Cyril of Jerusalem: 'Know that thou hast a soul possessed of free will; for thou dost not sin by birth (κατὰ γένεσιν), nor by fortune, but we sin by free choice.' *All* the Latin Fathers also maintained that free will was not lost after the fall. The Fathers also denied in part, that man is born infected with Adam's sin. Thus Athenagoras says in his Apology, 'Man is in a good state, not only in respect to his Creator, but also in respect to his natural generation.' "—Wiggers, *Augustinism and Pelagianism.* Translated by Rev. Ralph Emerson, Professor in the Theological Seminary, Andover, Mass.

90. "Abi ad Jordonum, et Trinitatem disce," was on early notion.

91. Dr. Horace Bushnell, a favorite authority with Dr. Huntington, whom Dr. Huntington quotes largely, and whose views he earnestly recommends, gives us his testimony to this point, thus ("God in Christ," pp. 130, 131):—

"A very large portion of Christian teachers, together with the general mass of disciples, undoubtedly hold three real living persons in the interior nature of God; that is, three consciousnesses, wills, hearts, understandings."

"*A very large portion of Christian teachers*" hold, then, to a belief in three Gods; and with them is joined "*the general mass of the disciples.*" The only Unity held by these teachers is, he goes on to say, "a social Unity." Father, Son, and Holy Ghost are, in their view, socially united only, and preside in that way, as a kind of celestial Tritheocracy, over the world. This heresy, he says, "because of its clear opposition to Unitarianism, is counted safe, and never treated as a heresy." That is, the Christian Church allows the belief in *three Gods*, and will not discipline those who hold that opinion; but, if you believe strictly and only in *one God*, you cannot be saved!

92. Dr. Bushnell goes on to say "While the Unity is thus confused and lost in the threeness, perhaps I should admit that the threeness sometimes appears to be clouded or obscured by the Unity. Thus it is sometimes protested, that in the word, 'person' nothing is meant beyond a threefold distinction; though it will always be observed, that nothing is really meant by the protestation; that the protester goes on to speak and to reason of the three, not as being only somewhats or distinctions, but as metaphysical and real persons.... Indeed, it is a somewhat curious fact in theology, that the class of teachers who protest over the word 'person,' declaring that they mean only a *threefold distinction*, cannot show that there is really a hair's breadth of difference between their doctrine and the doctrine asserted by many of the later Unitarians."

93. "It has often been asserted *and admitted*," says Tweaten, one of the strongest of modern Trinitarians, "that even the principal notions about which the Church doctrine turns are foreign to the New Testament; as οὐσία and ὑπόστασις, τρόπος ὑπάρξεως and ἀποκαλύψεως, τριάς and ὁμοούσια."(Twesten: Dogmatik, vol. ii. p. 281.)

94. "Who will venture to say that any of the definitions heretofore given of personality in the Godhead, in Itself considered,—such definitions as have their basis in the Nicene or Athanasian Creed,—are intelligible and satisfactory to the mind? At least, I can truly say, that I have not been able to find them, if they do in fact exist; nor, so far as I know, has any one been able, by any commentary on them, to make them clear and satisfactory." (Prof. Stuart, Biblical Repository, April, 1835. See Wilson, Trin. Test., p. 272.)

95. See the creed in Hagenbach (History of Doct., vol. i. p. 208): "Θεος ἐκ Θεοῦ, φῶς ἐκ φωτός, Θεον ἀληθινὸν ἐκ Θεοῦ ἀληθινοῦ."

96. Thus speaks Dr. Bushnell on this head ("God in Christ," p. 139):—

"Besides, it is another source of mental confusion, connected with this view of three metaphysical persons, that, though they are all declared to be infinite and equal, they really are not so. The proper deity of Christ is not held in this view. He is begotten, sent, supported, directed, by the Father, in such a sense as really annihilates his deity. This has been shown in a truly searching and convincing manner by Schleiermacher, in his historical essay on the Trinity; and, indeed, you will see at it at a glance, that this view of a metaphysical Trinity of persons breaks down in the very point which is commonly regarded as its excellence—its assertion of the proper deity of Christ."